Planning for Clima

This book provides an overview of the large and interdisciplinary literature on the substance and process of urban climate change planning and design, using the most important articles from the last 15 years to engage readers in understanding problems and finding solutions to this increasingly critical issue. The Reader's particular focus is how the impacts of climate change can be addressed in urban and suburban environments—what actions can be taken, as well as the need for and the process of climate planning. Both reducing greenhouse gas emissions as well as adapting to future climate are explored. Many of the emerging best practices in this field involve improving the green infrastructure of the city and region—providing better on-site stormwater management, more urban greening to address excess heat, zoning for regional patterns of open space and public transportation corridors, and similar actions. These actions may also improve current public health and livability in cities, bringing benefits now and into the future. This Reader is innovative in bringing climate adaptation and green infrastructure together, encouraging a more hopeful perspective on the great challenge of climate change by exploring both the problems of climate change and local solutions.

Elisabeth M. Hamin Infield is a Professor of Regional Planning at the University of Massachusetts Amherst, USA, in the Department of Landscape Architecture and Regional Planning, where she teaches graduate and undergraduate courses on climate change adaptation and land use planning.

Yaser Abunnasr is an Associate Professor of Landscape Architecture and Planning at the American University of Beirut in the Department of Landscape Design and Ecosystem Management, Beirut, Lebanon.

Robert L. Ryan is Professor and Chair of the Department of Landscape Architecture and Regional Planning, University of Massachusetts Amherst, USA, where he teaches courses on landscape planning and assessment, environment and behavior, and green infrastructure planning.

Planning for Climate Change

A Reader in Green Infrastructure and Sustainable Design for Resilient Cities

Edited by Elisabeth M. Hamin Infield, Yaser Abunnasr, and Robert L. Ryan

Routledge
Taylor & Francis Group

NEW YORK AND LONDON

First published 2019
by Routledge
711 Third Avenue, New York, NY 10017

and by Routledge
2 Park Square, Milton Park, Abingdon, Oxon, OX14 4RN

Routledge is an imprint of the Taylor & Francis Group, an informa business

© 2019 Taylor & Francis

The right of Elisabeth M. Hamin Infield, Yaser Abunnasr, Robert L. Ryan to be identified as the authors of the editorial material, and of the authors for their individual chapters, has been asserted in accordance with sections 77 and 78 of the Copyright, Designs and Patents Act 1988.

Library of Congress Cataloging-in-Publication Data
A catalog record for this book has been requested

ISBN: 978-0-8153-9167-8 (hbk)
ISBN: 978-0-8153-9168-5 (pbk)
ISBN: 978-1-351-20111-7 (ebk)

Typeset in Sabon
by Apex CoVantage, LLC

To the incredible mentors, teachers, and colleagues I have had along the way, without whom the road I've taken would have been much poorer.
To my amazing daughters Maia and Darya.
And to Gen Y and beyond, who will have the task of cleaning up the big mess of climate change previous generations have created. Hopefully, this book will be of some help.
Elisabeth M. Hamin Infield

To Maria, Zayn, and Jad for their love and patience
To Muna for her limitless giving
To the memory of Fadeel
Yaser Abunnasr

To Benjamin and Maggie, I hope this book will help make the world a better place for you and all the younger generation who are inheriting both the beauty and the challenge of the world we live in. To Janet who has always been there through the ups and downs of my professional and personal life, your love and support is what makes this all possible. Finally, to the many students throughout the years who have inspired and challenged me to explore the ways that green infrastructure can help address climate change.
Robert Ryan

Contents

Acknowledgments   *xxi*

Book Introduction   **1**
ELISABETH M. HAMIN INFIELD, YASER ABUNNASR, AND
ROBERT L. RYAN

SECTION I
**Understanding the Problem—Climate Change
and Urban Areas**   **7**

   Introduction   **9**
   ELISABETH M. HAMIN INFIELD

1 **Optimism and Hope in a Hotter Time**   **11**
   DAVID ORR
   Editor's Introduction   11
   Optimism and Hope in a Hotter Time   12

2 **Assessment Report 5: Summary for Policymakers**   **16**
   IPCC
   Editor's Introduction   16
   Assessment Report 5: Summary for Policymakers   18
   Introduction   18
   SPM 1. Observed Changes and Their Causes   19
     SPM 1.1 Observed Changes in the Climate System   19
     SPM 1.2 Causes of Climate Change   21
     SPM 1.3 Impacts of Climate Change   24
     SPM 1.4 Extreme Events   24
   SPM 2. Future Climate Changes, Risks and Impacts   26
     SPM 2.1 Key Drivers of Future Climate   26
     SPM 2.2 Projected Changes in the Climate System   26

SPM 2.3 Future Risks and Impacts Caused by a
Changing Climate   29
SPM 2.4 Climate Change Beyond 2100, Irreversibility
and Abrupt Changes   31
SPM 3. Future Pathways for Adaptation, Mitigation and
Sustainable Development   31
SPM 3.1 Foundations of Decision-Making About
Climate Change   31
SPM 3.2 Climate Change Risks Reduced by Mitigation
and Adaptation   32
SPM 4. Adaptation and Mitigation   33

3   A Review of Climate Change Impacts on
    the Built Environment   34
    ROBERT L. WILBY

    Editor's Introduction   34
    A Review of Climate Change Impacts on
      the Built Environment   35
    Introduction   35
    Changing Urban Climate   35
        Ventilation and Cooling   36
        Urban Drainage and Flood Risk   37
        Water Resources   38
        Outdoor Spaces (Air Quality and Biodiversity)   38
    Concluding Remarks   39

4   Practical Guide to Resiliency Project Evaluation   42
    REBECCA FRICKE AND ELISABETH M. HAMIN INFIELD

    Editor's Introduction   42
    Practical Guide to Resiliency Project Evaluation   43
    Purpose of this Guide   43
    Eight Gradients of Resiliency   43
    Example Questions to Ask   43
        Exposure Reduction   43
        Cost Efficiency   44
        Institutional Capacity   44
        Ecological Enhancement   44
        Adaptation Over Time   45
        Greenhouse Gas Reduction and Sustainable Materials   45
        Participatory Process   46
        Social Benefits   46

The Evaluation Process   46
   Step 1. Form an Evaluation Team   46
   Step 2. Collect Relevant Information   46
   Step 3. Score the Project   47
   Step 4. Present the Shared Averages for Each Gradient
     As a Visual   47
   Step 5. Move Forward   48
Materials Available   48

SECTION II
Introduction to Greenhouse Gas Mitigation in Urban Areas   49

Introduction   51
ELISABETH M. HAMIN INFIELD

5   **Stabilization Wedges: Solving the Climate Problem for the Next 50 Years With Current Technologies**   55
STEPHEN PACALA AND ROBERT SOCOLOW

   Editor's Introduction   55
   Stabilization Wedges: Solving the Climate Problem for
     the Next 50 Years With Current Technologies   56
   What Do We Mean by "Solving the Carbon and Climate Problem
     for the Next Half-Century"?   56
   The Stabilization Triangle   58
   What Current Options Could Be Scaled Up to Produce at Least
     One Wedge?   59
     Category I: Efficiency and Conservation   59
     Category II: Decarbonization of Electricity and Fuels   60
     Category III: Natural Sinks   60
   Conclusions   60

6   **Cities and Greenhouse Gas Emissions: Moving Forward**   62
DANIEL HOORNWEG, LORRAINE SUGAR AND CLAUDIA LORENA
TREJOS GÓMEZ

   Editor's Introduction   62
   Cities and Greenhouse Gas Emissions: Moving Forward   63
   Cities and Climate Change   63
   GHG Emissions: Assigning Responsibility   64
   Cities Are Major Players in Climate Change Mitigation   66
   Action Begins With a Greenhouse Gas Inventory   70
   Empowering Change Through Cities   70

7   The Influence of Urban Form on GHG Emissions in
    the U.S. Household Sector   72
    SUNGWON LEE AND BUMSOO LEE

    Editor's Introduction   72
    The Influence of Urgan Form on GHG Emissions
        in the U.S. Household Sector   73
    Introduction   73
    Urban Form and GHG emissions   73
    Research Methods   74
        Model Specification   74
    Results   75
        Household CO$_2$ Emissions in U.S. Urbanized Areas   75
    Conclusions   79

8   An Assessment of the Link Between Greenhouse Gas
    Emissions Inventories and Climate Action Plans   83
    MICHAEL R. BOSWELL, ADRIENNE I. GREVE, AND TAMMY L. SEALE

    Editor's Introduction   83
    An Assessment of the Link Between Greenhouse Gas Emissions
        Inventories and Climate Action Plans   84
    History and Purpose (of Climate Action Planning)   85
    The Greenhouse Gas Emissions Inventory Process   86
    Conclusion   88

9   Forces Driving Urban Greenhouse Gas Emissions   91
    DAVID DODMAN

    Editor's Introduction   91
    Forces Driving Urban Greenhouse Gas Emissions   92
    Introduction   92
    Assessing Urban Greenhouse Gas Emissions   92
    Factors Influencing Greenhouse Gas Emissions   95
    Underlying Drivers of Emissions   96
    Conclusion: Addressing Climate Change Mitigation in Urban Areas 97

10 Climate Change and Health in Cities: Impacts of Heat
    and Air Pollution and Potential Co-Benefits from Mitigation
    and Adaptation   98
    SHARON L. HARLAN AND DARREN M. RUDDELL

    Editor's Introduction   98
    Climate Change and Health in Cities: Impacts of Heat
        and Air Pollution and Potential Co-Benefits from
        Mitigation and Adaptation   99
    Introduction   99

Changes in the Climate of Cities 99
    Extreme Heat 100
    Air Pollution 100
    Variable Health Risks Within Cities 101
Potential Health Co-Benefits Through Mitigation and Adaptation 101
Conclusions 102

SECTION III
Adaptation, Risk, and Resilience 105

    Introduction 107
    YASER ABUNNASR

11 **IPCC, 2012: Summary for Policymakers: Managing the**
   Risks of Extreme Events and Disasters to Advance Climate
   Change Adaptation 111
   CHRISTOPHER B. FIELD, VICENTE BARROS, THOMAS F. STOCKER,
   QIN DAHE, DAVID JON DOKKEN, KRISTIE L. EBI, MICHAEL D.
   MASTRANDREA, KATHARINE J. MACH, GIAN-KASPER PLATTNER,
   SIMON K. ALLEN, MELINDA TIGNOR, AND PAULINE M. MIDGLEY (EDS.)

    Editor's Introduction 111
    Managing the Risks of Extreme Events and Disasters to
       Advance Climate Change Adaptation: 2012 Special Report
       of Working Groups I and II of the IPCC 112
    Context 112
    Observations of Exposure, Vulnerability, Climate Extremes,
       Impacts, and Disaster Losses 116
       Exposure and Vulnerability 116
       Climate Extremes and Impacts 116
       Disaster Losses 117
    Disaster Risk Management and Adaptation to Climate Change:
       Past Experience With Climate Extremes 117
    Future Climate Extremes, Impacts, and Disaster Losses 118
       Climate Extremes and Impacts 118
    Managing Changing Risks of Climate Extremes and Disasters 119
       Implications for Sustainable Development 127

12 **Temporal and Spatial Changes in Social Vulnerability to**
   Natural Hazards 129
   SUSAN L. CUTTER AND CHRISTINA FINCH

    Editor's Introduction 129
    (2008) Temporal and Spatial Changes in Social Vulnerability to
       Natural Hazards 130

Results   131
  Consistency of Principal Components   131
  Mapping Social Vulnerability   132
  Local Places, Local Changes   133
  Anticipating Future Vulnerability   134
Discussion   135

**13 The Climate Gap: Inequalities in How Climate Change
Hurts Americans and How to Close the Gap   138**
RACHEL MORELLO FROSCH, MANUEL PASTOR, JIM SADD
AND SETH SHONKOFF

Editor's Introduction   138
(2009) the Climate Cap: Inequalities in How Climate Change
  Hurts Americans and How to Close the Gap   139
Methodology   139
Introduction   139
Key Findings   140
  The Climate Gap in Extreme Heat Waves   140
  The Climate Gap in Health Hazards from Increased
    Air Pollution   140
  The Climate Gap in How Much Some People Pay for
    Basic Necessities   141
  The Climate Gap in Job Opportunities   141
  The Climate Gap in Extreme Weather Insurance   142
How to Close the Climate Gap   142
  Close the Climate Gap by Auctioning Permits or Establishing
    a Fee and Invest in Communities That Will Be Hardest Hit   143
  Close the Climate Gap by Maximizing Reductions in
    Greenhouse Gas Emissions and Toxic Air Pollution in
    Neighborhoods With the Dirtiest Air   143
  Why We Can't Afford to Focus Only on Regional Greenhouse
    Gas Reductions   144
  Ensuring New Fuels Don't Increase Pollution in Low-Income
    and Minority Communities   145
Other Key Recommendations to Close the Climate Gap   145
  Close the Health Impacts Gap Between People of Color and
    the Poor, and the Rest of the Population 145
  Develop Policies That Close the Gap Between the Economic
    Disparities Faced by People of Color and the Poor, and the
    Rest of the Population   146
  Close the Conversation Gap   147
Conclusions   147

14 Social-Ecological Resilience to Coastal Disasters 151

W. NEIL ADGER, TERRY P. HUGHES, CARL FOLKE, STEPHEN R. CARPENTER, AND JOHAN ROCKSTRÖM

Editor's Introduction 151
(2005) Social-Ecological Resilience to Coastal Disasters 152
Coastal Hazards and Resilience 152
Responding to Change in Coastal Areas 154
    The 2004 Asian Tsunami 154
    Coping and Adapting to Hurricanes 156
Conclusions 158

15 Traditional Peoples and Climate Change 160

JAN SALICK AND NANCI ROSS

Editor's Introduction 160
(2009) Traditional Peoples and Climate Change 161

SECTION IV
Green Infrastructure, Urban Form, and Adaptation 167

Introduction 169

YASER ABUNNASR

16 Landscape Planning, Design, and Green Infrastructure 173

DAVID ROUSE AND IGNACIO BUNSTER-OSSA

Editor's Introduction 173
(2013) Green Infrastructure: A Landscape Approach 174
Definitions of Landscape and Green Infrastructure 174
Key Concepts 176
    Sustainability: Realizing the Multiple Benefits of Green
        Infrastructure 176
    Public Health: Expanding the Scope of Green
        Infrastructure 178
    Green Infrastructure and Systems Thinking 179

17 The Green Infrastructure Transect: An Organizational Framework for Mainstreaming Adaptation Planning Policies 184

YASER ABUNNASR AND ELISABETH M. HAMIN INFIELD

Editor's Introduction 184
(2012) The Green Infrastructure Transect: An Organizational
    Framework for Mainstreaming Adaptation Planning Policies 185

Introduction   185
The Green Infrastructure Transect   186
Boston Metropolitan Region   189
Conclusion   193

18 **Adapting Cities for Climate Change: The Role of the**
    Green Infrastructure   **195**
    SUSANNAH E. GILL, JOHN F. HANDLEY, ADRIAN R. ENNOS
    AND STEPHAN PAULEIT

    Editor's Introduction   195
    Adapting Cities for Climate Change: The Role of
        the Green Infrastructure   196
    Introduction   196
    Case Study Site   198
    Urban Characterization   198
    Quantifying the Environmental Functions   199
    Climate Adaptation via the Green Infrastructure   200
    Conclusion   202

19 **Climate Change in Suburbs: An Exploration of**
    Key Impacts and Vulnerabilities   **206**
    ROBIN M. LEICHENKO AND WILLIAM D. SOLECKI

    Editor's Introduction   206
    (2013) Climate Change in Suburbs: An Exploration of
        Key Impacts and Vulnerabilities   207
    Introduction   207
    Vulnerabilities and Impacts in Suburban New Jersey   208
        Key Vulnerabilities and Impacts in High-Density
            Suburbs   209
        Key Vulnerabilities and Impacts in Medium-Density
            Suburbs   212
        Key Vulnerabilities and Impacts in Low-Density
            Suburbs   214

SECTION V
Green Infrastructure for Urban Heat and Stormwater   **219**

    Introduction   **221**
    ROBERT L. RYAN

    Urban Heat   221
    Stormwater Management   223

20 Avoided Heat-Related Mortality Through Climate
    Adaptation Strategies in Three US Cities   225
    BRIAN STONE JR., JASON VARGO, PENG LIU, DANA HABEEB,
    ANTHONY DELUCIA, MARCUS TRAIL, YONGTAO HU, AND
    ARMISTEAD RUSSELL

    Editor's Introduction   225
    Avoided Heat-Related Mortality Through Climate Adaptation
        Strategies in Three US Cities   226
    Introduction   226
    Methods   227
        Land Cover Modeling   227
        Global and Regional Climate Modeling   228
        Health Effects Modeling   228
    Results   230
    Discussion   231
    Conclusions   232

21 Planning for Cooler Cities: A Framework to Prioritise
    Green Infrastructure to Mitigate High Temperatures in
    Urban Landscapes   233
    BRIONY A. NORTON, ANDREW M. COUTTS, STEPHEN J. LIVESLEY,
    RICHARD J. HARRIS, ANNIE M. HUNTER AND NICHOLAS
    S.G. WILLIAMS

    Editor's Introduction   233
    Planning for Cooler Cities: A Framework to Prioritise
        Green Infrastructure to Mitigate High Temperatures
        in Urban Landscapes   234
    Abstract   234
    Introduction   234
    A Framework for Using UGI to Mitigate Excess Urban Heat   236
        Step 1—Identify Priority Urban Neighbourhoods   236
        Step 2—Characterise UGI and Grey Infrastructure   238
        Step 3—Maximise the Cooling Benefit from Existing UGI 238
        Step 4—Develop a Hierarchy of Streets for New UGI Integration 239
        Step 5—Select New UGI Based on Site Characteristics and
            Cooling Potential   240
        Urban Green Open Spaces   241
        Green Facades   241
        Green Roofs   242
    Discussion   242
    Conclusions   243
    Acknowledgements   244

22 How to Make a City Climate-Proof: Addressing the
    Urban Heat Island Effect   250
    LAURA KLEEREKOPER, MARJOLEIN VAN ESCH AND
    TADEO BALDIRI SALCEDO

    Editor's Introduction   250
    Cities and Climate—Causes of the Urban Heat Island Effect   251
        Health Effects of Heat Stress   252
        Climate Change and Predicted Effects   252
    Tools for Urban Design and Strategies for Implementation   252
        Vegetation   253
        Water   254
        Built Form   255
        Material   256
    Transfer of Knowledge   257
    Case Study of Existing Urban Fabrics in Den Haag and Utrecht   257
        Ondiep   258
    Conclusion   261

23 Urban Design and Adapting to Flood Risk: The Role
    of Green Infrastructure   263
    MICK LENNON, MARK SCOTT AND EOIN O'NEILL

    Editor's Introduction   263
    Urban Design and Adapting to Flood Risk: The Role of Green
        Infrastructure   264
    Introduction   264
    Designing for Flood Risk Management   265
        Persistence   266
        Adaptation   266
        Transformation   267
    The Green Infrastructure (GI) Approach   267
    Conclusions   269

24 Green Infrastructure: A Landscape Approach   273
    DAVID C. ROUSE AND IGNACIO BUNSTER-OSSA

    Editor's Introduction   273
    Green Infrastructure: A Landscape Approach   274
    Planning and Design Principles   274
        Multi-Functionality   274
        Connectivity   275
        Habitability   275
        Resiliency   275
        Identity   275
        Return on Investment   276

Green Infrastructure in Philadelphia 276
   Making the Case for Green Infrastructure: GreenPlan
     Philadelphia 276
Lessons Learned 279
   Leadership and Vision Are Key 279
   Green Infrastructure Requires Partnerships 280
   Multiple Benefits Are a Plus 280
   Passion and Patience Are Needed 280
   Allow Flexible Approaches 280
   Back It up With Research and Data 280

SECTION VI
Introduction to Green Infrastructure for Rising Sea Levels
and Coastal Risks 283

Introduction 285
ELISABETH M. HAMIN INFIELD

25 **Managing Shoreline Retreat: A US Perspective** 290
CAROLYN KOUSKY

   Editor's Introduction 290
   Managing Shoreline Retreat: A US Perspective 291
   Introduction 291
   Reducing or Restricting New Development in High-Risk Areas 292
   Backing Away from the Shore 294
   Using Disasters as Opportunities 295
   Discussion: Achieving Institutional Change 296

26 **Breaking the Waves** 299
GABRIEL POPKIN

   Editor's Introduction 299
   Breaking the Waves 299

27 **Interdependencies of Urban Climate Change Impacts**
and Adaptation Strategies: A Case Study of Metropolitan
Boston, USA 306
PAUL KIRSHEN, MATTHIAS RUTH, AND WILLIAM ANDERSON

   Editor's Introduction 306
   Interdependencies of Urban Climate Change Impacts
     and Adaptation Strategies 307
   Introduction 307
   The CLIMB Project 308

Methodology   308
Interdependencies of Impacts and Adaptation Actions   311
Conclusions   314

28 **Sustainable Tourism, Climate Change and Sea Level Rise
    Adaptation Policies in Barbados**   315
    MICHELLE MYCOO

    Editor's Introduction   315
    Sustainable Tourism, Climate Change and Sea Level Rise
      Adaptation Policies in Barbados   316
    Introduction   316
    Research Methods   317
    Background on Barbados Tourism Sector   317
    Sustainable Tourism, Physical Planning Policy and Practice
      and Climate Change Adaptation   318
    Integrated Coastal Zone Management Policies and Projects,
      Sustainable Tourism and Climate Change Adaptation   319
        Protection Measures   320
        Planned Retreat   320
        Beach Nourishment   320
        Ecosystem-Based Adaptation   320
    Policy Recommendations for SIDS   321
        Physical Planning Policies, Risk Assessment and Hazard Mapping 321
        ICZM, Sustainable Tourism and Climate Change Adaptation
          Strategies   321
        Infrastructure Policies and Projects   322
        Water Conservation   322
        Capacity-Building and Institutional Reform   322
    Conclusion   324

SECTION VII
Implementing the Vision   327

    Introduction   329
    ROBERT L. RYAN

29 **Urban Form and Climate Change: Balancing Adaptation
    and Mitigation in the U.S. and Australia**   332
    ELISABETH M. HAMIN INFIELD AND NICOLE GURRAN

    Editor's Introduction   332
    Urban Form and Climate Change: Balancing Adaptation
      and Mitigation in the U.S. and Australia   332

Introduction 332
Research Question and Method 333
Mitigation Policy Goals 334
Adaptation 335
Mitigation, Adaptation, and Land-Use Conflict 336
Two Examples of Conflicts Between Adaptation and Mitigation 336
Significance 337

30 **Explaining Progress in Climate Adaptation Planning
   Across 156 U.S. Municipalities** **340**
   LINDA SHI, ERIC CHU AND JESSICA DEBATS GARRISON

   Editor's Introduction 340
   Explaining Progress in Climate Adaptation Planning
       Across 156 U.S. Municipalities 340
   Progress and Barriers to Local Government Adaptation 341
   Resources 342
   Local Leadership 343
   Information and Communication 343
   State Policy Framework 343
   Survey of Adaptation Planning Progress 344
   Constructing the Model 345
   Modeling Results 345
   Implications for Policymakers and Planners 346
   Acknowledgments 347

31 **Urban Wildscapes and Green Spaces in Mombasa and
   Their Potential Contribution to Climate Change Adaptation
   and Mitigation** **352**
   ANNA LYTH AND JUSTUS KITHIIA

   Editor's Introduction 352
   Urban Wildscapes and Green Spaces in Mombasa and
       Their Potential Contribution to Climate Change
       Adaptation and Mitigation 353
   Introduction 353
   Green Landscapes in the Context of Mombasa 354
   From Wildscape to Greenscape: Mombasa's Haller Park 355
       History: Quarry to Park 356
       Current Status 357
   Discussing the Lafarge Ecosystems Programme and Related
       Activities in the Context of Climate Change Risk Response
       and Other Socio-Ecological Benefits 357
   Conclusions 359

32 Making Climate Change Visible: A Critical Role for
    Landscape Professionals   **361**
    STEPHEN R.L. SHEPPARD

    Editor's Introduction   361
    Introduction   362
    Problems and Principles in Engaging Society on Climate Change   362
    The Special Role of Landscape in Engaging Society on
        Climate Change   363
    Learning to Recognize Climate Change Holistically in
        Our Landscapes   365
    Critical Roles for Landscape Professionals   366
        Landscape Messaging on Climate Change   367
        Visualization and Other Visual Learning Tools   369
        Visioning Studies for Planning and Decision-Making   370
        Fostering Local Learning and Community Action on
            Climate Change   371
    Conclusions   372

    List of Articles   *376*
    Editor Biographies   *378*
    Index   *380*

Acknowledgments

This book has benefited enormously from the hard work and organizational skill of Rebecca Fricke, and all the editors are most grateful. August Williams-Eynon provided background research and gave great feedback on section introductions, and we likewise appreciate his hard work. Several doctoral students also provided helpful background work through "Lab 'n' Lunch" readings and discussion, and Arlen Marielos Marin helped with initial organization. Funding support was provided by the National Science Foundation's National Science Foundation Research Collaboration Network program grant "Sustainable Adaptive Gradients in the Coastal Environment (SAGE)" (ICER-1338767), as well as the United States Department of Agriculture HATCH grant #MAS00458, the University of Massachusetts Amherst's subvention program, the American University of Beirut Long term faculty development grants program, and the Landscape Architecture and Regional Planning Department at UMass. We extend our appreciation to Kathryn Schell and Krystal LaDuc of Taylor and Francis. The book would not have been possible without all of this support.

Book Introduction

*Elisabeth M. Hamin Infield, Yaser Abunnasr,
and Robert L. Ryan*

The world's climate is the bedrock of all of our civilizations. No matter how encased we humans are in our technological world, it is the benefits and resources derived from ecosystems that give us the necessary ingredients of life: water, air, food, and energy. So it should come as no surprise that when climate changes rapidly, these goods and services are threatened and impact ecological and human systems. The bedrock shifts, and we shift with it, whether we wish it or not. Farming is less predictable; people migrate toward areas they perceive as less hazardous; wildfires and hurricanes wreak havoc and require responses; ocean and land species need room and time to respond in their own ways to change. In cities with their hard infrastructure of buildings, roads, and waste and energy systems, change in engineering, design, and planning is required. The question, then, becomes one of minimizing human causes of climate change, and also adapting to this new reality—seeking approaches that will allow societies to become better, not worse, with change. Reducing the causes and minimizing the effects of climate change is the grand challenge of the 21st century.

Climate change has been referred to as not just a 'wicked' problem, but a 'super wicked' one (Lazarus, 2009). Problems in this category defy resolution because they have significant interdependencies among those who must act, complicating negotiations; there is uncertainty about how much change is acceptable and the specifics of what it will take to minimize that change; and the interests of different stakeholders can collide, such as the goals of the coal industry and the solar industry. The issue of time makes matters worse. The longer it takes for emissions to be reduced, the more they have to be reduced since greenhouse gases accumulate. Climate catastrophes in the meantime may make it harder to organize for action. As one last complicating feature, those who did the most to create the problem are not the ones most impacted—historically high-emitting nations like the United States have enjoyed the economic benefits of the carbon economy and now have more capacity to withstand the negative effects from it (Howard, 2009). Poor countries which have emitted little will likely experience the worst of it. It is extremely unfortunate that globally we have not moved more aggressively to reduce emissions, but as the complexity above highlights, it is perhaps understandable. Despite these challenges, most countries now have signed onto the Paris Climate Accords, committing to reduce their emissions over time. But this is a slow process, and one thing we know about climate change is that it is consistently ahead of schedule (McKibben, 2011). We cannot wait until some future time to act.

Cities are a particularly important and appropriate arena for action. The United Nations reports:

> Cities are major contributors to climate change: although they cover less than 2 per cent of the earth's surface, cities consume 78 per cent of the world's energy and produce more than 60 per cent of all carbon dioxide and significant amounts of other greenhouse gas emissions, mainly through energy generation, vehicles, industry, and biomass use.[1]

This, of course, is not because cities are bad. It is because cities are where the majority of people live.[2] The density of infrastructure, people, and key societal function such as governance in urban areas makes urban areas particularly vulnerability to hazardous events such as hurricanes, heat waves, flooding, and drought. Fortunately, this is a sphere where aggressive climate change action is happening. Local politicians, designers, technical experts and activists, are finding innovative approaches to achieving climate goals. Cities, towns, and regions across the globe are reducing their emissions and preparing for the climate change that is already entrained for the future. This book is dedicated to expanding knowledge of these innovative and essential solutions.

Over the last ten or twenty years, designers have developed the concepts and practice of 'green infrastructure' to improve city function. At the site scale this might be using on-site stormwater management rather than moving water as fast as possible off site to some distant site, or more urban greening to address excess heat, and similar actions. At the city and regional scales, green infrastructure is the networks of open space that structure the city and provide ecological as well as recreational benefit (Rouse & Bunster-Ossa, 2013). In just the last few years, these two big ideas have come together: using green infrastructure to address climate change. Green infrastructure, along with other regulatory and social actions and grey infrastructure where needed, provide a set of solutions that can reduce greenhouse gas emissions and improve adaptation to future climate change in urban areas. This is the intersection this book explores. This reader provides an overview of the large and interdisciplinary literature on the substance and process of urban climate change planning and design, using key articles to engage readers in understanding problems and finding solutions to this increasingly critical issue. The Reader's particular focus is how the impacts of climate change can be addressed in the urban and suburban environments—what actions can be taken, as well as the need for and the process of climate planning.

Climate change planning is generally divided into adaptation, defined as actions taken to address the impacts of coming climate changes, and mitigation, the reduction of greenhouse gases so as to minimize the need for adaptation. In plain language, mitigation also means the reduction of risk, oftentimes leading to confusion in language, especially as scholars and practitioners coming from the disaster reduction area use mitigation to mean reducing the impact of a harmful event, and writing on disaster reduction and climate planning are (or at least should be) interlinked. Nevertheless, for this text, we follow the International Panel on Climate Change (IPCC) and use mitigation in a focused way to mean the reduction of current and future greenhouse gas emissions.

There are several implicit perspectives that guide our work and the selection of readings here. First is that climate change should be integrated into planning, design, and engineering in way that makes it a standard variable to consider, in the same way that demography, economics, cost effectiveness and existing land use inform a local plan. Plans, policies, and designs can be evaluated on hazard resilience and fitness to future climate in the same way that they are currently evaluated on how well they will work for the size of the population anticipated in twenty years, or the employment projections. Climate planning also needs to integrate with general land use and development planning to be meaningful and to be implemented. Stand-alone climate plans can be helpful for getting a big view of goals, but implementation happens when climate concern is mainstreamed into policy.

A second key point is that climate-beneficial actions can also be people-beneficial actions. Improving transit saves emissions, and also helps people get to work. Adding trees to the urban environment cools the air, but also improves people's connection to their neighborhood. Reducing local carbon emissions often also reduces particulate emissions, bringing air quality benefits that can reduce asthma in poor neighborhoods. And so on. In the field, these are called co-benefits, the desirable outcomes from a design or policy that go beyond addressing climate change. Many actions are no-regret policies; in other words, doing them achieves enough current goals that the climate change benefits can themselves be considered the bonus. Co-benefits help build coalitions for climate action, such as partnerships between climate justice and public health activists. Identifying or increasing co-benefits of climate actions or choosing no-regret policies will help enormously in getting climate actions through the political process, whether at the local or national level. Early on in the Reader, we present original research on how these various goals can be included and visualized, and we hope that this sets a tone for the rest of the book of looking for solutions that solve many problems at once.

Climate impacts are not evenly distributed across regions or populations. The disadvantaged tend to be concentrated in areas with lower property values, which are often areas that flood, have landslides, and have poor urban tree cover for cooling. Recovery from hurricanes is slower for populations with fewer resources, and more poor people die from intense and lengthy heat waves. But the disadvantaged are not just a passive object of concern; they are active participants in the push for climate action and in finding solutions that work for their own regions and communities. Indigenous peoples and the emerging climate justice movement provide key political organization for change. We highlight attention to vulnerable populations, public health and climate justice throughout the Reader, and provide a balance of readings from developed and developing countries to suggest the diversity, but also the similarity, of issues and approaches in each.

Perhaps the most essential core value inherent in the book is that it is hopeful. There are solutions out there, and there are more being invented and designed each day. This is a moment when old patterns of practice are being reconsidered and there is great opportunity to make a difference. A lot of the work will happen within professions, and even more through the collaboration of different professions. But because most of these actions are through the public sphere, getting them in place also requires public engagement and support. Even if you, our reader, do not end up working in this field, we hope that you will feel empowered to argue for change at the local, regional, state, and national level. Indeed, one of the reasons we authors love the field of planning and design is because it enables, even empowers, citizens to feel that they can have an impact on their world. This Reader is designed to provide enough technical knowledge and inspiration that a hopeful future can be pictured. Because what can be pictured can also be achieved.

The book is organized into seven sections. Early chapters introduce fundamental knowledge that will inform the rest of the readings. In the first section, we introduce climate science and some of the core issues highlighted in this introduction. The International Panel on Climate Change (IPCC) is the most respected international body on this topic, and has rigorously evaluated research on the process of and causes for climate change, and so we read their core report in its original. Other articles in this section describe hope in the face of uncertainty, the ways that climate change particularly affects urban areas, and a reading introducing the range of values that resilient infrastructure can achieve and be evaluated upon. The second section focuses on climate change mitigation—the reduction of greenhouse gases at the city and building level. Readings present the impacts that built-form and urban systems have on levels of emissions in different cities, and highlight steps that will ensure that new construction and urban form will help reduce future emissions rather than enshrine a highly carbon-intensive region. The third section introduces basic concepts of risk and resilience, mapping how climate impacts differentially affect regions and populations. We again turn to the IPCC for its scientifically rigorous view on these social issues, while other readings introduce the climate justice movement and indigenous populations as active participants in creating knowledge and taking action.

In the fourth section, the Reader turns to built-form responses to the hazards of climate change, and in particular green infrastructure and planning approaches. Section IV focuses on overall urban form, demonstrating how the shape of a city region can help or hinder its adaptation to climate change. Regional level networks of green and open space, along with transportation routes, structure the overall form of the city. For many inland cities, the primary challenges climate change will bring are managing floodwater and heat, and it is to these that Section V is addressed, primarily focusing on the site scale. Section VI also looks at the site scale, but investigates responses to rising sea levels and coastal risks. Included here are case studies from Barbados as well as Boston (USA). The final section lays out the current status of adaptation and principles for implementation of all the great ideas developed in the previous sections. Process will vary by place, and so we present literature from developed countries as well as less developed regions. The book concludes with an argument for the role of professionals in addressing climate change at the local level.

We hope that these readings leave you convinced of the importance and feasibility of addressing climate change at the local level, and inspired to make change in your communities.

NOTES

1. UN-Habitat (2012).
2. World Health Organization (2018).

REFERENCES

Howard, J. (2009). Climate Change Mitigation and Adaptation in Developed Nations: A Critical Perspective on the Adaptation Turn in Urban Climate Planning. In S. Davoudi, J. Crawford & A. Mehmood (Eds.), *Planning for Climate Change: Strategies for Mitigation and Adaptation*. London: Earthscan.

Lazarus, R. J. (2009). Super Wicked Problems and Climate Change: Restraining the Present to Liberate the Future. *Cornell Law Review*, 94, 1153–1234.

McKibben, B. (2011). *Eaarth: Making a Life on a Tough New Planet*. New York: Henry Holt and Company.

Rouse, D. C., AICP, & Bunster-Ossa, I. (2013). *Green Infrastructure: A Landscape Approach (PAS Report 571)*. Chicago: American Planning Association.

UN-Habitat. (2012). *Climate Change* [webpage]. Retrieved from https://unhabitat.org/urban-themes/climate-change/

World Health Organization. (2018). *Urban Population Growth* [webpage]. Retrieved from http://www.who.int/gho/urban_health/situation_trends/urban_population_growth_text/en/

Section I

Understanding the Problem—Climate Change and Urban Areas

Introduction

Elisabeth M. Hamin Infield

The fundamental principles underlying this book are that climate change impacts cities in unique ways, and that both the causes and consequences of it can be addressed in those same locations using innovative approaches. Some context on the challenge at hand will help. Before industrialization, the earth's atmosphere naturally contained about 595 gigatonnes of carbon in the form of carbon dioxide.[1] Currently, the atmosphere contains about 850 gigatonnes, a 43% increase over pre-industrial levels. A widely used threshold of 'acceptable' climate change is a 2° Celsius overall global warming compared to pre-industrial levels; this 2° goal is at the center of the United Nations Framework on Climate Change. For those on the Fahrenheit system, this is about 3.6°F. Annual emissions add up to a 'carbon budget'—the total amount of carbon that can be released before we cross that 2°C threshold. The international scientific community estimates this budget to be 1 trillion tons of carbon (PgC). As of 2011, we had already burned through 52% of this budget. Estimates suggest we will use up the remaining 455 PgC by 2045 if emissions continue unchanged. To avoid more than 2° of warming, global emissions must fall by an average of 50% below 1990 levels by 2050.[2,3]

As is likely to clear to most readers of the news, impacts from climate change are already being felt. Globally, the ten hottest years on record have all occurred since 1998, with 2014 previous records, 2015 breaking 2014's record, and 2016 breaking 2015's record.[4] A 2017 report by the US National Climate Assessment found that US temperatures on average have increased by 1°C already, with Alaska warming twice as much. Seas have already risen by an observed 7–8 inches since 1900, a greater rate of rise than the globe has seen in at least 2,800 years. Generally, things are worse at the higher and lower latitudes, although impacts are being experienced all over the globe.[5]

There is some good news. A recent World Resources Institute paper finds that 57 countries have either reached their peak greenhouse gas (GHG) emissions or have a commitment that implies a peak in the future. This is up from just 19 countries in 1990. Some of the world's biggest emitters peaked by 2010, including almost all of Europe, the former Soviet republics, the United States, Russia, Japan, and Brazil; China and Mexico are expected to peak by 2030. WRI estimates that the US reached peak emission in 2007, and has declined slightly since then.[6] At the local level, as of November 2017, 684 cities representing over 500 million people globally have signed on to the Compact of Mayors. Committing to the compact requires a city to take a GHG inventory using standard methods, create reduction targets and establish a system of measurement, identify adaptation needs, and establish an action plan.[7]

The situation is dire, but not hopeless, and being able to take action in the face of these difficult facts is the subject of our first article by David Orr. Orr argues that "hope is a verb with its sleeves rolled up" and ready to work, which is the position we hope our readers will also take. The section then presents some basic information on the causes and consequences of global climate change. The second section reading comes from the International Panel on Climate Change (IPCC), the leading authority on climate change, and explains the basic climate situation. Because the IPCC's work is so central to global scientific understanding, it is helpful to get acquainted with the particular communication style of the IPCC. IPCC terminology will be used throughout the book, as it forms a common language across fields and thus encourages interdisciplinary understanding. In particular, the term 'mitigation' is used to mean the reduction of greenhouse gases, while the term 'adaptation' is used to mean actions that will reduce the impact of the increased hazards caused by climate change. In the third reading by Wilby, we begin to hone in on cities and green infrastructure as the topic of inquiry. He provides a sound general overview of the impacts of climate change in urban areas, impacts we will return to in more detail and with more solutions in the rest of the book. The final reading is a practical guide to thinking through the various goals and values that projects can achieve, including technical as well as social and ecological goals. Setting this wide framework helps to keep hope in view, as actions taken for climate change can achieve a range of other social goals.

NOTES

1. A metric ton = 10^3 kilograms, or 2,205 metric pounds. A gigaton = 10^9, or one billion (1,000,000,000) tons. A gigaton (Gt) and a petagram (Pg) of carbon are the same thing. A trillion = 10^{12}, or 1,000,000,000,000, so a PgC or GtC is about 2.2 trillion pounds.
2. IPCC (2014). Climate Change 2014: Synthesis Report. Contribution of Working Groups I, II and III to the Fifth Assessment Report of the Intergovernmental Panel on Climate Change [Core Writing Team, R.K. Pachauri and L.A. Meyer (eds.)]. IPCC, Geneva, Switzerland, 151 pp.
3. Bradbury, James and C. Forbes Thompkins. (2013). "5 Major Takeaways from the IPCC Report on Global Climate Change" [blog]. Retrieved from World Resources Institute: http://www.wri.org/blog/2013/09/5-major-takeaways-ipcc-report-global-climate-change
4. National Aeronautics and Space Administration (2017). "NASA, NOAA Data Show 2016 Warmest Year on Record Globally" [webpage]. Retrieved from https://www.nasa.gov/press-release/nasa-noaa-data-show-2016-warmest-year-on-record-globally
5. IPCC (2014).
6. Levin, Kelly and David Rich. (2017). "Turning Points: Trends in Countries' Reaching Peak Greenhouse Gas Emissions Over Time." Working Paper. Washington, D.C.: World Resources Institute.
7. Compact of Mayors. (2015). Retrieved from https://data.bloomberglp.com/mayors/sites/14/2015/07/Compact-of-Mayors-Full-Guide_July2015.pdf

1 Optimism and Hope in a Hotter Time

David Orr

EDITOR'S INTRODUCTION

Addressing climate change requires accepting the reality of the science, but also having the faith and knowledge that change is within the power of our societies and of us as individuals. Without this sense of empowerment, the slow grinding of the daily bad news wins, as we read about hurricane after hurricane, heat wave after heat wave, drought after drought, wildfires out of control, arctic ice sheets calving country-sized icebergs, and the poor suffering the most. Given the severity of the problem, it is tempting to be a Cassandra calling for only doom, but people do not typically respond well to cries of apocalypse; they either ignore them or hunker down and focus on their own near term. Local politicians, in particular, get elected on platforms of better times ahead, shared goals that people recognize as good for themselves and their neighbors. The question becomes how to frame and understand climate change in a way that enables us to address it, rather than ignore it. David Orr's answer is hope. He presents a hefty challenge for society: to face climate change honestly, without illusions about its causes or the level of reorganization necessary to stave off catastrophe, but nevertheless to take action. Orr argues that "Optimism is the recognition that the odds are in your favor; hope is the faith that things will work out whatever the odds. Hope is a verb with its sleeves rolled up." Against the scale of the problem of climate change, hope is foundational to creating solutions. He argues that hope can and must be found by each of us. The work of minimizing climate change, he explains, is to create a vision of a post-consumer society, vibrant sustainable communities and livable environments, and then work toward that vision. Climate change is a technical and scientific problem, but also a problem of values. Most people value a well-rounded, full life rather than one with just more stuff, but we need to do a better job of expressing those values and influencing policy to achieve them. David Orr is the Paul Sears Distinguished Professor of Environmental Studies and

Politics at Oberlin College, and serves as senior adviser to the college president. He is widely recognized as a leading scholar on the pedagogy of sustainability, and has authored seven books and numerous articles, book chapters, and other publications.

OPTIMISM AND HOPE IN A HOTTER TIME

Fraudulent hope is one of the greatest malefactors, even enervators, of the human race, concretely genuine hope its most dedicated benefactor.
Ernst Bloch (1986, quoted in Solnit 2004)

We like optimistic people. They are fun, often funny, and very often capable of doing amazing things otherwise thought to be impossible. Were I stranded on a life raft in the middle of the ocean and had a choice of a companion between an optimist and pessimist, I'd want an optimist, providing he did not have a liking for human flesh. *Optimism*, however, is often rather like Yankee fans believing that the team can win the game when it's the bottom of the ninth; they're up by a run, have two outs, a two-strike count against a .200 hitter, and Mariano Rivera in his prime is on the mound. They are optimistic for good reason. Red Sox fans, on the other hand, believe in salvation by small percentages and hope for a hit to get the runner home from second base and tie the game.[1] *Optimism* is the recognition that the odds are in your favor; *hope* is the faith that things will work out whatever the odds. *Hope* is a verb with its sleeves rolled up. Hopeful people are actively engaged in defying or changing the odds. *Optimism* leans back, puts its feet up, and wears a confident look knowing that the deck is stacked.

I know of no good reason for anyone to be optimistic about the human future, but I know a lot of reasons to be hopeful. How can one be optimistic, for example, about global warming? First, it isn't a "warming," but rather a total destabilization of the planet brought on by the behavior of one species: us. Whoever called this "warming" must have worked for the advertising industry or the northern Siberian Bureau of Economic Development. The Intergovernmental Panel on Climate Change—the thousand-plus scientists who study climate and whose livelihoods depend on authenticity, replicability, data, facts, and logic—put it differently. A hotter world means rising odds of more heat waves and droughts; more and larger storms; bigger hurricanes; forest dieback; changing ecosystems; more tropical diseases in formerly temperate areas; rising ocean levels (faster than once thought); losing many things nature once did for us; more and nastier pests; food shortages due to drought, heat, and more and nastier pests; more human deaths from climate driven weather events; more refugees fleeing floods, rising seas, drought, and expanding deserts; international conflicts over energy, food, and water; and if we do not act quickly and wisely, runaway climate change resulting in some new stable state, possibly without humans.

Some of these changes are inevitable, given the volume of heat-trapping gases we have already put into the atmosphere. There is a lag of several decades between the emission of carbon dioxide and other heat-trapping gases and the weather headlines, and still another lag until we experience their full economic and political effects. The sum total of the opinions of climate experts is that the planet has already warmed 0.8°C; it will warm another ~0.6°C; it is too late to avoid trauma, but probably not too late to avoid global catastrophe, which includes the possibility of runaway climate change; there are no easy answers or magical solutions; it is truly a global emergency.

Whether we can escape global catastrophe is anyone's guess, because the level of heat-trapping gases is higher than it has been in the past 650,000 years and quite likely for a great deal longer. We are playing a global version of Russian roulette, and no one knows for certain what the safe thresholds of various heat-trapping gases might be. Scientific certainty about the pace of climate change over the past three decades has a brief shelf-life, but the pattern is clear. As scientists learn more, what they are finding is that the situation is worse than they previously thought. Ocean acidification went from being a problem a century or two hence to being a crisis in a matter of decades. Melting of the Greenland and Antarctic ice sheets went from being possible hundreds of years hence to a matter of decades and a century or two. The threshold of perceived safety went down from perhaps 560 ppm CO_2 to perhaps 450 ppm CO_2, and so forth.

Optimism in these circumstances is like whistling while walking past the graveyard at midnight. There is no good case to be made for it, but the sound of whistling sure beats the sound of rustling in the bushes beside the fence. But whistling does not change the probabilities one iota or much influence any lurking goblins. Nonetheless, we like optimism and optimistic people. They soothe, reassure, and sometimes motivate us to accomplish a great deal more than we otherwise might. But sometimes optimism misleads, and on occasion badly so. This is where *hope* enters.

Hope, however, requires us to check our optimism at the door and enter the future without illusions. It requires a level of honesty, self-awareness, and sobriety that is difficult to summon and sustain. I know a great many smart people and many very good people, but I know far fewer people who can handle hard truth gracefully without despairing. In such circumstances it is tempting to seize on anything that distracts us from unpleasant things. The situation is rather like that portrayed in the movie "A Few Good Men" in which a beleaguered Marine Corps officer tells the prosecuting attorney: "You can't handle the truth!" T.S. Eliot (1971), less dramatically, noted the same tendency: "Human kind cannot bear very much reality" (*Four Quartets: Burnt Norton*). Authentic hope, in other words, is made of sterner stuff than optimism. It must be rooted in the truth as best we can see it, knowing that our vision is always partial. Hope requires the courage to reach farther, dig deeper, confront our limits and those of nature, work harder, and dream dreams. Optimism does not require much effort because one is likely to win anyway, but hope has to hustle, scheme, make deals, and strategize. [. . .]

I propose that those of us concerned about climate change, environmental quality, and equity treat the public as intelligent adults who are capable of understanding the truth and acting creatively and courageously in the face of necessity—much as a doctor talking to a patient with a potentially terminal disease. There are many good precedents for telling the truth. Abraham Lincoln, for one, did not pander, condescend, evade, or reduce moral and political issues to economics, jobs, and happy talk. Rather he described slavery as a moral disaster for slaves and slave owners alike. Similarly, Winston Churchill in the dark days of the London blitzkrieg in 1940 did not talk about defeating Nazism at a profit and the joys of urban renewal. Instead he offered the British people "blood, toil, tears, and sweat." And they responded with heart, courage, stamina, and sacrifice. At the individual level, faced with a life-threatening illness, people more often than not respond heroically. Every day soldiers, parents, citizens, and strangers do heroic and improbable things in the full knowledge of the price they will pay.

Telling truth means the people must be summoned to a level of extraordinary greatness appropriate to an extraordinarily dangerous time. [. . .]

Telling the truth means we will have to speak clearly about the causes of our failures that have led us to the brink of disaster. If we fail to deal with causes, there are no band-aids that will save us for long. The problems can in one way or another be traced to the irresponsible exercise of power that has excluded the rights of the poor, the disenfranchised, and every generation after our own. That this has happened is in no small way a direct result everywhere of money in politics, which has aided and abetted the theft of the public commons, including the airwaves where deliberate misinformation is a growing industry. Freedom of speech, as Lincoln said in 1860, does not include "the right to mislead others, who have less access to history and less leisure to study it." The rights of capital over the media now trump those of honesty and fair public dialogue and will continue to do so until the public reasserts its legitimate control over the public commons including the airwaves.

Telling the truth means summoning people to a higher vision than that of the affluent consumer society. Consider the well-studied but little-noted gap between the stagnant or falling trend line of happiness in the last half century and that of rising gross national product. That gap ought to have reinforced the ancient message that, beyond some point, more is not better. If we fail to see a vision of a livable decent future beyond the consumer society, we will never summon the courage, imagination, or wit to do the obvious things to create something better than what is in prospect. So, what does a carbon-neutral society and increasingly sustainable society look like? It has front porches; public parks; local businesses; windmills and solar collectors; local farms and better food; better woodlots and forests; local employment; more bike trails; summer sports leagues; community theaters; better poetry; neighborhood book clubs; bowling leagues; better schools; vibrant and robust downtowns with sidewalk cafes and great pubs serving microbrews; more kids playing outdoors; fewer freeways, shopping malls, and sprawl; less television; and no more wars for oil or anything else.

Nirvana? Hardly. Humans have a remarkable capacity to screw up good things. But it is still possible to create a future that is a great deal better than what is in prospect. Ironically, what we must do to avert the worst effects of climate change are mostly the same things we would do to build sustainable communities, improve environmental quality, build prosperous economies, and improve the prospects for our children. [. . .]

Hope, authentic hope, can be found only in our capacity to discern the truth about our situation and ourselves and summon the fortitude to act accordingly. We have it on high authority that the truth will set us free from illusion, greed, and ill will, and perhaps with a bit of luck it will save us from self-imposed destruction.

NOTE

1. Editor's note: This may have been written before the Sox's curse-breaking 2004 comeback against the Yankees leading to a World Series Championship, or the 2007 and 2013 series titles as well.

REFERENCES

Eliot, T. S. 1971. *The complete poems and plays*. Harcourt, Brace, & World, New York.
Solnit, R. 2004. *Hope in the dark*. Nation Books, New York.

2 Assessment Report 5
Summary for Policymakers

IPCC

EDITOR'S INTRODUCTION

The AR5, or the Fifth Assessment Report of the Intergovernmental Panel on Climate Change (IPCC), is the latest release of the most comprehensive, authoritative and well-researched report available on climate science. The IPCC is the leading international body for the assessment of climate change. It was founded in 1988 by the United Nations Environment Programme and the World Meteorological Organization, and is endorsed by the United Nations General Assembly. The process of writing an Assessment report is quite unique. These reports involve no new research; in fact, the IPCC funds no research. Instead, the reports synthesize thousands of research papers that have already gone through the peer-review process. Physical and social scientists from all over the world volunteer their time and expertise to contribute to IPCC reports as authors, contributors and reviewers. The IPCC (2014) notes:

> More than 830 Authors and Review Editors from over 80 countries were selected to form the Author teams that produced the Fifth Assessment Report (AR5). They in turn drew on the work of over 1,000 Contributing Authors and about 2,000 expert reviewers who provided over 140,000 review comments.

This thoroughness means the reports do not happen quickly. The first Assessment report was published in 1990, followed by reports in 1995, 2001, 2007, and now the fifth report in 2013/2014. AR6 is expected to be finalized in 2022.

Writing for the AR5 was divided up into working groups (WG): Physical Science Basis (WGI); Climate Change Impacts, Adaptation and Vulnerability (WGII), and Mitigation of Climate Change (WGIII). Each working group prepares a report following a painstaking process of writing, review by external experts from around the world, rewriting, review by more experts plus governmental officials worldwide, and final approval by the overall IPCC body. These working group reports are then synthesized into one Assessment Report, and from that Assessment Report an Executive Summary is prepared. The reports synthesize the most credible evidence from global research on the observed and predicted impacts of climate change, spanning the geosciences, agriculture, biodiversity and conservation, urban ecology, sociology, development studies and economics. The IPCC also prepares occasional "special reports," one of which is included in a later section of this reader.

Generally, the IPCC holds itself to a very high standard of caution in its claims so as to avoid controversy. They want their reports to be as unassailable as possible, which leads to a level of conservatism that can frustrate those who are more alarmed by current policies and trends. That unassailability, however, has provided the IPCC with a strong scientific and moral ground and contributed immensely to a saner climate conversation based on shared facts. For this reason, in 2007 the IPCC was awarded the Nobel Peace Prize (2007) "for their efforts to build up and disseminate greater knowledge about man-made climate change, and to lay the foundations for the measures that are needed to counteract such change."

The reports seek to be very transparent about what claims are well-grounded in science, and what claims have less evidence to support them. It is helpful to quote the report here:

> The IPCC . . . defines a common approach to evaluating and communicating the degree of certainty in findings of the assessment process. Each finding is grounded in an evaluation of underlying evidence and agreement. In many cases, a synthesis of evidence and agreement supports an assignment of confidence, especially for findings with stronger agreement and multiple independent lines of evidence. The degree of certainty in each key finding of the assessment is based on the type, amount, quality and consistency of evidence (e.g., data, mechanistic understanding, theory, models, expert judgment) and the degree of agreement. The summary terms for evidence are: limited, medium or robust. For agreement, they are low, medium or high. Levels of confidence include five qualifiers: very low, low, medium, high and very high, and are typeset in italics, e.g., medium confidence. The likelihood, or probability, of some well-defined outcome having occurred or occurring in the future can be described quantitatively through the following terms: virtually certain, 99–100% probability; extremely likely, 95–100%; very likely, 90–100%; likely, 66–100%; more likely than not, >50–100%; about as likely as not, 33–66%; unlikely, 0–33%; very unlikely, 0–10%; extremely unlikely, 0–5%; and exceptionally unlikely, 0–1%.
>
> (AR5 pg. 37)

In other words, confidence in a finding is based on whether there is sufficient evidence, and whether that evidence agrees. When AR5 reports a finding as very low or low it means either that there is not a lot of data (evidence), or the data disagree (agreement). If the report states that confidence is very high, there is both a lot of peer-reviewed articles on that topic (evidence) and the reports almost all find the same thing (agreement). Specific data claims like the percentage of decrease in summer sea-ice per decade are given likelihoods such as "very likely." More information on each of these can be found in the relevant underlying working group report. In this way, readers can understand the scientific strength of any particular finding.

The Assessment Reports are known for establishing the four Representative Concentration Pathways (RCPs), future scenarios of climate change that depend on the speed and degree of reduction in global emissions, which range from immediate, drastic reduction to "business as usual"—a continuation of unrestricted emissions and development patterns. These scenarios have been widely adopted in understanding the various paths the global social-ecological system could take over the next century, and, along with the documented and projected impacts related in the AR5, are essential knowledge for anyone concerned with climate adaptation and mitigation.

Included here are selections from the Executive Summary from the Synthesis Report from the 2014 AR5. The first half of the reading introduces the basic science of climate change, including the extent of change that has already occurred and expectations for future change. The second half of the reading, beginning with a section entitled Summary for Policy Makers (SPM) 3, focuses on policy and decision-making on adaptation, mitigation and the relationship of these to sustainable development. The numbers in braces "{}" tell the section number in the underlying report from which the information was drawn. The full reports as well as background material and any updates are available on the IPCC website at www.ipcc.ch/.

ASSESSMENT REPORT 5: SUMMARY FOR POLICYMAKERS

INTRODUCTION

This Synthesis Report is based on the reports of the three Working Groups of the Intergovernmental Panel on Climate Change (IPCC), including relevant Special Reports. It provides an integrated view of climate change as the final part of the IPCC's Fifth Assessment Report (AR5).

This summary follows the structure of the longer report which addresses the following topics: Observed changes and their causes; Future climate change, risks and impacts; Future pathways for adaptation, mitigation and sustainable development; Adaptation and mitigation.

In the Synthesis Report, the certainty in key assessment findings is communicated as in the Working Group Reports and Special Reports. It is based on the author teams' evaluations of underlying scientific understanding and is expressed as a qualitative level of confidence (from very low to very high) and, when possible, probabilistically with a quantified likelihood (from exceptionally unlikely to virtually certain). Where appropriate, findings are also formulated as statements of fact without using uncertainty qualifiers.

This report includes information relevant to Article 2 of the United Nations Framework Convention on Climate Change (UNFCCC).

SPM 1. OBSERVED CHANGES AND THEIR CAUSES

Human influence on the climate system is clear, and recent anthropogenic emissions of greenhouse gases are the highest in history. Recent climate changes have had widespread impacts on human and natural systems. {1}

SPM 1.1 Observed Changes in the Climate System

Warming of the climate system is unequivocal, and since the 1950s, many of the observed changes are unprecedented over decades to millennia. The atmosphere and ocean have warmed, the amounts of snow and ice have diminished, and sea level has risen. {1.1}

Each of the last three decades has been successively warmer at the Earth's surface than any preceding decade since 1850. The period from 1983 to 2012 was likely the warmest 30-year period of the last 1400 years in the Northern Hemisphere, where such assessment is possible (medium confidence). The globally averaged combined land and ocean surface temperature data as calculated by a linear trend show a warming of 0.85 [0.65 to 1.06] °C over the period 1880 to 2012, when multiple independently produced datasets exist. See Figure 2.1.

[...]

Ocean warming dominates the increase in energy stored in the climate system, accounting for more than 90% of the energy accumulated between 1971 and 2010 (high confidence), with only about 1% stored in the atmosphere. On a global scale, the ocean warming is largest near the surface, and the upper 75 m warmed by 0.11 [0.09 to 0.13] °C per decade over the period 1971 to 2010. It is virtually certain that the upper ocean (0–700 m) warmed from 1971 to 2010, and it likely warmed between the 1870s and 1971. {1.1.2}

Averaged over the mid-latitude land areas of the Northern Hemisphere, precipitation has increased since 1901 (medium confidence before and high confidence after 1951). For other latitudes, area-averaged long-term positive or negative trends have low confidence. Observations of changes in ocean surface salinity also provide indirect evidence for changes in the global water cycle over the ocean (medium confidence). It is very likely that regions of high salinity, where evaporation dominates, have become more saline, while regions of low salinity, where precipitation dominates, have become fresher since the 1950s. {1.1.1, 1.1.2}

Since the beginning of the industrial era, oceanic uptake of CO_2 has resulted in acidification of the ocean; the pH of ocean surface water has decreased by 0.1 (high confidence), responding to a 26% increase in acidity, measured as hydrogen ion concentration. {1.1.2}

Over the period 1992 to 2011, the Greenland and Antarctic ice sheets have been losing mass (high confidence), likely at a larger rate over 2002 to 2011. Glaciers have continued to shrink almost worldwide (high confidence). Northern

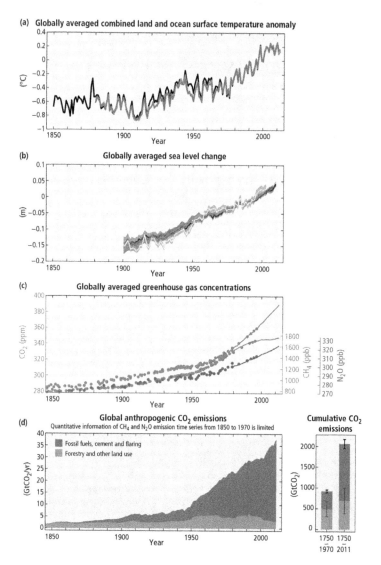

Figure 2.1 (SPM.1) The complex relationship between the observations (panels a, b, c) and the emissions (panel d) is addressed in Section 1.2. Observations and other indicators of a changing global climate system. Observations: (a) Annually and globally averaged combined land and ocean surface temperature anomalies relative to the average over the period 1986 to 2005. (b) Annually and globally averaged sea level change relative to the average over the period 1986 to 2005 in the longest-running dataset. Colours indicate different datasets. All datasets are aligned to have the same value in 1993, the first year of satellite altimetry data (red). Where assessed, uncertainties are indicated by shading. (c) Atmospheric concentrations of the greenhouse gases carbon dioxide (CO_2), methane (CH_4) and nitrous oxide (N_2O) determined from ice core data (dots) and from direct atmospheric measurements (lines). Indicators: (d) Global anthropogenic CO_2 emissions from forestry and other land use as well as from burning of fossil fuel, cement production and flaring. Cumulative emissions of CO_2 from these sources and their uncertainties are shown as bars and whiskers, respectively, on the right hand side. The global effects of the accumulation of CH_4 and N_2O emissions are shown in panel c. Greenhouse gas emission data from 1970 to 2010 are shown in Figure 2.2. {Figures 1.1, 1.3, 1.5}

Hemisphere spring snow cover has continued to decrease in extent (high confidence). There is high confidence that permafrost temperatures have increased in most regions since the early 1980s in response to increased surface temperature and changing snow cover. {1.1.3}

The annual mean Arctic sea-ice extent decreased over the period 1979 to 2012, with a rate that was very likely in the range 3.5 to 4.1% per decade. Arctic sea-ice extent has decreased in every season and in every successive decade since 1979, with the most rapid decrease in decadal mean extent in summer (high confidence). [. . .]

Over the period 1901 to 2010, global mean sea level rose by 0.19 [0.17 to 0.21] m. The rate of sea level rise since the mid-19th century has been larger than the mean rate during the previous two millennia (high confidence). {1.1.4}

SPM 1.2 Causes of Climate Change

Anthropogenic greenhouse gas (GHG) emissions since the pre-industrial era have driven large increases in the atmospheric concentrations of carbon dioxide (CO_2), methane (CH_4) and nitrous oxide (N_2O). Between 1750 and 2011, cumulative anthropogenic CO_2 emissions to the atmosphere were 2040 ± 310 $GtCO_2$ [Editors' note: $GtCO_2$ are billions of tons of carbon]. About 40% of these emissions have remained in the atmosphere (880 ± 35 $GtCO_2$); the rest was removed from the atmosphere and stored on land (in plants and soils) and in the ocean. The ocean has absorbed about 30% of the emitted anthropogenic CO_2, causing ocean acidification. About half of the anthropogenic CO_2 emissions between 1750 and 2011 have occurred in the last 40 years (high confidence). {1.2.1, 1.2.2}. See Figure 2.2.

Total anthropogenic GHG emissions have continued to increase over 1970 to 2010 with larger absolute increases between 2000 and 2010, despite a growing number of climate change mitigation policies. Anthropogenic GHG emissions in 2010 have reached 49 ± 4.5 $GtCO_2$-eq/yr. Emissions of CO_2 from fossil fuel combustion and industrial processes contributed about 78% of the total GHG emissions increase from 1970 to 2010, with a similar percentage contribution for the increase during the period 2000 to 2010 (high confidence) (Figure 2.2). Globally, economic and population growth continued to be the most important drivers of increases in CO_2 emissions from fossil fuel combustion. The contribution of population growth between 2000 and 2010 remained roughly identical to the previous three decades, while the contribution of economic growth has risen sharply. Increased use of coal has reversed the long-standing trend of gradual decarbonization (i.e., reducing the carbon intensity of energy) of the world's energy supply (high confidence). {1.2.2}

The evidence for human influence on the climate system has grown since the IPCC Fourth Assessment Report (AR4). It is extremely likely that more than half of the observed increase in global average surface temperature from 1951 to 2010 was caused by the anthropogenic increase in GHG concentrations and other anthropogenic forcings together. The best estimate of the human-induced contribution to

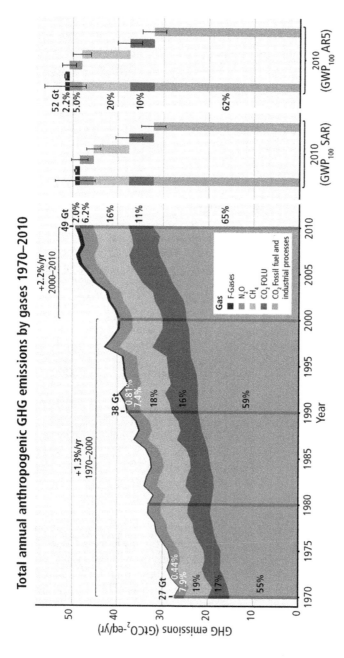

Figure 2.2 (SPM.2) Total annual anthropogenic greenhouse gas (GHG) emissions (gigatonne of CO_2-equivalent per year, $GtCO_2$-eq/yr) for the period 1970 to 2010 by gases: CO_2 from fossil fuel combustion and industrial processes; CO_2 from Forestry and Other Land Use (FOLU); methane (CH_4); nitrous oxide (N_2O); fluorinated gases covered under the Kyoto Protocol (F-gases). Right hand side shows 2010 emissions, using alternatively CO_2-equivalent emission weightings based on IPCC Second Assessment Report (SAR) and AR5 values. Unless otherwise stated, CO_2-equivalent emissions in this report include the basket of Kyoto gases (CO_2, CH_4, N_2O as well as F-gases) calculated based on 100-year Global Warming Potential (GWP100) values from the SAR (see Glossary). Using the most recent GWP100 values from the AR5 (right hand bars) would result in higher total annual GHG emissions (52 $GtCO_2$-eq/yr) from an increased contribution of methane, but does not change the long-term trend significantly. [Figure 1.6, Box 3.2]

warming is similar to the observed warming over this period (Figure 2.3). Anthropogenic forcings have likely made a substantial contribution to surface temperature increases since the mid-20th century over every continental region except Antarctica. Anthropogenic influences have likely affected the global water cycle since 1960 and contributed to the retreat of glaciers since the 1960s and to the increased surface melting of the Greenland ice sheet since 1993. Anthropogenic influences have very likely contributed to Arctic sea-ice loss since 1979 and have very likely made a substantial contribution to increases in global upper ocean heat content (0–700 m) and to global mean sea level rise observed since the 1970s. {Figure 2.3}

Contributions to observed surface temperature change over the period 1951–2010

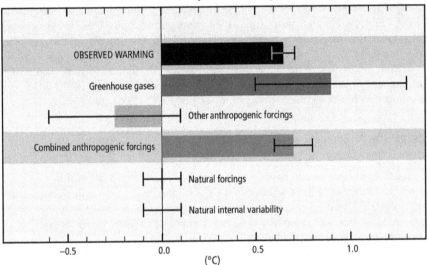

Figure 2.3 (SPM.3) Assessed likely ranges (whiskers) and their mid-points (bars) for warming trends over the 1951–2010 period from well-mixed greenhouse gases, other anthropogenic forcings (including the cooling effect of aerosols and the effect of land use change), combined anthropogenic forcings, natural forcings and natural internal climate variability (which is the element of climate variability that arises spontaneously within the climate system even in the absence of forcings). The observed surface temperature change is shown in black, with the 5 to 95% uncertainty range due to observational uncertainty. The attributed warming ranges (colours) are based on observations combined with climate model simulations, in order to estimate the contribution of an individual external forcing to the observed warming. The contribution from the combined anthropogenic forcings can be estimated with less uncertainty than the contributions from greenhouse gases and from other anthropogenic forcings separately. This is because these two contributions partially compensate, resulting in a combined signal that is better constrained by observations. {Figure 1.9}

SPM 1.3 Impacts of Climate Change

In recent decades, changes in climate have caused impacts on natural and human systems on all continents and across the oceans. Impacts are due to observed climate change, irrespective of its cause, indicating the sensitivity of natural and human systems to changing climate. {1.3.2}

Evidence of observed climate change impacts is strongest and most comprehensive for natural systems. In many regions, changing precipitation or melting snow and ice are altering hydrological systems, affecting water resources in terms of quantity and quality (medium confidence). Many terrestrial, freshwater and marine species have shifted their geographic ranges, seasonal activities, migration patterns, abundances and species interactions in response to ongoing climate change (high confidence). Some impacts on human systems have also been attributed to climate change, with a major or minor contribution of climate change distinguishable from other influences (Figure 2.4). Assessment of many studies covering a wide range of regions and crops shows that negative impacts of climate change on crop yields have been more common than positive impacts (high confidence). Some impacts of ocean acidification on marine organisms have been attributed to human influence (medium confidence). {1.3.2}. *See Figure 2.4.*

SPM 1.4 Extreme Events

Changes in many extreme weather and climate events have been observed since about 1950. Some of these changes have been linked to human influences, including a decrease in cold temperature extremes, an increase in warm temperature extremes, an increase in extreme high sea levels and an increase in the number of heavy precipitation events in a number of regions. {1.4}

It is very likely that the number of cold days and nights has decreased and the number of warm days and nights has increased on the global scale. It is likely that the frequency of heat waves has increased in large parts of Europe, Asia and Australia. It is very likely that human influence has contributed to the observed global-scale changes in the frequency and intensity of daily temperature extremes since the mid-20th century. It is likely that human influence has more than doubled the probability of occurrence of heat waves in some locations. There is medium confidence that the observed warming has increased heat-related human mortality and decreased cold-related human mortality in some regions. {1.4}

There are likely more land regions where the number of heavy precipitation events has increased than where it has decreased. Recent detection of increasing trends in extreme precipitation and discharge in some catchments implies greater risks of flooding at regional scale (medium confidence). It is likely that extreme sea levels (for example, as experienced in storm surges) have increased since 1970, being mainly a result of rising mean sea level. {1.4}

Impacts from recent climate-related extremes, such as heat waves, droughts, floods, cyclones and wildfires, reveal significant vulnerability and exposure of some ecosystems and many human systems to current climate variability (very high confidence). {1.4}

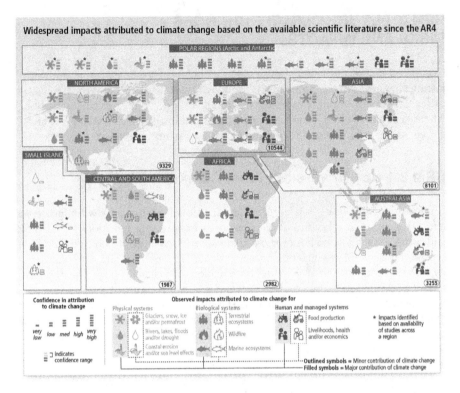

Figure 2.4 (SPM.4) Based on the available scientific literature since the IPCC Fourth Assessment Report (AR4), there are substantially more impacts in recent decades now attributed to climate change. Attribution requires defined scientific evidence on the role of climate change. Absence from the map of additional impacts attributed to climate change does not imply that such impacts have not occurred. The publications supporting attributed impacts reflect a growing knowledge base, but publications are still limited for many regions, systems and processes, highlighting gaps in data and studies. Symbols indicate categories of attributed impacts, the relative contribution of climate change (major or minor) to the observed impact and confidence in attribution. Each symbol refers to one or more entries in WGII Table SPM.A1, grouping related regional-scale impacts. Numbers in ovals indicate regional totals of climate change publications from 2001 to 2010, based on the Scopus bibliographic database for publications in English with individual countries mentioned in title, abstract or key words (as of July 2011). These numbers provide an overall measure of the available scientific literature on climate change across regions; they do not indicate the number of publications supporting attribution of climate change impacts in each region. Studies for polar regions and small islands are grouped with neighbouring continental regions. The inclusion of publications for assessment of attribution followed IPCC scientific evidence criteria defined in WGII Chapter 18. Publications considered in the attribution analyses come from a broader range of literature assessed in the WGII AR5. See WGII Table SPM.A1 for descriptions of the attributed impacts. {Figure 1.11}

SPM 2. FUTURE CLIMATE CHANGES, RISKS AND IMPACTS

Continued emission of greenhouse gases will cause further warming and long-lasting changes in all components of the climate system, increasing the likelihood of severe, pervasive and irreversible impacts for people and ecosystems. Limiting climate change would require substantial and sustained reductions in greenhouse gas emissions which, together with adaptation, can limit climate change risks. {2}

SPM 2.1 Key Drivers of Future Climate

Cumulative emissions of CO_2 largely determine global mean surface warming by the late 21st century and beyond. Projections of greenhouse gas emissions vary over a wide range, depending on both socio-economic development and climate policy. {2.1}

Anthropogenic GHG emissions are mainly driven by population size, economic activity, lifestyle, energy use, land use patterns, technology and climate policy. The Representative Concentration Pathways (RCPs), which are used for making projections based on these factors, describe four different 21st century pathways of GHG emissions and atmospheric concentrations, air pollutant emissions and land use. The RCPs include a stringent mitigation scenario (RCP2.6), two intermediate scenarios (RCP4.5 and RCP6.0) and one scenario with very high GHG emissions (RCP8.5). Scenarios without additional efforts to constrain emissions ("baseline scenarios") lead to pathways ranging between RCP6.0 and RCP8.5. RCP2.6 is representative of a scenario that aims to keep global warming likely below 2°C above pre-industrial temperatures. The RCPs are consistent with the wide range of scenarios in the literature as assessed by WGIII.

Multiple lines of evidence indicate a strong, consistent, almost linear relationship between cumulative CO_2 emissions and projected global temperature change to the year 2100 in both the RCPs and the wider set of mitigation scenarios analysed in WGIII. Any given level of warming is associated with a range of cumulative CO_2 emissions, and therefore, e.g., higher emissions in earlier decades imply lower emissions later. {2.2.5}

Multi-model results show that limiting total human-induced warming to less than 2°C relative to the period 1861–1880 with a probability of >66% would require cumulative CO_2 emissions from all anthropogenic sources since 1870 to remain below about 2900 $GtCO_2$ (with a range of 2550 to 3150 $GtCO_2$ depending on non-CO_2 drivers). About 1900 $GtCO_2$ had already been emitted by 2011. {2.2.5}

SPM 2.2 Projected Changes in the Climate System

Surface temperature is projected to rise over the 21st century under all assessed emission scenarios. It is very likely that heat waves will occur more often and last longer, and that extreme precipitation events will become more intense and frequent in many regions. The ocean will continue to warm and acidify, and global mean sea level to rise. {2.2}

The projected changes in Section SPM 2.2 are for 2081–2100 relative to 1986–2005, unless otherwise indicated.

Future climate will depend on committed warming caused by past anthropogenic emissions, as well as future anthropogenic emissions and natural climate variability. The global mean surface temperature change for the period 2016–2035 relative to 1986–2005 is similar for the four RCPs and will likely be in the range 0.3°C to 0.7°C (medium confidence). This assumes that there will be no major volcanic eruptions or changes in some natural sources (e.g., CH_4 and N_2O), or unexpected changes in total solar irradiance. By mid-21st century, the magnitude of the projected climate change is substantially affected by the choice of emissions scenario. {2.2.1}

[. . .]

The increase of global mean surface temperature by the end of the 21st century (2081–2100) relative to 1986–2005 is likely to be 0.3°C to 1.7°C under RCP2.6, 1.1°C to 2.6°C under RCP4.5, 1.4°C to 3.1°C under RCP6.0 and 2.6°C to 4.8°C under RCP8.5. The Arctic region will continue to warm more rapidly than the global mean. {2.2.1}. *See Figures 2.5 and 2.6.*

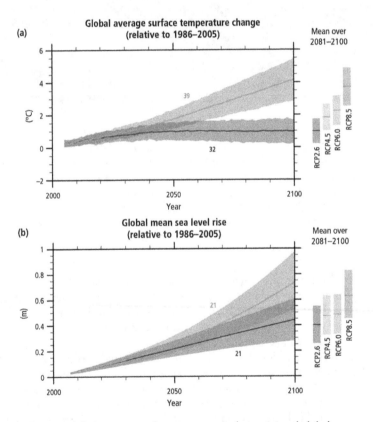

Figure 2.5 (SPM.5) Global average surface temperature change (a) and global mean sea level rise10 (b) from 2006 to 2100 as determined by multi-model simulations. All changes are relative to 1986–2005. Time series of projections and a measure of uncertainty (shading) are shown for scenarios RCP2.6 (blue) and RCP8.5 (red). The mean and associated uncertainties averaged over 2081–2100 are given for all RCP scenarios as coloured vertical bars at the right hand side of each panel. The number of Coupled Model Intercomparison Project Phase 5 (CMIP5) models used to calculate the multi-model mean is indicated. {2.2, Figure 2.1}

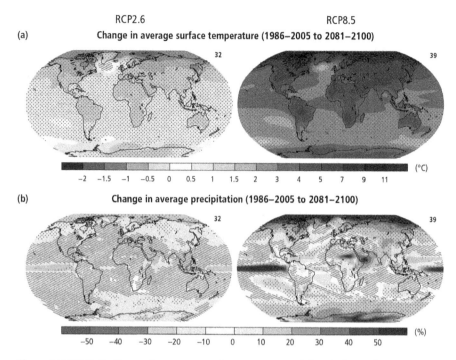

Figure 2.6 (SPM.6) Change in average surface temperature (a) and change in average precipitation (b) based on multi-model mean projections for 2081–2100 relative to 1986–2005 under the RCP2.6 (left) and RCP8.5 (right) scenarios. The number of models used to calculate the multi-model mean is indicated in the upper right corner of each panel. Stippling (i.e., dots) shows regions where the projected change is large compared to natural internal variability and where at least 90% of models agree on the sign of change. Hatching (i.e., diagonal lines) shows regions where the projected change is less than one standard deviation of the natural internal variability. {2.2, Figure 2.2}

It is virtually certain that there will be more frequent hot and fewer cold temperature extremes over most land areas on daily and seasonal timescales, as global mean surface temperature increases. It is very likely that heat waves will occur with a higher frequency and longer duration. Occasional cold winter extremes will continue to occur. {2.2.1}

Changes in precipitation will not be uniform. The high latitudes and the equatorial Pacific are likely to experience an increase in annual mean precipitation under the RCP8.5 scenario. In many mid-latitude and subtropical dry regions, mean precipitation will likely decrease, while in many mid-latitude wet regions, mean precipitation will likely increase under the RCP8.5 scenario. Extreme precipitation events over most of the mid-latitude land masses and over wet tropical regions will very likely become more intense and more frequent. {2.2.2}

The global ocean will continue to warm during the 21st century, with the strongest warming projected for the surface in tropical and Northern Hemisphere subtropical regions. {2.2.3}

[. . .]

Year-round reductions in Arctic sea-ice are projected for all RCP scenarios. A nearly ice-free Arctic Ocean in the summer sea-ice minimum in September before mid-century is likely for RCP8.5 (medium confidence). {2.2.3}

It is virtually certain that near-surface permafrost extent at high northern latitudes will be reduced as global mean surface temperature increases, with the area of permafrost near the surface (upper 3.5 m) projected to decrease by 37% (RCP2.6) to 81% (RCP8.5) for the multi-model average (medium confidence). {2.2.3}

The global glacier volume, excluding glaciers on the periphery of Antarctica (and excluding the Greenland and Antarctic ice sheets), is projected to decrease by 15 to 55% for RCP2.6 and by 35 to 85% for RCP8.5 (medium confidence). {2.2.3}

There has been significant improvement in understanding and projection of sea level change since the AR4. Global mean sea level rise will continue during the 21st century, very likely at a faster rate than observed from 1971 to 2010. For the period 2081–2100 relative to 1986–2005, the rise will likely be in the ranges of 0.26 to 0.55 m for RCP2.6, and of 0.45 to 0.82 m for RCP8.5 (medium confidence). Sea level rise will not be uniform across regions. By the end of the 21st century, it is very likely that sea level will rise in more than about 95% of the ocean area. About 70% of the coastlines worldwide are projected to experience a sea level change within ±20% of the global mean. {2.2.3}

SPM 2.3 Future Risks and Impacts Caused by a Changing Climate

Climate change will amplify existing risks and create new risks for natural and human systems. Risks are unevenly distributed and are generally greater for disadvantaged people and communities in countries at all levels of development. {2.3}. [. . .]

Risk of climate-related impacts results from the interaction of climate-related hazards (including hazardous events and trends) with the vulnerability and exposure of human and natural systems, including their ability to adapt. Rising rates and magnitudes of warming and other changes in the climate system, accompanied by ocean acidification, increase the risk of severe, pervasive and in some cases irreversible detrimental impacts. Some risks are particularly relevant for individual regions, while others are global. The overall risks of future climate change impacts can be reduced by limiting the rate and magnitude of climate change, including ocean acidification. The precise levels of climate change sufficient to trigger abrupt and irreversible change remain uncertain, but the risk associated with crossing such thresholds increases with rising temperature (medium confidence). For risk assessment, it is important to evaluate the widest possible range of impacts, including low-probability outcomes with large consequences. {1.5, 2.3, 2.4, 3.3}

A large fraction of species faces increased extinction risk due to climate change during and beyond the 21st century, especially as climate change interacts with other stressors (high confidence). Most plant species cannot naturally shift their geographical ranges sufficiently fast to keep up with current and high projected rates of climate change in most landscapes; most small mammals and freshwater molluscs will not be able to keep up at the rates projected under RCP4.5 and above in flat landscapes in this century (high confidence). [. . .]

Climate change is projected to undermine food security. Due to projected climate change by the mid-21st century and beyond, global marine species redistribution and marine biodiversity reduction in sensitive regions will challenge the sustained provision of fisheries productivity and other ecosystem services (high confidence). For wheat, rice and maize in tropical and temperate regions, climate change without adaptation is projected to negatively impact production for local temperature increases of 2°C or more above late 20th century levels, although individual locations may benefit (medium confidence). Global temperature increases of ~4°C or more above late 20th century levels, combined with increasing food demand, would pose large risks to food security globally (high confidence). Climate change is projected to reduce renewable surface water and groundwater resources in most dry subtropical regions (robust evidence, high agreement), intensifying competition for water among sectors (limited evidence, medium agreement). {2.3.1, 2.3.2}

Until mid-century, projected climate change will impact human health mainly by exacerbating health problems that already exist (very high confidence). Throughout the 21st century, climate change is expected to lead to increases in ill-health in many regions and especially in developing countries with low income, as compared to a baseline without climate change (high confidence). By 2100 for RCP8.5, the combination of high temperature and humidity in some areas for parts of the year is expected to compromise common human activities, including growing food and working outdoors (high confidence). {2.3.2}

In urban areas climate change is projected to increase risks for people, assets, economies and ecosystems, including risks from heat stress, storms and extreme precipitation, inland and coastal flooding, landslides, air pollution, drought, water scarcity, sea level rise and storm surges (very high confidence). These risks are amplified for those lacking essential infrastructure and services or living in exposed areas. {2.3.2}

Rural areas are expected to experience major impacts on water availability and supply, food security, infrastructure and agricultural incomes, including shifts in the production areas of food and non-food crops around the world (high confidence). {2.3.2}

Aggregate economic losses accelerate with increasing temperature (limited evidence, high agreement), but global economic impacts from climate change are currently difficult to estimate. From a poverty perspective, climate change impacts are projected to slow down economic growth, make poverty reduction more difficult, further erode food security and prolong existing and create new poverty traps, the latter particularly in urban areas and emerging hotspots of hunger (medium confidence). International dimensions such as trade and relations among states are also important for understanding the risks of climate change at regional scales. {2.3.2}

Climate change is projected to increase displacement of people (medium evidence, high agreement). Populations that lack the resources for planned migration experience higher exposure to extreme weather events, particularly in developing countries with low income. Climate change can indirectly increase risks of violent conflicts by amplifying well-documented drivers of these conflicts such as poverty and economic shocks (medium confidence). {2.3.2}

SPM 2.4 Climate Change Beyond 2100, Irreversibility and Abrupt Changes

Many aspects of climate change and associated impacts will continue for centuries, even if anthropogenic emissions of greenhouse gases are stopped. The risks of abrupt or irreversible changes increase as the magnitude of the warming increases. {2.4} Warming will continue beyond 2100 under all RCP scenarios except RCP2.6. [. . .]

SPM 3. FUTURE PATHWAYS FOR ADAPTATION, MITIGATION AND SUSTAINABLE DEVELOPMENT

Adaptation and mitigation are complementary strategies for reducing and managing the risks of climate change. Substantial emissions reductions over the next few decades can reduce climate risks in the 21st century and beyond, increase prospects for effective adaptation, reduce the costs and challenges of mitigation in the longer term and contribute to climate-resilient pathways for sustainable development. {3.2, 3.3, 3.4}

SPM 3.1 Foundations of Decision-Making About Climate Change

[. . .]
    Sustainable development and equity provide a basis for assessing climate policies. Limiting the effects of climate change is necessary to achieve sustainable development and equity, including poverty eradication. Countries' past and future contributions to the accumulation of GHGs in the atmosphere are different, and countries also face varying challenges and circumstances and have different capacities to address mitigation and adaptation. Mitigation and adaptation raise issues of equity, justice and fairness. Many of those most vulnerable to climate change have contributed and contribute little to GHG emissions. Delaying mitigation shifts burdens from the present to the future, and insufficient adaptation responses to emerging impacts are already eroding the basis for sustainable development. Comprehensive strategies in response to climate change that are consistent with sustainable development take into account the co-benefits, adverse side effects and risks that may arise from both adaptation and mitigation options. {3.1, 3.5, Box 3.4}
    [. . .]
    Climate change has the characteristics of a collective action problem at the global scale, because most GHGs accumulate over time and mix globally, and

emissions by any agent (e.g., individual, community, company, country) affect other agents. Effective mitigation will not be achieved if individual agents advance their own interests independently. Cooperative responses, including international cooperation, are therefore required to effectively mitigate GHG emissions and address other climate change issues. The effectiveness of adaptation can be enhanced through complementary actions across levels, including international cooperation. The evidence suggests that outcomes seen as equitable can lead to more effective cooperation. {3.1}

SPM 3.2 Climate Change Risks Reduced by Mitigation and Adaptation

Without additional mitigation efforts beyond those in place today, and even with adaptation, warming by the end of the 21st century will lead to high to very high risk of severe, widespread and irreversible impacts globally (high confidence). Mitigation involves some level of co-benefits and of risks due to adverse side effects, but these risks do not involve the same possibility of severe, widespread and irreversible impacts as risks from climate change, increasing the benefits from near term mitigation efforts. {3.2, 3.4}

Mitigation and adaptation are complementary approaches for reducing risks of climate change impacts over different timescales (high confidence). Mitigation, in the near term and through the century, can substantially reduce climate change impacts in the latter decades of the 21st century and beyond. Benefits from adaptation can already be realized in addressing current risks, and can be realized in the future for addressing emerging risks. {3.2, 4.5} [. . .].

Greater rates and magnitude of climate change increase the likelihood of exceeding adaptation limits (high confidence). Limits to adaptation emerge from the interaction among climate change and biophysical and/or socio-economic constraints. Further, poor planning or implementation, overemphasizing short-term outcomes or failing to sufficiently anticipate consequences can result in maladaptation, increasing the vulnerability or exposure of the target group in the future or the vulnerability of other people, places or sectors (medium evidence, high agreement). Underestimating the complexity of adaptation as a social process can create unrealistic expectations about achieving intended adaptation outcomes. {3.3} [. . .]

Transformations in economic, social, technological and political decisions and actions can enhance adaptation and promote sustainable development (high confidence). At the national level, transformation is considered most effective when it reflects a country's own visions and approaches to achieving sustainable development in accordance with its national circumstances and priorities. Restricting adaptation responses to incremental changes to existing systems and structures, without considering transformational change, may increase costs and losses and miss opportunities. Planning and implementation of transformational adaptation could reflect strengthened, altered or aligned paradigms and may place new and increased demands on governance structures to reconcile different goals and visions for the future and to address possible equity and ethical implications. Adaptation pathways are enhanced by iterative learning, deliberative processes and innovation. {3.3} [. . .].

SPM 4. ADAPTATION AND MITIGATION

Many adaptation and mitigation options can help address climate change, but no single option is sufficient by itself. Effective implementation depends on policies and cooperation at all scales and can be enhanced through integrated responses that link adaptation and mitigation with other societal objectives. {4} [. . .]

REFERENCES

IPCC (2014). IPCC Press Release: Concluding Instalment of the Fifth Assessment Report: Climate Change Threatens Irreversible and Dangerous Impacts, but Options Exist to Limit Its Effects. Retrieved 8 January 2017 from https://www.ipcc.ch/pdf/ar5/prpc_syr/11022014_syr_copenhagen.pdf

"The Nobel Peace Prize 2007." Nobelprize.org. Nobel Media AB 2014. Web. 5 July 2018. http://www.nobelprize.org/nobel_prizes/peace/laureates/2007/

3 A Review of Climate Change Impacts on the Built Environment

Robert L. Wilby

EDITOR'S INTRODUCTION

Previous readings in this section have introduced the overall picture of climate change. In this reading by Wilby, we begin to consider its effects on the focus of this reader—cities, city residents, and the infrastructure that supports them. Although sea level rise, shrinking polar ice, and major storms usually dominate climate change-related headlines, there are other wide-reaching impacts of a warmer globe that will be felt especially acutely in cities. Wilby covers the documented and projected effects of climate change on urban heat and cooling, drainage and flooding, water resources, outdoor spaces, air quality and biodiversity, and provides approaches for mitigating each impact. He begins with the dangerous heat stress increasing temperatures will impose on city residents, as they produce and retain greater amounts of heat than their rural surroundings, causing greater dependence on air conditioning or urban vegetation for cooling. Flood risk from intensifying rainfall patterns will increase, requiring changes in building design, more defensive infrastructure or stricter development controls in flood-prone areas. Decreased water supplies and threats to water quality are also likely, straining water supply and filtration systems, as well as resource governance. Last, cities will need more green spaces like gardens, parks and green roofs to promote cooling and reduce air pollution exacerbated by rising temperatures. Although these effects of climate change are numerous and challenging, Wilby ends on a note of hope, stating that careful planning measures and reduced resource use will be powerful tools for mitigating and adapting to climate change.

R.L. Wilby currently serves as Associate Dean for Research in the School of Social, Political and Geographical Sciences and is a Professor of hydroclimatic modelling at Loughborough University, where his research focuses on management of freshwater resources and climate risk assessment.

A REVIEW OF CLIMATE CHANGE IMPACTS ON THE BUILT ENVIRONMENT

INTRODUCTION

Increasing attention is being paid to the potential impacts of climate change on urban environments. At present, roughly 50 per cent of the world's population live in cities, but this figure is expected to rise to more than 60 per cent over the next 30 years. Most of the future growth of the urban population is anticipated in the developing world. [. . .]

The vulnerable populations of many low-income countries are already exposed to shortages of clean drinking water and poor sanitation, and often occupy high-risk areas such as floodplains and coastal zones (Haines et al., 2006). As the concentration of urban populations and their assets is increasingly juxtaposed with growing risks of extreme events, so the re-insurance industry is suffering rising costs of weather-related losses (Berz, 1997).

[. . .]

CHANGING URBAN CLIMATE

Detection of climate-driven trends at the scale of individual cities is problematic due to the high inter-annual variability of local weather and confounding factors such as land-use change or urbanization effects. It has long been recognized that built areas can have urban heat islands (UHI) that may be up to 5–6°C warmer than surrounding countryside (Oke, 1982). Compared with vegetated surfaces, building materials retain more solar energy during the day, and have lower rates of radiant cooling during the night. Urban areas also have lower wind speeds, less convective heat losses and evapotranspiration, yielding more energy for surface warming. Artificial space heating, air conditioning, transportation, cooking and industrial processes introduce additional sources of heat into the urban environment, causing distinct weekly cycles in UHI intensity (Wilby, 2003). [. . .]

The physical constituents of built areas and human activities within urban centres also interact with other climate drivers. For example, runoff from impervious surfaces can have dramatic effects on downstream risks of flooding and erosion (Hollis, 1988), as well as modifying river temperatures and water quality via uncontrolled discharges of stormwater (Paul and Meyer, 2001). Urban air pollution concentrations may also increase during heat waves with significant consequences for mortality, as in the summer of 2003 (Stedman, 2004). This is because high temperatures and solar radiation stimulate the production of photochemical smog as well as ozone precursor biogenic volatile organic compounds (VOCs) by some plants. Conversely, urban vegetation can deliver lower energy demands for air conditioning and help reduce health hazards by removal of air pollutants (Solecki et al., 2005).

Ventilation and Cooling

As noted above, city centres can be several degrees warmer than surrounding rural areas due to the UHI effect. Detailed temperature monitoring in London has established that the heat island is most pronounced at night, that it weakens with increasing wind speed and distance from the city centre, and that the location of the thermal maximum shifts with changes in wind direction (Graves et al., 2001). [. . .]

Heat waves are expected to increase in frequency and severity in a warmer world (Meehl and Tebaldi, 2004). Urban heat islands will exacerbate the effects of regional warming by increasing summer temperatures relative to outlying rural districts. [. . .]

If realized, these projected trends could have significant consequences. The cooling potential of natural ventilation falls with rising outdoor temperatures, so the demand for summer cooling could grow as internal temperatures rise during heat waves. For example, a study of energy demand in Athens showed a 30 per cent increase in energy demand by the 2080s during July and August (Giannakopoulos and Psiloglou, 2006). Mortality is also known to increase in hot weather especially amongst the elderly (Haines et al., 2006). As witnessed during the major European heat wave of 2003, urban centres such as Paris were particularly affected due to extreme day-time temperatures and by lack of relief from high nocturnal temperatures (Vandentorren et al., 2004). Thus, even in the absence of climate change, summer heat waves combined with the UHI effect can trigger major public-health crises in largely urbanized populations (see Table 3.1). Using present-day relationships between extreme heat and summer excess mortality for the Los Angeles metropolitan area, heat-related deaths were found to increase by up to seven times by the 2090s even with acclimatization (Hayhoe et al., 2004).

Table 3.1 Excess mortality attributed to the 2003 heat wave in Europe.

Location	Date	Excess mortality	% increase
England and Wales	Aug 4–13	2091	17
France	Aug 1–20	14802	60
Germany	Aug 1–24	1410	—
Italy	Jun 1–Aug 15	3134	15
Netherlands	Jun–Sep	1400–2200	—
Portugal	Aug	1854	40
Spain	Jul–Aug	4151	11
Switzerland	Jun–Sep	975	7

Source: Adapted from (Haines et al., 2006)

Urban Drainage and Flood Risk

Long-term observations support the view that the frequency and intensity of heavy rainfall increased in many regions during the twentieth century (Groisman et al., 1999), and regional climate models suggest that intensities will continue to increase over coming decades (Ekström et al., 2005). [. . .]

Assessing urban flood risk is further complicated by the performance of the urban drainage system, which responds to highly localized effects such as blocked culverts or overwhelming of the hydraulic capacity of sewers (Ashley et al., 2005). Urban drainage in cold regions dominated by snowmelt may be especially vulnerable to climate change (Semadeni-Davis, 2004). There is also a wide variety of tangible and non-tangible secondary impacts associated with flooding in urban areas (Table 3.2). [. . .]

Many of the world's major cities are located on low-lying areas near coasts and estuaries and are threatened by long-term sea level rise (Nicholls, 2004). Assessments of future flood risk for these cities bring the added complexity of interactions between sea level rise, tidal surges and storminess, combined with fluvial flooding and coastal erosion (Lowe et al., 2001; Svensson and Jones, 2002; Woth, 2005). Given such large and multiple uncertainties, some flood risk managers are turning to the use of precautionary allowances and sensitivity testing as a means of factoring climate change into urban development control or engineering designs. For example, in the UK, a 20 per cent sensitivity allowance is applied to daily rainfall, peak river flow volumes and urban drainage volumes to account for climate change by 2050 (Hawkes et al., 2003). Contingency allowances are also provided for sea level rise, offshore wind speeds and wave heights.

Detailed cost analysis has also shown that adaptation of existent flood protection measures is much more expensive than incorporating climate change effects at the planning stage. [. . .]

Table 3.2 Potential consequences of sea level rise and increased fluvial flood risk in London identified by stakeholders.

- Loss of freshwater/riparian habitats (see next section)
- Saline intrusion further up estuary and into adjacent freshwater marshland
- Greater demands placed upon emergency services
- Disrupted operations in floodplain landfill sites or loss of potential landfill sites
- Higher costs of flood protection for new developments
- Mortgage and insurance difficulties leading to blighting of some communities
- Flooding of the London Underground (already being pumped)
- Greater threat to riverside developments and inundation of major assets such as sewage treatment works
- Access and aesthetics impaired by raised flood defences
- More foul water flooding
- Severe disruption to utilities and transport systems
- Disruption to river-based activities such as navigation
- Stress to flood victims

Source: Adapted from (LCCP, 2002)

Water Resources

Water resources planning has traditionally viewed climate as stationary, a position that is increasingly untenable given that infrastructure can be in place for many decades, even centuries. The latest macro scale models driven by future rainfall scenarios show increasing water scarcity around the Mediterranean, parts of Europe, Central and South America, and southern Africa (Arnell, 2004; Milly et al., 2005). Long-term planning taking into account climate variability and change must also accommodate the various, and often conflicting, demands for water, as well as the need to protect the wider environment. In developing countries, failure of water supplies and irrigation systems can lead to poor sanitation in urban areas, as well as food shortage and reduced power generation (Magadza, 2000). Reduced reliability of surface water supplies could shift reliance to groundwater resources that are already over exploited as in the case of many agricultural areas of California (Hayhoe et al., 2004). [. . .]

In addition to water availability and impact on the natural environment, climate change also affects water resource planning through changing patterns of water consumption (Herrington, 1996) and patterns of seniority in water rights (Hayhoe et al., 2004). Domestic water use is expected to increase as a result of hotter summers leading to increased garden watering and personal washing. [. . .]

Outdoor Spaces (Air Quality and Biodiversity)

Green space is regarded by many as a crucial component of urban landscapes, not least for countering the UHI, reducing flood risk, improving air quality and promoting habitat availability/connectivity (Defra, 2005; Solecki et al., 2005; Wilby and Perry, 2006). Gardens can cover a significant proportion of urban areas and their conservation value should not be underestimated (Rudd et al., 2002). But like other habitats, gardens are also susceptible to climate change (Bisgrove and Hadley, 2002).

Developers and design teams are already encouraged to incorporate green space in their plans, and to make good use of shading and green roofs to help reduce the UHI (GLA, 2005). This provision is also made on the understanding that urban populations will want more access to outdoor natural spaces as temperatures increase. [. . .] Green roofs are regarded as a Sustainable Drainage System (SUDS) technique, and can help attenuate surface runoff, as well as trap pollutants and promote groundwater recharge (GLA, 2005) [. . .] and pollution episodes, and hence the health of urban populations as witnessed during the 2003 heat wave (Stedman, 2004). Several studies have indicated that weather patterns favouring air stagnation, heat waves, lower rainfall and ventilation could become more frequent in the future, leading to deteriorating air quality (e.g., Langner et al., 2005; Leung and Gustafson, 2005; Wilby, 2003). Under existing air pollution abatement policies, 311,000 premature deaths are projected in 2030 due to ground-level ozone and fine particles (EEA, 2006). Full implementation of measures to achieve the EU's long-term climate objective of limiting global mean temperature increases to 2°C would reduce premature deaths by over 20,000 by 2030. Other ancillary benefits of this 'climate action scenario' include lower costs of controlling air pollutant emissions as well as improved health of ecosystems impacted by acidification and eutrophication.

Despite the benefits associated with green spaces, urban wildlife could still suffer serious threats from degradation and/or loss of habitat, the introduction and spread of problem species, water pollution, unsympathetic management and the encroachment of inappropriate development (Wilby and Perry, 2006). Climate change could add to these problems through competition from exotic species, the spread of disease and pests, increased summer drought stress for wetlands and woodland and sea level rise threatening rare coastal habitats. Earlier springs, longer frost-free seasons, or reduced snowfall could further affect species phenology (such as the dates of egg-laying, emergence, first flowering or leafing of plants). Conversely, some small birds and naturalized species could benefit from warmer winters associated with the combined effect of regional climate change and enhanced UHI (LCCP, 2002).

CONCLUDING REMARKS

There is no doubt that the populations, infrastructure and ecology of cities are at risk from the impacts of climate change. However, tools are becoming available for addressing some of the worst effects. For example, appropriate building design and climate sensitive planning, avoidance of high-risk areas through more stringent development control, incorporation of climate change allowances in engineering standards applied to flood defences and water supply systems, and allocating green space for urban cooling and flood attenuation. [. . .] Citizens also have a responsibility to mitigate their collective impact on the local and global environment through reduced resource consumption and changed behaviour (Hunt, 2004).

Above all, there is an urgent need to translate awareness of climate change impacts into tangible adaptation measures at all levels of governance. [. . .] The next challenge is to integrate measures across sectors so that such responses are implemented in a coordinated and cost-effective way.

REFERENCES

Arnell, N.W. (2004) Climate change and global water resources: SRES emissions and socio economic scenarios. *Global Environmental Change*, 14, pp. 31–52.

Ashley, R.M., Balmforth, D.J., Saul, A.J. and Blanskby, J.D. (2005) Flooding in the future-predicting climate change, risks and responses in urban areas. *Water Science and Technology*, 52, pp. 265–273.

Berz, G.A. (1997) Catastrophes and climate change: Risks and (re-)actions from the viewpoint of an international reinsurer. *Eclogae Geologicae Helvetiae*, 90, pp. 375–379.

Bisgrove, R. and Hadley, R. (2002) *Gardening in the Global Greenhouse: The Impacts of Climate Change on Gardens in the UK*. Technical Report. Oxford: UKCIP.

Defra (2005) *Making Space for Water*. London: Department of Environment, Food and Rural Affairs.

EEA (European Environment Agency) (2006) *Air Quality and Ancillary Benefits of Climate Change Policies*. EEA Technical Report 4/2006. Copenhagen: European Environment Agency.

Ekström, M., Fowler, H.J., Kilsby, C.G. and Jones, R.D. (2005) New estimates of future changes in extreme rainfall across the UK using regional climate model integrations: 2. Future estimates and use in impact studies. *Journal of Hydrology*, 300, pp. 234–251.

Giannakopoulos, C. and Psiloglou, B.E. (2006) Trends in energy load demand for Athens, Greece: Weather and non-weather related factors. *Climate Research*, 31, pp. 97–108.

GLA (Greater London Authority) (2005) *Adapting to Climate Change: A Checklist for Development*. London: London Climate Change Partnership.

Graves, H.M., Watkins, R., Westbury, P. and Littlefair, P.J. (2001) *Cooling Buildings in London*. BR 431. London: CRC Ltd.

Groisman, P.Y. *et al.* (1999) Changes in the probability of heavy precipitation: Important indicators of climate change. *Climatic Change*, 42, pp. 243–283.

Haines, A., Kovats, R.S., Campbell-Lendrum, D. and Corvalan, C. (2006) Climate change and human health: Impacts, vulnerability, and public health. *Lancet*, 367, pp. 2101–2109.

Hawkes, P., Surendran, S. and Richardson, D. (2003) Use of UKCIP02 climate change scenarios in flood and coastal defence. *Water and Environmental Management Journal*, 17, pp. 214–219.

Hayhoe, K., Cayan, D., Field, C.B. *et al.* (2004) Emission pathways, climate change and impacts on California. *PNAS*, 101, pp. 12422–12427.

Herrington, P. (1996) *Climate Change and the Demand for Water*. London: HMSO.

Hollis, G.E. (1988) Rain, roads, roofs and runoff: Hydrology in cities. *Geography*, 73, pp. 9–18.

Hunt, J. (2004) How can cities mitigate and adapt to climate change? *Building Research and Information*, 32, pp. 55–57.

Langner, J., Bergström, R. and Foltescu, V. (2005) Impact of climate change on surface ozone and deposition of sulphur and nitrogen in Europe. *Atmospheric Environment*, 39, pp. 1129–1141.

LCCP (London Climate Change Partnership) (2002) *London's Warming: The Impacts of Climate Change on London*. Final Technical Report. London: Entec UK Ltd.

Leung, L.R. and Gustafson, W.I. (2005) Potential regional climate change and implications to US air quality. *Geophysical Research Letters*, 32, p. L16711, doi:10.1029/2005GL022911.

Lowe, J.A., Gregory, J.M. and Flather, R.A. (2001) Changes in the occurrence of storm surges around the UK under a future climate scenario using a dynamic storm surge model driven by the Hadley Centre climate models. *Climate Dynamics*, 18, pp. 179–188.

Magadza, C.H.D. (2000) Climate change impacts and human settlements in Africa: Prospects for adaptation. *Environmental Monitoring and Assessment*, 61, pp. 193–205.

Meehl, G.A. and Tebaldi, C. (2004) More intense, more frequent, and longer lasting heat-waves in the 21st century. *Science*, 305, pp. 994–997.

Milly, P.C.D., Dunne, K.A. and Vecchia, A.V. (2005) Global pattern of trends in streamflow and water availability in a changing climate. *Nature*, 438, pp. 347–350.

Nicholls, R.J. (2004) Coastal flooding and wetland loss in the 21st century: Changes under the SRES climate and socio-economic scenarios. *Global Environmental Change*, 14, pp. 69–86.

Oke, T.R. (1982) The energetic basis of the urban heat island. *Quarterly Journal of the Royal Meteorological Society*, 108, pp. 1–24.

Paul, M.J. and Meyer, J.L. (2001) Streams in the urban landscape. *Annual Review of Ecology and Systematics*, 32, pp. 333–365.

Rudd, H., Vala, J. and Scaefer, V. (2002) Importance of backyard habitat in a comprehensive bio diversity conservation strategy: A connectivity analysis of urban green spaces. *Restoration Ecology*, 10, pp. 368–375.

Semadeni-Davis, A. (2004) Urban water management vs. climate change: Impacts on cold region waste water inflows. *Climatic Change*, 64, pp. 102–126.

Solecki, W.D., Rosenzweig, C., Parshall, L., Popec, G., Clark, M., Cox, J. and Wiencke, M. (2005) Mitigation of the heat island effect in urban New Jersey. *Environmental Hazards*, 6, pp. 39–49.

Stedman, J.R. (2004) The predicted number of air pollution related deaths in the UK during the August 2003 heatwave. *Atmospheric Environment*, 38, pp. 1083–1085.

Svensson, C. and Jones, D.A. (2002) Dependence between extreme sea surge, river flow and precipitation in eastern Britain. *International Journal of Climatology*, 22, pp. 1149–1168.

Vandentorren, S., Suzan, F., Medina, S. *et al.* (2004) Mortality in 13 French cities during the August 2003 heat wave. *American Journal of Public Health*, 94, pp. 1518–1520.

Wilby, R.L. (2003) Weekly warming. *Weather*, 58, pp. 446–447.

Wilby, R.L. and Perry, G.L.W. (2006) Climate change, biodiversity and the urban environment: A critical review based on London, UK. *Progress in Physical Geography*, 30, pp. 73–98.

Woth, K. (2005) North Sea storm surge statistics based on projections in a warmer climate: How important are the driving GCM and the chosen emission scenario? *Geophysical Research Letters*, 32, p. 22708, doi:10.1029/2005GL023762.

4 Practical Guide to Resiliency Project Evaluation

Rebecca Fricke and Elisabeth M. Hamin Infield

EDITOR'S INTRODUCTION

We started this section arguing that as bad as climate change is, moving toward action requires facing it with a sense of hope of creating better futures. In this final selection for the section, we present a decision guide that illuminates the range of outcomes that are possible from green infrastructure and climate change policies. These include technical requirements: reducing the impact of hazards such as flooding and hurricanes, achieving goals in a cost-effective manner, being suited to the institutional capacity of the implementing agency, responding well over time and as climate and social conditions change, and a participatory process. But outcomes can also include valued co-benefits such as ecological improvement, greenhouse gas reduction and improvements in social equity. The priorities for different situations will vary. Some communities will be more interested in hazard reduction and others more focused on ecological enhancement, but all will benefit from a conscious discussion of the range of goals that could be prioritized and the expected outcomes on those goals. Explicitly highlighting the range of benefits that can be included helps to create that sense of hope and potential for change. Thinking about climate change policies this way also implicitly encourages viewing them as just another part of infrastructure and policy, integrated into other actions the city or agency is considering. We believe this 'normalizing' of climate change will increase consideration and action. The reading ahead is a guide designed for use by communities, and therefore is in simple language with clear steps for action. The authors of the underlying research include the three co-editors for this volume, along with a wide range of experts from many disciplines and geographic regions of the world. The overall research project is the SAGE (Adaptive Gradients in the Coastal Environment Research Collaboration Network), funded by the US National Science Foundation, Award Number: ICER-1338767. Rebecca Fricke, Project Manager for SAGE, is first author on the guide.

She is a long-time community activist and artist with professional experience in the US and the Caribbean. Co-author Elisabeth M. Hamin Infield is a professor of Regional Planning, first editor on this book and the Principal Investigator on the SAGE project. The research underlying the practical guide can be viewed on the website: www.resilient-infrastructure.org, along with case studies and templates. The principles of looking for co-benefits and considering a wide range of policy goals should inform readers' approaches to the policies and ideas in the rest of the book.

PRACTICAL GUIDE TO RESILIENCY PROJECT EVALUATION

PURPOSE OF THIS GUIDE

Our climate is changing. Storms are increasing in strength and numbers. Sea levels are rising, and days of extreme heat are increasing. It is time for communities to better manage their futures. While we cannot control the weather, municipalities and community groups can build infrastructure to be more resilient. What does this mean? A community or project that is resilient can adapt to environmental, social and economic change. Infrastructure and other resiliency moves can also serve current goals, like improving ecology, equity and participation, and reducing greenhouse gases. The best projects achieve multiple goals, but only the community can decide how to weight the importance of these.

This guide is designed to help communities evaluate proposed projects, infrastructure and otherwise. One goal of this guide is to encourage communities to consider greener infrastructure choices by illuminating the range of values that projects serve. Every location, every group of people, every town, has its own set of characteristics that will need to be taken into account as the evaluation process is followed. The process requires cooperation, creativity, time and work, but at the end you will have the information you need to make the best decisions for your community and the environment.

EIGHT GRADIENTS OF RESILIENCY

Eight components capture the various goals and requirements of a good resiliency project, shown below. We call these 'gradients' to highlight that they are not 1/0 items, but instead occur along ranges of values.

EXAMPLE QUESTIONS TO ASK

Exposure Reduction

Does the project's technical plan include materials and a design that will reduce the consequences of a hazardous event? How effective is the design likely to be in reducing risks to the humans in the area, to the local ecology, to local businesses? This question is often answered in engineering or other technical studies.

Table 4.1 Eight Gradients of Resiliency

GRADIENT	GRADIENT DEFINITION
Exposure Reduction	The technical or engineering components of the project that reduce the consequences of hazardous event on human, ecological, social and economic resources.
Cost Efficiency	Positive benefit-cost outcomes. Least-cost or low-cost solutions.
Institutional Capacity	Project development and long-term management/maintenance requirements suit the organizational capacity of the responsible parties. Funding methods appear suitable for the host agency.
Ecological Enhancement	Project preserves and supports the long-standing ecology of the area or creates/mimics/replaces native ecological systems.
Adaptation over Time	Expected ability to respond to a changing climate, as well as other social, economic and ecological variation over time, either as a function of design or through anticipated monitoring and assessment.
Greenhouse Gas Reduction	Project will minimize current or future greenhouse gases, including low embodied energy, long-term efficiencies, or carbon sequestration. General sustainability of materials used.
Participatory Process	Community involvement and public transparency in planning, design and implementation of the project; whether participation changed project plans.
Social Benefits	Project achieves justice goals, often measured by benefit to disadvantaged communities. Project provides co-benefits to local communities such as jobs, public health, or other locally desired outcomes.

Cost Efficiency

What are the costs involved? How do they compare to other options? The costs will depend on the materials and the amount of construction involved. Some materials might cost more up front, but are cheaper in the long run. Benefit-cost analysis could be used, or measures of cost per foot or bid price. Be sure to consider maintenance.

Institutional Capacity

Who is going to plan, build and maintain the site? How will the project be funded through the planning, implementing and then upkeep stages? Does this strain available resources, like staff or bonding capacity? Will it depend on volunteers? Who will organize the volunteers? Consider financial, staff and long-term impacts.

Ecological Enhancement

Does the project protect a natural area? Does the project help to regenerate a natural area? Or does it recreate a natural area that will enhance the local ecology? Conservation commissioners or similar staff and volunteers may be able to comment on this.

Figure 4.1 There are different kinds of infrastructure. Some are built completely of manmade materials like concrete and steel. Other plans might include planting gardens or creating wetlands, dunes and grasslands. Plans can include non-structural items too, like changes to zoning and set-backs or supporting community groups to maintain a project.

Adaptation Over Time

Will the project respond to the changing climate? Are the plans and funds for testing how well the project is doing? Will the project be flexible and responsive to shifts in water, temperature and natural surrounding materials?

Are the planting species going to do well in the future local climate? Highly technical climate projections are not necessary, but the project should make some plan for increased sea level rise, rain, drought, heat and storms over time.

Greenhouse Gas Reduction and Sustainable Materials

Will the project minimize greenhouse gases (GHG)? Does the plan involve vegetation that will help sequester carbon? Are the materials being used sustainable? Are they local or imported? Is the vegetation being used native to the area? Can the materials be reused or recycled as they are replaced? No project is perfect, but some do more (and less) than others on this count.

Participatory Process

How will the community be involved in the planning and implementation of the project? Are all people in the community welcome and encouraged to take part in the planning and design of the project? Is the decision-making process transparent? Are the meetings advertised and held in different places and at different times and in languages that match the local population? If the planning process has happened already, did participant comments change the design of the project?

Social Benefits

It is helpful to consciously consider the questions of who pays, and who benefits in what ways, and whether that matches broader goals. Does the project provide benefits beyond its immediate purpose? Does it create more recreational space? Does it create jobs? Health benefits? Beauty? Safety? Are cultural assets protected? Is there an appropriate match of who pays and who benefits? Do project benefits go to less-advantaged populations?

THE EVALUATION PROCESS

Step 1. Form an Evaluation Team

In order to begin evaluating a proposed or a built project, it is important to organize a group of people with varying interests, abilities and specialties. In order to do the project evaluation, this team of people will need to collect information that applies to each area. It helps if there are people who are have knowledge of and interest in each of the gradients. For this quick evaluation process, we suggest teams are made up of relatively unbiased experts in the various areas, such as a coastal ecologist and a landscape architect and an engineer and a social scientist. Teams should meet with and in the end present their findings to representatives of the affected communities, who will be the ones who use the results to identify desired changes in the project. If the project involves a Native American historical site, for instance, be sure to include a tribal representative. If the project impacts a neighborhood, be sure to include representatives from the neighborhood association. If the community prefers, stakeholders can be included in the evaluation team itself. We find teams of 8–12 to be effective.

Step 2. Collect Relevant Information

This process can be done with just a project proposal and basic background information on the site and community. If an Environmental Impact Statement or similar reports have been done, these will be useful. Compile basic information organized into each of the gradients. Make the information accessible to everyone in the group. Once all of the information is collected, the group should meet and look through the files. Your information will be imperfect—information always is. Decide what is good enough for your purposes.

Step 3. Score the Project

Keep the rating system simple. We suggest asking people to score each project gradient using:

1 = low
2 = medium
3 = high
.5 = if people said something in between

Score the project twice. The first scoring should be done individually based on the data. The team gets together for the second round, and discusses their scores. Allow people to change their individual scores, but there is no pressure to have consensus—it is appropriate that different people score items differently.

Collect the scores and find the average for each gradient. The group can score different scenarios of a proposed project to see how the project's resiliency changes depending on planning and design.

Step 4. Present the Shared Averages for Each Gradient As a Visual

We like the spider diagram, shown here. The wider the web, the higher the resiliency of the project. Using the spider, people can see the strengths and weaknesses of the project.

Table 4.2 Scoring the Project

8 Gradients	Team Member 1	Team Member 2	Team Member ...	Average Score	Comments
Exposure Reduction					
Cost Efficiency					
Institutional Capacity					
Ecological Enhancement					
Adaptation Over Time					
GHG Reduction					
Participatory Process					
Equitable Outcomes					

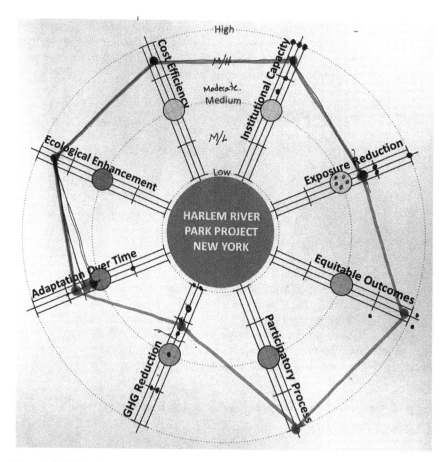

Figure 4.2 Spider diagram a simple visual to communicate final scores.
Source: Yaser Abunnasr

Step 5. Move Forward

Use the spider diagram and a brief write-up of the research and conversation that went into scoring to educate the decision-makers and the community involved. It can be helpful to write up a one-page summary to share with decision-makers, including your spider diagram summary of various proposals.

MATERIALS AVAILABLE

On our website you can find the full article "Pathways to Coastal Resiliency: The Adaptation Gradients Framework" describing the gradients approach, sample templates for recording data and scoring, and a PowerPoint for the spider diagram. See: www.resilient-infrastructure.org

Section II

Introduction to Greenhouse Gas Mitigation in Urban Areas

Introduction

Elisabeth M. Hamin Infield

One of the themes of this reader is that urban form is intimately connected to environmental performance, and in particular the ability to address climate change through mitigation and adaptation. In this section we focus on the issue of mitigation—the reduction of greenhouse gas emissions. Inventorying and then reducing greenhouse gas emissions at the local level has been a widely, although clearly not universally, accepted goal for at least a decade. As the first section of the Reader showed, there is a high degree of consensus on the facts of climate change and the ways that climate is changing as carbon builds up in the atmosphere. Similarly, a high degree of consensus has emerged on how urban areas can reduce their greenhouse gas emissions—in other words, how to achieve mitigation. The first step is to understand the past and projected future contributions of emissions from urban and other sources broadly through comparative analysis, and locally through greenhouse gas inventories. From there, policies can be designed that will be effective in the circumstances of the local place.

This section of the Reader introduces key concepts regarding how urban areas can reduce energy use and emissions, how emissions are accounted for, and what other benefits reductions are likely to provide. As the articles in this section show, without addressing land use, transportation, and building efficiency, it will be very difficult to achieve stabilization of overall global greenhouse gases discussed in the first section of the Reader. In this section, the first article is a widely cited and influential paper by Pacala and Socolow that sets out a very straight-forward way to think about what will be required to halt the increase in carbon build up in the atmosphere. They suggest we think about reductions as 'wedges', with each wedge a sector for action using existing technology and policy that could be scaled up to meet emissions reduction goals. Several of the leading actions they include are reducing reliance on cars, building more energy efficient structures, improving natural sinks—all of which are in the purview of planning, design, and construction fields. Each wedge area has a contribution to make, and all of them will be required for climate stabilization.

While not a specific 'wedge' in the Pacala and Socolow scheme, urban form itself influences greenhouse gas use, and thus can be used as a lever for reduction.

As further described in the article by Lee and Lee, research-tested methods for reducing overall urban emissions include improving biking and public transit so that residents drive less; building in fairly dense but still attractive ways to encourage the density needed for public transit, as well as allowing shared-wall housing styles; better managing waste streams; and then identifying steps appropriate to different cities' needs and goals.

One of the long-recognized challenges of mitigation is that the costs tend to be local, while the benefits are global. For example, a municipality that wants to reduce greenhouse gases by switching to electric new buses incurs all the cost, potentially resulting in higher local taxes, while the local direct benefit of the climate change prevented from that action may be very small—distribution of costs and benefits do not match up. Overcoming this perception has been critical to encouraging widespread mitigation action, and happens on several fronts. Perhaps most persuasive at the local level, reducing emissions also often leads to a higher quality of life for urban residents, as argued by Dodman. Money is saved on energy bills from conservation and good building design, as described by Lee and Lee. Harlan and Ruddell demonstrate that public health is improved when the particulates that get emitted alongside carbon are prevented. These and other strong local benefits to mitigation can create a persuasive case for politicians to take action.

Beyond the important questions of what will work to prevent future emissions are questions of who is responsible for the mess we are in now. To understand this, it is important to recognize the difference between current and cumulative emissions. The problem with carbon is that it breaks down very slowly, thus accumulating over time. Global North countries have cumulatively emitted most of the excess carbon in the atmosphere. The United States, for instance, is the world's largest cumulative greenhouse gas emitter at 29.3% of global emissions measured from 1850–2002, followed closely by the EU-25, 25 countries that together make up Europe. The whole Global South contributed only 24% excluding land use change. Emissions patterns change over time; for example, in recent years the annual total emissions from China have exceeded U.S. emissions.[1]

Another way to look at the issue is on a per capita basis, and there we see that in 2014 the average U.S. resident emitted 4.43 metric tons of carbon annually, Taiwanese residents emitted an average of 3.08 tons of carbon, the average Qatari emitted a startling 13.54 metric tons, while emissions from a resident of Kiribati, an island nation at risk of disappearing from rising seas, is so vanishingly small it is 0.15 metric tons.[2] Several points can be inferred or argued from this. Factually, those who contributed least to the problem are often the ones who are most at risk from it. We believe the data show there is a strong responsibility for those who have contributed the most to the climate crisis to take steps to reduce their future harm. As elegantly explained by Dodman in the reading in this section, developed countries need to reduce their emissions, and developing countries need to make choices that do not put them on track for rapid increases in per capita emissions while still achieving public health goals.

As former New York City mayor Michael Bloomberg notes, it is hard to manage what you haven't measured.[3] Local mitigation usually begins with a greenhouse gas inventory, in which municipalities attempt to measure the greenhouse gases

which come from their municipal actions (e.g., their bus fleets, building operations, waste sites) and often those of their residents as well. With inventories in
hand, municipalities can identify steps they themselves can take to reduce emissions. A couple of common examples are investing in hybrid bus fleets, or insulat-
ing municipal buildings. Campuses also do greenhouse gas inventories and for the
same reason. Inventories are not easy, however. A first consideration is whether a
municipality will include only the emissions its city government actually creates.
This is called 'Scope 1'—emissions that are the responsibility of the measuring
body. A broader perspective is 'Scope 2', which seeks to include emissions of the
people who live or work in that geography. Even more far-reaching is what is
called 'Scope 3', which seeks to include not just what gets produced in the area,
but also emissions from items purchased from elsewhere—the power brought in
from international sources, the manufactured goods residents buy from newly
developing countries. The Hoornweeg et al. and Dodman articles explore these
classifications as well as the difficulty in measuring Scope 3.

There are fairly well established international protocols for inventories, as
explained in the Boswell article. Many communities purchase a membership in
the non-profit ICLEI: Local Governments for Sustainability[4] when they are ready
to do an inventory, and use the ICLEI method to provide comparable and repro-
ducible results. Alternatively or in conjunction, many cities sign on to the Global
Covenant of Mayors for Climate & Energy, which also provides a free municipal
GHG inventory tool.[5] The Boswell et al. article explores how climate action planning is occurring in the U.S. A greenhouse gas emissions inventory is often part of
a Climate Action Plan, which includes steps to take to reach municipal goals. This
requires that municipal departments take the recommendations from the climate
action plans and build them into their departmental plans, including land use
plans and zoning regulations. As Boswell et al. report, stakeholder participation
and buy-in from the mayor through department heads and the broader public is
what moves plans into action. This is a theme we return to in the last section of
the book on implementation.

It has taken steady scholarly attention to develop and test these principles. The
articles in this section demonstrate how an intellectual argument to inform public
policy is built. The article by Lee and Lee shows the kind of steady and careful
scholarship that tests and builds the factual case regarding what sort of emissions
reduction can be expected from municipal actions, while articles by Hoornweg
et al., Dodman, and Harlen and Ruddell demonstrate how primary research gets
synthesized and contextualized to make broader policy arguments. The article by
Boswell et al. demonstrates the social science research that can encourage effective
implementation of policy.

Policy and planning influence individual and corporate actions—much of
land use in general and mitigation in particular is the sum of individual actions.
But individual voter support for these policies is what encourages politicians to
address them. And individual level action can happen with or without municipal
policies. At the individual level, you can choose a home in an area served by public
transit, drive less, buy energy-efficient cars and appliances, reduce consumption in
general, do activism for climate issues, and take the many other steps that improve
individual sustainability. For purposes here, this section focuses primarily on local

governments reducing their own emissions and creating the regulatory and fiscal conditions that will encourage individuals to make climate-smart choices. We do hope, however, that learning about what really works will encourage you to choose a lower-emissions lifestyle. Lessons we hope you take away from this section include that mitigation actions taken locally are critical for preventing even more future climate change and also have very tangible current benefits, that these actions start with a municipal greenhouse gas inventory, and that our ability to precisely identify the benefits of effective policies is improving with strong modeling. The green infrastructure of urban form has an important role to play in combating greenhouse gases and climate change.

NOTES

1. Baumert, K.A., Herzog, T., and Pershing, J. (2005). *Navigating the Numbers: Greenhouse Gas Data and International Climate Policy.* Washington, D.C.: World Resources Institute, Retrieved from pdf.wri.org/navigating_numbers_chapter6.pdf
2. Boden, T.A., Marland, G., and Andres, R.J. (2017). *National CO2 Emissions from Fossil-Fuel Burning, Cement Manufacture, and Gas Flaring: 1751–2014,* Carbon Dioxide Information Analysis Center, Oak Ridge National Laboratory, U.S. Department of Energy, doi: 10.3334/CDIAC/00001_V2017.
3. Bloomberg, M. and C. Pope (2017). *Climate of Hope.* New York, NY, Time-Life Inc.
4. ICLEI: Local Governments for Sustainability (2018). Retrieved from http://www.iclei.org/
5. Global Covenant of Mayors for Climate & Energy (2018). https://www.globalcovenant ofmayors.org/

5 Stabilization Wedges
Solving the Climate Problem for the Next 50 Years With Current Technologies

Stephen Pacala and Robert Socolow

EDITOR'S INTRODUCTION

The goal of carbon stabilization to a level that can prevent the most damaging climate change can seem distant and unobtainable if we conceptualize it only as a problem of global governance through international agreements, or as requiring currently unrealized technological break-throughs. There is a tendency to view addressing climate change as a problem for someone else to do, some other profession, some central government. In this article, authors Pacala and Socolow argue that long-term stabilization is achievable with current technology. The key is that emissions reduction has to occur across a range of sectors. They conceptualize these as "wedges," with each wedge having a role to play. Emissions stabilization and then reduction will occur as each of these wedges is addressed. Energy efficiency, switching to low-carbon energy sources, and biological storage are the three core components for the wedges. For urban planning generally and this book in particular, a core point of the reading is that our work can contribute in meaningful, significant ways to this key challenge. We are not bit players in this international and intergenerational drama of climate change. Instead, many of the solutions can only be achieved with good urban planning and good urban policy. Urban form matters; building more energy-efficient urban form will reduce reliance on cars and energy use in buildings. Public transportation and non-motorized commuting matters; denser urban form both requires and supports lower-carbon transportation. Municipal power sources matter; communities can choose low-carbon power sources. Green infrastructure matters; urban greening can help with sequestration of carbon. This field needs to be one of the wedges.

Stephen Pacala is the Frederick D. Petrie Professor in Ecology and Evolutionary Biology at Princeton University and for many years was the director of the Princeton

Environmental Institute. He is a fellow of the National Academy of Sciences, the American Association for the Advancement of Science, and the American Academy of Arts and Sciences, and continues research to model the global carbon cycle at many scales.

Robert Socolow trained as a physicist and is now Professor Emeritus of Mechanical and Aerospace Engineering at Princeton University. He is a member of the American Academy of Arts and Sciences, an associate of the National Research Council of the National Academies, a fellow of the American Physical Society, a fellow of the American Association for the Advancement of Science, and the recipient of the Leo Szilard Lectureship Award by the American Physical Society. His research seeks to anticipate key issues associated with low-carbon futures.

STABILIZATION WEDGES: SOLVING THE CLIMATE PROBLEM FOR THE NEXT 50 YEARS WITH CURRENT TECHNOLOGIES

Humanity already possesses the fundamental scientific, technical, and industrial know-how to solve the carbon and climate problem for the next half-century. A portfolio of technologies now exists to meet the world's energy needs over the next 50 years and limit atmospheric CO_2 to a trajectory that avoids a doubling of the preindustrial concentration. Every element in this portfolio has passed beyond the laboratory bench and demonstration project; many are already implemented somewhere at full industrial scale. Although no element is a credible candidate for doing the entire job (or even half the job) by itself, the portfolio as a whole is large enough that not every element has to be used.

The debate in the current literature about stabilizing atmospheric CO_2 at less than a doubling of the preindustrial concentration has led to needless confusion about current options for mitigation. On one side, the Intergovernmental Panel on Climate Change (IPCC) has claimed that "technologies that exist in operation or pilot stage today" are sufficient to follow a less-than-doubling trajectory "over the next hundred years or more" [(1), p. 8]. On the other side, a recent review in *Science* asserts that the IPCC claim demonstrates "misperceptions of techno- logical readiness" and calls for "revolutionary changes" in mitigation technology, such as fusion, space-based solar electricity, and artificial photosynthesis (2). We agree that fundamental research is vital to develop the revolutionary mitigation strategies needed in the second half of this century and beyond. But it is important not to become beguiled by the possibility of revolutionary technology. Humanity can solve the carbon and climate problem in the first half of this century simply by scaling up what we already know how to do.

WHAT DO WE MEAN BY "SOLVING THE CARBON AND CLIMATE PROBLEM FOR THE NEXT HALF-CENTURY"?

Proposals to limit atmospheric CO_2 to a concentration that would prevent most damaging climate change have focused on a goal of 500 ± 50 parts per million (ppm), or less than double the preindustrial concentration of 280 ppm (3–7).

The current concentration is ~375 ppm. The CO_2 emissions reductions necessary to achieve any such target depend on the emissions judged likely to occur in the absence of a focus on carbon (called a business-as-usual [BAU] trajectory), the quantitative details of the stabilization target, and the future behavior of natural sinks for atmospheric CO_2 (i.e., the oceans and terrestrial biosphere). We focus exclusively on CO_2, because it is the dominant anthropogenic greenhouse gas; industrial-scale mitigation options also exist for subordinate gases, such as methane and N_2O.

Very roughly, stabilization at 500 ppm requires that emissions be held near the present level of 7 billion tons of carbon per year (GtC/year) for the next 50 years, even though they are currently on course to more than double (Figure 5.1A).

[. . .]

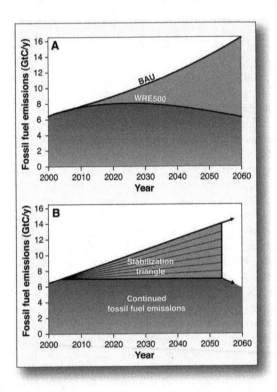

Figure 5.1 (A) The top curve is a representative BAU emissions path for global carbon emissions as CO_2 from fossil fuel combustion and cement manufacture: 1.5% per year growth starting from 7.0 GtC/year in 2004. The bottom curve is a CO_2 emissions path consistent with atmospheric CO_2 stabilization at 500 ppm by 2125 [. . .] The area between the two curves represents the avoided carbon emissions required for stabilization. (B) Idealization of (A): A stabilization triangle of avoided emissions (green) and allowed emissions (blue). The allowed emissions are fixed at 7 GtC/year beginning in 2004. The stabilization triangle is divided into seven wedges, each of which reaches 1 GtC/year in 2054. With linear growth, the total avoided emissions per wedge is 25 GtC, and the total area of the stabilization triangle is 175 GtC. The arrow at the bottom right of the stabilization triangle points downward to emphasize that fossil fuel emissions must decline substantially below 7 GtC/year after 2054 to achieve stabilization at 500 ppm.

THE STABILIZATION TRIANGLE

We idealize the 50-year emissions reductions as a perfect triangle. Stabilization is represented by a "flat" trajectory of fossil fuel emissions at 7 GtC/year, and BAU is represented by a straight-line "ramp" trajectory rising to 14 GtC/year in 2054. The "stabilization triangle," located between the flat trajectory and BAU, removes exactly one-third of BAU emissions.

To keep the focus on technologies that have the potential to produce a material difference by 2054, we divide the stabilization triangle into seven equal "wedges." A wedge represents an activity that reduces emissions to the atmosphere that starts at zero today and increases linearly until it accounts for 1 GtC/year of reduced carbon emissions in 50 years. It thus represents a cumulative total of 25 GtC of reduced emissions over 50 years. In this paper, to "solve the carbon and climate problem over the next half-century" means to deploy the technologies and/or lifestyle changes necessary to fill all seven wedges of the stabilization triangle.

Stabilization at any level requires that net emissions do not simply remain constant, but eventually drop to zero. For example, in one simple model (8) that begins with the stabilization triangle but looks beyond 2054, 500-ppm stabilization is achieved by 50 years of flat emissions, followed by a linear decline of about two-thirds in the following 50 years, and a very slow decline thereafter that matches the declining ocean sink. To develop the revolutionary technologies required for such large emissions reductions in the second half of the century, enhanced research and development would have to begin immediately.

Policies designed to stabilize at 500 ppm would inevitably be renegotiated periodically to take into account the results of research and development, experience with specific wedges, and revised estimates of the size of the stabilization triangle. But not filling the stabilization triangle will put 500-ppm stabilization out of reach. In that same simple model (8), 50 years of BAU emissions followed by 50 years of a flat trajectory at 14 GtC/year leads to more than a tripling of the preindustrial concentration.

It is important to understand that each of the seven wedges represents an effort beyond what would occur under BAU. Our BAU simply continues the 1.5% annual carbon emissions growth of the past 30 years. This historic trend in emissions has been accompanied by 2% growth in primary energy consumption and 3% growth in gross world product (GWP) (Section 1 of Supporting Online Material, available at www.sciencemag.org/cgi/content/full/305/5686/968/). If carbon emissions were to grow 2% per year, then [about] 10 wedges would be needed instead of seven, and if carbon emissions were to grow at 3% per year, then [about] 18 wedges would be required (Section 1 of SOM text). Thus, a continuation of the historical rate of decarbonization of the fuel mix prevents the need for three additional wedges, and ongoing improvements in energy efficiency prevent the need for eight additional wedges. Most readers will reject at least one of the wedges listed here, believing that the corresponding deployment is certain to occur in BAU, but readers will disagree about which to reject on such grounds. On the other hand, our list of mitigation options is not exhaustive.

WHAT CURRENT OPTIONS COULD BE SCALED UP TO PRODUCE AT LEAST ONE WEDGE?

Wedges can be achieved from energy efficiency, from the decarbonization of the supply of electricity and fuels (by means of fuel shifting, carbon capture and storage, nuclear energy, and renewable energy), and from biological storage in forests and agricultural soils. We will discuss 15 different examples of options that are already deployed at an industrial scale and that could be scaled up further to produce at least one wedge. Although several options could be scaled up to two or more wedges, we doubt that any could fill the stabilization triangle, or even half of it, alone.

Because the same BAU carbon emissions cannot be displaced twice, achieving one wedge often interacts with achieving another. The more the electricity system becomes decarbonized, for example, the less the available savings from greater efficiency of electricity use, and vice versa. [. . .]

Category I: Efficiency and Conservation

Improvements in efficiency and conservation probably offer the greatest potential to provide wedges. For example, in 2002, the United States announced the goal of decreasing its carbon intensity (carbon emissions per unit GDP) by 18% over the next decade, a decrease of 1.96% per year. An entire wedge would be created if the United States were to reset its carbon intensity goal to a decrease of 2.11% per year and extend it to 50 years, and if every country were to follow suit by adding the same 0.15% per year increment to its own carbon intensity goal. However, efficiency and conservation options are less tangible than those from the other categories. Improvements in energy efficiency will come from literally hundreds of innovations that range from new catalysts and chemical processes, to more efficient lighting and insulation for buildings, to the growth of the service economy and telecommuting. Here, we provide four of many possible comparisons of greater and less efficiency in 2054. (See references and details in Section 2 of the SOM text.)

> *Option 1: Improved fuel economy.* Suppose that in 2054, 2 billion cars (roughly four times as many as today) average 10,000 miles per year (as they do today). One wedge would be achieved if, instead of averaging 30 miles per gallon (mpg) on conventional fuel, cars in 2054 averaged 60 mpg, with fuel type and distance traveled unchanged.
> *Option 2: Reduced reliance on cars.* A wedge would also be achieved if the average fuel economy of the 2 billion 2054 cars were 30 mpg, but the annual distance traveled were 5,000 miles instead of 10,000 miles.

Option 3: More efficient buildings. According to a 1996 study by the IPCC, a wedge is the difference between pursuing and not pursuing "known and established approaches" to energy-efficient space heating and cooling, water heating, lighting, and refrigeration in residential and commercial buildings. These approaches reduce mid-century emissions from buildings by about one-fourth. About half of potential savings are in the buildings in developing countries (1).

Option 4: Improved power plant efficiency. In 2000, coal power plants, operating on average at 32% efficiency, produced about one-fourth of all carbon emissions: [. . .]

Category II: Decarbonization of Electricity and Fuels

[Editors' note: in this section authors suggest as Options 5–13 actions such as substituting natural gas for coal, utilizing carbon capture, and increasing low-carbon energy sources such as wind and other renewables]

Category III: Natural Sinks

Although the literature on biological sequestration includes a diverse array of options and some very large estimates of the global potential, here we restrict our attention to the pair of options that are already implemented at large scale and that could be scaled up to a wedge or more without a lot of new research. (See Section 4 of the SOM text for references and details.)

Option 14: Forest management. Conservative assumptions lead to the conclusion that at least one wedge would be available from reduced tropical deforestation and the management of temperate and tropical forests. [. . .]

Option 15: Agricultural soils management. When forest or natural grassland is converted to cropland, up to one-half of the soil carbon is lost, primarily because annual tilling increases the rate of decomposition by aerating undecomposed organic matter. About 55 GtC, or two wedges' worth, has been lost historically in this way. Practices such as conservation tillage (e.g., seeds are drilled into the soil without plowing), the use of cover crops, and erosion control can reverse the losses. [. . .]

CONCLUSIONS

In confronting the problem of greenhouse warming, the choice today is between action and delay. Here, we presented a part of the case for action by identifying a set of options that have the capacity to provide the seven stabilization wedges and solve the climate problem for the next half-century. None of the options is a pipe dream or an unproven idea. Today, one can buy electricity from a wind turbine, PV array, gas turbine, or nuclear power plant. One can buy hydrogen produced with the chemistry of carbon capture, biofuel to power one's car, and hundreds of devices that improve energy efficiency. One can visit tropical forests where clear-cutting has ceased, farms practicing conservation tillage, and facilities that inject carbon into geologic reservoirs. Every one of these options is already implemented at an industrial scale and could be scaled up further over 50 years to provide at least one wedge.

REFERENCES

1. IPCC, *Climate Change 2001: Mitigation*, B. Metz *et al.*, Eds. (IPCC Secretariat, Geneva, Switzerland, 2001); available at www.grida.no/climate/ipcc_tar/wg3/index.htm.
2. M. I. Hoffert et al., *Science* **298**, 981 (2002).
3. R. T. Watson et al., *Climate Change 2001: Synthesis Report. Contribution to the Third Assessment Report of the Intergovernmental Panel on Climate Change* (Cambridge Univ. Press, Cambridge, UK, 2001).
4. B. C. O'Neill, M. Oppenheimer, *Science* **296**, 1971 (2002).
5. Royal Commission on Environmental Pollution, *Energy: The Changing Climate* (2000); available at www.rcep.org.uk/energy.htm.
6. Environmental Defense, *Adequacy of Commitments—Avoiding "Dangerous" Climate Change: A Narrow Time Window for Reductions and a Steep Price for Delay* (2002); available at www.environmentaldefense.org/documents/2422_COP_time.pdf.
7. "Climate Options for the Long Term (COOL) synthesis report," *NRP Rep. 954281* (2002); available at www.wau.nl/cool/reports/COOLVolumeAdef.pdf.
8. R. Socolow, S. Pacala, J. Greenblatt, *Proceedings of the Seventh International Conference on Greenhouse Gas Control Technology*, Vancouver, Canada, 5 to 9 September, 2004.

6 Cities and Greenhouse Gas Emissions

Moving Forward

Daniel Hoornweg, Lorraine Sugar and Claudia Lorena Trejos Gómez

EDITOR'S INTRODUCTION

The article by Hoornweg, Sugar and Gomez provides an excellent introduction to some of the issues and challenges faced when considering climate mitigation at the local level. The importance of action at the urban level is hard to overstate—as they note, by 2050 the world will be 70 percent urban with a potential for 76 percent of energy-related global GHG by 2030. To achieve sustainable development goals, in their words, "cities must be efficient and well managed, and need to protect much better their most vulnerable populations. They also need to emit far less GHGs." The article establishes that per-person average emissions vary wildly from place to place, both between countries and within them. Much of this is climate-related; it simply takes more energy to heat homes in Canada than it does in California. But much of it is not dependent on climate, and instead is influenced by a wide range of factors, many of them based on the type of neighbourhood one chooses for home and work. As they report:

> The neighbourhood with the lowest emissions per capita is a high-density apartment complex within walking distance of a shopping centre and public transit. The average emissions per capita neighbourhood consists of high-density single family homes close to the downtown core and with access to public transit. The highest emissions per capita neighbourhood is located in the suburbs, consisting of large, low-density single family homes, distant from commercial activity.

They provide an illuminating list of example actions that cities have already taken, showing that change is entirely possible, and also that different places will require different practices.

Daniel Hoornweg is currently Professor and Jeff Boyce Research Chair, University of Ontario Institute of Technology, with a background in earth sciences and civil and environmental engineering. He was the World Bank's Lead Urban Specialist in Cities and Climate Change until his retirement from there in 2012. Co-author Lorraine Sugar also worked for the World Bank as a climate change specialist, and now pursues her Ph.D. in civil engineering at the University of Toronto. Claudia Lorena Trejos Gómez is a Senior Disaster Risk Management Specialist consultant for the World Bank.

CITIES AND GREENHOUSE GAS EMISSIONS: MOVING FORWARD

CITIES AND CLIMATE CHANGE

Climate change and urbanization are two of the most important phenomena facing the world today, and they are inextricably linked. Poverty reduction and sustainable development remain as core global priorities but, as the World Development Report 2010 emphasizes, climate change now threatens to undermine the progress achieved by low- and middle-income countries, and the poorest populations are most vulnerable.

The World Development Report 2009 presented a new development paradigm: harnessing the growth and development benefits of urbanization while proactively managing its negative effects. Urbanization likely presents the best chance for the world's poorest, however up to now most GHG emissions (and solid waste) are byproducts of the associated increase in affluence that usually accompanies urbanization. These emissions are particularly worrisome when they exceed the earth's assimilative capacity. In a fast-approaching world with 9 billion people, 70 percent of whom are expected to live in urban areas by 2050, cities must be efficient and well managed, and need to protect much better their most vulnerable populations. They also need to emit far less GHGs.

A large share of global greenhouse gas emissions is attributable to cities (World Bank, 2010). The International Energy Agency (IEA) estimates that urban areas currently account for more than 71 percent of energy-related global greenhouse gases, and this is expected to rise to 76 percent by 2030 (IEA, 2008), making energy-related emissions the largest single source of GHG emissions from a production-based perspective (i.e. allocating emissions to the places where they are generated). Taking a consumption-oriented perspective (where emissions are allocated to the persons whose consumption caused the emissions), total GHG emissions rates would exceed this when the emissions associated with products consumed by urban residents are included, e.g. agriculture, forestry and commodities [. . .].

City administrations and their citizens will be tasked with achieving the largest share of GHG emissions reductions. Using available GHG emissions data, this paper presents a possible path forward: clearly measure and communicate what is happening, tackle the largest issues first and get help from citizens, other cities and national governments. Cities will likely address the challenge of GHG mitigation in the same pragmatic manner they have approached other issues such as solid waste management, water supply and, hopefully, better services to and inclusion of the urban poor.

GHG EMISSIONS: ASSIGNING RESPONSIBILITY

When it comes to the causes of climate change, statements have been made suggesting that up to 80 percent of the world's anthropogenic greenhouse gas emissions are attributable to cities. In contrast, arguments have been made against blaming cities for climate change based on observations such as: most emissions can occur outside the specific legislative boundary of cities, e.g. for electricity generation; and that urban living is more environmentally efficient than suburban and rural living at similar levels of affluence. The conflict between these two perspectives represents the difference between production based and consumption-based GHG attribution [. . .]

Consider the sheer magnitude of some larger world cities. Shanghai's population and greenhouse gas emissions would place it in the world's top 40 if it were a separate country. In terms of economic significance, Tokyo and New York both have GDPs greater than Canada's. Based on GHG emissions per GDP, citizens of Tokyo are 5.6 times more efficient than Canadians. [The C40 is an international group of cities who have voluntarily committed to tackling climate change; see http://www.c40cities.org/.] Combined, all member cities of the C40 represent 291 million people, at least 1,747 megatonnes of greenhouse gas emissions and more than US$10.8 trillion (PPP) total GDP, placing the combined 40 cities among the top four countries in the world for each category (Table 6.1).

[. . .]

Table 6.1 Rank of C40 member cities relative to the world's top nations in terms of population, GHG emissions and GDP

Population (millions)	GHG emissions (MtCO$_2$e)	GDP (billion $ PPP)
(1) China: 1,191.8	(1) USA: 7,107.2	(1) USA: 14,202
(2) India: 915.7	(2) China: 4,057.6	(2) C40 cities: 10,875
(3) USA: 301.3	(3) Russian Federation: 2,192.8	(3) China: 7,903
(4) C40 cities: 291.0	(4) C40 cities: 1,747.2	(4) Japan: 4,354
(5) Indonesia: 190.0	(5) Japan: 1,374.3	(5) India: 3,388

Sources: GDP calculated using data from Hawksworth, John, Thomas Hoehn and Anmol Tiwari (2009), "Which are the largest city economies in the world and how might this change by 2025?" in Price Waterhouse Coopers (PwC), *UK Economic Outlook November 2009*, London, pages 20–34 (conservatively scaled by population with national data for cities not included in Hawksworth et al.). GHG emissions calculated using data from Table 6.2 and United Nations Framework Convention on Climate Change (UNFCCC) (2005), "Sixth compilation and synthesis of initial national communications from Parties not included in Annex I to the Convention," United Nations Office at Geneva, Geneva, 20 pages; also United Nations Framework Convention on Climate Change (UNFCCC) (2009), "National greenhouse gas inventory data for the period 1990–2007," United Nations Office at Geneva, Geneva, 27 pages. Population figures for nations are from the World Bank (2009), *World Development Report 2010: Development and Climate Change*, The World Bank, Washington DC, 417 pages, and for cities from C40 Cities: Climate Leadership Group (2010), "C40 cities: participating cities," accessed October 2010 at www.c40cities.org/cities.

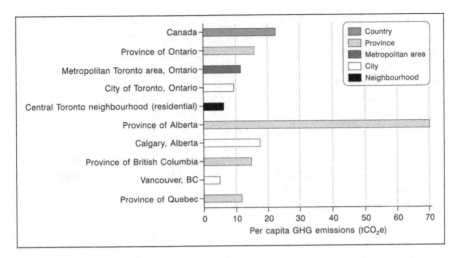

Figure 6.1 Disaggregated per capita emissions for various Canadians*

Note: *National and provincial emissions are production based; city emissions are production based for fossil fuel combustion and industrial processes, and consumption based for electricity and waste; neighbourhood emissions are production based for transportation, and consumption based for household energy.

Sources: National and provincial data from Environment Canada (2010), "Canada's greenhouse gas inventory: national/provincial/territorial tables," accessed October 2010 at www.ec.gc.ca/ges-ghg/default.asp?lang=En&n=83A34A7A-1. Metropolitan Toronto data from Kennedy, C, J Steinberger, B Gasson, Y Hansen, T Hillman, M Havranek, D Pataki, A Phdungsilp, A Ramaswami and G Villalba Mendez (2009), "Greenhouse gas emissions from global cities," *Environmental Science and Technology* Vol 43, No 19, October, pages 7297–7302; also City of Toronto (2007), "Greenhouse gases and air pollutants in the city of Toronto, 2004," accessed March 2010 at www.toronto.ca/teo/pdf/ghg-aq-inventory-june2007.pdf. Neighbourhood data from VandeWeghe, Jared R and Christopher Kennedy (2007), "A spatial analysis of residential greenhouse gas emissions in the Toronto census metropolitan area," *Journal of Industrial Ecology* Vol 11, No 2, pages 133–144.

Figure 6.1 provides disaggregated per capita emissions for various Canadians. All are accurate, yet these averages vary from a low of 6.4 tCO$_2$e per capita in a central neighbourhood in Toronto to a high of 70.1 tCO$_2$e per capita for an Albertan. There are variations within provinces and cities, and the same person can have different emissions depending on the geographical area used. For example, the same Toronto resident's per capita emissions are 6.42 tCO$_2$e for their household emissions, 9.5 tCO$_2$e for citywide emissions, 11.6 tCO$_2$e for the Greater Toronto metropolitan area, 16.0 tCO$_2$e as a resident of the province of Ontario and 22.65 tCO$_2$e as an average Canadian.

Per capita estimates of emissions represent not only an individual's lifestyle choices, but also the nature of the infrastructure and the structure of the economy in the geographical region. [. . .]

Emissions also vary significantly at the neighbourhood level [. . .] A close examination of the GHG attribution by census tract reveals interesting correlations between per capita GHG emissions, urban form and service access. Satellite imagery of three Toronto census tracts: the tract with the lowest per capita emissions, a tract with the average per capita emissions and the tract with the highest per capita emissions. The neighbourhood with the lowest emissions per capita is a high-density apartment complex within walking distance of a shopping centre and public transit. The average emissions per capita neighbourhood consists of high-density single family homes close to the downtown core and with access to public transit. The highest emissions per capita neighbourhood is located in the suburbs, consisting of large, low-density single family homes, distant from commercial activity. This heterogeneity of per capita emissions is not unique to Canada. [. . .]

CITIES ARE MAJOR PLAYERS IN CLIMATE CHANGE MITIGATION

Global trends and cultural shifts now arise exclusively through cities. Globalization is anchored through the growing connectivity of about 75 "global cities." Through their economic heft and trend-setting nature, these "country-lites" act as portals in determining much of our collective civilization.

By their nature, as national governments deal with more intractable geopolitical issues, cities are often able to better cooperate with each other than their host countries. Cities often express the aspirations of their citizens more succinctly and more quickly than higher levels of government, and when these rising voices are credibly articulated, their global impact is considerable. The global response to climate change is illustrative. In the US, for example, 1,017 cities have signed up to meet or exceed Kyoto Protocol targets to reduce GHG emissions, even though the national government refused to sign the protocol.

Because of their proximity to the public and the focus on providing day-to-day services, cities tend to be more pragmatic than senior levels of government. National governments may set the rules of the game, but it is cities that are the athletes. [. . .]

Table 6.2 provides an array of policy tools that are being implemented by cities. Some examples of municipal policies leading to reductions in emissions include congestion pricing (Singapore and Stockholm), dense and integrated land use (Barcelona and São Paulo), and provision of good public transit (Zurich and Curitiba).

In cities, there is the potential to capitalize on the co-benefits of mitigation, adaptation and improved access to services. Cities with excellent services are resilient cities: advanced drainage systems can alleviate flooding during intense storms; robust healthcare services are equipped to respond in emergency situations; warning systems and transportation infrastructure allow citizens to evacuate in response to risk.

Table 6.2 Policy tools for local-level action on climate change

Policy goals	Policy tools	Policy sector	Purpose	Mode of governance	Complementary with policy tools that:
Reduce trip lengths	Restructure land value tax to increase value of land closer to urban core, jobs or services	Land use zoning	Mitigation	Regulatory	Increase mass transit use*
	Mixed use zoning to shorten trip distances	Land use zoning	Mitigation	Regulatory	Discourage vehicle use;* support non-motorized means of travel
Increase mass transit use	Transit-oriented development zones	Land use zoning	Mitigation	Regulatory	Increase mass transit use;* discourage vehicle use*
	Restructure land value tax to increase value of land served by public transportation	Land use zoning	Mitigation	Regulatory	Increase mass transit use*
	Tax incentives to developers near public transportation	Land use zoning	Mitigation	Regulatory	Increase mass transit use*
	Improve quality of public transportation	Transportation	Mitigation	Service provision	Discourage vehicle use*
	Provide linkages with multiple modes of travel	Transportation	Mitigation	Service provision	Discourage vehicle use;* support non-motorized means of travel*
	Expand mass transit service	Transportation	Mitigation	Service provision	Discourage vehicle use*
	Employee transport plans	Transportation	Mitigation	Facilitative	Improve quality of public transportation; provide linkages with multiple modes of travel; expand mass transit service
Discourage vehicle use	Traffic calming to discourage driving	Land use Zoning	Mitigation	Regulatory/ service provision	Improve quality of public transportation; provide linkages with multiple modes of travel; expand mass transit service
	Driving and parking restrictions in certain zones	Transportation	Mitigation	Regulatory	Improve quality of public transportation; provide linkages with multiple modes of travel; expand mass transit service

(Continued)

Table 6.2 (Continued)

Policy goals	Policy tools	Policy sector	Purpose	Mode of governance	Complementary with policy tools that:
Support non-motorized means of travel	Traffic calming and increase in bike lanes	Transportation	Mitigation	Regulatory/service provision	Discourage vehicle use*
Increase vehicle efficiency and alternative fuels use	Special parking privileges for alternative fuel or hybrid vehicles	Transportation	Mitigation	Regulatory	Driving and parking restrictions in certain zones
Efficiency and alternative fuels use	Purchase of fuel efficient, hybrid or alternative fuel vehicles for city fleet	Transportation	Mitigation	Self-governance	—
Increase building energy efficiency	Zoning regulation to promote multi-family and connected residential housing	Land use zoning	Mitigation	Regulatory	Increase attractiveness of higher-density developments through policy tools that: increase neighbourhood open space; improve quality of public transportation; provide linkages with multiple modes of travel; expand mass transit service; tree-planting programmes
	Energy efficiency requirements in building codes	Building	Mitigation	Regulatory	Coordination of public-private retrofitting programmes; stringent enforcement policies; national building codes
	Coordination of public-private retrofitting programmes	Building	Mitigation	Service provision	Energy efficiency requirements in building codes
Increase local share of renewable and captured energy generation	Building codes requiring a minimum share of renewable energy	Building	Mitigation	Regulatory	Technical support to developers and property owners
	District heating and cooling projects	Building	Mitigation	Regulatory/service provision	Remove regulatory barriers to requiring connection to district heating/cooling system
	Waste-to-energy programmes	Waste	Mitigation	Service provision	Strictly regulate incinerator emissions; remove recyclables from waste stream

Reduce vulnerability to flooding and increased storm events	Zoning regulation to create more open space	Land use zoning	Adaptation	Regulatory	Zoning regulation to promote multi-family and connected residential housing
	Retrofitting and improvements to mass transit systems to reduce potential damage from flooding	Transportation	Adaptation	Service provision	Improve quality of public transportation; provide linkages with multiple modes of travel; expand mass transit service
	Designation of open space as buffer zones for flooding	Natural resources	Adaptation	Regulatory	Zoning regulation to create more open space; zoning regulation to promote multi-family and connected residential housing
	Building codes requiring minimum ground clearance	Building	Adaptation	Regulatory	Designation of open space as buffer zones for flooding
Reduce urban heat-island effects and vulnerability to extreme heat	Retrofitting and improvements to mass transit systems to reduce potential damage from extreme temperatures	Transportation	Adaptation	Service provision	Improve quality of public transportation; provide linkages with multiple modes of travel; expand mass transit service
	Tree-planting programmes	Natural resources	Mitigation and adaptation	Self-governance	Increase attractiveness of higher-density developments
	Building codes requiring design materials that reduce heat-island effects	Building	Adaptation	Regulatory	Energy efficiency requirements in building codes
	Building codes requiring "green roofs" with vegetation or white surfaces	Building	Mitigation and adaptation	Regulatory	Energy efficiency requirements in building codes

Note: Denotes all policy tools listed under a policy goal.

Source: Kamal-Chaoui, Lamia and Alexis Robert (editors) (2009), "Competitive cities and climate change", OECD Regional Development Working Paper No 2, OECD Publishing, 172 pages.

ACTION BEGINS WITH A GREENHOUSE
GAS INVENTORY

The mitigation process to reduce GHG emissions should begin with a good understanding of emissions sources. This is accomplished with a clear and comprehensive greenhouse gas inventory. Greenhouse gas inventories for local jurisdictions identify emissions by source and report them in per capita terms. By identifying sectors with high levels of emissions, cities can determine where best to direct mitigation efforts. Regular updating is also needed to monitor the impact of policy initiatives. Even with the complexity of the systems and dynamics found in cities, greenhouse gas emissions reflect well the multi-faceted nature of urban activity. GHGs are waste products expelled into the atmosphere as a result of various activities. The level of economic and social activity, as well as the systems and structures that enable activities, determine the amount of greenhouse gases produced. Therefore, GHG emissions provide a clear link between daily life and climate change.

Per capita estimates of urban GHG emissions largely reflect the nature and economic structure of their respective cities. For example, a city with heavy industry, high car usage and coal-generated electricity will have higher per capita emissions than a city with a knowledge-based industry, good public transit and electricity drawn from hydropower. More research is needed, the variations between cities may be as wide as within cities. Emissions are likely most closely correlated to affluence, and low neighbourhood-level emissions might offset the higher global emissions resulting from air travel or second homes. [. . .]

Low- and middle-income countries tend to have lower per capita emissions than high-income countries; dense cities tend to have relatively lower per capita emissions (particularly those with good transportation systems); cities tend to have higher emissions if in a cold climate zone. The most important observation is that there is no single factor that can explain variations in per capita emissions across cities; they are agglomerations of a variety of physical, economic and social factors specific to their unique urban life. The details of each inventory and its ability to undergo peer review, however, are critical to the development and monitoring of an effective mitigation strategy.

The city of Toronto, for which some of the most comprehensive spatial data is now available, provides an important observation: in the total emissions per capita value for citywide (9.5 tCO_2e) and metropolitan (11.6 tCO_2e), residential contributions account for approximately 68 percent and 57 percent, respectively (Kennedy et al., 2009). The "low" and "high" neighbourhoods vary by as much as a factor of 10. This suggests that what you buy is important, but what type of housing and neighbourhood you live in is much more important.

EMPOWERING CHANGE THROUGH CITIES

Cities are the optimum scale for integrated policy development and action on climate change mitigation. [. . .]

GHG mitigation strategies will likely evolve along two complementary parallel tracks. The first—and largely led by individual cities—will focus on urban form, with a keen interest in housing type and on integrated transport systems. The second track will require cooperative efforts between cities and countries, and will encourage less carbon-intense electricity, greater efficiency for all products and activities (for example, international air travel), and likely a particular focus on the poor in cities in low-income and many middle-income nations, who emit virtually no emissions yet, but will be most impacted.

REFERENCES

International Energy Agency (IEA) (2008), *World Energy Outlook 2008*, IEA, Paris, 569 p.

Kamal-Chaoui, Lamia and Alexis Robert (editors) (2009), "Competitive cities and climate change", *OECD Regional Development Working Paper No 2*, OECD Publishing, 172 p.

Kennedy, Christopher, Steinberger, Julia, Gasson, Barrie, Hansen, Yvonne, Hillman, Timothy, Havránek, Miroslav, Pataki, Diane, Phdungsilp, Aumnad, Ramaswami, Anu and Villalba Mendez, Gara (2009), Greenhouse Gas Emissions from Global Cities. *Environmental Science & Technology* 2009 43 (19), 7297–7302. DOI: 10.1021/es900213p

World Bank (2010), *Cities and Climate Change: An Urgent Agenda*, The World Bank, Washington, DC.

7 The Influence of Urban Form on GHG Emissions in the U.S. Household Sector

Sungwon Lee and Bumsoo Lee

EDITOR'S INTRODUCTION

Common sense suggests that providing an urban form dense enough to make using the bus convenient will reduce emissions, but exactly how much of change is possible has been a contested area. Can we cut driving in half? By just a little? Similarly, it makes sense that homes with shared walls (apartments, condos, and such) which tend to predominate in denser urban areas are more energy efficient. But how much more, on average? The answers matter in terms of policy investment in money, time, and political will, and in the actual contributions of such actions to goals of carbon reduction. Attempting to quantitatively evaluate the role of density and building form is fraught with complexity, leading to some of the most contentious moments in planning scholarship in recent years. The challenge is isolating the contribution of urban form on what are very interrelated emissions outcomes. It is into these difficult waters that Lee and Lee plunged in their 2014 article. Their modeling shows that shifting to a more compact urban form helps both by reducing trips taken and vehicle miles traveled, and in residential energy use. Doubling population-weighted density is associated with a reduction in CO_2 emissions of 48% of household travel and 35% of household residential energy use. Doubling density is a highly ambitious goal in many contexts. Less ambitiously, increasing population-weighted density by 10% leads to a reduction in CO_2 emissions by 4.8% and 3.5% from household travel and residential building energy use, respectively. These numbers aren't huge, but they contribute substantially to the urban areas carbon stabilization 'wedge' as described in this section's first reading, and with minimal change in the urban form. Beyond density, they find that policies that work in urban areas include providing cleaner energy sources especially for electricity, transportation investments to encourage public transit, and improving building efficiency.

Sungwon Lee is Associate Research Fellow in the Smart & Green City Research Center at the Korea Research Institute for Human Settlements. His research interests lie in spatial and temporal aspects of development to attain energy efficient and productive cities. Currently he focuses on smart city policies such as how information and communication technology effectively contribute to accomplish sustainable and livable cities. Bumsoo Lee is an Associate Professor of Urban and Regional Planning at the University of Illinois at Urbana-Champaign, and currently serves as its Director of the Masters in Urban Planning, and has research interests in the relationships between urban spatial structure and various urban indicators such as productivity, travel behavior, pollution, and greenhouse gas emissions; the influences of urban form on health related behavior and obesity; and economic impact modeling for man-made and natural disasters.

THE INFLUENCE OF URGAN FORM ON GHG EMISSIONS IN THE U.S. HOUSEHOLD SECTOR

INTRODUCTION

Experts widely agree that the global mean temperature (GMT) should be kept within a maximum of 2°C above preindustrial levels to prevent potentially catastrophic consequences for human society and natural ecosystems (Smith et al., 2009). [. . .] Reducing individual energy consumption through shifts in behavior represents one opportunity to mitigate GHG emissions. This option is compelling given that households, as an end-user sector, account for 42% of total U.S. carbon dioxide emissions from fossil fuel combustion, combining emissions from residential buildings (22%) and passenger travel (20%) (U.S. Environmental Protection Agency, 2012). While various factors such as energy price, income, and weather affect household energy consumption, a growing body of literature has linked compact urban development to more carbon efficient lifestyles, including less driving and more energy efficient housing choices (Ewing et al., 2008a, 2008b). [. . .]

This study investigates the paths by which urban form influences household sector carbon dioxide emissions in the 125 largest urbanized areas (UAs) in the U.S. We estimate individual household carbon emissions from travel and home energy use by processing household surveys, including the census, and quantify spatial structure of urbanized areas in several dimensions beyond a simple population density measure. Using this data, combined with a multilevel structural equation model (SEM), we demonstrate that shifting toward more compact urban form can significantly reduce energy consumption and CO_2 emissions in the household sector. Our analysis shows that increasing population-weighted density by 10% leads to a reduction in CO_2 emissions by 4.8% and 3.5% from household travel and residential building energy use, respectively. The effects of other spatial variables are estimated to be small.

URBAN FORM AND GHG EMISSIONS

Connections between urban form and GHG emissions have been studied in the fields of transportation and building energy research. In the transportation sector, research has typically focused on the influence of the built environment on travel demand, often measured in vehicle miles traveled (VMT). In the absence of adequate emissions data at individual and even urban area levels, emissions are often assumed to be a function of VMT, given the current or a target fuel efficiency and fuel carbon content (Mui et al., 2007). Despite earlier skepticism (Boarnet and Crane, 2001; Boarnet and Sarmiento, 1998), many recent empirical studies have found that urban form variables significantly influence travel behavior, including mode choice, trip frequency, trip distance, and, ultimately, VMT. These variables include density, land use diversity, street design; Cervero and Kockelman, 1997), destination accessibility, and distance to transit (additional 2Ds; Cervero et al., 2009). A growing body of literature shows that residents in more compact and transit-friendly neighborhoods drive considerably less than those living in sprawling neighborhoods. Moreover, the travel impacts of neighborhood characteristics are found to be significant, even after controlling for the effects of residential self-sorting by preferences and environmental attitudes (Cao et al., 2009; Mokhtarian and Cao, 2008).

[. . .]

Urban form also affects energy consumption, and hence GHG emissions in residential buildings, through two paths: housing choices—sizes and types—and, potentially, urban heat island (UHI) effects. Households in multifamily housing units, characterized by shared walls and typically smaller floor space, consume less energy for space heating, cooling, and all other purposes than do households in detached single-family homes, when controlling for the age of housing structures as a proxy of construction technology (Brown and Southworth, 2005; Holden and Norland, 2005; Myors et al., 2005; Perkins et al., 2009). An analysis of the U.S. Residential Energy Consumption Survey (RECS) data shows that single-family home residents consume 54% more energy for home heating and 26% more energy for home cooling than do comparable multifamily housing units (Ewing and Rong, 2008). The same study also shows that doubling home size is associated with the use of 16% more energy for heating and 13% more energy for cooling. [. . .]

This study examines the effects of urbanized area level urban form on individual household level carbon dioxide emissions, accounting for both transportation and residential energy uses. [. . .]

RESEARCH METHODS

Model Specification

Our basic approach is a multilevel structural equation model (SEM), which simultaneously tests multiple causal relations between urban spatial structure and household CO_2 emissions. SEM is an increasingly popular statistical method in various disciplines, including travel behavior research. [. . .] We use the 2000 Census Public Use Microdata Sample (PUMS) for residential carbon emission models and the 2001 National Household Travel Survey for analyzing CO_2 emissions from travel. The unit of analysis in both models is individual households nested within the 125 largest urbanized areas in the United States. [. . .]

RESULTS

Household CO_2 Emissions in U.S. Urbanized Areas

The average annual CO_2 emission of U.S. households in the largest 125 urban areas is estimated at 49,733 lbs., as shown in Table 7.1, combining emissions from driving, public transit use, home heating, and electricity use.

[. . .]

Private vehicle driving is a predominant source (97.5%) of carbon emissions from household travel simply because it is the dominant travel mode (88.2%). Switching from driving to riding public transit has a good potential for reducing carbon emissions. Our data show that average public transit produces about 53% less CO_2 per passenger mile than a single-occupancy private vehicle and 26% less than an average occupancy vehicle. However, public transit is not cleaner than private vehicles in all cities. In 91 of the 125 urbanized areas in our sample, public

Table 7.1 Average annual CO_2 emission per household in the largest 125 U.S. urbanized areas, 2000[c].

	Transportation CO_2		Residential CO_2		Total
	Private vehicle	Public transit	Heating	Electricity	
CO_2 emissions per household (lbs)	21,155 (44.6%)	538 (1.1%)	11,160 (23.5%)	14,615 (30.8%)	47,468 (100%)
Household travel					
Annual miles traveled per household[a]	19,706	211			
CO_2 emissions per VMT (lbs)[b]	1.07				
CO_2 emissions per PMT (lbs)[b]	0.69	0.51			
Residential energy use					
Energy consumption (kWh)			24,528 (67.3%)	11,934 (32.7%)	36,462 (100%)
CO_2 emissions per kWh (lbs)			0.45	1.22	

a Vehicle miles traveled (VMT) for private vehicle use and person miles traveled (PMT) for public transit use.

b The average occupancy rate of 1.56 per private vehicle and fuel efficiency of 20.96 mpg from the 2001 NHTS are applied to convert VMT to CO_2 emissions.

c Transportation CO_2 is estimated for 2001 while residential CO_2 is estimated using the 2000 census data.

transit emits more CO_2 per passenger mile—the result of low occupancy rates of transit modes in small and medium-sized cities. This does not mean that we should discourage public transportation in small and medium-sized cities. Rather, it implies an even larger potential in GHG reduction of switching from driving to transit riding when threshold passenger loads are ensured by supporting land use and transportation policies.

Regarding residential energy consumption, it should be noted that more CO_2 is produced from electricity consumption (including electricity for home cooling) than from home heating, even as home heating accounts for double the energy use. In other words, on average, the current portfolio of power generation relies on much dirtier energy sources than does individual residential home heating. It is also notable that there is wide variation in the resources mix, and the relative carbon intensity of power generation, across the eGRID subregions. The amount of CO_2 emissions per MWh of electricity ranges from 775 lbs in the SERC Tennessee Valley to 2,283 lbs in the Southwest Power Pool (SPP) North. [. . .] The result also suggests that switching to an alternative resource mix from coal in power generation should be a priority in warmer regions where the demand for home cooling is high.

The geographic pattern of urbanized area carbon footprints shown in Figure 7.1 is consistent with previous studies (Brown et al., 2008; Glaeser and Kahn, 2010). The average household carbon dioxide emissions are considerably lower in UAs of the West Coast and Florida, with good climatic conditions, and Northeastern cities that are transit dependent. Many UAs in the Midwest and Southeast that are automobile-oriented and/or carbon intense in power generation have the largest carbon footprints per household.

Figure 7.2 presents the negative relationship between average annual household CO_2 emissions and population-weighted density, the most basic urban form indicator urban form indicator. The estimated elasticity of CO_2 emissions with regard to density is about 17.34% at the aggregate level when no other covariates are included. However, population density explains only 18% of the variation in average carbon dioxide emissions at the aggregate level. In the following section, we will investigate the true relationship between urban form and CO_2 emissions after controlling for demographic and socio-economic conditions at the individual household level, along with other UA level characteristics such as climate conditions and transportation infrastructure.

[. . .]

Results for Transportation CO_2 Emissions

Combining all direct and indirect elasticities, a 10% increase in population-weighted density is associated with a 4.8% reduction in CO_2 emissions from travel, all else being equal. Most of the density effect occurs via the VMT path, as shown by the indirect composite elasticity of 0.398 (-0.986×0.404). High-density developments reduce household VMT by promoting alternative transportation modes and bringing trip origins and destinations closer together. In addition, people tend to own more fuel-efficient vehicles, and public transit is more carbon efficient per passenger mile, due to higher passenger loads in higher-density

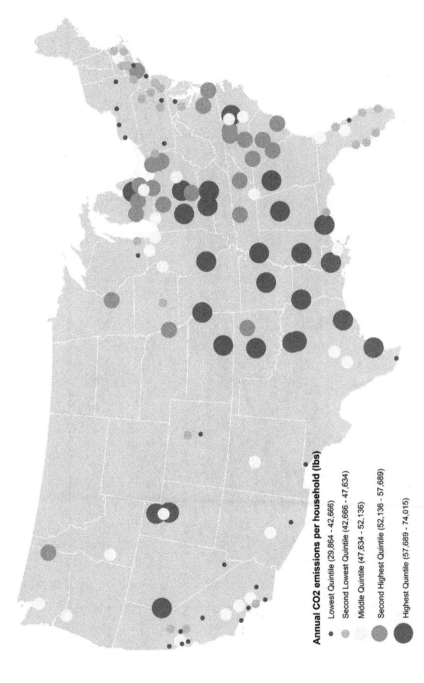

Annual CO2 emissions per household (lbs)

·   Lowest Quintile (29,864 - 42,666)

•   Second Lowest Quintile (42,666 - 47,634)

●   Middle Quintile (47,634 - 52,136)

⬤   Second Highest Quintile (52,136 - 57,689)

⬤   Highest Quintile (57,689 - 74,015)

Figure 7.1 The geography of carbon footprints in U.S. urbanized areas, 2000.

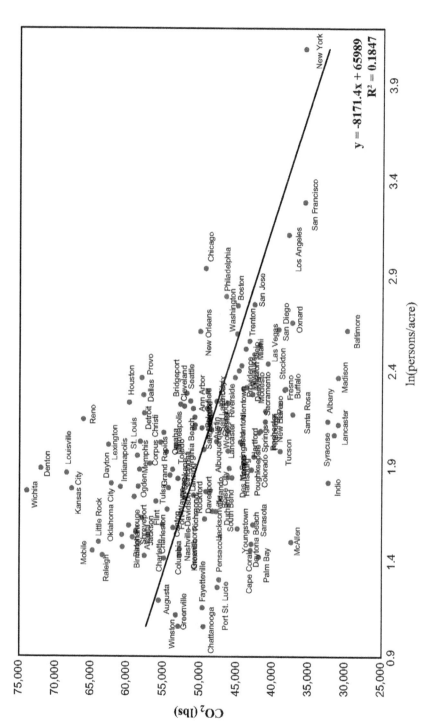

Figure 7.2 The relationship between population-weighted density and annual household CO_2 emissions.

communities. These additional effects are captured by the direct impact of density in our model.

[. . .] The impacts of the other two urban form variables are estimated to be moderate. Consistent with our expectation, centralized population distribution, given the same population and density, significantly reduces the amount of vehicle travel, by promoting public transportation and reducing trip distances. The elasticity is estimated at about 0.09. Thus, both overall population density in an urbanized area and the density near the central location are important in reducing carbon dioxide emissions from household travel.

As discussed earlier, a polycentric structure is expected to have dual effects. On the one hand, it can potentially shorten commute distances, given more decentralized population and employment; on the other, it can make serving urban activities by public transportation more difficult. The net effect is estimated to be moderately positive in this study, suggesting that the effect of discouraging transit use dominates in medium and large U.S. urbanized areas. This finding implies that increasing employment density near the central business district CBD can also be beneficial in terms of CO_2 emission reduction. However, it should be noted that polycentric structure is a spatial adjustment to cope with negative externalities of city size (Fujita and Ogawa, 1982; McMillen and Smith, 2003). Empirical studies have associated polycentric metropolitan structure with higher productivity (Meijers and Burger, 2010), and decentralized employment has often been connected with a shorter average commute time (Crane and Chatman, 2003; Gordon and Lee, 2014). Thus, developing public transportation networks that can efficiently serve polycentrized urban regions would be a better policy solution (Brown and Thompson, 2008) than discouraging transformation from a monocentric to polycentric urban area.

This policy implication is further articulated by the significance of the transit subsidy variable. Doubling transit subsidy per capita is associated with nearly 46% lower VMT and an 18% reduction in CO_2 emissions. [. . .]

Residential CO_2 Emissions

High-density development also contributes to energy saving and CO_2 emission reduction in residential buildings. A 10% increase in population-weighted density is associated with a 3.5% reduction in residential CO_2 emissions (the reduction is 3.1% when accounting for only statistically significant path coefficients). While this elasticity is slightly smaller than the impact on transportation CO_2 emissions, it is still a considerable effect that deserves policy attention.

[. . .]

CONCLUSIONS

To enhance our understanding of the role of sustainable urban development in GHG mitigation, this study investigated the paths via which urban form influences household carbon dioxide emissions in the 125 largest urbanized areas in the United States. Toward that end, we estimated individual household level CO_2

emissions from travel and residential energy consumption based on the 2001 National Household Travel Survey and the 2000 Census PUMS data. Estimates show that an average U.S. household in large and medium size urban areas annually produces 49,733 lbs. of CO_2, combining emissions from travel (45.7%) and residential energy consumption (54.3%). It is notable that the carbon intensity of electricity is about 2.7 times that of home heating energy on average and has wide variation from region to region.

The results of multilevel SEM analyses show that doubling population-weighted density is associated with a reduction in CO_2 emissions from household travel and residential energy consumption by 48% and 35%, respectively. Population density is believed to function as a catchall variable for compact urban form, which may also include land use mix and alternative urban design elements, although several additional UA-level urban form variables are included in our models. In any case, our analysis presents considerably larger elasticities than previous estimates by using population-weighted density instead of a conventional density measure. Furthermore, though not included in our analysis, compact urban form can also contribute to reducing energy use and GHG emissions in commercial buildings that may be comparable to carbon savings from residential buildings shown in this study.

The other two urban form variables were only moderately significant: centralized population distribution helps reduce VMT and hence transportation CO_2 emissions, while polycentric structure is associated with an opposite outcome. Perhaps more importantly in terms of policy implications, we also found that public transportation policy can play a significant role in lowering VMT. Doubling the per capita transit subsidy is associated with a nearly 46% lower VMT and an 18% reduction in transportation CO_2 emissions. A caveat, though, is that the transit subsidy variable in our parsimonious model seems to capture the impacts of various factors that affect transit mode shares.

A notable limitation of the present analysis is that our urban form measures focus only on the macro spatial structure at the urbanized area level, leaving out other urban form dimensions such as land use mix and street connectivity. There is a promising research opportunity in the future in which one can examine urban form effects at both neighborhood and urban area levels in a three-level hierarchical model.

Given that household travel and residential energy use account for 42% of total U.S. carbon dioxide emissions, our research findings corroborate that urban land use and transportation policies to build more compact cities should play a crucial part of any strategic efforts to mitigate GHG emissions and stabilize climate at all levels of government. Changing urban settlement forms certainly require long-term efforts. Researchers can only offer a wide range of scenarios regarding the percent of all new development by 2050 which is compact: between 25% and 75% (Transportation Research Board, 2009) or between 60% and 90% (Ewing et al., 2008b). However, studies show that there are latent demands for more sustainable developments in light of demographical and socio-economic changes (Nelson, 2009). Our findings using population-weighted density highlight that concentrating density in central areas by strategic infill (re)development will be particularly beneficial. In recent years, smart growth principles aimed at reversing the long-standing trend of sprawled development in U.S. urban areas have been increasingly adopted by urban planners and environmentalists. While these efforts to create more compact, mixed-use and transit-oriented urban areas have produced some evident changes in pioneering regions such as Portland, Oregon, smart growth still remains an unrealized vision in many other parts of urban America (Downs, 2005). Federal and state level policies and programs are needed to support local and regional efforts to implement smart growth.

[. . .] Switching to alternative power resources should take high priority in warm regions, where the demand for home cooling is high. In low density urban areas with currently high VMT, tighter vehicle fuel efficiency standards and alternative fuel policies are necessary in the short run, while well-coordinated smart growth policies to create sustainable urban environment should follow in the long run.

REFERENCES

Boarnet, M.G., Crane, R., 2001. *Travel by Design: The Influence of Urban form on Travel.* Oxford University Press, New York.

Boarnet, M.G., Sarmiento, S., 1998. Can land-use policy really affect travel behavior? A study of the link between non-work travel and land-use characteristics. *Urban Stud.* 35, 1155–1169.

Brown, J., Thompson, G., 2008. Service orientation, bus–rail service integration, and transit performance: Examination of 45 U.S. metropolitan areas. *Transp. Res. Record: J. Transp. Res. Board* 2042, 82–89.

Brown, M.A., Southworth, F., Stovall, T., 2005. *Towards a Climate-Friendly Built Environment.* Oak Ridge, CA: Pew Center on Global Climate Change.

Brown, M.A., Southworth, F., Sarzynski, A., 2008. *Shrinking the Carbon Footprint of Metropolitan America.* Brookings Institution, Washington, DC.

Cao, X.Y., Mokhtarian, P.L., Handy, S.L., 2009. Examining the impacts of residential self-selection on travel behaviour: A focus on empirical findings. *Transp. Rev.* 29, 359–395.

Cervero, R., Kockelman, K., 1997. Travel demand and the 3Ds: Density, diversity, and design. *Transp. Res.* D 2, 199–219.

Cervero, R., Sarmiento, O.L., Jacoby, E., Gomez, L.F., Neiman, A., 2009. Influences of built environments on walking and cycling: Lessons from Bogotá. *Int. J. Sustainable Transp.* 3, 203–226.

Crane, R., Chatman, D., 2003. Traffic and sprawl: Evidence from U.S. commuting, 1985 to 1997. *Plan. Mark.* 6, 14–22.

Downs, A., 2005. Smart growth: Why we discuss it more than we do it. *J. Am. Plan. Assoc.* 71, 367–378.

Ewing, R., Bartholomew, K., Winkelman, S., Walters, J., Anderson, G., 2008a. Urban development and climate change. *J. Urbanism* 1, 201–216.

Ewing, R., Bartholomew, K., Winkelman, S., Walters, J., Chen, D., 2008b. *Growing Cooler: The Evidence on Urban Development and Climate Change.* Urban Land Institute, Washington, DC.

Ewing, R., Rong, F., 2008. The impact of urban form on US residential energy use. *Hous. Policy Debate* 19, 1–30.

Fujita, M., Ogawa, H., 1982. Multiple equilibria and structural transition of nonmonocentric urban configurations. *Reg. Sci. Urban Eco.* 12, 161–196.

Glaeser, E.L., Kahn, M.E., 2010. The greenness of cities: Carbon dioxide emissions and urban development. *J. Urban Eco.* 67, 404–418.

Gordon, P., Lee, B., 2014. Chapter 4: Spatial structure and travel-Trends in commuting and non-commuting travels in US metropolitan areas. In: Hickman, R., Bonilla, D., Givoni, M., Banister, D. (Eds.), *International Handbook on Transport and Development*. Edward Elgar Publishing, Cheltenham, UK. (in press).

Holden, E., Norland, I.T., 2005. Three challenges for the compact city as a sustainable urban form: Household consumption of energy and transport in eight residential areas in the greater Oslo region. *Urban Stud.* 42, 2145.

McMillen, D.P., Smith, S.C., 2003. The number of subcenters in large urban areas. *J. Urban Eco.* 53, 321–338.

Meijers, E., Burger, M., 2010. Spatial structure and productivity in US metropolitan areas. *Environ. Plan.* A 42, 1383–1402.

Mokhtarian, P.L., Cao, X.Y., 2008. Examining the impacts of residential self-selection on travel behavior: A focus on methodologies. *Transp. Res. B – Methodol.* 42, 204–228.

Mui, S., Alson, J., Ellies, B., Ganss, D., 2007. *A Wedge Analysis of the US Transportation Sector*.

Myors, P., O'Leary, R., Helstroom, R., 2005. Multi unit residential buildings energy and peak demand study. *Energy News* 23, 113–116.

Nelson, A.C., 2009. The new urbanity: The rise of a New America. *Ann. Am. Acad. Political Soc. Sci.* 626, 192.

Perkins, A., Hamnett, S., Pullen, S., Zito, R., Trebilcock, D., 2009. Transport, housing and urban form: The life cycle energy consumption and emissions of city centre apartments compared with suburban dwellings. *Urban Policy Res.* 27, 377–396.

Smith, J.B., Schneider, S.H., Oppenheimer, M., Yohe, G.W., Hare, W., Mastrandrea, M.D., Patwardhan, A., Burton, I., Corfee-Morlot, J., Magadza, C.H.D., 2009. Assessing dangerous climate change through an update of the Intergovernmental Panel on Climate Change (IPCC) "reasons for concern". *Proc. Natl. Acad. Sci.* 106, 4133.

Transportation Research Board, 2009. *Driving and the Built Environment: The Effects of Compact Development on Motorized Travel, Energy Use, and CO2 Emissions*. National Research Council, National Academy of Sciences, Washington, DC.

U.S. Environmental Protection Agency, 2012. *Inventory of U.S. Greenhouse Gas Emissions and Sinks: 1990–2010*. U.S. Environmental Protection Agency, Washington, DC.

8 An Assessment of the Link Between Greenhouse Gas Emissions Inventories and Climate Action Plans

Michael R. Boswell, Adrienne I. Greve, and Tammy L. Seale

EDITOR'S INTRODUCTION

When a community becomes serious about addressing climate change, the first step is often to do a greenhouse gas inventory, which measures current emissions in the community, sets goals for reductions over time, and identifies key actions to take to achieve those goals. Those inventories become the starting point of broader climate action plans. This article by Boswell, Greve, and Seale provides some starting points for how an inventory is done. Generally, an inventory starts with a baseline, forecast for how key demographic variables (population, jobs, housing) are expected to change over the time of the plan, and then establishes a business-as-usual forecast of current emissions and how they would likely grow over time, without intervention. From there the next steps are to choose a reduction target for the forecast year, usually a percentage relative to the baseline year. Finally, the plan needs to identify ways to achieve those reduction goals. The low-hanging fruit often involves focusing on the biggest emitters first (electrical energy providers, transportation, etc.), and taking a close look at municipal operations. Steps such as switching the municipal fleet of cars and buses from diesel to hybrid or electric, improving insulation and lighting efficiency in municipal buildings, reducing methane releases at municipal waste sites, and similar actions enable the city or town to lead by example. It is essential, though, that these plans also relate to land use, building codes, and zoning in the community, to ensure the long-term efficiency of urban form and buildings. In Massachusetts, for instance, communities can adopt "stretch codes" which are building codes with more rigorous expectations for energy efficiency. The analysis process requires many assumptions, as the article's authors point out, and the more transparent these can be, the better. It is essential that these plans are done with buy-in from elected officials, agency, and staff that will have to implement their recommendations, and the public who need to weigh in on evaluating the tradeoffs in implementation choices. Despite the complexity, greenhouse gas inventories and resulting climate action plans are essential for progress at the local level, and can be avenues to empower citizens to be more active and engaged in solving the climate crisis.

Michael R. Boswell is Department Head and Professor in City and Regional Planning at California Polytechnic State University (Cal Poly) in San Luis Obispo. Dr. Boswell currently serves as an expert advisor on Guidelines for City Climate Action Plans for the UN Habitat Cities and Climate Change Initiative. He and his co-authors wrote the text *Local Climate Action Planning* for Island Press (2011). Adrianne Greve is an associate professor of in the same program at Cal Poly. Tammy Seale is an Associate Principal for Climate Action and Resiliency for Placeworks Consulting.

AN ASSESSMENT OF THE LINK BETWEEN GREENHOUSE GAS EMISSIONS INVENTORIES AND CLIMATE ACTION PLANS

In this article, we review local climate action plans and their associated greenhouse gas (GHG) emissions inventories from 30 U.S. cities in order to assess the degree to which climate action plans are informed by such inventories and to identify choices and assumptions the inventories require that may influence climate action plan policies and proposed actions. We hope this will help planners preparing climate action plans make informed, clear, and defensible choices, as well as optimize policy development and implementation in their communities. In addition, we hope that this research will contribute to refining future GHG emissions inventory protocols and climate action planning methods.

Communities wanting to address the problem of climate change increasingly do so by preparing local climate action plans. Such plans contain policies and propose actions designed to reduce the community's GHG emissions and are usually based on GHG emissions inventories (APA, 2008; International Council for Local Environmental Initiatives [ICLEI], n.d., 2010; National Wildlife Federation, 2008; Natural Capital Solutions, 2007; United Nations, 1998). A GHG emissions inventory aims to identify and calculate a community's current and projected emissions, which requires making some choices and assumptions. The advantage of using such an inventory as the basis for climate action planning is that it provides a quantitative baseline from which to measure progress on plan implementation, something that is uncommon in other types of planning.

[. . .]

HISTORY AND PURPOSE (OF CLIMATE ACTION PLANNING)

The rise of climate action planning at the community level can be traced to the emergence of the idea of "sustainable development" established in 1983 by the Brundtland Commission, also called the United Nations World Commission on Environment and Development. The Brundtland Commission report (World Commission on Environment and Development, 1987) embraced the concept of thinking globally but acting locally, which is key to the climate action planning movement. However, climate change was only one of many issues raised by the sustainability movement; it only garnered brief mention in the Brundtland Commission report. Not until the United Nations Conference on Environment and Development (also called the Earth Summit) in Rio de Janeiro in 1992, and the signing of the United Nations Framework Convention on Climate Change (UNFCCC: United Nations, 1992b), did climate change become distinct from the larger issue of sustainability. The UNFCCC led to the ICLEI Cities for Climate Protection campaign and its Local Agenda 21 Model Communities Program (ICLEI, 2008a, 2008b; United Nations, 1992a), President Clinton's *Climate Change Action Plan* (Clinton & Gore, 1993), and the Kyoto Protocol (United Nations, 1998). These events inspired an initial round of climate action plans, some of which were incorporated into existing sustainability planning efforts and Local Agenda 21 plans, and others that were stand-alone climate action plans (also known as local action plans, GHG reduction plans, and CO_2 reduction plans). During this period, the Intergovernmental Panel on Climate Change (IPCC) had been establishing consensus on climate change science, bringing attention to the effects of climate change and the options for mitigation and adaptation (IPCC, n.d.).

Over the last decade, other developments made community-level climate action planning a common endeavor. The New England governors collaborated with premiers of eastern Canadian provinces on a plan released in 2001 that set in motion a round of climate action planning in the northeastern United States (Committee on the Environment and the Northeast International Committee on Energy of the Conference of New England Governors and Eastern Canadian Premiers, 2001). The U.S. Conference of Mayors adopted its own Climate Protection Agreement (U.S. Conference of Mayors, 2005) to support the Kyoto Protocol standards and commit cities to reducing CO_2 emissions to 7% below 1990 levels by 2012. This agreement continues to prompt mayors to initiate planning efforts in their communities. In 2007, the IPCC produced its fourth assessment report (IPCC, 2007) which concluded that "warming of the climate system is unequivocal" (p. 5), most of it due to human-caused GHG emissions, and that this has the potential to impact social, physical, and biological systems. Many local governments have joined the ICLEI Local Governments for Sustainability Cities for Climate Protection (CCP) campaign in the last decade and committed to ICLEI's Five Milestones for Climate Mitigation methodology (ICLEI, 2010). Joining ICLEI not only commits cities to an established GHG inventory protocol, but provides access to GHG accounting software.

Despite this history, as of April 2010, only about 80 cities in the United States had adopted climate action plans based on GHG emissions inventories, although many more are in development. Researchers have found that communities are more likely to adopt climate mitigation policies and actions if they have higher proportions of their registered voters in the Democratic Party, higher risks of climate-related natural hazards (Hanak, Bedsworth, Swanbeck, & Malaczynski, 2008; Zahran, Brody, Vedlitz, Grover, & Miller, 2008), more staff assigned to energy or climate planning, higher levels of local government environmental awareness, and higher levels of community environmental activism (Pitt, 2009).

THE GREENHOUSE GAS EMISSIONS INVENTORY PROCESS

[. . .] The process of preparing a GHG emissions inventory entails decisions and procedural steps that have been codified through a variety of GHG emissions inventory protocols and related software developed by national and international organizations (see California Air Resources Board [CARB], 2008; ICLEI, 2009). Because choices made during inventory development influence climate action plan content, the best practice is for all assumptions to be documented and justified (Institute for Local Self Reliance, 2007) [. . .] An inventory should encompass all the GHG emissions associated with activities in the community (CARB, 2008; ICLEI, 2009), including indirect emissions associated with sources such as electricity generation. Clear articulation of the sources included in the inventory is critical, as only these will be subject to the reduction measures in the climate action plan. By identifying the GHG emissions sources and quantifying the total, an emissions inventory provides a foundation for projecting future emissions and setting a reduction target (EPA, 2009b). These data are the benchmarks against which the success of proposed GHG emissions reduction measures can be assessed. [. . .]

The success of a climate action plan is measured against a GHG emissions forecast from a baseline year. [. . .] The plan also requires a business-as-usual forecast of future emissions that assumes no new action to mitigate GHG emissions, prepared using local forecasts for population, jobs, and housing. The choice of the inventory forecast year establishes the planning horizon of the climate action plan (CARB, 2008; ICLEI, 2009). After the business-as-usual forecast is complete, the GHG emissions reduction target for the forecast year is chosen and the difference between these establishes the GHG reduction that must be achieved by the associated climate action plan. Such a target is most often expressed as the percentage by which emissions will be reduced relative to the baseline year (e.g., 15% reduction from baseline year by 2020; CARB, 2008; ICLEI, 2009). Reduction targets may be short-, mid-, or long-term, and the period will influence the range of actions and policy options used to achieve the targets.

There are several types of exogenous change that may affect future levels of GHG emissions in a community and, thus, should be accounted for in the GHG emissions forecast and setting of the reduction target: technological, social/behavioral, legislative and regulatory, demographic, and economic. Technological innovation and change may influence automotive technology and fuels, electricity generation and fuels, and building technology. Social and behavioral changes may include commuting habits, household energy use, or purchasing habits. Potential legislative and regulatory change may include cap-and-trade legislation, renewable energy portfolio standards, and fuel efficiency standards (e.g., the federal Corporate Average Fuel Economy [CAFE] standard). Demographic changes that have the potential to influence GHG emissions include population growth, poverty level, and housing tenure and occupancy. Long-term GHG emissions may also be influenced by economic changes in gross domestic product, industrial and manufacturing mix, and balance of trade. This sampling of issues shows that considerable uncertainty exists in forecasting future levels of GHG emissions, particularly at the community level.

It is common to address uncertainty in forecasting either by ignoring it and assuming a continuation of current trends, or by varying the assumptions and developing multiple forecasts or scenarios. The problem with the former is that change seems almost certain at this point. For example, public transit ridership is at its highest level in 52 years (Sun, 2009), bicycle commuting has jumped 43% since 2000 (League of American Bicyclists, 2009), and solar and wind power had their highest growth years to date in 2008 (American Wind Energy Association, 2009; U.S. installed solar capacity up 17 percent in 2008, 2009). Emissions forecasts that assume long-term trends will persist, and do not take into account the potential for the kind of dramatic short-term changes these examples illustrate, are likely to overestimate future emissions. The policy implications could include the setting of overly conservative reduction targets, sticker-shock reactions to how much effort would be required to meet aggressive reduction targets, or despondency created from a sense that the future is inevitable.

Additionally, assuming no exogenous changes may cause communities to misjudge the amount of local mitigation needed. With too little mitigation, the community will miss its reduction target, but too much mitigation may cause it to incur high costs (an economically inefficient outcome), upset community members, or bear an unfairly large share of the state and national effort. [. . .]

The problem with addressing uncertainty by developing multiple forecasts or scenarios is that making assumptions about critical future changes would exceed the capabilities of most local governments. Moreover, no standardized approach for addressing this has been developed for community level emissions inventories. Wing and Eckaus (2007) observe:

> Perhaps the thorniest problem is the issue of how to model the effect of technological progress, which, some have argued, has been the major influence on the intensity of fossil fuel use. But the projection of technological change is, in turn, one of the most difficult tasks that economists have undertaken, and the literature is strewn with efforts that are at best only partially successful.
>
> (p. 5267)

Once the GHG emissions forecast is complete and the reduction target is established, mitigation actions to reduce the community's GHG emissions must be developed and adopted. For the plan to be effective, adopted mitigation actions must cumulatively reach the GHG emissions reduction target identified in the inventory. To assess whether or not mitigations will be adequate to reach the target, they must be quantified. Estimating the emissions reduction associated with each mitigation action requires that assumptions be made about implementation, phasing, and emissions conversion factors (CARB, 2008; ICLEI, n.d., 2010; National Wildlife Federation, 2008). For example, estimating the emissions reduction that will result from improved bicycle infrastructure requires assumptions, such as the percentage of the population that will change behavior, the VMT reduction associated with the behavior change, and the emissions resulting from the reduced VMT. Such assumptions should be transparent, to make it easier to recognize when they are violated, to recognize the changes that would needed to meet reduction targets if this were the case, and to facilitate development of monitoring programs to track progress.

[. . .]

CONCLUSION

Best-practice standards for GHG emissions inventories and climate action plans are changing and improving on a regular basis. Our review of 30 local climate action plans and their associated GHG emissions inventories from a variety of U.S. cities shows mixed adherence to these standards. Although most communities preparing climate action plans do begin with a GHG emissions inventory, many fail to follow through on conducting adequate emissions forecasts, setting meaningful reduction targets, or linking their mitigation measures to these forecasts and targets. Since the choices and assumptions made in GHG emissions inventories, forecasts, and reduction targets influence selection and implementation of climate action plan policies and actions, these plans may not effectively address the climate change problem, as Wheeler (2008) also concluded. We hope that the city planning profession can take a more prominent role in bringing principles of good planning to the emerging field of climate action planning. We encourage the American Planning Association, college and university departments of city planning, and other professional planning organizations to take a more active role in the education of planners, allied professionals, local officials, and citizens on the possibility of meaningful local planning for solving the climate crisis.

REFERENCES

American Planning Association. (2008). *Policy guide on planning and climate change.* Washington, DC: Author.
American Wind Energy Association. (2009). *Wind energy grows by record 8,300 MW in 2008.* Retrieved October 28, 2009, from http://www.awea.org/newsroom/releases/wind_energy_growth2008_27Jan09.html

Boswell, M. R., Greve, A. I., & Seale, T. L. (2012). *Local climate action planning*. Washington DC: Island Press.

California Air Resources Board. (2008). *Local government operations protocol for the quantification and reporting of greenhouse gas emissions inventories*. Sacramento, CA: Author.

Clinton, W. J., & Gore, A., Jr. (1993). *The climate change action plan*. Washington, DC: The White House.

Committee on the Environment and the Northeast International Committee on Energy of the Conference of New England Governors and Eastern Canadian Premiers. (2001). *Climate change action plan 2001*. Retrieved June 9, 2010, from http://www.negc.org/documents/NEG-ECP%20CCAP.PDF

Hanak, E., Bedsworth, L., Swanbeck, S., & Malaczynski, J. (2008). *Climate policy at the local level: A survey of California's cities and counties*. San Francisco, CA: Public Policy Institute of California.

Institute for Local Self Reliance. (2007). *Lesson from the pioneers: Tackling global warming at the local level*. Minneapolis, MN: Author.

Intergovernmental Panel on Climate Change. (2007). Summary for policymakers. In S. Solomon, D. Qin, M. Manning, Z. Chen, M. Marquis, K. B. Avery, . . . H. L. Miller (Eds.), *Climate change 2007: The physical science basis: Contribution of Working Group I to the fourth assessment report of the Intergovernmental Panel on Climate Change* (pp. 1–18). Cambridge, UK: Cambridge University Press.

Intergovernmental Panel on Climate Change. (n.d.). *History*. Retrieved June 1, 2010, from www.ipcc.ch/organization/organization_history.htm

International Council for Local Environmental Initiatives. (2008a). *ICLEI climate program*. Retrieved May 11, 2010, from http://www.iclei.org/index.php?id=800

International Council for Local Environmental Initiatives. (2008b). *Local agenda 21 (LA21) campaign*. Retrieved May 11, 2010, from http://www.iclei.org/index.php?id=798

International Council for Local Environmental Initiatives. (2009). *International local government GHG emissions analysis protocol (IEAP) Version 1.0*. Retrieved March 3, 2010, from http://www.iclei.org/fileadmin/user_upload/documents/Global/Progams/CCP/Standards/ICLEI_IEAP_2009.pdf

International Council for Local Environmental Initiatives. (2010). *ICLEI's five milestones for climate mitigation*. Retrieved May 11, 2010, from http://www.icleiusa.org/action-center/getting-started/iclei2019s-five-milestones-for-climate-protection/

International Council for Local Environmental Initiatives. (n.d.). *U.S. Mayors' Climate Protection Agreement: Climate action handbook*. Retrieved May 29, 2009, from http://www.seattle.gov/climate/docs/ClimateActionHandbook.pdf

League of American Bicyclists. (2009). *43% increase in bicycle commuting since 2000*. Retrieved October 20, 2009, from http://www.bikeleague.org/blog/2009/09/43increase-in-bicycle-commuting-since-2000/

National Wildlife Federation. (2008). *Guide to climate action planning: Pathways to a low-carbon campus*. Reston, VA: Author.

Natural Capital Solutions. (2007). *Climate protection manual for cities*. Eldorado Springs, CO: Author.

Pitt, D. (2009, October). *The diffusion of climate protection planning among U.S. municipalities*. Paper presented at the Association of Collegiate Schools of Planning Conference, Crystal City, VA.

Sun, L. H. (2009, March 9). Public transit ridership rises to highest level in 52 years. *The Washington Post*. Retrieved June 9, 2010, from http://www.washingtonpost.com/wp-dyn/content/article/2009/03/08/AR2009030801960.html

United Nations. (1992a). *Agenda 21*. Retrieved October 20, 2009, from http://www.unep.org/Documents.Multilingual/Default.asp?documentID=52

United Nations. (1992b) *United Nations framework convention on climate change*. Retrieved June 9, 2010, from http://unfccc.int/resource/docs/convkp/conveng.pdf

United Nations. (1998). *Kyoto protocol to the United Nations framework convention on climate change*. Retrieved October 20, 2009, from http://unfccc.int/resource/docs/convkp/kpeng.pdf

U.S. Conference of Mayors. (2005). *The U.S. Mayors Climate Protection Agreement*. Retrieved June 9, 2010, from http://www.usmayors.org/climateprotection/documents/mcpAgreement.pdf

U.S. Environmental Protection Agency State and Local Climate and Energy Program. (2009b). *From inventory to action: Putting greenhouse gas inventories to work (EPA-430-F-09-002)*. Washington, DC: Author.

U.S. installed solar capacity up 17 percent in 2008. (2009, March 20). Retrieved June 9, 2010, from http://www.reuters.com/article/GCA-BusinessofGreen/idUSTRE52J5VW20090320

Wheeler, S. M. (2008). State and municipal climate change plans: The first generation. *Journal of the American Planning Association, 74*(4), 481–496.

Wing, S., & Eckaus, R. S. (2007). The implications of the historical decline in U.S. energy intensity for long-run CO2 emission projections. *Energy Policy, 35*(11), 5267–5286.

World Commission on Environment and Development. (1987). *Our common future*. Oxford, UK: Oxford University Press.

Zahran, S., Brody, S. D., Vedlitz, A., Grover, H., & Miller, C. (2008). Vulnerability and capacity: Examining local commitment to climate change policy. *Environment and Planning C: Government and Policy, 26*(3), 544–562.

9 Forces Driving Urban Greenhouse Gas Emissions

David Dodman

EDITOR'S INTRODUCTION

In this article, David Dodman explores some of the theoretical and practical difficulties experienced when urban areas undertake greenhouse gas emissions inventories. Inventories have difficulties in overcoming what are called 'boundary problems'—that the physical site of emissions such as power plants and manufacturing processes that benefit a location may not be within the physical boundary of the reporting area. The luggage I buy was made in China—who is responsible for the emissions from production, the purchaser (me) or the manufacturer (in China)? The electricity that lights my home comes from a power plant in Canada. Who should be responsible for reporting the emissions, the user or the producer? He brings in important language used to communicate about these issues: "Scope 1 emissions represent direct emissions from within a given geographical area; Scope 2 emissions are those associated with electricity, heating, and cooling; and Scope 3 emissions include those that are indirect or embodied". Theoretically, Scope 3 is the strongest, as it asks people and the city to account for their purchases, and when divided into per capita numbers, gives a standard carbon footprint that is easy to compare and generally fairly easy for the public to understand. But the reporting challenges and assumptions required to accomplish that are many, and so most entities use Scope 1 or 2. Another way to think about this is to ask whether a report is based on consumption, or production. Some city-regions have a primarily services-based economy, which tends toward lower emissions; other city-regions have strong manufacturing or mining industries, and will have higher emissions. Identifying equitable ways to address these disparities will help make GHG inventories more representative. These issues can seem quite technical, but are important for several reasons. One is that the same ideas are relevant when individuals make decisions about their lifestyles and purchases, or think about their own carbon footprints. Secondly, preparing climate action plans and their underlying emissions inventories are growing fields of practice and research and, importantly for students, professional positions. Finally, transparency in the assumptions underlying an inventory enables stakeholders to really understand and engage in the process, which benefits everyone.

David Dodman is the Director of Human Settlements for the International Institute for Environment and Development. He is widely published in the areas of climate change vulnerability, risk and resilience, and the intersection of these with settlements and sustainable development. He is passionate in his advocacy for vulnerable populations in the low-income countries of the Global South. He also serves as an expert with the IPCC.

FORCES DRIVING URBAN GREENHOUSE GAS EMISSIONS

INTRODUCTION

The contribution of cities to global greenhouse gas emissions has become a hotly contested area of debate, as has the allocation of responsibility for climate change. The almost universal acceptance of the need to reduce atmospheric concentrations of greenhouse gases has lent these discussions particular importance as new mechanisms are sought to achieve this objective. Of course, a wide range of activities that take place in urban areas—including electricity generation, construction, manufacturing and service industries, and transportation—generate greenhouse gases. At the same time, towns and cities rely on inward flows of food, water, and consumer goods from elsewhere—whether rural areas, other urban areas, or overseas. Because of this, it is perhaps more appropriate to examine the underlying forces that drive greenhouse gas emissions—wherever the geographical location of their actual release. Measuring and understanding these forces is extremely important in the process of developing urban and global policies to respond to climate change [. . .].

This paper first summarizes current mechanisms used to assess greenhouse gas emissions from urban areas, and reviews the findings from several attempts to provide accurate inventories. However, its primary focus is on the factors that shape city emission profiles, and the underlying drivers of these. It concludes by reviewing recent arguments that suggest meaningful long-term mitigation of climate change will require addressing patterns of consumption, particularly in middle-income and high-income countries.

ASSESSING URBAN GREENHOUSE GAS EMISSIONS

Climate change is caused by the increased atmospheric concentration of greenhouse gases, including carbon dioxide, nitrous oxide, methane, and ozone. The Intergovernmental Panel on Climate Change (IPCC) identifies as the main

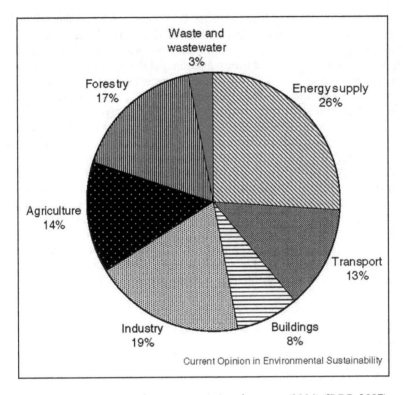

Figure 9.1 Anthropogenic greenhouse gas emissions by sector (2004) (IPCC, 2007).

contributors to this process energy supply, transportation, buildings, industry, agriculture, forestry, and waste and wastewater; and their relative contribution to global emissions is shown in Figure 9.1.

The United Nations Framework Convention for Climate Change (UNFCCC) supervises the assessment of national greenhouse gas inventories, based on the assumption that a nation is responsible for all emissions produced within its area of jurisdiction. However, as many polluting and carbon-intensive manufacturing processes are no longer located in Europe or North America, but have been sited elsewhere in the world to take advantage of lower labour costs and less rigorous enforcement of environmental regulations, the underlying drivers of emissions are not adequately taken into account.

For towns and cities, the responsibility for emissions is even less clear for two main reasons. First, local government authorities have only very limited levels of control over emissions, lacking the legal powers to set targets or regulations on this issue. Secondly, a focus solely on the emissions emitted from within the identifiable territorial boundaries of an urban area is likely to misrepresent the responsibility for these emissions. In general, the smaller the scale, the greater the challenges posed by 'boundary problems' in which it is increasingly hard to identify which emissions ought or ought not to be allocated to a particular place. At the most basic level, electricity generation often takes place outside urban administrative boundaries, yet is supplied to and consumed by industries, businesses, and households within the urban area. More complex relationships exist around the production of other goods and services outside towns and cities—including food production and transportation and the manufacture of many consumer goods—which are consumed in urban areas. However, although residents of cities in high-income countries are responsible for a very large share of greenhouse gas emissions, the increasing demand for energy (particularly household electricity) and private transportation in low-income and middle-income cities means that assessing and addressing the contribution of these urban centres to climate change will become increasingly important in the years to come.

As a result of this, various frameworks have been proposed to enable cities to produce robust and comparable accounts of their contribution to climate change, including an 'International Standard for Determining Greenhouse Gas Emissions for Cities' produced by UNEP, UN Habitat, and the World Bank. Other frameworks, such as the one developed by ICLEI Local Governments for Sustainability, identify urban emissions as coming either from 'government operations' or from 'community activities' (Table 9.1). Within each of these, emissions can be seen as belonging to several different 'scopes', depending on how directly their

Table 9.1 Emission scopes for local authorities (ICLEI, 2008)

	Definitions	Examples
Government operation emissions		
Scope 1	Direct emission sources owned or operated by the local government	A municipal vehicle powered by gasoline or a municipal generator powered by diesel fuel
Scope 2	Indirect emission sources limited to electricity, district heating, steam, and cooling consumption	Purchased electricity used by the local government, which is associated with the generation of greenhouse gas emissions at a power plant
Scope 3	All other indirect or embodied emissions over which the local government exerts significant control or influence	Emissions resulting from contracted waste hauling services
Community-scale emissions		
Scope 1	All direct emission sources located within the geopolitical boundary of the local government	Use of fuels such as heavy fuel oil, natural gas or propane used for heating
Scope 2	Indirect emissions that result as a consequence of activity within the jurisdiction's geopolitical boundary limited to electricity, district heating, steam, and cooling consumption	Purchased eletricity used within the geopolitical boundaries of the jurisdiction associated with the generation of greenhouse gases at the power plant
Scope 3	All other indirect and embodied emissions that occur as a result of activity within the geopolitical boundary	Methane emissions from solid waste generated within the community which decomposes at landfills either inside or outside of the community's geopolitical boundary

production is linked to a particular location. Scope 1 emissions represent direct emissions from within a given geographical area; Scope 2 emissions are those associated with electricity, heating, and cooling; and Scope 3 emissions include those that are indirect or embodied. In practice, greenhouse gas emission inventories from urban areas that include Scope 3 emissions are very rare—the point to which these Scope 3 emissions are included is very arbitrary and there is no agreement as to a comparable framework to compare emissions of this type between urban areas. If Scope 3—or embodied emissions are included, it is likely that the per capita emission of greenhouse gases allocated to a city will increase significantly—particularly if the city is large, well-developed and with a predominance of service and commercial activities. In addition, it is almost impossible to compile a comprehensive inventory of Scope 3 emissions that takes into account all the consumption of all the individuals living in an urban area. In other words, "emissions can be attributed either to the spatial location of actual release or to the spatial location that generated activity that led to the actual release". A detailed Scope 3 inventory should also subtract the embodied energy in goods made in that city and subsequently exported.

FACTORS INFLUENCING GREENHOUSE GAS EMISSIONS

However, this process still only assesses the location of emissions, and not the underlying processes which drive these. These can be seen as either direct factors (related to geographic context, urban form and density, and economic activities) or underlying drivers (which require a careful examination of the differences between 'production'-based and 'consumption'-based approaches to measuring greenhouse gas emissions).

Various aspects of geography affect the contribution of urban areas to climate change. The geographical location of any given urban area affects energy demands for heating, cooling, and lighting. In the United States, areas with lower temperatures in January have higher emissions associated with home heating, while areas with warmer summers have higher electricity consumption associated with space cooling. Geographical location also influences the fuels used for electricity generation, and hence the levels of greenhouse gas emissions from this process. Rio de Janeiro and São Paulo in Brazil both have relatively low levels of emissions, as they receive a large proportion of their electricity from hydroelectric generation, whereas many Chinese cities have high emissions associated with electricity generated by coal-fired plants.

Urban form and urban spatial organization can have a wide range of implications for a city's greenhouse gas emissions. The proximity of homes and businesses in dense urban areas can encourage walking, cycling, and the use of mass transport in place of private motor vehicles. Research by Gottdiener and Budd (2005) suggests that the doubling of neighbourhood density can decrease per-household vehicle use by 20–40% with a corresponding decline in greenhouse gas emissions, while an influential paper by Newman and Kenworthy suggested that gasoline use per capita declines with increasing urban density. More compact housing also requires less energy for heating: US households living in single-family detached housing consume 35% more energy for heating and 21% more energy for cooling than comparable households in other forms of house. Dense urban settlements can therefore be seen to enable lifestyles that reduce per capita greenhouse gas emissions through the concentration of services that reduces the need to travel large distances, the (generally) better provision of public transportation networks, and the constraints on the size of residential dwellings imposed by the scarcity and high cost of land.

The types of economic activities that take place within urban areas also influence greenhouse gas emissions. Extractive activities and energy-intensive manufacturing are obviously associated with higher levels of emissions, especially when the energy for these is supplied from fossil fuels. The influence of the urban economy on patterns of emissions can be seen in the large variations in the proportion of a city's greenhouse gas emissions that can be attributed to the industrial sector. Industrial activities were responsible for 80% of Shanghai's emissions and 65% of Beijing's (figures from 1999). In contrast, greenhouse gas emissions from the industrial sector in cities elsewhere are much lower, generally reflecting a transition to service-based urban economies: 0.04% in Washington, DC; 6.2% in Rio de Janeiro; 7% in London; 9.7% in Sao Paulo; and 10% in Tokyo and New York City (Dodman, 2009).

UNDERLYING DRIVERS OF EMISSIONS

[. . .]

The previous discussion uses a 'production-based' approach to assess greenhouse gas emissions—based on the spatial location of the actual release of the gases. Yet this can lead to perverse and negative effects, as cities (or countries) create disincentives for activities that generate high levels of greenhouse gases, that merely result in these activities being moved to elsewhere in the world—a process referred to as carbon leakage (Hertwich and Peters, 2009). In cities where service industries are more important, emissions associated with consumption are more important than those generated by production.

In contrast, a 'consumption-based' approach attempts to address the underlying drivers of emissions in a more complete way. This strategy attempts to identify a city or individual's carbon footprint [. . .]—the total set of greenhouse gases released by all the items consumed, wherever these emissions were produced geographically. These approaches have greater degrees of uncertainty, as there are many more systems to be incorporated, and there are high margins of uncertainty and a much higher potential for calculation error. Despite this, they provide considerable insight into climate policy and mitigation and should probably be used at least as a complementary indicator to help analyse and inform climate policy.

[. . .]

Policy responses to urban greenhouse gas emissions need to take into account both production and consumption approaches. Strategies to reduce emissions from within urban areas are more easily implementable and measurable. But if these rely on legislation and financial instruments that merely serve to encourage heavily emitting activities to move elsewhere—to places with less stringent regulations—then the net impact on global carbon emissions will be non-existent. On the other hand, strategies to promote responsible consumption are much more difficult to measure. Bridging these two issues will require urban and national authorities from both low-income and high-income nations to work collaboratively with a range of stakeholders to develop innovative approaches: for example, through supporting the use of low-carbon technologies in manufacturing and service industries in low-income towns and cities as a development strategy.

CONCLUSION: ADDRESSING CLIMATE CHANGE MITIGATION IN URBAN AREAS

Assessing the sources of greenhouse gas emissions, or of the underlying drivers of these, is a purely academic exercise unless this information is used to develop effective, locally appropriate strategies for climate change mitigation. Two general lessons can be drawn from this. First, there is a need for more active engagement by city authorities in the processes of urban and global governance for climate change mitigation. Local governments are able to shape the behaviour of citizens and industry through a combination of incentives and regulations, and thereby address the drivers of greenhouse gas emissions directly. Second, there is a need for deeper awareness and action by urban residents, particularly wealthy citizens of high-income countries. The consumption habits of these individuals acts to generate greenhouse gas emissions both directly (e.g. through emissions associated with transportation) and through the emissions embedded in the products they choose to buy [. . .] When greenhouse gas emissions and climate change are seen in a global context, rather than simply as a matter of meeting targets at the urban or national level, then assessing and addressing these underlying drivers acquires true importance.

REFERENCES

Dodman D: Blaming cities for climate change? An analysis of urban greenhouse gas emissions. *Environ Urban* 2009, 21:185–201.

Gottdiener M, Budd L: *Key Concepts in Urban Studies*. London: Sage; 2005.

Hertwich E, Peters G: Carbon footprint of nations: a global, trade-linked analysis. *Environ Sci Technol* 2009, 43:6414–6420.

Intergovernmental Panel on Climate Change (IPCC): Summary for policymakers. In *Climate Change 2007: The Physical Science Basis. Contribution of Working Group I to the Fourth Assessment Report of the Intergovernmental Panel on Climate Change*. Edited by Solomon S, Qin D, Manning M, Chen Z, Marquis M, Averyt K, Tignor M, Miller H. Cambridge: Cambridge University Press; 2007.

ICLEI Local Governments for Sustainability: International Local Government GHG Emissions Analysis Protocol. Release Version 1.0. 2008: Available online: http://www.iclei.org/fileadmin/user_upload/documents/Global/Progams/GHG/LGGHGEmissionsProtocol.pdf (accessed 29.07.09).

10 Climate Change and Health in Cities

Impacts of Heat and Air Pollution and Potential Co-Benefits from Mitigation and Adaptation

Sharon L. Harlan and Darren M. Ruddell

EDITOR'S INTRODUCTION

In the article by Harlan and Ruddell, we turn from considering how to address emissions at the urban scale to why cities should do this, introducing public health as a major theme that continues throughout the Reader. Reducing local emissions of GHGs improves human health in several ways. First, reducing emissions reduces the pollution and related particulates that can compromise respiratory health. This is an important equity issue, since poor air quality is not evenly distributed, and neither are its impacts. Within a city-region, poorer neighborhoods often have worse air, as they may be located close to highways, trucking facilities, and manufacturing and repair facilities. Reducing emissions leading to reduced particulates can help with asthma, a particular scourge among the young in low-income neighborhoods. Second, heat is a byproduct of most fuel combustion and consumption—think about walking outdoors past window air conditioner outlets and how hot that is, or the heat thrown off by cars on a busy summer street. Reducing emissions also reduces these sorts of human-caused (anthropogenic) heat, reducing intensity of and risks for extreme heat waves in urban areas. As these authors note, when mitigation costs are calculated, they should be reduced by the public health benefits to morbidity (sickness) and mortality (death). Later articles in this reader will describe in some detail the steps that cities are taking to address these issues. For this article, the key lesson is that addressing local mitigation also brings local benefits for something everyone cares about—their health—as well as the health of poorer, more vulnerable populations. These facts also have political relevance. Framing emissions reduction as a justice and public health issue widens the political support for emissions reduction among stake-holders, activists, and the public. Broader constituencies and current benefits give policy-makers a reason to act now.

Sharon Harlan is a Professor of Health Sciences and Sociology at Northeastern University. Her research explores the human impacts of climate change that are dependent upon people's positions in social hierarchies, places in built environments of unequal quality, and policies that improve or impede human adaptive capabilities. Darren Ruddell is an Associate Professor of Spatial Sciences at the University of Southern California, with particular expertise in using geospatial technologies to investigate issues of urban sustainability and resiliency.

CLIMATE CHANGE AND HEALTH IN CITIES: IMPACTS OF HEAT AND AIR POLLUTION AND POTENTIAL CO-BENEFITS FROM MITIGATION AND ADAPTATION

INTRODUCTION

[. . .]

This review will summarize epidemiological studies primarily from 2005–2010 on mortality and morbidity related to two climate hazards in cities: increasing temperatures and the modifying influence of air pollution. Heat exposure and related illnesses are under intensive investigation worldwide because they affect cities in all types of climate regimes. Air quality, a long-standing environmental issue, has improved in many cities in high-income countries because of government regulations and advances in technology. Nevertheless, respiratory illnesses are still a major global urban health burden.

Many cities are designing and implementing strategic risk management action plans to lessen the impacts of climate change. These plans may have health co-benefits, such as reducing illnesses related to heat and air pollution, as well as other diseases associated with urban lifestyles. This review reports on climate mitigation and adaptation strategies in cities and assesses their potential to improve urban health. Although cities face other risks from climate change, such as flooding and sea level rise (Huq et al., 2007; De Sherbinin et al., 2007), this review concentrates on climate risks related to rising temperatures and air pollution.

CHANGES IN THE CLIMATE OF CITIES

Human and natural systems in cities are tightly coupled in synergistic and dynamic relationships embedded within a global environment that is rapidly changing. In urban social-ecological systems, human activities are causing rising temperatures and other climatic changes, which in turn affect human health and well-being. [. . .] During the 20th century, temperatures increased significantly faster in cities compared to nearby rural areas due to the urban heat island (UHI) effect. The transformation of native landscapes into dense urban settlements of heat-retaining impervious surfaces and building materials that inhibit night-time cooling is the most significant anthropogenic driver of urban climate change in cities around the world.

Warmer baseline temperatures in cities are further elevated by extreme heat events (EHEs) or heat waves, which are projected to strike with increasing frequency and intensity in the 21st century. Moreover, meteorology influences air quality, such that elevated temperatures during the summer can contribute to air pollution that exacerbates harmful impacts of heat on human health. Coupled global and regional model simulations show that global warming will probably result in deteriorating urban air quality, including increased surface ozone levels and particulate matter (PM), smoke from wildfires, and some pollens in certain regions of the world. The largest effects of climate change on air quality will be experienced in northern mid-latitude cities during high pollution episodes.

Extreme Heat

Studies consistently show a strong relationship between high temperatures and excess all-cause mortality with city-specific thresholds that vary according to latitude and normal average temperatures. The range of temperature thresholds indicates variability in human acclimatization and availability of adaptations, such as air conditioning. Moreover, cities on nearly every inhabited continent have experienced EHEs in the 21st century that collectively have resulted in tens, perhaps hundreds, of thousands of excess deaths directly due to heat and its consequences or indirectly due to disease. In North America, extreme heat is the most common cause of death among all weather-related disasters. Additional research is needed on how mortality estimates vary with definitions of heat waves and whether advance warning systems prevent deaths.

[. . .]

Air Pollution

The impacts of air quality on urban health outcomes are more complex than temperature impacts, owing to the variable distribution and behavior of a large number of pollutants that affect different disease categories, such as respiratory and cardiovascular illnesses and allergies. Stricter air quality standards have improved health in many high-income countries; for example, between 1970 and 2000, reductions in fine PM accounted for as much as 15 percent of the overall increase in life expectancy in 51 US metropolitan areas (Pope et al., 2009). In cities of low-income and middle-income countries, however, air quality continues to deteriorate and to impose increasingly greater health burdens on growing populations that use large amounts of energy to meet domestic and industrial needs (Chan and Yao, 2008; Kan et al., 2009; Romero Lankao, 2007).

At present, there is scientific consensus that extreme heat and air pollution separately cause significant urban health problems, and the negative impact of each is expected to intensify with climate change. There is not consensus, however, on whether air pollution is a modifying influence that interacts with temperature to produce an even larger negative impact on human health. In some studies, air pollution is a significant modifier of high temperature on mortality, but in others, the interaction effects are negligible or only appear during some heat events. Others find heterogeneity among cities in the magnitude of joint effects and relative contributions of temperature and air quality to mortality rates. More research is required to understand the coupled relationship between emissions and weather in an era of increasing climate change.

Variable Health Risks Within Cities

Health risks from extreme heat and air pollution differ among cities depending on geography, climate, wealth, and a number of other factors. Owing to a robust research tradition in environmental justice, race, and air pollution in the US and advances in socio-spatial analysis of fine-scale social, ecological, and weather data, we are beginning to understand the distribution of health risks for urban subpopulations within individual cities.

Health risk factors related to climate change include differences in physiological sensitivity to high temperature and air pollution, socio-economic variables that modify exposure levels to hazards, and spatial locations that are hazardous living spaces. Individuals at risk for increased exposure and susceptibility to extreme heat and air pollution include the elderly, very young, socially isolated, poor, racial/ethnic minorities, and those with pre-existing illnesses or no access to air conditioning. Many recent studies compare the vulnerability of neighborhoods within cities, correlating fine-scale measurements of microclimate temperatures or air pollution with neighborhood biophysical and social variables, such as amount of vegetation, open space, and socio-economic composition of the population. Several studies reveal spatial variation in intra-urban environmental quality, but more studies are needed that include spatial measures of human health.

POTENTIAL HEALTH CO-BENEFITS THROUGH MITIGATION AND ADAPTATION

[. . .]

Reducing fossil fuel consumption in cities has significant health co-benefits, especially in developing nations, and the estimated net costs of climate policies would be substantially reduced if the co-benefits of improved air quality were fully valued. In fact, most studies that have quantitatively assessed health co-benefits focus on air pollution, particularly PM2.5 and ozone. Using a variety of air pollution and epidemiological models and assumptions about policy scenarios, estimates of co-benefits have been derived for scenarios of reduced GHG emissions in electricity production, household energy use, and transportation.

Controlling emissions in cities will also decrease the amount of anthropogenic heat released into the atmosphere, thereby reducing contributions to global warming and the UHI effect, while having the co-benefit of preventing heat-related illnesses and deaths. Cities that promote an energy generation transition from fossil fuels to renewable sources should reap the benefits of a cleaner living environment and restored ecosystems, which will foster co-benefits of a healthier and more active lifestyle for residents. For example, improved air quality will reduce respiratory illnesses and increased physical activity should reduce 'lifestyle' diseases, such as obesity, cardiovascular disease, and social isolation, while also improving mental health.

Many cities have developed risk management action plans that include mitigation and adaptation strategies to reduce key vulnerabilities to climate change. If these plans are implemented, positive environmental impacts and health co-benefits that improve the well- being of urban residents are very likely to occur. [. . .]

The development of city action plans is an important step toward reducing human vulnerability to climate change, but a number of challenges and tradeoffs are already apparent in the implementation phase. For example, implementing the plans requires an initial financial investment, which many local elected officials and decision-makers are reluctant to make, particularly in a depressed economy. Many cities in developing and industrial countries alike face the difficult choice between pursing economic development in the short-term or reducing environmental degradation and associated public health risks. There are institutional barriers to establishing trust and collaboration between the public and private sectors, grassroots campaigns, and scientific enterprises in order to effectively and equitably carry out risk management tactics. A serious problem is that many programs do not specifically target marginalized and/or segregated communities in high-income, middle-income, or low-income countries. Neglect of the most vulnerable populations and places will exacerbate uneven development and social inequality at the submetropolitan scale.

[. . .]

CONCLUSIONS

Excessive heat and air pollution increase mortality and morbidity in cities on six continents. Research during the past decade has created a sense of urgency among public health professionals because future scenarios predict warming urban temperatures and increasing frequency and intensity of EHEs (Extreme Heat Events) due to the interaction of global climate change and UHIs (Urban Heat Islands).

Research that identifies the most vulnerable populations and places within cities—heterogeneity of risks—is crucial because health burdens fall disproportionately on urban residents who are physiologically susceptible, socio-economically disadvantaged, and live in the most degraded environments. The most 'actionable' research findings emerge from studies of specific cities because researchers find so much variation in local meteorology, level of emissions, capabilities of governments, and acclimatization of residents.

City risk management strategies for mitigating and adapting to climate change propose to reduce GHG emissions and cool the city through changes in the built environment, land use, and transportation. Implementing these plans could provide health co-benefits for residents, including reductions in heat-related and respiratory illnesses, as well as 'lifestyle' diseases. Many cities have adopted surveillance, warning, and alert systems to trigger emergency responses to EHEs and poor air quality days. However, there is little research to evaluate whether other strategies have been implemented or whether health co-benefits have been realized. There are impediments to implementing costly aspects of city mitigation and adaptation plans under current economic conditions and further research is needed on how much health co-benefits reduce the cost of climate policies.

REFERENCES

Chan SK, Yao ZX: Air pollution in mega cities in China. *Atmospheric Environment* 2008, 42:1–42.

De Sherbinin A, Schiller A, Pulsipher A: The vulnerability of global cities to climate hazards. *Environment and Urbanization* 2007, 19:39–64.

Huq S, Kovats S, Reid H, Satterthwaite D: Reducing risks to cities from disasters and climate change. *Environment and Urbanization* 2007, 19:3–15.

Kan H, Huang W, Chen B, Zhao N: Impact of outdoor air pollution on cardiovascular health in mainland China. *CVD Prevention and Control* 2009, 4:71–78.

Pope CA III, Essati M, Dockery DW: Fine-particulate air pollution and life expectancy in the United States. *The New England Journal of Medicine* 2009, 360:376–386.

Romero Lankao P: Are we missing the point? Particularities of urbanization, sustainability and carbon emissions in Latin American cities. *Environment and Urbanization* 2007, 19:159–175.

Section III

Adaptation, Risk, and Resilience

Introduction

Yaser Abunnasr

Historic and continuing carbon emissions have placed cities in a position where modifications of urban systems to the impacts of a new climate reality are inevitable. Physical, social, and economic infrastructure will need to be adjusted to absorb the potential human and material costs resulting from increased temperatures, erratic weather events, drought, flooding, and rising sea levels. The course of adaptation to new climate realities is defined as "the process of adjustment to actual or expected climate and its effects, in order to moderate harm or exploit beneficial opportunities" (IPCC, 2012, p. 3). Achieving adaptation requires a resilient and equitable approach to city planning and design. Central is the understanding of the internal interdependencies across risk, exposure, and vulnerability as well as exogenous influences, such as climate variability and contemporary city development dynamics.

Internal interdependencies are complex, context specific, and dependent on community capacities. Risk is defined as the probability of a community to witness severe alterations and changes over a specified period of time due to natural and/or anthropogenic weather events (IPCC, 2012). This predisposition to risk and the magnitude of ensuing impacts depend on understanding the extent of exposure and vulnerability. Exposure is the extent that communities are in harm's way of an identified risk (IPCC, 2012). For example, communities located within a river flood plain with a projected increase in precipitation will probably face high levels of flooding due to unprecedented storm events. On the other hand, vulnerability is defined as the tendency of a community and its systems to be adversely affected (IPCC, 2012). This tendency can be attributed to the internal social, economic, and environmental structure and capacities within a community. To follow with the same example, when human and financial resources are not allocated for a disaster plan for an out-of-the-ordinary flooding event and the community includes a significant number of low-income families, then this community will not be able to respond appropriately. As such, it is high on the vulnerability scale. The combined variation of levels of exposure and vulnerability determine the level of risk. It follows that a community with high exposure and vulnerability will be at high risk with high potential impacts on physical, social, economic, and ecological systems; and vice versa applies. The level of risk is further influenced by climate variability and contemporary city development dynamics.

Climate variability increases risk, regardless of the existing levels of exposure and vulnerability, and hinders future planning due to uncertainty of events. Climate variability is the unpredictability of climate events manifested in the magnitude and return frequency compared to historic data. As recent as 2017, a series of three Category 4 and 5 hurricanes hit the Caribbean and Southern USA within 24 days with unprecedented strength. The average global temperatures have been steadily increasing with 2016 being the hottest increase on record of 14.8°C (NOAA, 2016). Even normal weather regimes have been changing upsetting water reservoirs, crop growth, and in many areas leading to water scarcity (Bates et al., 2008). As a result, future prediction of how weather events will manifest has become uncertain. For example, environmental engineers use a scale (i.e. 50-year or 100-year event) that describes the intensity and rate of return of storm events indicating an expected volume of precipitation important to the design of stormwater infrastructure. These scales suggest high predictability of future conditions. An unpredictable climate will probably result in a 50-year event occurring more frequently, releasing higher amounts of water than expected rendering current stormwater systems inadequate. If we take a broader look, FEMA (Federal Emergency Management Agency) applies these scales to develop flood maps across the USA determining varying levels of exposure to flooding. FEMA maps contribute to the structure of home insurance rates as well. As uncertainty of weather events become more frequent, FEMA maps will require continuous revisions. Accordingly, insurance rates will change and vary contributing to the uncertainty of cost of risk aversion. Climate variability points to a new reality in which futures are dynamic and cannot be predicted with certainty. This will require city planners and policy makers to adopt adaptive and flexible approaches across urban systems to accommodate these changes.

Cities have expanded exponentially during the last century increasing risk in many ways. The percentage of world urban population from total world population has increased from 30% in 1950 (750 million of 2.5 billion) to 54% in 2014 (3.83 billion of 7.1 billion) and projected at 66% by 2050 (UN, 2014). In addition to population increase, the fast and expansive urbanization process can also be attributed to shifts in local and global economies, land speculation, real estate development, and rural-urban migration. Coupled with technological advances comes the development of extensive and fast infrastructure systems growing land consumption toward locations that increase exposure of urban communities. This condition is more pressing when considering socially and economically disadvantaged populations. A significant percentage of the population settling in cities tend to be either poor, from minority groups, elderly, and, in many cultures, women seeking to improve their livelihoods. Due to land speculation and high real estate prices, vulnerable populations tend to settle in locations that are cheaper and correspond to highly exposed locations such as flood plains, coastal areas, and on steep slopes. When weather events occur (even if not extreme), communities in these locations will be the first to feel the high impact of floods and landslides, resulting in human and material losses. The combination of specific socio-economic status and location render these communities at high risk especially that adequate physical, social, and economic infrastructure are often not available. Examples of such settlements include the favelas in Brazil; "Cities of the Dead" informal settlements in Cairo; and African American and Hispanic working communities in the USA. The prevalence of informal settlements in many contemporary cities and extensive land development along high exposure locations increase levels of risk making contemporary city making process an essential contributor to increasing risk.

The combined effect of variability of weather events and contemporary market based city development processes render conventional planning approaches somewhat obsolete, requiring city planners, engineers, architects, landscape architects, and policy makers to shift toward adaptive and resilient approaches to climate-proof cities. The concept of resilience is rooted in the field of ecology and defined as the inherent capability of ecological systems to rebound from disturbance (i.e. extreme events or disasters) over time. In human systems, disasters are usually associated with negative impacts, while in natural systems these could be moments of rebirth and rejuvenation. Fires tend to burn large territories of forest turning life into ashes. While the process is destructive, it eliminates disease and rejuvenates soils preparing the ground for new growth. Forests usually recover over long periods of time, a luxury that human systems cannot afford.

In the context of city planning for climate change, resilience takes a somewhat variegated definition. It is defined as:

> the ability of a system and its component parts to anticipate, absorb, accommodate, or recover from the effects of a hazardous event in a timely and efficient manner, including through ensuring the preservation, restoration, or improvement of its essential basic structures and functions.
>
> (IPCC, 2014, p. 3)

Resilience in human systems differs from ecological systems in that it is not inherent and should be intentionally planned and implemented. This translates into the ability of a community and its leaders to understand current threats, exposure, and vulnerabilities of their own context to define applicable levels of risk. Resources are then allocated to put in place plans that either reduce levels of risk or recover urban systems when risks exceed expectation. When considering resiliency plans in tandem with uncertainty, deterministic plans will be hard to develop because of the difficulty of projecting futures and collecting reliable data. As a result, much of the proposed resiliency planning is characterized with flexibility (to adjust plans as threats emerge and develop), defining scenarios (to anticipate all possible futures and actions), redundancy (to ensure continuity when failure of certain systems occur in one location or sector), participation (ensuring equity), and monitoring (to ensure that data and implementation of plans are continuously updated with developing events). These principles apply to physical, social, economic, and ecological infrastructure planning to ensure adaptive responses to climate events. While these principles are important when planning to climate-proof cities, uptake by policy makers remains slow as immediate benefits cannot be easily realized.

This section presents the concepts of risk, adaptation, and resilience, with a special focus on social vulnerability. The editors would like to underscore the significance of vulnerable communities in climate planning because they are the first and most affected social groups during disasters. The first article by the

International Panel on Climate Change (IPCC) provides an overview of risk and adaptation as well as related action strategies. Social vulnerability and its causes are then introduced by Susan Cutter and Christina Finch with a special focus on spatial distribution across the USA. The concept of "climate gap" by Rachel Morello-Frosch and co-authors is introduced highlighting the impacts of climate change on vulnerable communities of color and low socio-economic status as well as how to close this gap. The concept of social-ecological resilience in coastal contexts is then discussed by Neil W. Adger and co-authors to demonstrate that the synergy between communities and their land can lead to resilient and sustainable results when faced with extreme events. We conclude with a hardly addressed topic in climate resilience planning by Jan Salick and Nanci Ross, highlighting beneficial lessons on climate adaptation from indigenous peoples' traditional knowledge and collective memory in responding to impacts of change on social-ecological systems. In many ways, addressing social vulnerability and its flip side, social capacity, underpins successful and resilient adaptation to climate change impacts.

REFERENCES

Bates, B.C., Z.W. Kundzewicz, S. Wu and J.P. Palutikof, Eds. (2008) *Climate Change and Water: Technical Paper of the Intergovernmental Panel on Climate Change*, IPCC Secretariat, Geneva, 210 pp.

NOAA (2016). Global Climate Report for Annual 2016, published online January 2017, retrieved January 5, 2018 from www.ncdc.noaa.gov/sotc/global/201613.

IPCC (2012). *Managing the Risks of Extreme Events and Disasters to Advance Climate Change Adaptation. A Special Report of Working Groups I and II of the Intergovernmental Panel on Climate Change* [Field, C.B., V. Barros, T.F. Stocker, D. Qin, D.J. Dokken, K.L. Ebi, M.D. Mastrandrea, K.J. Mach, G.-K. Plattner, S.K. Allen, M. Tignor, and P.M. Midgley (eds.)]. Cambridge University Press, Cambridge, UK, and New York, NY, USA, 582 pp.

IPCC (2014). *Summary for Policymakers from Climate Change 2014: Synthesis Report. Contribution of Working Groups I, II and III to the Fifth Assessment Report of the Intergovernmental Panel on Climate Change* [Core Writing Team, Pachauri, R.K. and Meyer, L. (eds.)]. IPCC, Geneva, Switzerland.

UN (2014). The UN World Urbanization Prospects Report. Department of Economic and Social Affairs, Population Division, New York.

11 IPCC, 2012: Summary for Policymakers

Managing the Risks of Extreme Events and Disasters to Advance Climate Change Adaptation

Christopher B. Field, Vicente Barros,
Thomas F. Stocker, Qin Dahe,
David Jon Dokken, Kristie L. Ebi,
Michael D. Mastrandrea, Katharine J. Mach,
Gian-Kasper Plattner, Simon K. Allen,
Melinda Tignor, and Pauline M. Midgley (eds.)

EDITOR'S INTRODUCTION

The Intergovernmental Panel on Climate Change (IPCC) periodically develops an assessment of the state of the climate. The current report was developed in 2012, including a new section (from previous reports) on climate adaptation. This summary introduces readers to the ideas of and the relationships across risk, exposure, vulnerability, adaptive capacity, and resilience. The discussion is based on scientific consensus to date across several disciplines regarding how these elements affect each other.

The major lesson from this summary focuses on the relationship between climate extremes, exposure, and vulnerability and their impact on managing risk. The degree to which a climate hazard, like a heat wave or hurricane, becomes a disaster (defined by the authors as a hazard that causes "widespread damage . . . and severe alterations in the normal functioning of communities or societies") is determined by hazards experienced (exposures) and the vulnerability of the people affected.

Other key lessons are the compounding effects of multiple exposures on each other, and on a community's ability to adapt. For example, the greater risk of wildfire caused by extreme heat, or the impact of experiencing repeated storms in a short period. The authors also find that while economic losses from disasters are higher in developed countries, fatality rates are higher in developing countries, mostly due to increased exposure. Vulnerability and exposure are greatly affected by social inequalities like wealth or gender (a concept that the next article by Cutter and Finch will expand upon), and can be reduced through adaptation practices and policies.

These include actions can begin with "low-regrets" policies, which are adaptation steps that reduce risk to current *and* future climate hazards while providing co-benefits in other areas, like health or economic development. Conducting adaptation in a way that addresses various hazards simultaneously and delivers these co-benefits is found to be most effective. Last, this summary relates the need for both incremental and transformational adaptation to climate impacts, noting that in places with low adaptive capacity, transformative approaches may be more necessary.

This summary for policy makers references the Fourth Assessment Synthesis Report by the Intergovernmental Panel on Climate Change (2012). The editors chose to maintain the original references to the full report to allow further in-depth reading. References in brackets refer to figures and section number in the full report at the following link: https://www.ipcc.ch/publications_and_data/ar4/syr/en/main.html. All figure references in parentheses refer to figures within this text, while references in brackets [] refer to the full IPPC reports from which the information in this summary document is sourced.

MANAGING THE RISKS OF EXTREME EVENTS AND DISASTERS TO ADVANCE CLIMATE CHANGE ADAPTATION: 2012 SPECIAL REPORT OF WORKING GROUPS I AND II OF THE IPCC

CONTEXT

The character and severity of impacts from climate extremes depend not only on the extremes themselves but also on exposure and vulnerability. In this report, adverse impacts are considered disasters when they produce widespread damage and cause severe alterations in the normal functioning of communities or societies. Climate extremes, exposure, and vulnerability are influenced by a wide range of factors, including anthropogenic climate change, natural climate variability, and socio-economic development (Figure 11.1). Disaster risk management and adaptation to climate change focus on reducing exposure and vulnerability and increasing resilience to the potential adverse impacts of climate extremes, even though risks cannot fully be eliminated. Although mitigation of climate change is not the focus of this report, adaptation and mitigation can complement each other and together can significantly reduce the risks of climate change. [SYR AR4, 5.3] [. . .]

This report integrates perspectives from several historically distinct research communities studying climate science, climate impacts, adaptation to climate change, and disaster risk management. Each community brings different viewpoints, vocabularies, approaches, and goals, and all provide important insights

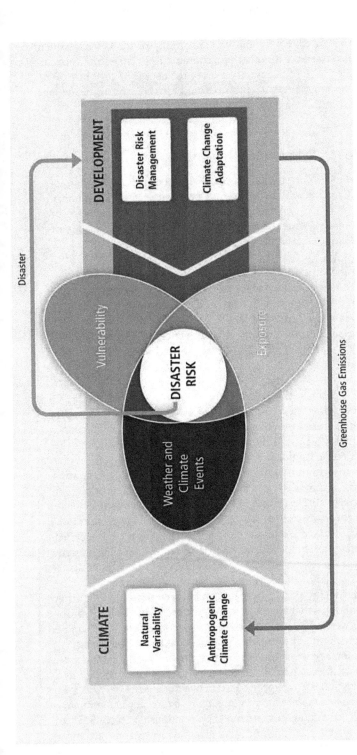

Figure 11.1 (SPM.1) Illustration of the core concepts of SREX. The report assesses how exposure and vulnerability to weather and climate events determine impacts and the likelihood of disasters (disaster risk). It evaluates the influence of natural climate variability and anthropogenic climate change on climate extremes and other weather and climate events that can contribute to disasters, as well as the exposure and vulnerability of human society and natural ecosystems. It also considers the role of development in trends in exposure and vulnerability, implications for disaster risk, and interactions between disasters and development. The report examines how disaster risk management and adaptation to climate change can reduce exposure and vulnerability to weather and climate events and thus reduce disaster risk, as well as increase resilience to the risks that cannot be eliminated. Other important processes are largely outside the scope of this report, including the influence of development on greenhouse gas emissions and anthropogenic climate change, and the potential for mitigation of anthropogenic climate change. [1.1.2, Figure 1-1]

into the status of the knowledge base and its gaps. Many of the key assessment findings come from the interfaces among these communities. These interfaces are also illustrated in Table 11.1. To accurately convey the degree of certainty in key findings, the report relies on the consistent use of calibrated uncertainty language, introduced in Box 11.1 and Figure 11.2 (Box SPM.2).

Box 11.1 (SPM.2) | Treatment of Uncertainty

Based on the Guidance Note for Lead Authors of the IPCC Fifth Assessment Report on Consistent Treatment of Uncertainties,[1] this Summary for Policymakers relies on two metrics for communicating the degree of certainty in key findings, which is based on author teams' evaluations of underlying scientific understanding:

- Confidence in the validity of a finding, based on the type, amount, quality, and consistency of evidence (e.g. mechanistic understanding, theory, data, models, expert judgment) and the degree of agreement. Confidence is expressed qualitatively.
- Quantified measures of uncertainty in a finding expressed probabilistically (based on statistical analysis of observations or model results, or expert judgment).

This Guidance Note refines the guidance provided to support the IPCC Third and Fourth Assessment Reports. Direct comparisons between assessment of uncertainties in findings in this report and those in the IPCC Fourth Assessment Report are difficult, if not impossible, because of the application of the revised guidance note on uncertainties, as well as the availability of new information, improved scientific understanding, continued analyses of data and models, and specific differences in methodologies applied in the assessed studies. For some extremes, different aspects have been assessed and therefore a direct comparison would be inappropriate.

Each key finding is based on an author team's evaluation of associated evidence and agreement. The confidence metric provides a qualitative synthesis of an author team's judgment about the validity of a finding, as determined through evaluation of evidence and agreement. If uncertainties can be quantified probabilistically, an author team can characterize a finding using the calibrated likelihood language or a more precise presentation of probability. Unless otherwise indicated, *high* or *very high confidence* is associated with findings for which an author team has assigned a likelihood term.

The following summary terms are used to describe the available evidence: *limited, medium,* or *robust;* and for the degree of agreement: *low, medium,* or *high.* A level of confidence is expressed using five qualifiers: *very low, low, medium, high,* and *very high.* The accompanying figure depicts summary statements for evidence and agreement and their relationship to confidence. There is flexibility in this relationship; for a given evidence and agreement statement, different confidence levels can be assigned, but increasing levels of evidence and degrees of agreement are correlated with increasing confidence.

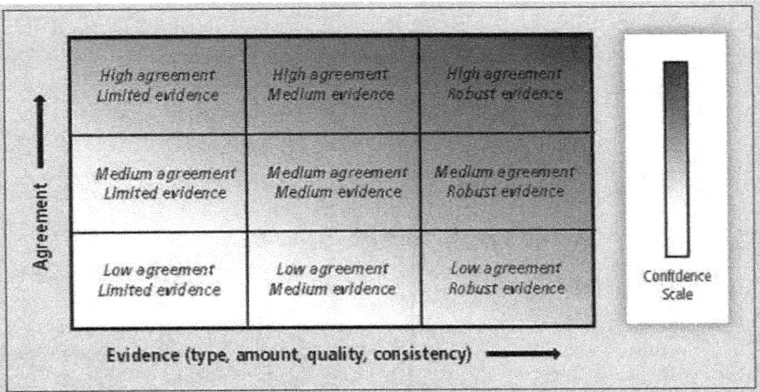

The following terms indicate the assessed likelihood:

Term*	Likelihood of the Outcome
Virtually certain	99–100% probability
Very likely	90–100% probability
Likely	66–100% probability
About as likely as not	33–66% probability
Unlikely	0–33% probability
Very unlikely	0–10% probability
Exceptionally unlikely	0–1% probability

* Additional terms that were used in limited circumstances in the Fourth Assessment Report (*extremely likely*: 95–100% probability, *more likely than not*: >50–100% probability, and *extremely unlikely*: 0–5% probability) may also be used when appropriate.

High agreement Limited evidence	High agreement Medium evidence	High agreement Robust evidence
Medium agreement Limited evidence	Medium agreement Medium evidence	Medium agreement Robust evidence
Low agreement Limited evidence	Low agreement Medium evidence	Low agreement Robust evidence

Agreement ←

Evidence (type, amount, quality, consistency) →

Confidence Scale

A depiction of evidence and agreement statements and their relationship to confidence. Confidence increases toward the top-right corner as suggested by the increasing strength of shading. Generally, evidence is most robust when there are multiple, consistent independent lines of high-quality evidence.

Figure 11.2 (SPM.2)

[. . .]

Exposure and vulnerability are key determinants of disaster risk and of impacts when risk is realized. For example, a tropical cyclone can have very different impacts depending on where and when it makes landfall. Similarly, a heat wave can have very different impacts on different populations depending on their vulnerability. Extreme impacts on human, ecological, or physical systems can result from individual extreme weather or climate events. Extreme impacts can also result from non-extreme events where exposure and vulnerability are high or from a compounding of events or their impacts. For example, drought, coupled with extreme heat and low humidity, can increase the risk of wildfire.

Extreme and non-extreme weather or climate events affect vulnerability to future extreme events by modifying resilience, coping capacity, and adaptive capacity. In particular, the cumulative effects of disasters at local or sub-national levels can substantially affect livelihood options and resources and the capacity of societies and communities to prepare for and respond to future disasters.

[. . .]

OBSERVATIONS OF EXPOSURE, VULNERABILITY, CLIMATE EXTREMES, IMPACTS, AND DISASTER LOSSES

The impacts of climate extremes and the potential for disasters result from the climate extremes themselves and from the exposure and vulnerability of human and natural systems. Observed changes in climate extremes reflect the influence of anthropogenic climate change in addition to natural climate variability, with changes in exposure and vulnerability influenced by both climatic and non-climatic factors.

Exposure and Vulnerability

- Exposure and vulnerability are dynamic, varying across temporal and spatial scales, and depend on economic, social, geographic, demographic, cultural, institutional, governance, and environmental factors (high confidence).
- Settlement patterns, urbanization, and changes in socio-economic conditions have all influenced observed trends in exposure and vulnerability to climate extremes (high confidence).

Climate Extremes and Impacts

- There is evidence from observations gathered since 1950 of change in some extremes. Confidence in observed changes in extremes depends on the quality and quantity of data and the availability of studies analyzing these data, which vary across regions and for different extremes. Assigning "low confidence" in observed changes in a specific extreme on regional or global scales neither implies nor excludes the possibility of changes in this extreme.

- There is evidence that some extremes have changed as a result of anthropogenic influences, including increases in atmospheric concentrations of greenhouse gases.

Disaster Losses

- Economic losses from weather- and climate-related disasters have increased, but with large spatial and inter-annual variability (high confidence, based on high agreement, medium evidence).
- Economic, including insured, disaster losses associated with weather, climate, and geophysical events are higher in developed countries. Fatality rates and economic losses expressed as a proportion of gross domestic product (GDP) are higher in developing countries (high confidence).
- Increasing exposure of people and economic assets has been the major cause of long-term increases in economic losses from weather- and climate-related disasters (high confidence). Long-term trends in economic disaster losses adjusted for wealth and population increases have not been attributed to climate change, but a role for climate change has not been excluded (high agreement, medium evidence).

DISASTER RISK MANAGEMENT AND ADAPTATION TO CLIMATE CHANGE: PAST EXPERIENCE WITH CLIMATE EXTREMES

Past experience with climate extremes contributes to understanding of effective disaster risk management and adaptation approaches to manage risks.

- The severity of the impacts of climate extremes depends strongly on the level of the exposure and vulnerability to these extremes (high confidence).
- Trends in exposure and vulnerability are major drivers of changes in disaster risk (high confidence).
- Development practice, policy, and outcomes are critical to shaping disaster risk, which may be increased by shortcomings in development (high confidence).
- Data on disasters and disaster risk reduction are lacking at the local level, which can constrain improvements in local vulnerability reduction (high agreement, medium evidence).
- Inequalities influence local coping and adaptive capacity, and pose disaster risk management and adaptation challenges from the local to national levels (high agreement, robust evidence).

- Humanitarian relief is often required when disaster risk reduction measures are absent or inadequate (high agreement, robust evidence).
- Post-disaster recovery and reconstruction provide an opportunity for reducing weather- and climate-related disaster risk and for improving adaptive capacity (high agreement, robust evidence).
- Risk sharing and transfer mechanisms at local, national, regional, and global scales can increase resilience to climate extremes (medium confidence).
- Attention to the temporal and spatial dynamics of exposure and vulnerability is particularly important given that the design and implementation of adaptation and disaster risk management strategies and policies can reduce risk in the short term, but may increase exposure and vulnerability over the longer term (high agreement, medium evidence).
- National systems are at the core of countries' capacity to meet the challenges of observed and projected trends in exposure, vulnerability, and weather and climate extremes (high agreement, robust evidence).
- Closer integration of disaster risk management and climate change adaptation, along with the incorporation of both into local, sub-national, national, and international development policies and practices, could provide benefits at all scales (high agreement, medium evidence).

FUTURE CLIMATE EXTREMES, IMPACTS, AND DISASTER LOSSES

Future changes in exposure, vulnerability, and climate extremes resulting from natural climate variability, anthropogenic climate change, and socio-economic development can alter the impacts of climate extremes on natural and human systems and the potential for disasters.

Climate Extremes and Impacts

- Confidence in projecting changes in the direction and magnitude of climate extremes depends on many factors, including the type of extreme, the region and season, the amount and quality of observational data, the level of understanding of the underlying processes, and the reliability of their simulation in models.
- Models project substantial warming in temperature extremes by the end of the 21st century.
- It is likely that the frequency of heavy precipitation or the proportion of total rainfall from heavy falls will increase in the 21st century over many areas of the globe.
- Average tropical cyclone maximum wind speed is likely to increase, although increases may not occur in all ocean basins. It is likely that the global frequency of tropical cyclones will either decrease or remain essentially unchanged.

- There is medium confidence that there will be a reduction in the number of extratropical cyclones averaged over each hemisphere.
- There is medium confidence that droughts will intensify in the 21st century in some seasons and areas, due to reduced precipitation and/or increased evapotranspiration.
- Projected precipitation and temperature changes imply possible changes in floods, although overall there is low confidence in projections of changes in fluvial floods.
- It is very likely that mean sea level rise will contribute to upward trends in extreme coastal high water levels in the future.
- There is high confidence that changes in heat waves, glacial retreat, and/or permafrost degradation will affect high mountain phenomena such as slope instabilities, movements of mass, and glacial lake outburst floods.
- There is low confidence in projections of changes in large-scale patterns of natural climate variability.

Human Impacts and Disaster Losses
- Extreme events will have greater impacts on sectors with closer links to climate, such as water, agriculture, and food security, forestry, health, and tourism. . . .
- In many regions, the main drivers of future increases in economic losses due to some climate extremes will be socio-economic in nature (medium confidence, based on medium agreement, limited evidence). . . .
- Increases in exposure will result in higher direct economic losses from tropical cyclones. Losses will also depend on future changes in tropical cyclone frequency and intensity (high confidence). . . .
- Disasters associated with climate extremes influence population mobility and relocation, affecting host and origin communities (medium agreement, medium evidence).

MANAGING CHANGING RISKS OF CLIMATE EXTREMES AND DISASTERS

Adaptation to climate change and disaster risk management provide a range of complementary approaches for managing the risks of climate extremes and disasters. Effectively applying and combining approaches may benefit from considering the broader challenge of sustainable development.

- Measures that provide benefits under current climate and a range of future climate change scenarios, called low-regrets measures, are available starting points for addressing projected trends in exposure, vulnerability, and climate extremes. They have the potential to offer benefits now and lay the foundation for addressing projected changes (high agreement, medium evidence). Many of these low-regrets strategies produce co-benefits; help address other development goals, such as improvements in livelihoods,

human well-being, and biodiversity conservation; and help minimize the
scope for maladaptation.

> Potential low-regrets measures include early warning systems; risk
> communication between decision makers and local citizens; sustainable
> land management, including land use planning; and ecosystem
> management and restoration. Other low-regrets measures include
> improvements to health surveillance, water supply, sanitation, and
> irrigation and drainage systems; climate-proofing of infrastructure;
> development and enforcement of building codes; and better education
> and awareness.

- **Effective risk management generally involves a portfolio of actions
  to reduce and transfer risk and to respond to events and disasters, as
  opposed to a singular focus on any one action or type of action (high
  confidence).** Such integrated approaches are more effective when they
  are informed by and customized to specific local circumstances (high
  agreement, robust evidence). Successful strategies include a combination
  of hard infrastructure-based responses and soft solutions such as
  individual and institutional capacity building and ecosystem-based
  responses.
- **Multi-hazard risk management approaches provide opportunities to
  reduce complex and compound hazards (high agreement, robust evidence).**
  Considering multiple types of hazards reduces the likelihood that risk
  reduction efforts targeting one type of hazard will increase exposure and
  vulnerability to other hazards, in the present and future.
- **Opportunities exist to create synergies in international finance for disaster
  risk management and adaptation to climate change, but these have not yet
  been fully realized (high confidence).** International funding for disaster risk
  reduction remains relatively low as compared to the scale of spending on
  international humanitarian response. Technology transfer and cooperation
  to advance disaster risk reduction and climate change adaptation are
  important. Coordination on technology transfer and cooperation
  between these two fields has been lacking, which has led to fragmented
  implementation.
- **Stronger efforts at the international level do not necessarily lead to
  substantive and rapid results at the local level (high confidence).** There
  is room for improved integration across scales from international to
  local.
- **Integration of local knowledge with additional scientific and technical
  knowledge can improve disaster risk reduction and climate change
  adaptation (high agreement, robust evidence).** Local populations document
  their experiences with the changing climate, particularly extreme weather
  events, in many different ways, and this self-generated knowledge can
  uncover existing capacity within the community and important current

shortcomings. Local participation supports community-based adaptation to benefit management of disaster risk and climate extremes. However, improvements in the availability of human and financial capital and of disaster risk and climate information customized for local stakeholders can enhance community-based adaptation (medium agreement, medium evidence).

- **Appropriate and timely risk communication is critical for effective adaptation and disaster risk management (high confidence).** Explicit characterization of uncertainty and complexity strengthens risk communication. Effective risk communication builds on exchanging, sharing, and integrating knowledge about climate-related risks among all stakeholder groups. Among individual stakeholders and groups, perceptions of risk are driven by psychological and cultural factors, values, and beliefs.

- **An iterative process of monitoring, research, evaluation, learning, and innovation can reduce disaster risk and promote adaptive management in the context of climate extremes (high agreement, robust evidence).** Adaptation efforts benefit from iterative risk management strategies because of the complexity, uncertainties, and long time frame associated with climate change (high confidence) [1.3.2]. Addressing knowledge gaps through enhanced observation and research can reduce uncertainty and help in designing effective adaptation and risk management strategies.

- **Table 11.1 presents examples of how observed and projected trends in exposure, vulnerability, and climate extremes can inform risk management and adaptation strategies, policies, and measures.** The importance of these trends for decision making depends on their magnitude and degree of certainty at the temporal and spatial scale of the risk being managed and on the available capacity to implement risk management options.

(see Table 11.1)

The examples were selected based on availability of evidence in the underlying chapters, including on exposure, vulnerability, climate information, and risk management and adaptation options. They are intended to reflect relevant risk management themes and scales, rather than to provide comprehensive information by region. The examples are not intended to reflect any regional differences in exposure and vulnerability, or in experience in risk management.

The confidence in projected changes in climate extremes at local scales is often more limited than the confidence in projected regional and global changes. This limited confidence in changes places a focus on low-regrets risk management options that aim to reduce exposure and vulnerability and to increase resilience and preparedness for risks that cannot be entirely eliminated. Higher-confidence projected changes in climate extremes, at a scale relevant to adaptation and risk management decisions, can inform more targeted adjustments in strategies, policies, and measures. [3.1.6, Box 3–2,6.3,1,6.5.2]

Table 11.1 (SPM.1) | Illustrative examples of options for risk management and adaptation in the context of changes in exposure, vulnerability, and climate extremes. In each example, information is characterized at the scale directly relevant to decision-making. Observed and projected changes in climate extremes at global and regional scales illustrate that the direction or magnitude of, and/or degree of certainty for changes may differ across scales.

Example	Exposure and vulnerability at scale of risk management in the example	Information on Climate Extreme Across Spatial Scales			Options for risk management and adaptation in the example
		GLOBAL Observed (since 1950) and projected (to 2100) global changes	REGIONAL Observed (since 1950) and projected (to 2100) changes in the example	SCALE OF RISK MANAGEMENT Available information for the example	
Inundation related to **extreme sea levels** in tropical small island developing states	Small island states in the Pacific, Indian, and Atlantic oceans, often with low elevation, are particularly vulnerable to rising sea levels and impacts such as erosion, inundation, shoreline change, and saltwater intrusion into coastal aquifers. These impacts can result in ecosystem disruption, decreased agricultural productivity, changes in disease patterns, economic losses such as in tourism industries, and population displacement—all at which reinforce vulnerability to extreme weather events. [3.5.5, Box 3–4, 4.3.5, 4.4.10, 9.2.9]	**Observed:** *Likely* increase in extreme coastal high water worldwide related to increases in mean sea level. **Projected:** *Very likely* that mean sea level rise will contribute to upward trends in extreme coastal high water levels. *High confidence* that locations currently experiencing coastal erosion and inundation will continue to do so due to increasing sea level, in the absence of changes in other contributing factors. *Likely* that the global frequency of tropical cyclones will either decease or remain essentially unchanged.	**Observed:** Tides and El Niño-Southern Oscillation have contributed to the more frequent occurrence of extreme coastal high water levels and associated flooding experienced on some Pacific Islands in recent years. **Projected:** The *very likely* contribution of mean sea level rise to increased extreme coastal high water levels, coupled with the *likely* increase in tropical cyclone maximum wind speed, is a specific issue for tropical small island states.	Sparse regional and temporal coverage of terrestrial-based observation networks and limited in situ ocean observing network, but with improved satellite-based observations in recent decades. While changes in storminess may contribute to changes in extreme coastal high water levels, the limited geographical coverage of studies to date and the uncertainties associated with storminess charges overall mean that a general assessment of the effects of storminess changes on storm surge is not possible at this time. [Box 3–4, 3.5.3]	Low-regrets options that reduce exposure and vulnerability across a range of hazard trends: • Maintenance of drainage systems • Well technologies to limit saltwater contamination of groundwater • Improved early warning systems • Regional risk pooling • Mangrove conservation, restoration, and replanting Specific adaptation options include, for instance, rendering national economies more climate-independent and adaptive management involving iterative learning. In some cases, there may be a need to consider relocation, for example, for atolls where

Flash floods in informal settlements in Nairobi, Kenya					storm surges may completely inundate them. [4.3.5, 4.4.10, 5.2.2, 6.3.2, 6.5.2, 6.6.2, 7.4.4, 9.2.9, 9.2.11, 9.2.13]
Flash floods in informal settlements in Nairobi, Kenya	Rapid expansion of poor people living in informal settlements around Nairobi has led to houses of weak building materials being constructed immediately adjacent to rivers and to blockage of natural drainage areas, increasing exposure and vulnerability. [6.4.2, Box 6–2]	*Likely* increase in average tropical cyclone maximum wind speed, although increases may not occur in all ocean basins. [Table 3–1, 3.4.4, 3.5.3, 3.5.5] **Observed:** *Low confidence* at global scale regarding (climate-driven) observed changes in the magnitude and frequency of floods. **Projected:** *Low confidence* in projections of changes in floods because of limited evidence and because the causes of regional changes are complex. However, *medium confidence* (based on physical reasoning) that projected increases in heavy precipitation will contribute to rain-generated local flooding in some catchments or regions. [Table 3–1, 3.5.2]	See global changes column for information on global projections for tropical cyclones. [Box 3–4, 3.4.4, 2.5.3] **Observed:** *Low confidence* regarding trends in heavy precipitation in East Africa, because of insufficient evidence. **Projected:** *Likely* increase in heavy precipitation indicators in East Africa. [Table 3–2, Table 3–3, 3.3.2]	Limited ability to provide local flash flood projections. [3.5.2]	Low-regrets options that reduce exposure and vulnerability across a range of hazard trends: • Strengthening building design and regulation • City-wide drainage and sewerage improvements • Poverty reduction schemes The Nairobi Rivers Rehabilitation and Restoration Programme includes installation of riparian buffers, canals, and drainage channels, and clearance of existing channel; attention to climate variability and change in the location and design of wastewater infrastructure; and environmental monitoring for flood early warning. [6.3, 6.4.2, Box 6–2, Box 6–6]

(Continued)

Table 11.1 (SPM.1) (Continued)

Example	Exposure and vulnerability at scale of risk management in the example	Information on Climate Extreme Across Spatial Scales			Options for risk management and adaptation in the example
		GLOBAL Observed (since 1950) and projected (to 2100) global changes	REGIONAL Observed (since 1950) and projected (to 2100) changes in the example	SCALE OF RISK MANAGEMENT Available information for the example	
Impacts of heat waves in urban areas in Europe	Factors affecting exposure and vulnerability include age, pre-existing health status, level of outdoor activity, socioeconomic factors including poverty and social isolation, access to and use of cooling, physiological, and behavioral adaptation of the population, and urban infrastructure. [2.5.2, 4.3.5, 4.3.6, 4.4.5, 9.2.1]	**Observed:** *Medium* confidence that the length or number of warm spells or heat waves has increased since the middle of the 20th century, in many (but not all) regions over the globe. *Very likely* increase in number of warm days and nights at the global scale. **Projected:** *Very likely* increase in length, frequency, and/or intensity of warm spells or heat waves over most land areas. *Virtually certain* increase in frequency and magnitude of warm days and nights at the global scale. [Table 3–1, 3.3.1]	**Observed:** *Medium* confidence in increase in heat waves or warm spells in Europe. *Likely* overall increase in warm days and nights over most of the continent. **Projected:** *Likely* more frequent, longer, and/or more intense heat waves or warm spells in Europe. *Very likely* increase in warm days and nights. [Table 3–2, Table 3-3.3.3.1]	Observations and projections can provide information for specific urban areas in the region, with increased heat waves expected due to regional trends and urban heat island effects. [3.3.1, 4.4.5]	Low-regrets options that reduce exposure and vulnerability across a range of hazard trends: • Early warning systems that reach particularly vulnerable groups (e.g., the elderly) • Vulnerability mapping and corresponding measures • Public information on what to do during heat waves, including behavioral advice • Use of social care networks to reach vulnerable groups Specific adjustments in strategies, policies, and measures informed by trends in heat waves include awareness raising of heat waves as a public health concern; changes in urban infrastructure and land use planning, for example, increasing urban green space; changes in approaches to cooling for public facilities; and adjustments in energy generation and transmission infrastructure. [Table 6–1, 9.2.1]

| Increasing losses from **hurricanes** in the USA and the Caribbean | Exposure and vulnerability are increasing due to growth in population and increase in property values, particularly along the Gulf and Atlantic coasts of the United States. Some of this increase has been offset by improved building codes.

[4.4.6] | **Observed:** *Low confidence* in any observed long-term (i.e., 40 years or more) increases in tropical cyclone activity, after accounting for past changes in observing capabilities.

Projected: *Likely* that the global frequency of tropical cyclones will either decrease or remain essentially unchanged. *Likely* increase in average tropical cyclone maximum wind speed, although increases may not occur in all ocean basins. Heavy rainfalls associated with tropical cyclones are *likely* to increase. Projected sea level rise is expected to further compound tropical cyclone surge impacts.

[Table 3–1, 3.4.4] | See global changes column for global projections. | Limited model capability to project changes relevant to specific settlements or other locations, due to the inability of global models to accurately simulate factors relevant to tropical cyclone genesis, track, and intensity evolution.

[3.4.4] | Low-regrets options that reduce exposure and vulnerability across a range of hazard trends:
• Adoption and enforcement of improved building codes
• Improved forecasting capacity and implementation of improved early warning systems (including evacuation plans and infrastructures)
• Regional risk pooling

In the context of high underlying variability and uncertainty regarding trends, options can include emphasizing adaptive management involving learning and flexibility (e.g., Cayman Islands National Hurricane Committee).

[5.5.3, 6.5.2, 6.6.2, Box 6–7, Table 6–1, 7.4.4, 9.2.5, 9.2.11, 9.2.13] |

(Continued)

Table 11.1 (SPM.1) (Continued)

Example	Exposure and vulnerability at scale of risk management in the example	Information on Climate Extreme Across Spatial Scales		SCALE OF RISK MANAGEMENT *Available information for the example*	Options for risk management and adaptation in the example
		GLOBAL *Observed (since 1950) and projected (to 2100) global changes*	REGIONAL *Observed (since 1950) and projected (to 2100) changes in the example*		
Droughts in the context of food security in West Africa	Less advanced agricultural practices render region vulnerable to increasing variability in seasonal rainfall, drought, and weather extremes. Vulnerability is exacerbated by population growth, degradation of ecosystems, and overuse of natural resources, as well as poor standards for health, education, and governance. [2.2.2, 2.3, 2.5, 4.4.2, 9.2.3]	**Observed:** *Medium confidence* that some regions of the world have experienced more intense and longer droughts, but in some regions, droughts have become less frequent, less intense, or shorter. **Projected:** *Medium confidence* in projected intensification of drought in some seasons and areas. Elsewhere there is overall *low confidence* due to inconsistent projections. [Table 3–1,3.5.1]	**Observed:** *Medium confidence* in an increase in dryness. Recent years characterized by greater interannual variability than previous 40 years, with the western Sahel remaining dry and the eastern Sahel returning to wetter conditions **Projected:** *Low confidence* due to inconsistent signal in model projections. [Table 3–2, Table 3–3, 3.5.1]	Sub-seasonal, seasonal, and interannual forecasts with increasing uncertainty over longer time scales. Improved monitoring, instrumentation, and data associated with early warning systems, but with limited participation and dissemination to at-risk populations [5.3.1, 5.5.3, 7.3.1, 9.2.3, 9.2.11]	Low-regrets options that reduce exposure and vulnerability across a range of hazard trends: • Traditional rain and groundwater harvesting and storage systems • Water demand management and improved irrigation efficiency measures • Conservation agriculture, crop rotation, and livelihood diversification • Increasing use of drought-resistant crop varieties • Early warning systems integrating seasonal forecasts with drought projections, with improved communication involving extension services • Risk pooling at the regional or national level [2.5.4, 5.3.1, 5.3.3, 6.5, Table 6–3, 9.2.3, 9.2.11]

Implications for Sustainable Development

- Actions that range from incremental steps to transformational changes are essential for reducing risk from climate extremes (high agreement, robust evidence). Incremental steps aim to improve efficiency within existing technological, governance, and value systems, whereas transformation may involve alterations of fundamental attributes of those systems. Transformations, where they are required, are also facilitated through increased emphasis on adaptive management and learning. Where vulnerability is high and adaptive capacity low, changes in climate extremes can make it difficult for systems to adapt sustainably without transformational changes. Vulnerability is often concentrated in lower-income countries or groups, although higher-income countries or groups can also be vulnerable to climate extremes.

- Social, economic, and environmental sustainability can be enhanced by disaster risk management and adaptation approaches. A prerequisite for sustainability in the context of climate change is addressing the underlying causes of vulnerability, including the structural inequalities that create and sustain poverty and constrain access to resources (medium agreement, robust evidence). This involves integrating disaster risk management and adaptation into all social, economic, and environmental policy domains.

- The most effective adaptation and disaster risk reduction actions are those that offer development benefits in the relatively near term, as well as reductions in vulnerability over the longer term (high agreement, medium evidence). There are tradeoffs between current decisions and long-term goals linked to diverse values, interests, and priorities for the future. Short- and long-term perspectives on disaster risk management and adaptation to climate change thus can be difficult to reconcile. Such reconciliation involves overcoming the disconnect between local risk management practices and national institutional and legal frameworks, policy, and planning.

- Progress toward resilient and sustainable development in the context of changing climate extremes can benefit from questioning assumptions and paradigms and stimulating innovation to encourage new patterns of response (medium agreement, robust evidence). Successfully addressing disaster risk, climate change, and other stressors often involves embracing broad participation in strategy development, the capacity to combine multiple perspectives, and contrasting ways of organizing social relations.

- The interactions among climate change mitigation, adaptation, and disaster risk management may have a major influence on resilient and sustainable pathways (high agreement, limited evidence). Interactions between the goals of mitigation and adaptation in particular will play out locally, but have global consequences.

There are many approaches and pathways to a sustainable and resilient future. However, limits to resilience are faced when thresholds or tipping points associated with social and/or natural systems are exceeded, posing severe challenges for adaptation. Choices and outcomes for adaptive actions to climate events must reflect divergent capacities and resources and multiple interacting processes. Actions are framed by tradeoffs between competing prioritized values and objectives, and different visions of development that can change over time. Iterative approaches allow development pathways to integrate risk management so that diverse policy solutions can be considered, as risk and its measurement, perception, and understanding evolve over time.

NOTE

1. Mastrandrea, M.D., C.B. Field, U. Stocker, O. Edenhofer, K.L. Ebi, D.J. Frame, H. Held, E. Kriegler, K.J. Mach, P.R. Matschoss, G.-K. Plattner, G.W. Yohe, and F.W. Zwiers, 2010. Guidance Note for Lead Authors of the IPCC Fifth Assessment Report on Consistent Treatment of Uncertainties. Intergovernmental Panel on Climate Change (IPCC), Geneva, Switzerland, www.1pcc.ch.

12 Temporal and Spatial Changes in Social Vulnerability to Natural Hazards

Susan L. Cutter and Christina Finch

EDITOR'S INTRODUCTION

Cutter and Finch define social vulnerability as an identification of "sensitive populations that may be less likely to respond to, cope with, and recover from a natural disaster," and lay out a comprehensive analysis of how it has been distributed across the United States from 1960 to 2000. Social vulnerability is distinct from geographic/environmental vulnerability, which refers to the natural hazards a population or place is likely to be exposed to. As this article makes clear, climate change will not impact everyone equally—even within the same geographic area. Understanding how social vulnerability varies dramatically based on socio-economic status, race, gender, age, and urban development is key to equitably improving resilience. The authors note the example of older populations being less mobile and less able to recover from financial losses if they live on a fixed income. Cutter and Finch use these factors to calculate the social vulnerability index of every county in the United States in 1960, 1970, 1980, 1990, and 2000, exploring some of the principal factors and determining how the distribution evolved throughout this period.

They find that high social vulnerability is most frequently associated with low socio-economic status, racial diversity, and high urban development, and has consistently been concentrated in Southwestern and northern Midwest counties. The single most vulnerable county across the studied years was New York County. They also find that social vulnerability shifted over time from New England and the Pacific Northwest into the Rocky Mountain states, particularly Colorado. One of their most important findings is that the causes of social vulnerability differ in each location. For example, high concentrations of elderly populations in the Midwest is attributed to the decline of the younger generation, while concentrations of poor Latino immigrants create high social vulnerability in California and along the Texas-Mexico border. This cements the localized nature of vulnerability, and demands deeply contextualized examinations of the social impacts of and approaches to addressing climate change. The authors conclude with predictions of future vulnerability distribution across the U.S.A. and a discussion of the challenges to validate the accuracy of the social vulnerability index.

Dr. Susan Cutter is a Carolina Distinguished Professor of Geography at the University of South Carolina, where she directs the Hazards and Vulnerability Research Institute with a focus on how vulnerability and resilience are measured, monitored, and assessed. Christina Finch is a project manager with the Federal Emergency Management Agency (FEMA) in the Risk Analysis Division.

(2008) TEMPORAL AND SPATIAL CHANGES IN SOCIAL VULNERABILITY TO NATURAL HAZARDS

Although significant advancements have been made in sustainability and vulnerability science, especially the conceptualization and representation of vulnerability within the human-environment system (1–6), nuanced differences in the definition of vulnerability between the risk-hazards and human-environmental research communities remain. The primary application arena also distinguishes these two communities. Human-environmental vulnerability research relates to large-scale global environmental processes, especially climate change and its local to global impacts (7, 8). Findings from natural hazards and disasters research on vulnerability and resilience are incorporated into emergency management and hazards mitigation (9–12). Despite differences between the two research communities, both acknowledge that the composition of vulnerability is driven by exposure, sensitivity, and response (carrying capacity or resilience), and it requires measurements of both environmental and social systems, the latter being less prevalent in the literature. This paper adds to the paucity of empirical literature on the vulnerability of social systems through an examination of the historical variability in natural hazard vulnerability, or social vulnerability.

Social vulnerability is a measure of both the sensitivity of a population to natural hazards and its ability to respond to and recover from the impacts of hazards. It is a multidimensional construct, one not easily captured with a single variable. There is ample field-based evidence for understanding the characteristics of people and social groups that make them more sensitive to the effects of natural hazards and reduce their ability to adequately respond and recover (13, 14). Race/ethnicity, socio-economic class, and gender are among the most common characteristics that define vulnerable populations, along with age (elderly and children), migration, and housing tenure (renter or owner). For example, the literature has cited many reasons why the elderly are more vulnerable in the event of a disaster: physical limitations that influence their inability or unwillingness to comply with mandatory evacuation orders; post-disaster psychological stress that impairs recovery and increases the need for additional social services, declining cognitive abilities to process hazard information necessitating specially targeted risk communication or warning messages, and fewer economic resources to repair damaged homes, especially by elderly residents on fixed incomes (15–18). Thus, the greater the proportion of elderly in a community, the more vulnerable it is and the longer it will take for the community to fully recover from the disaster's aftermath.

There have been some notable attempts to measure vulnerability. There are many national-level hazards and disasters indicator studies that incorporate social characteristics such as population numbers and distributions as a method for defining population exposures to a variety of hazard agents (19–25). Other studies incorporating vulnerability metrics focused on human-environmental systems at different subnational spatial scales: within India (26), U.S. watersheds (27), U.S. Great Plains counties (28), and the Yaqui Valley, Mexico (29). More detailed vulnerability metrics on human-environmental systems used subcounty enumeration units within the United States: Georgetown County, SC (30); Revere, MA (31); and Hampton Roads, VA (32). Methodological difficulties, data quality and access issues, and conceptual shortcomings within social vulnerability science limit the development of consistent measures of social vulnerability to natural hazards.

RESULTS

The shortcomings noted previously led to the development of the Social Vulnerability Index or SoVI (33). The SoVI provides a county-level comparative metric of social vulnerability to natural hazards based on the underlying socio-economic and demographic profile.

Consistency of Principal Components

The percentage of the variation among U.S. counties explained by the SoVI varies from 73–78%. The number of components changes slightly from decade to decade, ranging from 9–12. In all decades, the dominant component was socio-economic status. The remaining underlying dimensions of social vulnerability remain consistent during the decades as well. These components, broadly described as the level of development of the built environment, age, race/ethnicity, and gender, account for nearly half of the variability in social vulnerability among U.S. counties.

A number of unique components appear only in a single decade. Suburbanization (number of building permits) assumed importance in 1970. By 1980, gender, specifically high percentages of women in rural areas, emerges as a separate indicator, and extreme wealth and civic engagement (percent voting) became important, as well. In 1990, the economic value of industries and value of property surfaces as a driving force of social vulnerability. In the 2000 SoVI, aspects of immigration (foreign-born residents) assumed more importance as a unique component, as did the economic dependence of counties.

[. . .]

Mapping Social Vulnerability

To illustrate the geographic patterns in the county SoVI scores, we classified the visualization of mapped scores using standard deviations from the mean for each decade. Because our primary focus is on the extremes of the distribution, we define social high and low vulnerability as those counties with SoVI scores greater than two standard deviations from the mean (high vulnerability ≥ +2 SD; low vulnerability ≤ –2 SD).

[. . .]

Figure 12.1 shows the geographic pattern of social vulnerability for each decade. In 1960, the most socially vulnerable counties are concentrated in the Southwest, north-central Great Plains, lower Mississippi Valley, Florida, and Hawaii. The

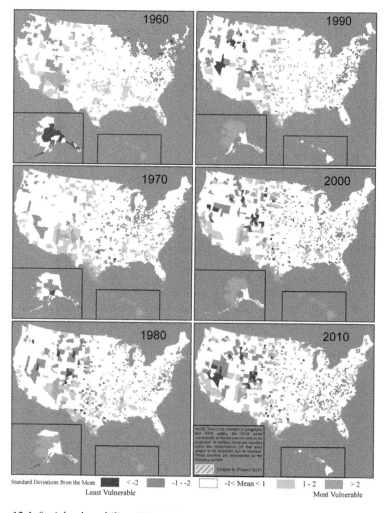

Figure 12.1 Social vulnerability 1960–2010.

least vulnerable counties in 1960 are in New England, the upper Great Lakes, the Pacific Northwest, and Alaska. For 1970, the pattern of high social vulnerability in the Southwest shrank, and a new area emerged along the U.S.-Mexico border regions of Texas. The lower Mississippi Valley and the Upper Great Plains retained their placement in the high vulnerability category. Interestingly, the pattern of low social vulnerability showed regional shifts, with many of the 1960 counties moving into the moderate or average range.

[. . .]

For 1980, the extremes in social vulnerability still showed some distinct spatial patterns. For example, the areas of high social vulnerability remained along the U.S.-Mexico border; in the Native American lands in the Southwest and Great Plains, in the lower Mississippi Valley, and in Alaska and Hawaii. The distribution of least vulnerable counties in 1980 continued a westward shift, showing concentrations in the Rocky Mountain and Great Basin areas (Figure 12.1). A vestige of low-social-vulnerability counties remained along the eastern flanks of the Appalachians in Virginia and North Carolina.

[. . .]

By 1990, the lower Mississippi Valley, the lower Rio Grande Valley, and the Great Plains continue to show greater social vulnerability. Most of Alaska remains in the highest category, but Hawaiian counties improve to average levels of vulnerability. There is an increase in the number of eastern counties in the least vulnerable category, and a decrease in the western counties in this same classification.

Finally, the 2000 SoVI shows a more dispersed pattern of social vulnerability nationally, although concentrations of high social vulnerability remain in the U.S.-Mexico border counties, the Deep South, the upper Great Plains, the Southwest, and in California (Figure 12.1).

[. . .]

Local Places, Local Changes

Although it is instructive to see the national pattern and trends in social vulnerability, more localized analyses provide an understanding of those places that are experiencing significant changes in their social vulnerability and show how such changes might influence emergency preparedness and response in the future. For example, has the social vulnerability of County A increased, decreased, or stayed relatively the same historically? More importantly, on the basis of this historical trend, what level of social vulnerability might be expected in County A in 2010?

[. . .]

Population change and population density have significant impact on the temporal trends of social vulnerability. Counties increasing in social vulnerability are doing so because of extreme depopulation or population growth. For example, the depopulation of the Great Plains had a direct influence on many components that increase social vulnerability that are evident from the mapped patterns (Figure 12.1). Consider McIntosh, Towner, and Divide counties in North Dakota. All of these counties experienced a 49–59% decrease in population from 1960–2000. As the counties lost younger people, the remaining population aged and eventually became dependent on social services and government support for their livelihoods. With fewer people, the civilian working force decreased, influencing the economic vitality of the county, and led to reduced access to critical facilities, such as hospitals and physicians. In 2000, Divide County's population was 27.6% elderly (65+ years of age) compared with the U.S. population distribution (12.4% elderly). The opposite influence of population change is represented in the counties that increased in social vulnerability through time.

Consider Orange County, CA, which was in the moderate vulnerability category in 1960 but by 2000 was among the most socially vulnerable in the nation. Orange County experienced significant population growth because of its proximity to Los Angeles, Long Beach, and Santa Ana. Since 1960, the population of Orange County, CA, increased by =300%. The population increase, largely the result of an influx of recent immigrants that resulted in a more diverse population, prompted more development; both factors contribute to social vulnerability to natural hazards.

There are also examples of counties experiencing socio-economic changes that decrease social vulnerability. In 1960, Teton County, WY; Pitkin County, CO; and Mono County, CA, were rural counties with small populations and were categorized with moderate levels of vulnerability. The counties experienced drastic increases in population over the 40-year time span, ranging from doubling to quintupling. Pitkin County's population increased by =525%, Teton County's increased by 496%, and Mono County's increased by 481%. Instead of increasing the vulnerability, the population growth actually reduced it because of the characteristics of in-migrants: white and wealthy individuals who helped stimulate an economic boom in the tourism sector, the predominant economic driver in the counties.

Population growth as a single variable tends to increase social vulnerability. Yet, one of the contributions of the SoVI is that it enables us to examine the multidimensionality of such growth by examining changes in the characteristics of the population and its subsequent impact on the county's overall vulnerability.

Anticipating Future Vulnerability

What might the social vulnerability of U.S. counties look like in 2010? On the basis of the linear trend for each county across the five time stamps (1960, 1970, 1980, 1990, and 2000), we expect 88 counties in the most vulnerable category, representing 2.8% of the total counties in 2010. We expect that the least vulnerable category will contain 55 counties or 1.8% of the total counties. The projected spatial pattern of social vulnerability in 2010 is similar to previous decades (Figure 12.1). There will be concentrations of high social vulnerability along the lower Mississippi River, the Southwest, the Texas-Mexico border, and California. However, the most dominant area of high social vulnerability will be located in the North Central United States. The counties with increased social vulnerability in 2010 are in North Dakota, South Dakota, and Montana, and are associated with Native American reservations or the depopulation of the Great Plains. As in all other decades, New York County, NY, will be the most vulnerable county in the predicted 2010 SoVI, followed by Kings County, NY; Bronx County, NY; and San Francisco County, CA.

The least vulnerable counties in 2010 will be located in the mountainous West, especially in Colorado, Nevada, and Idaho. The dominance of Colorado counties (Summit, Pitkin, Hinsdale, and San Miguel) as the least vulnerable will continue.

DISCUSSION

As the composition of American society changed during the past five decades, so too has our social vulnerability to natural hazards, as measured by the SoVI. Those most socially vulnerable populations were initially concentrated in the Deep South (race, gender, and socio-economic status), the Southwest (Native American lands), and in Florida (elderly), but over time, the pattern of social vulnerability to natural hazards in the United States changed. By 2000, the social vulnerability was greatest in the lower Mississippi Valley region, in South Texas border lands, in California's Central Valley, and in the upper Great Plains. Pockets of high social vulnerability remained in the Deep South and Southwest.

The driving forces behind increased social vulnerability vary between regions and across counties. For example, contributing components in the lower Mississippi Valley counties were race and socio-economic status; along the Texas-Mexico border counties, it was ethnicity and poverty; whereas in the Great Plains counties, it was a combination of economic dependence and an aging population brought on by depopulation. The overall result was a distinct geography of social vulnerability to natural hazards based on the SoVI metric.

Many counties in the United States are experiencing a significant increase or decrease in social vulnerability, suggesting that the county's susceptibility to hazards and their potential ability to recover from them has changed. On the basis of this analysis, 46 counties had significant increases in social vulnerability and 40 counties had significant decreases in social vulnerability from 1960–2000. As these counties experience changes over time attributable to components such as increasing development and diversity, the driving forces contributing to the social vulnerability need to be identified in current hazard assessment and mitigation plans to make them more responsive.

The projected social vulnerability in 2010 identified priority areas that should be addressed now, to improve the resilience of communities. The SoVI of 2010 projects that high-social-vulnerability concentrations will continue along the lower Mississippi River, the Texas-Mexico border, southern California, the northern Great Plains, and in the nation's largest metropolitan areas. Social vulnerability is born from inequality and its social and political consequences (37). In many ways, it mirrors the geography of inequality (38) and poverty (39). Within the context of natural hazards, the SoVI helps determine which places may need specialized attention during immediate response and long-term recovery after a natural hazard event, given the sensitivity of the populations and the lowered capacity to respond. Although not as readily apparent in the visualization of SoVI, metropolitan counties continue to be among the most socially vulnerable over time driven by components such as development density and large diverse populations. In a broader context of social policy, the SoVI has applicability in the identification of counties that are most in need for socially based services—health, welfare, housing, education—that would not improve the quality of life of residents but would improve their ability to respond to and recover from disaster events.

Although there is much exciting work on the development of vulnerability and resilience indices, there are serious obstacles to validating such metrics. First, the concepts of vulnerability and resilience are complex, and their meanings are often contested within their respective research communities. Thus, establishing viable metrics for measuring vulnerability and resilience and at the appropriate scale becomes problematic. Second, using natural hazard losses as validation is an oft-suggested approach, where losses would be correlated with social vulnerability. However, this approach assumes that the most socially vulnerable populations have the most to lose (economically), which is not the case. In correlating property losses with social vulnerability, we would expect an inverse relationship (high social vulnerability; low dollar losses), yet this assumes that the losses are evenly distributed throughout the nation, which they are not. Just as there is a spatial pattern of social vulnerability, there is a geographic distribution of natural hazard losses, with some regions exhibiting more hazard-proneness (e.g., coastal areas, seismic zones, and floodplains) or exposure than others (40, 41). Third, one could validate SoVI in a post event situation such as Hurricane Katrina, where we could predict the differential recovery outcomes on the basis of the preexisting social vulnerability. This natural experiment is under way and it is too soon to judge, but such an approach could provide for a true validation of the SoVI metric. Finally, once the 2010 Census is completed and released, we will be able to test how close our projected SoVI was to the actual computation.

The identification of socially vulnerable counties and regions and the components contributing to social vulnerability is a critical element for emergency preparedness, immediate response, mitigation planning, and long-term recovery from disasters. As we have shown, social vulnerability to natural hazards is dynamic. The temporal and spatial changes in social vulnerability based on our historic assessments suggest that for future preparedness, response, recovery, and mitigation planning, a one-size-fits-all approach may be ineffective in reducing social vulnerability or improving local resilience to the impacts of hazards. Instead, a more flexible approach that nests place-specific local variability within the broader federal policy guidelines and frameworks is suggested.

[. . .]

REFERENCES

1. Cutter SL (2006) *Hazards, Vulnerability and Environmental Justice* (Earthscan, Sterling, VA).
2. Eakin H, Luers AL (2006) *Annu Rev Environ Resour* 31:365–394.
3. Adger WN (2006) *Global Environ Change* 16:268–281.
4. Folke C (2006) *Global Environ Change* 16:253–267.
5. Cutter SL (2003) *Ann Assoc Am Geogr* 93:1–12.
6. Turner BL, II, Kasperson RE, Matson P, McCarthy JJ, Corell RW, Christensen L, Eckley N, Kasperson JX, Luers A, Martello ML, et al. (2003) *Proc Natl Acad Sci USA* 100:8074–8079.
7. Kasperson RE, Dow K, Archer E, Caceres D, Downing T, Elmqvist T, Eriksen S, Folke C, Han G, Iyengar K, et al. (2005) in *Ecosystems and Human Well-Being: Current State and Trends*, eds Hassan R, Scholes R, Ash N (Island Press, Washington, DC), Vol 1, pp 143–164.

8. Turner BL, Matson PA, McCarthy JJ, Corell RW, Christensen L, Eckley N, Hovelsrud-Broda GK, Kasperson JX, Kasperson RE, Luers A, et al. (2003) *Proc Natl Acad Sci USA* 100:8080–8085.
9. Blaikie P, Cannon T, Davies I, Wisner B (1994) *At Risk: Natural Hazards, People's Vulnerability and Disaster* (Routledge, London).
10. Bankoff G, Frerks G, Hilhorst D, eds (2004) *Mapping Vulnerability: Disasters, Development and People* (Earthscan, London).
11. Pelling M (2003) *The Vulnerability of Cities* (Earthscan, London).
12. Vale LJ, Campanella TJ (2005) *The Resilient City: How Modern Cities Recover from Disaster* (Oxford University Press, Oxford).
13. National Research Council (2006) *Facing Hazards and Disasters: Understanding Human Dimensions* (National Academic Press, Washington, DC).
14. Heinz Center (2002) *Human Links to Coastal Disasters* (The H. John Heinz III Center for Science, Economics and the Environment, Washington, DC).
15. Ngo EB (2001) *Nat Hazards Rev* 2:80–89.
16. Mayhorn CB (2005) *Nat Hazards Rev* 6:165–170.
17. Seplaki CL, Goldman N, Weinstein M, Lin Y-H (2006) *Soc Sci Med* 62:3121–3132.
18. Norris FH, Friedman MJ, Watson PJ (2002) *Psychiatry* 65:240 –260.
19. Esty DC, Levy M, Srebotnjak T, de Sherbinin A (2005) *2005 Environmental Sustainability Index: Benchmarking National Environmental Stewardship* (Yale Center for Environmental Law & Policy, New Haven, CT).
20. Inter-American Development Bank (2006) *Indicators of Disaster Risk and Risk Management: Summary Report* (Inter-American Development Bank, Washington, DC), www.iadb.org/exr/disaster/IDEA_IndicatorsReport.pdf?language_en&parid_6, pp 381, 388–389.
21. International Strategy for Disaster Reduction (2004) *Living with Risk: A Global Review of Disaster Reduction Initiatives* (United Nations, New York).
22. United Nations Development Programme (2004) *Reducing Disaster Risk: A Challenge for Development* (United Nations Development Programme, New York). Available at www.undp.org/bcpr/disred/rdr.htm.
23. Birkmann J (2007) *Measuring Vulnerability to Natural Hazards: Towards Disaster Resilient Societies* (United Nations Univ Press, Tokyo).
24. Dilley M, Chen RS, Deichmann U, Lerner-Lam AL, Arnold M (2005) *Natural Disaster Hot Spots: A Global Risk Analysis* (World Bank, Washington, DC).
25. Brooks N, Adger WN, Kelly PM (2005) *Global Environ Change* 15:151–163.
26. O'Brien KL, Leichenko R, Kelkarc U, Venemad H, Aandahl G, Tompkins H, Javed A, Bhadwal S, Barg S, Nygaard J, West J (2004) *Global Environ Change* 14:303–313.
27. Hurd B, Leary NA, Jones R, Smith J (1999) *J Am Water Res Assoc* 35:1399–1409.
28. Polsky C (2004) *Ann Assoc Am Geogr* 94:549–564.
29. Luers AL, Lobell DB, Sklar LS, Addams CL, Matson PA (2003) *Global Environ Change* 13:255–267.
30. Cutter SL, Mitchell JT, Scott MS (2000) *Ann Assoc Am Geogr* 90:713–737.
31. Clark GE, Moser S, Ratick S, Dow K, Meyer WB, Emani S, Jin W, Kasperson JX, Kasperson RE, Schwarz HE (1998) *Mitigation Adapt Strategies Global Change* 3:59–82.
32. Kleinosky LR, Yarnal B, Fisher A (2007) *Nat Hazards* 40:43–70.
33. Cutter SL, Boruff BJ, Shirley WL (2003) *Soc Sci Q* 84:242–261.
37. Neckerman KM, Torche F (2007) *Annu Rev Sociol* 33:3353–3357.
38. Massey DS, Fischer MJ (2003) in *Brookings–Wharton Papers on Urban Affairs 2003*, eds Gale WG, Jr, Pack JR (Brookings Institute, Washington, DC), pp 1–40.
39. Glasmeier AK (2006) *Poverty in America: One Nation, Pulling Apart, 1960–2003* (Routledge, New York).
40. Cutter SL, ed (2001) *American Hazardscapes: The Regionalization of Hazards and Disasters* (Joseph Henry/National Academic Science Press, Washington, DC).
41. Cutter SL, Emrich C (2005) *Eos Trans AGU* 86:381, 388–389.

13 The Climate Gap

Inequalities in How Climate Change Hurts Americans and How to Close the Gap

Rachel Morello Frosch, Manuel Pastor, Jim Sadd and Seth Shonkoff

EDITOR'S INTRODUCTION

This report relates the unequivocal finding that low-income people of color already experience, and will continue to experience, the greatest harm from climate change impacts. Focusing on California, the authors discuss the disproportionate health and economic consequences faced by African American and Latino communities from climate and environmental hazards like heat waves and air pollution. This disparate impact is what they term the "climate gap."

Examples of the climate gap include differences in mortality rates between racial groups during heat waves: African Americans in Los Angeles experience twice the mortality rate during extreme heat as the average Los Angeles resident. This increased likelihood of death extends to agricultural and construction workers, who are predominantly Latino.

The authors also address a key distinction between regional and local environmental/climate impacts and policies. While programs that reduce greenhouse gas emissions and air pollution in California have often been enacted at the regional scale, sources of emissions and pollution (like power plants) are local, as they are often located near low-income communities of color, causing greater health impacts in those neighborhoods. However, by focusing on total emissions or pollution levels in a region and failing to rein in specific emitters and polluters or focus on neighborhoods with the dirtiest air, policies may lower total emissions without changing the unequal distribution of health impacts.

Prioritizing the communities most affected by environmental hazards and avoiding an over-emphasis on regional solutions are two of several proposed equitable climate solutions, or ways to "close the climate gap." By concluding with these and several more approaches to reducing inequality, the authors reinforce the reality that action on climate change is possible, and if done right, can also reduce historical and current social inequalities.

The Climate Gap report is a publication of the Program for Environmental and Regional Equity (PERE) at the University of Southern California (USC). Dr. Morello-Frosch is Professor of Environmental Science, Policy and Management at UC Berkeley and an associate researcher with PERE; Dr. Manuel Pastor is Director of PERE and Professor of Sociology and American Studies & Ethnicity at USC; Dr. Jim Sadd is Professor of Environmental Science at Occidental College, and an associate researcher with PERE; Dr. Shonkoff is Executive Director of the Energy Science and Policy Institute, PSE Healthy Energy, and visiting scholar in the Department of Environmental Science, Policy and Management at UC Berkeley.

(2009) THE CLIMATE CAP: INEQUALITIES IN HOW CLIMATE CHANGE HURTS AMERICANS AND HOW TO CLOSE THE GAP

METHODOLOGY

This report analyzes currently available data on the disparate impacts of climate change and climate change mitigation policies on low socio-economic status (SES) groups in the United States that is relevant to the California context (Shonkoff et al. 2009). We have also drawn information from climate change policy, human health, and environmental justice literature to provide background and context for these issues. Our goal was to address some of the prominent public health, equity and regulatory issues that are pertinent to the policy deliberations surrounding the implementation of AB 32, The Global Warming Solutions Act, as well as federal climate change policy.

INTRODUCTION

What we used to think was tomorrow's climate crisis is here today. Heat waves, wildfires and floods are making headlines more often. **What hasn't made headlines—yet—is the climate gap: the disproportionate and unequal impact the climate crisis has on people of color and the poor.** Unless something is done, the consequences of America's climate crisis will harm all Americans—especially those who are least able to anticipate, cope with, resist and recover from the worst consequences. This analysis is of California, which in many ways is a microcosm of the entire United States.

Climate change is an issue of great importance for human rights, public health and social fairness because of its profound consequences overall and the very real danger that poor neighborhoods and people of color will suffer even worse harms and hazards than the rest of Americans. This "climate gap" is of special concern for California, home to one of the most ethnically and economically diverse populations in the country.

[...]

This report—an analysis and synthesis of available data—explores disparities in the impacts of climate change and the abilities of different groups to adapt to it. It also offers concrete recommendations for closing the climate gap, starting with insuring that climate solutions don't leave anyone behind.

KEY FINDINGS

The Climate Gap in Extreme Heat Waves

There is a climate gap. The health consequences of climate change will harm all Americans—but the poor and people of color will be hit the worst.

Extreme weather events, such as heat waves, droughts and floods are expected to increase in their frequency and intensity in the next hundred years due to climate change (IPCC 2007), which could increase the risk of illnesses and deaths linked to extreme heat.

- Extreme Heat Leads to Increased Illnesses and Deaths—Particularly among the Elderly, Infants and African Americans. [...]
- Risk Factors for Heat-Related Illness and Death Are Higher for Low-Income Neighborhoods and People of Color. [...]
- African Americans in Los Angeles Nearly Twice as Likely to Die from a Heat Wave. [...]
- Agricultural and Construction Workers Are Also at Increased Risk of Death. [...]
- Air Conditioning a Critical Coping Tool for Heat Waves—but Not Everyone Has Access. [...]
- Transportation Is Also a Critical Coping Tool During a Heat Wave—but African Americans, Latinos and Asians Less Likely to Have Access to a Car. [...]

The Climate Gap in Health Hazards from Increased Air Pollution

Research suggests that the majority of the health effects due to air pollution are caused by ozone (O_3) and particulate matter (PM) (Drechsler et al. 2006). However, it should be noted that many other pollutants that are associated with climate change, such as nitrogen dioxide, sulfur dioxide and carbon monoxide, also have health consequences (Drechsler et al. 2006).

Five of the ten most ozone-polluted metropolitan areas in the United States (Los Angeles, Bakersfield, Visalia, Fresno and Sacramento) are in California (Cordova et al. 2006; ALA 2008). Because of this, Californians already suffer a relatively high disease burden from air pollution—including 18,000 premature deaths each year and tens of thousands of other illnesses (CARB 2008a).

But climate change threatens to exacerbate California's dirty air problem. Higher temperatures hasten chemical interactions between nitrogen oxide, volatile organic gasses and sunlight that lead to increases in ambient ozone concentrations in urban areas (Jacobson 2008). In California, five of the smoggiest cities are also the locations with the highest projections of ambient ozone increases associated with climate change, as well as the highest densities of people of color and low-income residents.

People of color and the poor in these urban areas are likely to lack health insurance (Cordova et al. 2006). A lack of health insurance among vulnerable populations that are exposed to elevated levels of air pollutants may lead to greater health impacts from air pollution—particularly compared with those who have health insurance. [...]

The Climate Gap in How Much Some People Pay for Basic Necessities

There is a climate gap. The economic consequences of climate change will hit low-income neighborhoods and minorities the hardest.

- Prices for basic necessities are expected to skyrocket as a result of climate change.
- Low-income families already spend a bigger proportion of their income on food, energy and other household needs than higher-income families. With climate change, that spending gap will grow. [...]

The Climate Gap in Job Opportunities

Climate change will dramatically reduce job opportunities or cause major employment shifts in sectors that predominately employ low-income people of color.

The majority of jobs in sectors that will likely be significantly affected by climate change, such as agriculture and tourism, are held by low-income people of color (USCB 2005; EDD 2004). These workers would be the first to lose their jobs in the event of an economic downturn due to climatic troubles.

- **Fewer and Also More Dangerous Agriculture Jobs**

[...]

Research suggests that climate change will affect employment within the agricultural sector in three main ways:

1. Increases in the frequency and the intensity of extreme weather events will expose agriculture to greater productivity risks and (Lee et al. 2009) possible revenue losses that could lead to abrupt layoffs.

2. Changing weather and precipitation patterns could require expensive
    adaptation measures such as relocating crop cultivation, changing the
    composition or type of crops and increasing inputs such as pesticides
    to adapt to changes in ecological composition that lead to economic
    denigration and job loss (Cordova et al. 2006).
3. As climate change adversely affects agricultural productivity in California,
    laborers will be increasingly affected by job loss. For example, the two
    highest-value agricultural products in California's $30 billion agriculture
    sector are dairy products (milk and cream, valued at $3.8 billion annually)
    and grapes ($3.2 billion annually) (CASS 2002). Climate change is expected
    to decrease dairy production by between 7–22 percent by the end of the
    century (Pittock 2001). It is also expected to adversely affect the ripening of
    wine grapes, substantially reducing their market value (Hayhoe 2004).

[…]

•   There will be fewer jobs in tourism, an industry employing a high number
    of low-income people of color. […]

The Climate Gap in Extreme Weather Insurance

As extreme weather events such as wildfires, hurricanes and floods become more
common, severe damage and destruction to homes will also increase. Swiss Re
(2006) indicates that insurance losses have been on an upward trend since 1985.
During the years 1987–2004, property insurance losses due to natural disasters
averaged $23 billion per year and in 2005, losses rose to $83 billion, of which $60
billion was due to hurricanes Katrina, Rita and Wilma alone.

Households that have home or renters' insurance can, relatively rapidly, recuper-
ate and resume living much in the same way as prior to the disaster. In contrast,
low-income communities—which are often under-insured—may spend the rest
of their lives struggling to recover from property damage related to an extreme
weather event (Fothergill and Peek 2004; Blaikie et al. 1994; Thomalla et al. 2006).
[…]

HOW TO CLOSE THE CLIMATE GAP

[…]

At the federal and state levels, the United States is developing comprehensive
strategies to reduce climate change. Currently, the primary goal of such policy
is strictly to reduce carbon emissions, the leading cause of our deteriorating atmosphere. Yet closing the climate gap also needs to be a priority. Implementing policies
that protect the most vulnerable communities will better protect all Americans.

Currently, federal and state policymakers appear to be moving forward with a
framework that includes capping the total amount of greenhouse gas emissions,
lowering the cap over time and issuing permits as a way to ensure no one goes

over the limit. Yet few of the most prominent climate change mitigation strategies close the climate gap; and in some cases, policies may potentially widen the gap.

For example, one major concern with carbon emission reduction policies is that they will be regressive because the burden of rising costs will fall disproportionately on lower-income households (Walls and Hanson 1996; Hassett et al. 2008). A study by the Congressional Budget Office (2007a) shows how a program implemented to cut carbon dioxide (CO_2) emissions by 15 percent would cost 3.3 percent of the average income of households in the lowest income bracket as opposed to only 1.7 percent of the average income of households in the top income bracket.

Other policies that raise substantial climate gap issues are pollution credits allocated to facilities, as well as how revenues generated from fees on carbon emissions or the auctioning of emission credits will be distributed to society and individual consumers.

Close the Climate Gap by Auctioning Permits or Establishing a Fee and Invest in Communities That Will Be Hardest Hit

If emission credits are allocated for free, there is concern that these policies will be regressive (Dutzik et al. 2007). Alternatively, under cap-and-auction or fee-based strategies, the sale of emission credits to polluters could generate sizable revenues that could be used to offset higher costs—particularly for those who can least afford it (Hepburn et al. 2006). Revenues could be distributed to the public through tax cuts, investments in clean energy, high-value investments such as transportation, or through direct periodic dividends to consumers (CBO 2007).

Other reasons auctioning permits or establishing fees helps close the climate gap:

- Eliminates the need for emissions trading in comparison to free-allocation programs because industry is likely to buy only what it needs (Hepburn et al. 2006).
- Decreases financial incentives to keep old polluting facilities open by eliminating the grandfathering of old facilities.
- Decreases the problem of over-allocation and excessive banking and trading of emission credits.

Close the Climate Gap by Maximizing Reductions in Greenhouse Gas Emissions and Toxic Air Pollution in Neighborhoods With the Dirtiest Air

There is enormous potential to get more for our investments in climate change reduction by focusing on the dirtiest sources that cause both climate change and health problems locally. These sources are often concentrated in neighborhoods with the highest populations of low-income families and people of color, with local toxic air emissions that contribute to poor health. Policymakers have an opportunity to be efficient and effective stewards of taxpayer dollars by focusing on climate polluters disproportionately responsible for regional greenhouse gas emissions and dirtying the air in highly impacted neighborhoods.

[...]

In certain circumstances, cap-and-trade, the most prominent climate policy under consideration, may reduce climate emissions and toxic pollution region-ally. Yet there are no guaranteed reductions at any one source (O'Neill 2004). Communities with the dirtiest air are concerned that with the wrong approach, some polluters may maintain or increase their emissions, creating localized dirty air hotspots even if there are regional greenhouse gas reductions overall.

Instead, if directed in the right way, measures to reduce climate emissions could also reduce other types of dangerous pollution in the neighborhoods that need it most. In California, efforts should be directed to neighborhoods in close proximity to highways, ports and other sections of the transportation and goods-movement cor-ridors where air quality has been noted as among the worst in the state (CARB 2006; CARB 2008b; Morello-Frosch and Jesdale 2006; Morello-Frosch and Lopez 2006).

[...]

Such an approach might complicate the planning and implementation of mar-ket or fee systems, but the benefits for fairness and public health far outweigh the modest costs of extra complexity in the system. To facilitate this, a starting point would be developing mapping and analytical tools that allow policymakers to identify the neighborhoods with the greatest opportunities to maximize green-house gas emission reductions while also cleaning up toxic air pollution

Why We Can't Afford to Focus Only on Regional Greenhouse Gas Reductions

Today, most climate policy strategies focus exclusively on lowering greenhouse gasses, without regard to what other benefits we can achieve if we focus on reduc-ing greenhouse gasses from sources that also emit dangerous and toxic pollutants. In a struggling economy and as most Americans continue to rank air pollution as a leading concern, working to get more health and environmental benefits from one policy protection should be a goal of efficient, effective governments.

Failure to take under strong consideration sources that contribute to both cli-mate change and toxic air pollution can also lead to a widening of the climate gap between the health benefits achieved by some and the health consequences faced by others. It can mean that while regional air improves, the air in some neighbor-hoods gets dirtier.

For example, a study of the Regional Clean Air Incentives Market (RECLAIM), an emission trading system designed to lower nitrogen oxide emissions in South-ern California, indicates that the program may have increased nitrogen oxide emissions in Wilmington, California, while region-wide emission levels declined (Lejano and Hirose 2005). [...]

Ensuring New Fuels Don't Increase Pollution in Low-Income and Minority Communities

The lesson learned in California from the experiment with MTBE—a fuel additive that reduced air pollution, but was quickly banned after research found that it polluted drinking water—has critical implications for how we can close the climate gap.

Similarly, ethanol—a biofuel proposed for broader use by California and federal policymakers to help combat climate change—could reduce our dependence on oil. However, biofuel refineries could harm the health of adjacent communities by exposing them to the chemical and microbial byproducts of the distillation processes necessary for fuel production (Madsen 2006).

[...]

Last, it should be noted that growing crops for fuel will likely raise prices of food crops (Tenenbaum 2008). This would be most damaging to low-income consumers and low-income agricultural laborers who are most vulnerable to job loss and hunger (Tenenbaum 2008).

OTHER KEY RECOMMENDATIONS TO CLOSE THE CLIMATE GAP

More research is needed to look at the rates and impacts of climate change events that are projected to occur. Identifying possible mitigation and adaptation strategies that would reduce climate-related illnesses and deaths, particularly in the most vulnerable communities, should be a priority for the regulatory community as well as policymakers.

Close the Health Impacts Gap Between People of Color and the Poor, and the Rest of the Population

- **Focus Planning and Intervention in Poor and Minority Neighborhoods.** Because burdens of heat-related illness are borne disproportionately by groups of older residents, children and those of low socio-economic status (Knowlton et al. 2009; English 2007; Basu and Ostro 2008), preparedness strategies should include messages and information about avoiding extreme heat exposure that are disseminated and targeted toward parents and caregivers of young children, and the elderly (Knowlton et al. 2009). Climate change interventions to address the built environment should prioritize vulnerable groups who live in neighborhoods with high risks of heat island effects, poor housing quality and a lack of access to transportation to escape extreme weather events. These proactive strategies could go a long way to reduce the disproportionate burden of heat-related health effects on the poor and communities of color.
- **Use New Mapping Technologies to Identify Vulnerable Neighborhoods.** Differential exposures to the health-damaging impacts of climate change,

such as excessive heat and extreme weather events, could be examined from a geographical equity perspective by using GIS maps overlaid with vulnerability models and current socio-economic, racial/ethnicity and cultural group distributions in California. Interaction of these data layers should be taken into account when developing climate change policy (Elliott et al. 2005), so as to reduce the likelihood that future policies would create disproportionate burdens on already vulnerable populations.

- **Research the Potential Benefits and Harms of New Fuels.** Policymakers must take steps to better assess the effects of exposure to new fuels (i.e., ethanol), as well as increased emissions of other pollutants during combustion (Jacobson 2007) and production, on those already feeling the negative impact of the climate gap. More studies must also focus on the dangers of food shortages and food price increases associated with the production of ethanol and other biofuel crops (Tenenbaum 2008). Obtaining this information could illuminate whether biofuels are a viable solution or would simply widen the climate gap.

- **Measure the Success of Mitigation Strategies by Whether They Protect Everyone.** Runaway climate change, where positive feedback loops drive warming irrespective of human mitigation actions, could occur (NRC 2002; Gjerde et al. 1999; Pizer 2003). As we enact policies to reduce the chances that full-scale global warming will occur, we must also develop downstream adaptation strategies such as infrastructure protection, efficient and effective air-cooling technologies, and better surveillance for emerging infectious diseases. If we don't pay close attention to the climate gap from the beginning, disparities between populations of differing socio-economic status will likely increase.

- **Design Research that Identifies Opportunities for Targeting Greenhouse Gas Reductions to Reduce Toxic Air Emissions in Highly Polluted Neighborhoods.** In order to design proper policies and monitor the efficacy of climate policies, future research should: (1) explore how to characterize, quantify and maximize reducing both climate and toxic pollution in existing or new "toxic hotspots"; (2) determine the geographic scale at which these evaluations can take place given the data available; and (3) identify the data necessary to improve future evaluations.

Develop Policies That Close the Gap Between the Economic Disparities Faced by People of Color and the Poor, and the Rest of the Population

Because climate change and climate solutions are likely to negatively impact certain economic sectors more than others, policies must take into account how low-income families and people of color will be affected and what more can be done to help them adjust to major economic shifts. Some important policy directions include:

- Examine which greenhouse gas source sectors hold the most pollution reduction promise without economic disruption, both in terms of overall emission reductions and environmental health benefits (Prasad 2008).

- Anticipate and address inevitable job shifts and retraining needs to maximize opportunities for low-income communities and communities of color to successfully transition to and benefit from a new clean-energy economy.
- Ensure that revenue generated from climate policy will help high-poverty neighborhoods absorb the higher prices for energy and other basic necessities.

Close the Conversation Gap

Because climate change will affect some populations more than others, it is important to capture the specific vulnerabilities of different neighborhoods. Local expertise, community wisdom, and other contextual information are important to supplement technical knowledge. Researchers hoping to generate climate-change impact knowledge that is sensitive to community-specific concerns should integrate community participation in their studies (Morello-Frosch et al. 2005; Minkler and Wallerstein 2003; Corburn 2009). To proactively address the climate gap, ensure the effectiveness of preparedness and adaptation strategies, and alleviate environmental health inequalities, agency officials and policymakers must ensure that vulnerable communities play a prominent role in shaping future solutions to climate change in California (Elliott et al. 2005).

But it's more than just the regulatory agencies and affected communities. Policy differences between those who favor cap-and-trade and those who support carbon fees have led to tensions between advocates that share the goals of protecting the planet and protecting the poor. Concerns about whether climate policy will cost or create jobs have led to strains between those working to recover the economy and those working to save the planet. These tensions have led to a conversation gap.

One of the first steps to addressing the climate gap is addressing this conversation gap. Working together—across sectors and constituencies—and insuring that the effects of climate change and climate policy are not unequally felt by the poor and communities of color is exactly the recipe we need to cool the planet and create economic opportunities and health benefits for everyone.

CONCLUSIONS

This analysis of available data connects the dots between some facts we've known and others we haven't to reveal a hidden climate gap.

The climate gap means that climate change will more seriously affect the health of communities that are least likely to cope with, resist and recover from the impacts of extreme weather events and potential increases in air pollution compared to the rest of the population (Knowlton et al. 2004). Further, low-income and minority communities could be more seriously harmed by the economic shocks associated with climate change both in price increases for basic necessities (i.e., water, energy and food) and by threats of job loss due to economic and climatic shifts that affect industries such as agriculture and tourism (Stern 2008).

Policymakers have a clear choice: ignoring the climate gap could reinforce and amplify current—as well as future—socio-economic and racial disparities. On the other hand, policymakers can proactively close the climate gap through strategies that address the regressive economic and health impacts of climate change, and that lift all boats by ensuring that everyone shares equally in the benefits of climate solutions, and no one is left bearing more than their fair share of the burdens.

REFERENCES

ALA (American Lung Association). 2008. *State of the Air: 2008*. New York: American Lung Association.

Basu, R., and B. D. Ostro. 2008. "A multicounty analysis identifying the populations vulnerable to mortality associated with high ambient temperature in California." *Am J Epidemiol* 168(6): 632–637.

Blaikie, P., T. Cannon, I. Davis, and B. Wisner. 1994. *At Risk: Natural Hazards, People's Vulnerability, and Disasters*. New York: Routledge.

Cambone, Daniela. 2006. "Natural Catastrophes and Man-Made Disasters 2005: High Earthquake Casualties, New Dimension in Windstorm Losses." *The Insurance and Investment Journal*, January 26.

CARB (California Air Resources Board). 2006. *Quantification of the Health Impacts and Economic Valuation of Air Pollution from Ports and Goods Movement in California*. Appendix A in Emission Reduction Plan for Ports and Goods Movement (GMERP), Sacramento, CA.

CARB. 2008a. *Methodology for Estimating Premature Deaths Associated with Long-Term Exposure to Fine Airborne Particulate Matter in California*. California Air Resources Board, Sacramento, CA.

CARB. 2008b. *Diesel Particulate Matter Health Risk Assessment for the West Oakland Community: Preliminary Summary of Results*. California Environmental Protection Agency, Air Resources Board, Sacramento, CA.

CASS. 2002. California agriculture statistical review. Sacramento, California. California Agriculture Statistics Service.

CBO (Congressional Budget Office). 2007a. *Trade-Offs in Allocating Allowances for CO2 Emissions*. Washington, DC.

Corburn, J. 2009. Cities, climate change and urban heat island mitigation: Localizing global environmental science. *Urban Studies* 47(2), In press.

Cordova, R., M. Gelobter, A. Hoerner, J. R. Love, A. Miller, C. Saenger, and D. Zaidi. 2006. *Climate Change in California: Health, Economic and Equity Impacts*. Oakland, CA: Redefining Progress.

Drechsler, D., N. Motallebi, M. Kleema, D. Cayan, K. Hayhoe, L. S. Kalkstein, N. Miller, S. C. Sheridan, J. Jin, and R. A. VanCuren. 2006. *Public Health-Related Impacts of Climate Change in California*. California Energy Commission.

Dutzik, T., R. Sargent, and F. Figdor. 2007. *Cleaner, Cheaper, Smarter: The Case for Auctioning Pollution Allowances in a Global Warming Cap-and-Trade Program*. U.S. PIRG Education Fund.

EDD (California Employment Development Department). 2004. *Occupational Employment (2002) and Wage (2003) Data, Occupational Employment Statistics Survey Results*. Sacramento, CA.

Elliott, M., C. Saenger, and A. Hoerner. 2005. *Latinos and Climate Change: A Scoping Report*. Oakland, CA: Redefining Progress.

English, P., K. Fitzsimmons, S. Hoshiko, T. Kim, H. G. Margolis, T. E. McKone, M. Rotkin-Ellman, G. Solomon, R. Trent, and Z. Ross. 2007. *Public Health Impacts of Climate Change in California: Community Vulnerability Assessments and Adaptation Strategies*. Climate Change Public Health Impacts Assessment and Response Collaborative, California Department of Public Health Institute, Richmond, California.

Fothergill, A., and L. Peek. 2004. "Poverty and disasters in the United States: A review of recent sociological findings." *Natural Hazards Journal* 32(1): 89–110.

Gjerde, J., S. Grepperud, and S. Kverndokk. 1999. "Optimal climate policy under the probability of a catastrophe." *Resource and Energy Economics* 21: 289–317.

Hassett, K., A. Mathur, and G. Metcalf. 2008. *The Incidence of a U.S. Carbon Tax: A Lifetime and Regional Analysis*. Cambridge, MA: American Enterprise Institute for Public Policy Research.

Hayhoe, K., D. Cayan, C. B. Field, P. C. Frumhoff, E. P. Maurer, N. L. Miller, S. C. Moser, S. H. Schneider, K. N. Cahill, E. E. Cleland, L. Dale, R. Drapek, R. M. Hanemann, L. S. Kalkstein, J. Lenihan, C. K Lunch, R. P. Neilson, S. C. Sheridan, and J. H. Verville. 2004. "Emissions pathways, climate change, and impacts on California." *Proc Natl Acad Sci USA* 101(34): 12422–12427.

Hepburn, C., M. Grubb, K. Neuhoff, F. Matthes, and M. Tse. 2006. "Auctioning of EU ETS phase II allowances: How and why?" *Climate Policy* 6(1): 137–160.

IPCC (Intergovernmental Panel on Climate Change). 2007. *Working Group I Report: The Physical Science Basis*. Cambridge, UK and New York, NY: Cambridge University Press, 996 pp.

Jacobson, M. Z. 2007. "Effects of ethanol (E85) versus gasoline vehicles on cancer and mortality in the United States." *Environ Sci Technol* 41(11): 4150–4157.

Jacobson, M. Z. 2008. "On the causal link between carbon dioxide and air pollution mortality." *Geophys Res. Let.* 35(L03809).

Juhwan Lee, Steven De Gryze, and Johan Six "Effect of Climate Change on Field Crop Production in the Central Valley of California." Report from California Climate Change Center, March 2009, Draft Paper CEC-500-2009-041-D. Available at: http://www.energy.ca.gov/2009publications/CEC-500-2009--041-D.PDF

Knowlton, K., J. E. Rosenthal, C. Hogrefe, B. Lynn, S. Gaffin, R. Goldberg, C. Rosenzweig, K. Civerolo, J. Y. Ku, and P. L. Kinney. 2004. "Assessing ozone-related health impacts under a changing climate." *Environ Health Perspect* 112(15): 1557–1563.

Knowlton, K., M. Rotkin-Ellman, G. King, H. G. Margolis, D. Smith, G. Solomon, R. Trent, and P. English. 2009. The 2006 California heat wave: Impacts on hospitalizations and emergency department visits. *Environ Health Perspect* 117(1): 61–67.

Lejano, R., and R. Hirose. 2005. "Testing the assumptions behind emissions trading in non-market goods: The RECLAIM program in Southern California." *Environmental Science & Policy* 8: 367–377.

Madsen, A. M. 2006. "Exposure to airborne microbial components in autumn and spring during work at Danish biofuel plants." *Ann Occup Hyg* 50(8): 821–831.

Minkler, M., and N. Wallerstein. 2003. *Community-Based Participatory Research for Health*. San Francisco, CA: Jossey-Bass Press.

Morello-Frosch, R. A., and B. Jesdale. 2006. "Separate and Unequal: Residential segregation and estimated cancer risks associated with ambient air toxics in U.S. metropolitan areas." *Environmental Health Perspectives* 114(3): 386–393.

Morello-Frosch, R. A., and R. Lopez. 2006. "The riskscape and the color line: Examining the role of segregation in environmental health disparities." *Environmental Research* 102: 181–196.

Morello-Frosch, R. A., M. Pastor, J. Sadd, C. Porras, and M. Prichard. 2005. "Citizens, science, and data Judo: Leveraging community-based participatory research to build a regional collaborative for environmental justice in Southern California." In *Methods for Conducting Community-Based Participatory Research in Public Health*, B. Israel, et al., editors. University of Michigan, Jossey-Bass Press.

NRC (National Research Council). 2002 *Abrupt Climate Change: Inevitable Surprises*. Committee on Abrupt Climate Change. Washington, DC: National Academy Press.

O'Neill, C. 2004. "Mercury, risk and justice." *ELR News and Analysis* 34: 11070–11115.

Pittock, B., D. Wratt, R. Basher, B. Bates, M. Finlayson, H. Gitay, A. Woodward, A. Arthington, P. Beets, B. Biggs, et al. 2001. *Climate Change 2001: Impacts, Adaptation, and Vulnerability.* Cambridge, U.K.: Cambridge University Press.

Pizer, William. 2003. "Climate Change Catastrophes." *Discussion Papers dp-03-31.* Washington, DC: Resources for the Future.

Prasad, S. 2008. *Environmental Justice: Draft CEC PIER-EA Discussion Paper.* California Energy Commission, Public Interest Energy Research: Sacramento, CA.

Shonkoff, S., R. Morello-Frosch, M. Pastor, and J. Sadd. 2009. Environmental health and equity impacts from climate change and mitigation policies in California: A review of the literature. *Publication # CEC-500-2009-038-D.* Available at: http://www.climatechange.ca.gov/publications/cat/index.html

Stern, N. 2008. "Stern Review on the Economics of Climate Change." *American Economic Review: Papers & Proceedings* 98(2): 1–37.

Tenenbaum, D. 2008. "Food vs. fuel: Diversion of crops could cause more hunger." *Environ Health Perspect* 116(6): A254–A257.

Thomalla, F., and T. Downing, E. Spanger-Siegfried, G. Han, and J. Rockström. 2006. "Reducing hazard vulnerability: Towards a common approach between disaster risk reduction and climate adaptation." *Disasters* 30(1): 39–48.

USCB. 2005. *California-County: Percent of People Below Poverty Level in the Past 12 Months (For Whom Poverty Status is Determined).* Washington, DC: United States Census Bureau.

Walls, M., and J. Hanson. 1996. *Distributional Impacts of an Environmental Tax Shift: The Case of Motor Vehicle Emissions Taxes.* Washington, DC: Resources for the Future.

14 Social-Ecological Resilience to Coastal Disasters

W. Neil Adger, Terry P. Hughes, Carl Folke, Stephen R. Carpenter, and Johan Rockström

EDITOR'S INTRODUCTION

Although climate change will affect the entire globe, understanding and planning for its impacts on the world's coastlines is essential, given that—as the authors note—a majority of the world population will likely live within 100 km of the coast by 2030. Here, along the land's edge, is where threats like sea level rise, hurricanes, and typhoons loom.

Building resilience to these challenges is critical. This paper builds on previous definitions of resilience used in this section of the book and adds to the definition a system's ability to learn from experience and reorganize itself more suitably. Additionally, the authors make clear the major difference between resilience and sustainability: where sustainability focuses on maintaining ecological and human systems that are assumed to be inherently *stable*, resilience emphasizes the constantly changing nature of these systems and aims to help them adapt to uncertainty. Resilience is perhaps a more realistic approach in the age of climate change.

To help explain the concept of resilience, the authors compare impacts between Hurricane Andrew in Florida in 1992 to a typhoon of equivalent strength in Bangladesh in 1991. Twenty-three people died during Andrew, but the typhoon resulted in over 100,000 deaths and displaced millions more. The authors attribute the enormous difference in scale to Florida's higher resilience, derived from "strong institutions, early warning systems, and a high capacity to deal with the crisis".

Expanding on this comparison, the article examines case studies of the 2004 Asian tsunami and of coastal/island storm responses around the world to identify factors that make a place resilient to climate change. Both ecologically and socially, diversity and redundancy are key; diversity increases possible responses to disruption, while redundancy—for example, having multiple ways to generate power—can ensure that an entire system doesn't collapse at once during a crisis. Other lessons are also described, such as the role of responsive social institutions and incremental contributions to ecological health.

The authors conclude with a call to action: with greater and greater populations living on coastlines, and coastal storms increasing in frequency and strength, the need to bolster resilience is urgent.

Dr. Neil Adger is a Professor of Human Geography at the University of Exeter, United Kingdom. Dr. Terry Hughes is a Distinguished Professor of Marine Biology at James Cook University in Queensland, Australia. Dr. Carl Folke is the Science Director and co-founder of the Stockholm Resilience Center. Dr. Stephen Carpenter is the Stephen Alfred Forbes Professor of Integrative Biology at the University of Wisconsin–Madison, U.S.A.

(2005) SOCIAL-ECOLOGICAL RESILIENCE TO COASTAL DISASTERS

[. . .]

Human populations are concentrated along coasts, and consequently coastal ecosystems are some of the most impacted and altered worldwide. These areas are also sensitive to many hazards and risks, from floods to disease epidemics. Here, we explore how a better understanding of the linkages between ecosystems and human societies can help to reduce vulnerability and enhance resilience of these linked systems in coastal areas. By resilience, we mean the capacity of linked social-ecological systems to absorb recurrent disturbances such as hurricanes or floods so as to retain essential structures, processes, and feedbacks (1, 2). Resilience reflects the degree to which a complex adaptive system is capable of self-organization (versus lack of organization or organization forced by external factors), and the degree to which the system can build capacity for learning and adaptation (3, 4).

Part of this capacity lies in the regenerative ability of ecosystems and their capability in the face of change to continue to deliver resources and ecosystem services that are essential for human livelihoods and societal development. The concept of resilience is a profound shift in traditional perspectives, which attempt to control changes in systems that are assumed to be stable, to a more realistic viewpoint aimed at sustaining and enhancing the capacity of social-ecological systems to adapt to uncertainty and surprise.

COASTAL HAZARDS AND RESILIENCE

Natural hazards are an ongoing part of human history, and coping with them is a critical element of how resource use and human settlement have evolved (5, 6). Globally, 1.2 billion people (23% of the world's population) live within 100 km of the coast (7), and 50% are likely to do so by 2030. These populations are exposed to specific hazards such as coastal flooding, tsunamis, hurricanes, and transmission of marine-related infectious diseases. For example, today an estimated 10 million people experience coastal flooding each year due to storm surges and landfall typhoons, and 50 million could be at risk by 2080 because of climate change and increasing population densities (8). More and more, adaptive responses will be required in coastal zones to cope with a plethora of similar hazards arising as a result of global environmental change (9).

Hazards in coastal areas often become disasters through the erosion of resilience, driven by environmental change and by human action (10–12). For example, when Hurricane Andrew, a powerful category 5 storm, struck Florida in 1992, it caused devastation valued at $26.5 billion and 23 people lost their lives. An equivalent tropical typhoon that ravaged Bangladesh in 1991 resulted in over 100,000 deaths and the displacement of millions of individuals (13) from widespread flooding. In Florida, social resilience from strong institutions, early warning systems, and a high capacity to deal with the crisis confined the impact to manageable proportions, whereas social vulnerability in affected areas of Bangladesh caused a human disaster of a far greater scale. Yet adaptive capacity can be increased through purposeful action. Consequently, Bangladesh has reduced mortality associated with typhoons and flooding in the past decade through careful planning focused on the most vulnerable sectors of society (14, 15).

The resilience (or conversely, the vulnerability) of coastal societies is more tightly linked to larger-scale processes today than it was in the past. For example, economic linkages and the globalization of trade in commodities and ecological goods and services tie regions much more closely together than before (16–18). In coastal regions, this is often evident in the vulnerabilities created by global tourism (an ecosystem service), while the growing demands of visitors impact previously undeveloped coastal areas (19). Similarly, increased mobility of people has spread infectious diseases such as human immunodeficiency virus/acquired immune deficiency syndrome (which have high prevalence in some coastal fishing communities [20]), whereas global-scale environmental change is certain to exacerbate vulnerability to vector-borne diseases (e.g., malaria and cholera [21, 22]). Conversely, greater mobility, improved communications and awareness, and the growth of national and international NGOs that link societies can all strengthen resilience to crises and improve responses when they occur.

During periods of gradual or incremental change, many important sources of resilience may be unrecognized or dismissed as inefficient or irrelevant. Typically, therefore, components of resilience are allowed to decline or are deliberately eliminated because their importance is not appreciated until a crisis occurs. For example, chronic overfishing and declining water quality around coral reefs have made them more vulnerable to cyclones and global warming (23). Instead of absorbing recurrent disturbances as they have done for millennia, many overfished and polluted reefs have recently undergone radical regime shifts, where coral populations fail to rebuild after external shocks and have instead been replaced by fleshy seaweeds (24, 25). Rebuilding resilience, by improving water quality and maintaining adequate stocks of herbivores, can promote the regenerative capacity of corals after recurrent disturbances. Thus, loss of ecological and social resilience is often cryptic, and resilience can be eroded or bolstered accidentally or deliberately through human action (26).

Resilient social-ecological systems incorporate diverse mechanisms for coping with change and crisis (27, 28). In ecosystems, biodiversity, functional redundancy, and spatial pattern can all influence resilience. Biodiversity enhances resilience if species or functional groups respond differently to environmental fluctuations, so that declines in one group are compensated by increases in another (24, 29). Spatial heterogeneity can also confer resilience, as when refuge areas provide sources of colonists to repopulate disturbed regions (30). Similarly, in social systems, governance, and management frameworks can spread risk by diversifying patterns of resource use and by encouraging alternate activities and lifestyles. Such practices sustain ecosystem services, analogous to the way that management of a diverse portfolio sustains the growth of investments in financial markets (31).

After catastrophic change, remnants ("memory") of the former system become growth points for renewal and reorganization of the social-ecological system (28). Ecological memory is conferred by biological legacies that persist after disturbance, including mobile species and propagules that colonize and reorganize disturbed sites and refuges that support such legacies and mobile links (30, 32). Social memory comes from the diversity of individuals and institutions that draw on reservoirs of practices, knowledge, values, and worldviews and is crucial for preparing the system for change, building resilience, and for coping with surprises (33).

[. . .]

RESPONDING TO CHANGE IN COASTAL AREAS

How can coastal zones be transformed into systems that are more resilient and adaptive to a rising incidence of large disturbances? We review two case studies as examples. The first is the 2004 Asian tsunami, which shows that social-ecological resilience is an important determinant of both the impacts of the tsunami and of the reorganization by communities after the event. The second is from research on planning for and adapting to severe storms and climate change in coastal zones and on small islands. In both cases, individuals, and communities undertake adaptive strategies that involve the mobilization of assets, networks, and social capital both to anticipate and to react to potential disasters. Crucially, the causes of vulnerability are embedded in the political economy of resource use and the resilience of the ecosystems on which livelihoods depend.

The 2004 Asian Tsunami

On 26 December 2004, countries in South and Southeast Asia experienced an enormous tsunami associated with the second-largest earthquake in the instrumental record. Coastal areas in parts of Indonesia, Thailand, and Malaysia closest to the epicenter received little or no warning. A key lesson is that resilient social-ecological systems reduced vulnerability to the impacts of the tsunami and encouraged a rapid, positive response. This response needs to be sustained in the longer term, long after the tsunami fades from global news reports.

Chronic degradation of local environments has influenced the short- to medium-term impact of the tsunami, and will continue to shape the longer-term options for rebuilding. In Banda Aceh, Indonesia, the presence or absence of sand dunes, mangrove forests, and coral reefs made no difference in the impact of giant waves that penetrated kilometers inland. Further from the epicenter, however, in Sri Lanka, the energy of smaller waves was reduced by natural barriers (34, 35). Moreover, wherever ecosystems have been undermined, the ability to adapt and regenerate has been severely eroded. For example, throughout coastal Asia, deforestation of mangrove for intensive shrimp farming, a lucrative export industry, has reduced the livelihood options available to local farming and fishing communities (36). In many locations, environmental degradation such as land clearing, coastal erosion, overfishing, and coral mining has reduced the potential for economic recovery from the tsunami because of the loss of traditional income sources related to coastal ecosystems rich in biodiversity and ecological functions.

Social resilience, including institutions for collective action, robust governance systems, and a diversity of livelihood choices are important assets for buffering the effects of extreme natural hazards and promoting social reorganization (Table 14.1). Coastal communities harboring knowledgeable, prepared, and responsive institutions are more likely to be able to prevent the tsunami from making the transition from extreme natural hazard to longer-term social disaster (37). For instance, fishing communities on Simeulue Island, west of Sumatra and close to the epicenter of the earthquake causing the tsunami, and on Surin Island, Thailand, survived the tsunami thanks to inherited local knowledge of tsunamis and to institutional preparedness for disasters.

There has been a well-meaning rush by organizations and international aid agencies to apply engineering approaches to rebuilding coral reefs damaged by the tsunami by transplanting corals and constructing miniature artificial reefs. However, none of these engineering interventions actually work at meaningful scales or provide realistic solutions to the increased global threats to coral reefs. Fundamentally, the upsurge in investment in artificial rehabilitation of reefs is misguided because it fails to reverse the root causes of regional-scale degradation. Before the tsunami, runoff from land, overfishing, destructive fishing practices (bombing and poisoning), and climate change had already seriously degraded many reefs. Throughout the region, chronic pollution and overfishing of herbivorous fishes have promoted blooms of turfing and fleshy seaweed that overgrow and smother juvenile corals. Regeneration of damaged reefs continues to be impaired by these and other ongoing human impacts. Now the tsunami has added to the destruction in many locations, smashing corals and smothering reefs with choking sediments. Realistically, regeneration processes in the wider seascape are the only means by which coral reefs can reestablish after large-scale damage (25). Consequently, restoration efforts should focus on improving water quality and restoring depleted fish stocks to bolster the innate resilience of coral reefs (24). Scarce reconstruction aid should not be squandered on simplistic and ineffective reef rehabilitation projects. Rather, support should be directed to provide ecologically sustainable, long-term employment for coastal communities to eliminate poverty and to improve local and regional governance systems for managing the natural resilience of coral reefs.

The 2004 Asian tsunami tragedy demonstrates that formal and informal institutions with the capacity to respond to rapid change in environmental and social conditions are a key to mitigating the social effects of extreme natural hazards. Rather than attempting to reduce or eliminate inherent change and variability (the conventional engineering approach to "control" nature), governance systems—from governments through to local marine and land tenure systems—need to focus on sustaining and enhancing the sources of resilience of societies and their life-supporting ecosystems. The hidden success story of the tsunami was the prevention of widespread secondary mortality of injured and traumatized victims from infection and disease, due in large part to the unprecedented scale of national and international responses.

Coping and Adapting to Hurricanes

Hurricanes, typhoons, and their related impacts affect societies throughout the world. They do so both directly through acute damage on human settlement, often with major loss of life, and indirectly through their impact on coastal eco-systems such as coral reefs, seagrass beds, and mangroves (38, 39) that support local societies and economies. There is growing consensus than human-influenced climate changes are now evident in hurricane regions and are likely to affect hurricane intensity and rainfall (which cause much of the damage), although the effect of climate change on hurricane frequency in the future remains uncertain (40). Although the costs of weather and climate events in terms of economic damage and lives at risk are rising through time, the observed increases are caused by changing social vulnerabilities as much as by changing physical hazards (39).

In the Caribbean, responses to hurricanes and their effectiveness depend on social and ecological resilience. The Cayman Islands, for example, has implemented adaptation actions at national and community levels, building both preparedness and community resilience. The implementation of these activities followed economic and ecological impacts of three major hurricanes in 1988 (Gilbert), 1998 (Mitch), and 2000 (Michelle). The resilience of the islands was subsequently put to the test by Hurricane Ivan (2004), and was demonstrably improved. Adaptations included changes in the rules and governance of hurricane risk, change in organizations, establishment of early warning systems, and promotion of self-mobilization in civil society and private corporations. Social learning, the diversity of adaptations, and the promotion of strong local social cohesion and mechanisms for collective action have all enhanced resilience and continue to guide planning for future climate change (41). After Hurricane Ivan in 2004, private sector interests in tourism and banking accelerated recovery by rebuilding public infrastructure such as roads and electricity supply. In Trinidad and Tobago, networks associated with present-day coral reef management also play a key role in disaster preparedness and in building resilience (42, 43). Hence, social resilience to disasters in the Caribbean has been promoted through a wide diversity of institutional forms.

However, large sections of society in the Caribbean region remain vulnerable, and current adaptation processes are not always appropriate or effective. The impacts of Hurricane Mitch on Honduras, Nicaragua, and El Salvador in 1998 were exacerbated by unsound economic policies, such as export-driven agriculture. Farmers who had adopted modern management practices suffered greater losses than those who had more traditional agro-ecological practices (44). Industrialized agricultural practices also generated unexpected impacts and risks, such as the release of 70 tons of toxic pesticides into the environment in Honduras after the destruction of several warehouses, exposing rural populations to long-term harm (45). Even today, the lessons of implementing post disaster planning to increase adaptive capacity do not appear to have been learned by many of the states that were impacted by Hurricane Mitch.

In summary, the social-ecological resilience of regions affected by tsunamis and/or hurricanes or typhoons involves many elements and actions (Table 14.1), and each of these involves human agency. Exposure to hazards can often be modified through government interventions or informal norms that regulate the use of coastal ecosystems. Reducing the perverse incentives that destroy natural capital and thus exacerbate vulnerability in the first place should, in many cases, be the priority. Networks and institutions that promote resilience to present-day hazards also buffer against future risks, such as those associated with climate change. Effective multilevel governance systems are critical for building capacity to cope with changes in climate, disease outbreaks, hurricanes, global market demands, subsidies, governmental policies, and other large-scale changes. The challenge for social-ecological systems is to enhance the adaptive capacity to deal with disturbance and to build preparedness for living with change and uncertainty (28).

Table 14.1 Examples of local- and regional-scale actions to enhance resilience in social-ecological systems exposed to abrupt change.

Elements of vulnerability	Local action	National and international action
Exposure and sensitivity to hazard	Maintenance and enhancement of ecosystem functions through sustainable use Maintenance of local memory of resource use, learning processes for responding to environmental feedback and social cohesion	Mitigation of human-induced causes of hazard Avoidance of perverse incentives for ecosystem degradation that increase sensitivity to hazards Promotion of early warning networks and structures Enhancement of disaster recovery through appropriate donor response
Adaptive capacity	Diversity in ecological systems Diversity in economic livelihood portfolio Legitimate and inclusive governance structures and social capital	Bridging organizations for integrative responses Horizontal networks in civil society for social learning

CONCLUSIONS

The case for building resilience in coastal regions is urgent, given trends in human settlement, resource use, and global environmental change. Two-thirds of the coastal disasters recorded each year are associated with extreme weather events, such as storms and flooding, that are likely to become more pervasive threats because of anthropogenically driven shifts in Earth's climate and sea level rise. These risks in particular are exacerbated by human action, raising the possibility that greenhouse gas emitters may one day become legally liable for impacts (46). Clearly, the reduction of greenhouse gas emissions is necessary in this context, but not sufficient in the management of hazards in coastal regions. Already, the resilience of many social-ecological systems has been eroded, particularly in vulnerable, marginalized societies.

The capacity of coastal ecosystems to regenerate after disasters and to continue to produce resources and services for human livelihoods can no longer be taken for granted. Rather, socio-ecological resilience must be understood at broader scales and actively managed and nurtured. Incentives for generating ecological knowledge and translating it into information that can be used in governance are essential. Multilevel social networks are crucial for developing social capital and for supporting the legal, political, and financial frameworks that enhance sources of social and ecological resilience (33, 47). The sharing of management authority requires cross-level interactions and cooperation, not merely centralization or decentralization. In many cases, improved, strong leadership and changes of social norms within management organizations are required to implement adaptive governance of coastal social-ecological systems. There is no time to waste.

REFERENCES AND NOTES

* We thank the Christensen, McDonnell, and Packard foundations for support through the Resilience Alliance. W.N.A. acknowledges the U.K. Natural Environment Research Council, the Engineering and Physical Sciences Research Council, and the Economic and Social Research Council for financial support through the Tyndall Centre. C.F. acknowledges the support of the Swedish Research Council for Environment, Agricultural Sciences, and Spatial Planning. T.P.H. was supported by grants from the Australian Research Council (ARC) and an ARC Federation fellowship.

1. C. S. Holling, *Annu. Rev. Ecol. Syst.* 4, 1 (1973).
2. B. Walker, C. S. Holling, S. Carpenter, A. Kinzig, *Ecol. Soc.* 9(no. 2), U165 (2004), available online at www. ecologyandsociety.org/vol9/iss2/art5.
3. S. Carpenter, B. Walker, J. M. Anderies, N. Abel, *Ecosystems* 4, 765 (2001).
4. C. Folke et al., *Ambio* 31, 437 (2002).
5. J. Diamond, *Guns, Germs, and Steel* (Norton, New York, 1999).
6. R. C. Sidle et al., *Quat. Int.* 118–119, 181 (2004).
7. C. Small, R. J. Nicholls, J. *Coast. Res.* 19, 584 (2003).
8. R. J. Nicholls, *Glob. Environ. Change* 14, 69 (2004).
9. R. F. McClean, A. Tsyban, in *Climate Change 2001: Impacts, Adaptation, and Vulnerability: IPCC Working Group II*, J. J. McCarthy, O. Canziani, N. A. Leary, D. J. Dokken, K. S. White, Eds. (Cambridge University Press, Cambridge, 2001), pp. 345–379.

10. P. O'Keefe, K. Westgate, B. Wisner, *Nature* 260, 566 (1976).

11. P. Blaikie, T. Cannon, I. Davis, B. Wisner, *At Risk: Natural Hazards, People's Vulnerability, and Disasters* (Routledge, London, 1994).

12. B. L. Turner II et al., *Proc. Natl. Acad. Sci. U.S.A.* 100, 8074 (2003).

13. F. Miller, F. Thomalla, J. Rockström, *Sustainable Dev. Update* 1, 2 (2005).

14. M. M. Q. Mirza, *Clim. Policy* 3, 233 (2003).

15. S. Huq, Z. Karim, M. Asaduzzaman, F. Mahtab, Eds., *Vulnerability and Adaptation to Climate Change in Bangladesh* (Kluwer, Dordrecht, Netherlands, 1999).

16. K. O'Brien et al., *Glob. Environ. Change* 14, 303 (2004).

17. W. N. Adger, H. Eakin, A. Winkels, in *Global Environmental Change and the South-East Asian Region: An Assessment of the State of the Science*, L. Lebel, Ed. (Island Press, Washington, DC, in press).

18. W. N. Adger, N. Brooks, in *Natural Disasters and Development in a Globalising World*, M. Pelling, Ed. (Routledge, London, 2003), pp. 19–42.

19. K. Brown, R. K. Turner, H. Hameed, I. Bateman, *Environ. Conserv.* 24, 316 (1997).

20. E. H. Allison, J. A. Seeley, *Fish Fish.* 5, 215 (2004).

21. R. R. Colwell, *Science* 274, 2025 (1996).

22. C. D. Harvell et al., *Science* 285, 1505 (1999).

23. T. P. Hughes et al., *Science* 301, 929 (2003).

24. D. Bellwood, T. Hughes, C. Folke, M. Nyström, *Nature* 429, 827 (2004).

25. T. Hughes et al., *Trends Ecol. Evol.* 20, 380 (2005).

26. C. Folke et al., *Annu. Rev. Ecol. Evol. Syst.* 35, 557 (2004).

27. L. Gunderson, C. S. Holling, Eds., *Panarchy: Understanding Transformation in Human and Natural Systems* (Island Press, Washington, DC, 2002).

28. F. Berkes, J. Colding, C. Folke, Eds., *Navigating Social- Ecological Systems: Building Resilience for Complexity and Change* (Cambridge Univ. Press, Cambridge, 2003).

29. A. R. Ives, K. Gross, J. L. Klug, *Science* 286, 542 (1999).

30. M. Nyström, C. Folke, *Ecosystems* 4, 406 (2001).

31. R. Costanza et al., *Bioscience* 50, 149 (2000).

32. T. Elmqvist et al., *Front. Ecol. Environ.* 1, 488 (2003).

33. C. Folke, T. Hahn, P. Olsson, J. Norberg, Annu. Rev. Environ. Res., in press.

34. P. L.-F. Liu et al., *Science* 308, 1595 (2005).

35. F. Dahdouh-Guebas et al., *Curr. Biol.* 15, R443 (2005).

36. W. N. Adger, P. M. Kelly, N. H. Ninh, Eds., *Living with Environmental Change: Social Vulnerability, Adaptation and Resilience in Vietnam* (Routledge, London, 2001).

37. J. Colding, T. Elmqvist, P. Olsson, in *Navigating Social-Ecological Systems: Building Resilience for Complexity and Change*, F. Berkes, J. Colding, C. Folke, Eds. (Cambridge Univ. Press, Cambridge, 2003), pp. 163–185.

38. A. E. Lugo, C. S. Rogers, S. W. Nixon, *Ambio* 29, 106 (2000).

39. R. A. Pielke Jr. et al., *Nat. Hazards Rev.* 4, 101 (2003).

40. K. Trenberth, *Science* 308, 1753 (2005).

41. E. L. Tompkins, *Glob. Environ. Change* 15, 139 (2005).

42. E. L. Tompkins, W. N. Adger, *Ecol. Soc.* 9(no. 2), U190 (2004), available online at www.ecologyandsociety.org/ vol9/iss2/art10.

43. K. Brown, E. L. Tompkins, W. N. Adger, *Making Waves: Integrating Coastal Conservation and Development* (Earthscan, London, 2002).

44. E. Holt-Gimenez, *Agric. Ecosyst. Environ.* 93, 87 (2002).

45. K. Jansen, *Dev. Change* 34, 45 (2003).

46. M. R. Allen, R. Lord, *Nature* 432, 551 (2004).

47. T. Dietz, E. Ostrom, P. C. Stern, *Science* 302, 1907 (2003).

15 Traditional Peoples and Climate Change

Jan Salick and Nanci Ross

EDITOR'S INTRODUCTION

Despite being among the groups most vulnerable to environmental and climatic changes, indigenous peoples have historically and contemporarily been excluded from decision making and adaptation processes. Despite this inequality in treatment, indigenous peoples are closely connected to the patterns and changes in their local environments and have developed time-tested techniques for adapting to shifts in climate. The authors argue that this wealth of ecological knowledge and management ability has great value for providing much-needed phenological data and governance models, as well as a connection to the natural world that may help mobilize wider action on climate change.

This article, and the volume of essays it introduces, aims to shift the common perception of indigenous peoples as "helpless," passive observers to what the authors call "primary actors"—agents of change who are autonomous and capable both of directing their own responses and influencing global responses to climate monitoring, adaptation, and mitigation. They relate many of the environmental and social impacts already felt by indigenous peoples around the world, highlighting rapid losses of biological and cultural diversity and degradation of spiritual landscapes, and document some of the actions—both traditional and innovative—being taken in response to these shifts. They conclude with the message that indigenous peoples have much to teach regarding bridging the gap between preserving biodiversity and protecting vulnerable populations, as their main technique for self-preservation has been the protection of biodiversity itself.

The article introduces the special issue on indigenous people's knowledge on resilience where both authors are authors and guest editors. Jan Salick, Ph.D., is Senior Curator at the Missouri Botanical Garden, and researches climate change, ethnobotany, and traditional knowledge, often focusing on the Himalayan region of Tibet. Nanci Ross, Ph.D., is an Associate Professor of Ethnobotany at Drake University, where she researches and teaches long-term interactions between human cultures and ecosystems.

(2009) TRADITIONAL PEOPLES AND CLIMATE CHANGE

We are losing our cultural heritage at a rate that will seriously diminish our opportunities to achieve sustainability in the future.
                                        Kauai Declaration (2007, 11)

Indigenous and other traditional peoples are only rarely considered in academic, policy, and public discourses on climate change, despite the fact that they are and will be greatly impacted by present and impending changes. Symptomatic of the neglect of indigenous peoples, the recently released IPCC II (2007) report summary on climate change impacts makes only scarce mention of indigenous peoples, and then only in polar regions and merely as helpless victims of changes beyond their control. The IPCC III (2007) report on mitigation of climate change does not consider the role of indigenous peoples at all. This view of indigenous peoples as passive and helpless, at best, is not new, with roots going back to colonialism and reoccurring in contemporary discussions of development, conservation, indigenous rights, and indigenous knowledge.

In the original article's special issue, the authors shift the focus to indigenous people (the term broadly encompassing local and traditional cultures) as primary actors in terms of global climate change monitoring, adaptation, and mitigation in order to provide innovative perspectives that could contribute to global change efforts. Indigenous and other local peoples are vital and active parts of many ecosystems, and may help to enhance the resilience of these ecosystems. In addition, they interpret and react to climate change impacts in creative ways, drawing on traditional knowledge as well as new technologies to find solutions, which may help society at large to cope with the impending changes.

[. . .]

People have faced climate change and adapted to it since our species evolved. The invention of agriculture was almost certainly a major adaptation to climate change (Richerson et al., 2001); yet, much of what people have developed in response to disaster has also been lost: domesticated crops and land races have been lost (Altieri and Merrick, 1987; Salick and Merrick, 1990), many water harvesting techniques have been lost (Agarwal and Narain, 1997), and much dry land management has been lost (e.g., Lane, 1990).

[. . .]

We know above all, in times of disaster and climate change, that people depend on diversity—diversity of crops and their varieties, of wild plants, and of environments (Berkes et al., 2000). Indigenous peoples are fighting loss of biodiversity and adapting to climate change through migration, irrigation, water conservation techniques, and land reclamation, changing when, where, and at what elevation plants are cultivated, livelihood adaptation, and a myriad of other techniques (Macchi et al., 2008). Nonetheless, as climate change threatens biodiversity, it simultaneously removes the major defense that indigenous people have against variation and change. Their primary tool for adaptation is at risk.

For arctic peoples in polar regions, hunting and fishing strategies depend on stable ice; yet, temperatures in the arctic are predicted to rise by as much as 88°C in the 21st century under present conditions (IPCC, 2007). In alpine areas, global warming is causing the loss of alpine biodiversity. Upward movement of plants is measurable with the highest floras predicted to be displaced off the top of mountains, off their "sky islands" (Gottfried et al., 1999). On islands, many factors interact resulting in the greatest rates of extinction on earth: island ephemerality, habitat destruction, violent storms, salinization of ground water, over-exploitation, and invasive species—as well as climate change (Bergstrom and Chown, 1999). In deserts, both people and biodiversity cling to existence in small, dynamic, non-equilibrium patches which may be decimated by climate change. Tropical rainforests of the world are havens of outstanding biodiversity, as well as indigenous cultural diversity (Ramirez, 2005); as tropical rainforests are degraded, this heritage of biodiversity is threatened.

Climate change is projected on a global scale and is a global phenomenon. Different areas and different environments, however, exhibit much local and regional variation (Walther et al., 2002). While climate models can paint the bigger picture of climate change and provide estimates for the likely consequences of different future scenarios of human development, they are not very good at providing information about changes at the local level. From the British Columbia coast (Turner, 2009) to the Kalahari Desert to the English countryside (Lawrence, 2009, herein) and to the Himalayan Mountains (Salick et al., 2006, 2009), local people are experiencing local changes in climatic conditions.

Indigenous peoples are not only keen observers of climate changes, but they are also actively trying to adapt to the changing conditions (Salick and Byg, 2007; Macchi et al., 2008). In general, there appears to be a hierarchy of responses, whereby as conditions worsen, additional physical and biological responses are added, and social and political relations become more important for providing resources for basic survival. A diversified resource base is the first level of protection against environmental stochasticity utilized by indigenous groups across the globe. Indigenous groups also adjust the timing of activities and employ a variety of techniques which have developed over, in many cases, centuries of surviving changing conditions (Berkes et al., 2000).

The Stern review (Stern, 2006) and the Fourth Assessment Report by the Intergovernmental Panel on Climate Change (IPCC, 2007) have brought about changes in the climate change discussion. Both reports presented more and stronger evidence for the impacts of climate change on natural systems as well as on human activities in many parts of the world. Impacts are predicted to be especially large for poor countries as well as for many of the ecosystems that indigenous peoples inhabit—often economically and politically marginal areas in diverse, but fragile ecosystems.

[. . .]

Bridges and McClatchey (2009) illustrate the adaptive potential of indigenous cultures that have evolved in the marginal environments which are the first areas to experience the effects of climate change. Pacific Islanders living on atolls are already negatively affected by climate change, facing threats to available freshwater and food. Yet the long-term familiarity with the variable nature of the atoll environment, where survival is held in a tight feedback loop with this unforgiving environment, has led to the development of adaptive and flexible resource management regimes which could provide a model for global responses to climate change. The authors also identify another important aspect of climate change: scale. While climate change is a global phenomenon, human responses will be at the local scale. Bridges and McClatchey outline how the traditional ecological knowledge system of atoll dwellers allows them to observe and respond to subtle climate changes that have local impacts.

The concept of local versus global effects of climate change is expanded in the next two complementary papers focusing on the indigenous people living in the mountains of Eastern Tibet. Salick et al. (2009) describe the ecological implications of climate change in the alpine environment. They directly relate the gradients of local diversity—which are affected by biogeography, precipitation, and elevation—to Tibetan livelihoods. This paper provides quantification of how the indigenous Tibetan people living in the Himalayan biodiversity "hotspot" are more susceptible to climate change effects than less politically and geographically marginalized cultures; however, to address this inequality, we must assess the local perception and response to climate change impacts. Byg and Salick (2009) point out that while many scientific studies on climate change are at larger, regional scales, local perceptions and beliefs influence how people respond to climate change. Tibetans utilize a wide range of ecological zones, creating a land use model that is flexible and resilient to change (Salick et al., 2005). In Eastern Tibet, however, many landscape features have spiritual value (Anderson et al., 2005; Salick et al., 2007), so climate change effects can have significant social impacts. These impacts affect how Tibetans perceive, evaluate, and respond to climate change. The complexity of such local responses can have profound implications on efforts to combat the effects of global change in many areas of the world.

Concurrent with the loss of biodiversity is the loss of cultural diversity as globalization erodes the connections between indigenous knowledge systems and local environments (Toledo, 2001). This loss of indigenous cultural heritage, each culture evolved over generations in close association with a local environment, could result in a diminished capacity to recognize and implement sustainable environmental practices in the changing milieu of climate change (Kauai Declaration, 2007). Grabherr (2009) investigated the effects of climate change-induced pressure on biodiversity of alpine plants in the Alps. Similar to the climate change effects described in the Himalayas, warmer temperatures and a rising tree line are threatening alpine flora. Alpine plants are traditionally important for medicinal use (e.g., Salick et al., 2006) which leads to detailed observation of phenological patterns; however, the loss of traditional knowledge in "developed" areas such as Europe has led to a loss of knowledge and, perhaps more importantly, a loss of personal connection to local biodiversity. Interestingly, Grabherr found that climate change may be affecting a socially significant ornamental species, Edelweiss (*Leontopodium alpinum Cass.*). The iconic status of this species may allow it to provide a proxy for the traditionally utilized species and lead to public pressure for action to slow climate change and preserve this famous symbol of the Alps.

In the developed world, loss of traditional cultures and perspectives has led to a disconnect between people and nature. Indigenous peoples have often been found to have intimate familiarity with the natural rhythms and processes of their ecosystem (e.g., Vogt et al., 2002). When these cultures are lost, their traditional ecological knowledge system is also lost taking with it the storehouse of long-term phenological data that we so desperately need (see Barnard and Thuiller, 2008). The paper contributed by Lawrence (2009) offers a model to replace at least some of this knowledge. She looks at the collection of phenological data by "citizen scientists," i.e., amateur naturalists in Britain. This data provides in-depth observations of local effects of climate change; however, while scientists tend to view the data as the end goal, Lawrence explores the personal value the data collectors place on the experience of being directly involved in the generation of knowledge. She investigates the social significance of public participation in data collection in relation to the current global change debate suggesting that lack of public support for climate change mitigation efforts in areas of the developed world is not due necessarily to a lack of information. Rather, it is due to a lack of connection felt by the public to their environment.

Finally, Turner (2009) brings together these various lines of inquiry looking at climate change impacts at local and regional levels, the adaptive capacity of indigenous biodiversity management regimes, and indigenous perceptions and responses to climate change in the indigenous people of British Columbia, Canada. She documents clear examples of phenological changes observed by the local people on both land and sea and the adjustments made to resource harvesting and management in response. Turner suggests that indigenous and traditional ecological knowledge can be utilized as baseline long-term datasets developed over centuries of trial and error. She takes a close look at the nature of traditional ecological knowledge systems and how indigenous people view climate change. She also lays out areas where the input and participation of indigenous people should be encouraged so we can gain not only more data, but a richer, more nuanced perspective on our relationship with our environment.

The original article's special issue, although barely beginning a discussion on local peoples and climate change, nonetheless do highlight the myriad and varied aspects of global climate change, emphasizing the need to look beyond narrowminded perspectives. One perspective focuses on the preservation of global biodiversity, but searches for a solution using only the toolbox traditionally available to Western science. A second pursues the goal of protecting the world's most vulnerable peoples from climate change impacts, yet fails to consider the ability of those same people to help themselves and, indeed, us. The climate change research community must recognize the obvious bridge that indigenous and local peoples provide between climate change and biodiversity protection in the service of helping to preserve themselves. If we can expand our perspectives to learn the lessons that traditional cultures have to offer, we may find that they can teach us how to save ourselves.

REFERENCES

Agarwal, A., Narain, S., 1997. *Dying Wisdom*. Centre for Science and Environment. Thomson Press, Faridabad.

Altieri, M., Merrick, L., 1987. In situ conservation of crop genetic resources through maintenance of traditional farming systems. *Economic Botany* 41 (1), 86–96.

Anderson, D., Salick, J., Moseley, R.K., Xiaokun, O., 2005. Conserving the sacred medicine mountains: A vegetation analysis of Tibetan sacred sites in Northwest Yunnan. *Biodiversity and Conservation* 14, 3065–3091.

Barnard, P., Thuiller, W., 2008. Introduction: Global change and biodiversity: Future challenges. *Biology Letters* 4, 553–555.

Bergstrom, D.M., Chown, S.L., 1999. Life at the front: History, ecology and change on southern ocean islands. *Trends in Ecology and Evolution* 14, 472–476.

Berkes, F., Colding, J., Folke, C., 2000. Rediscovery of traditional ecological knowledge as adaptive management. *Ecological Applications* 10 (5), 1251–1262.

Bridges, K., McClatchey, W., 2009. Living on the margin: Ethnoecological insights from Marshall Islanders at Rongelap Atoll. *Global Environmental Change* 19, 140–146.

Byg, A., Salick, J., 2009. Local perspectives on a global phenomenon: Climate change in Eastern Tibetan villages. *Global Environmental Change* 19, 156–166.

Gottfried, M., Pauli, H., Reiter, K., Grabherr, G., 1999. A fine-scaled predictive model for changes in species distribution patterns of high mountain plants induced by climate warming. *Diversity and Distributions* 5, 241–251.

Grabherr, G., 2009. Biodiversity in the high ranges of the Alps: Ethnobotanical and climate change perspectives. *Global Environmental Change* 19, 167–172.

Intergovernmental Panel on Climate Change, Working Group I, 2007. *4th Assessment Report: The Physical Science Basis-Summary for Policy Makers.* http://www.ipcc.ch/pdf/assessment-report/ar4/wg1/ar4-wg1-spm.pdf (Online)

Intergovernmental Panel on Climate Change, Working Group II, 2007. *4th Assessment Report: Impacts, Adaptation, and Vulnerability-Summary for Policy Makers.* http://www.ipcc.ch/pdf/assessment-report/ar4/wg2/ar4-wg2-spm.pdf (Online)

Intergovernmental Panel on Climate Change, Working Group III, 2007. *4th Assessment Report: Mitigation of Climate Change-Summary for Policy Makers.* http://www.ipcc.ch/pdf/assessment-report/ar4/wg3/ar4-wg3-spm.pdf (Online)

Kauai Declaration, 2007. Ethnobotany, the science of survival: A declaration from Kaua'i. *Economic Botany* 61 (1), 1–2.

Lane, C., 1990. *Barabaig Natural Resource Management: Sustainable Land Use under Threat of Destruction.* United Nations Research Institute for Social Development (UNRISD). Discussion Paper Number 12.

Lawrence, A., 2009. The first Cuckoo in winter: Phenology, recording, credibility and meaning in Britain. *Global Environmental Change* 19, 173–179.

Macchi, M., Oviedo, G., Gotheil, S., Cross, K., Boedhihartono, A., Wolfangel, C., Howell, M., 2008. *Indigenous and Traditional Peoples and Climate Change.* IUCN Issues Paper. http://cmsdata.iucn.org/downloads (Online)

Ramirez, G.Z., 2005. Conservation of the biological and cultural diversity of the Colombian Amazon Piedmont: Dr. Schultes' legacy. *Ethnobotany Research and Applications* 3, 179–188.

Richerson, P.J., Boy, R., Bettinger, R.L., 2001. Was agriculture impossible during the Pleistocene, but mandatory during the Holocene? A climate change hypothesis. *American Antiquity* 66 (3), 387–411.

Salick, J., Amend, A., Anderson, D., Hoffmeister, K., Gunn, B., Fang, Z.D., 2007. Tibetan sacred sites conserve old growth trees in the Eastern Himalayas. *Biodiversity and Conservation* 16 (3), 693–706.

Salick, J., Amend, A., Gunn, B., Law, W., Schmidt, H., Byg, A., 2006. Tibetan medicine plurality. *Economic Botany* 60 (3), 227–253.

Salick, J., Byg, A. (Eds.), 2007. *Indigenous Peoples and Climate Change.* Tyndall Centre, Oxford, UK. http://www.tyndall.ac.uk/publications/Indigenouspeoples.pdf (Online)

Salick, J., Fang, Z., Byg, A., 2009. Eastern Himalayan alpine plant ecology, Tibetan ethnobotany, and climate change. *Global Environmental Change* 19, 147–155.

Salick, J., Merrick, L., 1990. Use and maintenance of genetic resources: Crops and their wild relatives. In: Carrol, C.R., Vandermeer, J.H., Rosset, P.M. (Eds.), *Agroecology.* McGraw Hill Publishing Company, New York.

Salick, J., Yang, Y.P., Amend, A., 2005. Tibetan land use and change in NW Yunnan. *Economic Botany* 59, 312–325.

Stern, N. (Ed.), 2006. *The Economics of Climate Change: The Stern Review.* Cambridge University Press, Cambridge, UK, p. 692.

Toledo, V., 2001. Indigenous people and biodiversity. In: Levin, S., Daily, G.C., Colwell, R.K., Lubchenco, J., Mooney, H.A., Schulze, E.D., Tilman, D. (Eds.), *Encyclopedia of Biodiversity.* Academic Press, San Diego, CA, pp. 451–463.

Turner, N., 2009. "It's so different today": Climate change and indigenous lifeways in British Columbia, Canada. *Global Environmental Change* 19, 180–190.

Vogt, K.A., Beard, K.H., Hammann, S., O'Hara Palmiotto, J., Vogt, D.J., Scatena, F.N., Hecht, B.P., 2002. Indigenous knowledge informing management of tropical forests: the link between rhythms in plant secondary chemistry and lunar cycles. *Ambio* 31, 485–490.

Walther, G.-R., Post, E., Convey, P., Menzel, A., Parmesan, C., Beebee, T.J.C., Fromentin, J.-M., Hoegh-Guldberg, O., Bairlein, F., 2002. Ecological responses to recent climate change. *Nature* 416, 389–395.

Section IV

Green Infrastructure, Urban Form, and Adaptation

Introduction

Yaser Abunnasr

The literature on adaptation planning is more frequently specifying Green Infra-structure (GI) as a viable adaptation tool capable of addressing current and future impacts of climate change. GI is a nature-based approach that incorporates ecological principles and formalizes the benefits that 'nature' freely provides into urban planning and design. While GI is a relatively new discipline, it builds on historical precedents and integrates principles from multiple disciplines including ecology, landscape ecology, planning, landscape architecture, and engineering. As a spatial planning tool, GI can enhance urban environments by incorporating networks of connected open spaces that enhance ecological processes to maximize ecosystem benefits. Ecosystem services are essential for cities as they provide a large suite of benefits such as clean air and water, local food, amelioration of the urban micro-climate, improved health, and enhanced biodiversity. These benefits are essential for urban areas and are considered essential and therefore 'infrastructural'. On the other hand, climate change will increase temperatures, exacerbate pollution, and increase precipitation/flooding. The complementarity between the provision of ecosystem benefits and climate change impacts make GI a suitable response for urban adaptation planning and design.

The 'infrastructural' understanding of ecological systems is not new. GI builds on historical precedents and associated disciplines. Eisenman (2016) attributes the earliest case of GI to Fredrick Law Olmsted's work in the late 19th century. The Emerald Necklace in Boston, a project begun in 1878, is a series of open spaces connected by linear park elements that were transformed from a marshy area of the Back Bay and The Fens into a much needed linear recreational park system simultaneously using the landscape as a water infrastructure system drain-ing, cleaning, and mitigating floodwaters. Olmsted progressed to apply his ideas in many cities across the United States. The idea of networked open space systems was further developed by Charles Eliot's Plan for the Metropolitan Park System of Boston (1899) at the city scale followed by Charles Eliot II's Open Space Plan for the Commonwealth of Massachusetts (1928) at the state scale, and Warren Manning's plan of 1923 identified connected green corridors across the USA to define future urban, commercial, and recreational areas. Olmsted's idea of an infrastructural landscape was prevented for decades (i.e. due to urban planning focus on transport and grey infrastructure) until it reemerged in the later part of the 20th century as an urban planning and design approach in response to the negative effects of development. Ian McHarg's book *Design with Nature* (1969) established the idea that nature could be the basis of urban development. He developed a suitability analysis method for land development where natural assets are mapped and overlaid to determine the most suitable locations for development, safeguarding natural systems and its benefits. McHarg's ideas were further developed by Anne Spirn's *The Granite Garden: Urban Nature and Human Design* (1984), which focused on urban ecology where impacts on the environment from urban morphology (i.e. pollution, noise, dust, stormwater runoff) can be addressed using natural systems that are incorporated within the urban landscape.

In contemporary planning and design, the GI concept emerged in the early 1990s from land conservation plans for the states of Maryland and Florida in the USA. GI was identified as one of the five primary sustainable development goals set by President Clinton's Towards a Sustainable America Report (PSC, 1999). The first formal and comprehensive definition was developed by Benedict and McMahon (2006) stating that GI is:

> an interconnected network of natural areas and other open spaces that conserves natural ecosystem values and functions, sustains clean air and water, and provides a wide array of benefits to people and wildlife. Used in this context, green infrastructure is the ecological framework for environmental, social, and economic health—in short, our natural life-support.
>
> (p. 1)

The push to reconsider natural systems as essential elements of urban contexts has been gaining greater urgency. Open space planning gained prominence in recent decades as a means to protect natural, agricultural, and other open spaces at city and regional scales. Variations of open space plans include parks and recreation plans, resource conservation plans, and greenway and trail plans. Specifically, Greenway plans (i.e. precursor of GI) of linear open space corridors (i.e. waterways and abandoned rail lines) have gained more prominence providing ecological, recreational, economic, and cultural/historic values (Fabos and Ryan, 2006). In the past ten years, the planning profession has witnessed the repurposing of open space and greenway plans as green infrastructure emphasizing environmental, economic, and social benefits. At the site scale, GI is often used to signify stormwater practices that mimic natural hydrological processes as opposed to grey infrastructure solutions.

As a spatial planning tool, GI is based on the landscape ecological concept of patch-corridor-matrix developed by Forman and Gordon (1986). When well planned and implemented, a GI system is composed of a network of patches (i.e. parks, forests, green roofs) that are connected by corridors (i.e. river systems, planted streets, trails) within a contextual matrix of dominant land uses (i.e. commercial, residential, agriculture). Depending on the urban context (urban core-suburban), morphology (densely or sparsely built) and availability of space, GI networks vary in composition, scale, and the delivery of ecosystem service types. At the metropolitan scale, urban forests and large parks can reduce the differential temperature due to the urban heat island phenomenon. At the urban scale, urban parks, street trees, and green roofs can provide ancillary space for water collection in case of extreme flooding. Within urban coastal areas, sand dunes and mangrove plantations attenuate the impacts of storm surges and rising sea levels. At the site scale, trees, community gardens, and vegetated ground cover can increase outdoor comfort levels and provide locally grown food. As an essential urban system, the interconnected and multifunctional characteristics of GI provide the necessary spatial and functional benefits needed to climate-proof cities.

As a networked system, GI is multifunctional because it provides several ecosystems services within the same landscape element (i.e. park, green roof, etc.). Ecosystem services can be categorized into four types: provisioning, such as the production of food and water; regulating, such as the control of climate and disease; supporting, such as nutrient cycles and crop pollination; and cultural, such as spiritual and recreational benefits (MEA, 2005). Ecosystem services are the result of ecological processes that manifest within an ecosystem—in this case, the GI landscape element. Usually, several processes occur simultaneously generating multiple benefits. This multi-functionality is an important quality because it renders GI effective, when compared to a single-use grey infrastructure (i.e. domestic water network). For example, the urban tree canopy (i.e. trees along streets, tree-planted parks, and trees in private yards) intercepts rainfall, reducing runoff; acts as a carbon sink; reduces the impact of increased temperature by providing shade and absorbing the sun's energy; and mitigates flooding by providing temporary water ponding. The same applies to forests, wetlands, agricultural lands, green roofs, and green facades. It is these same ecosystems services that make GI inherently compatible with climate adaptation in cities because it has the capacity to address the same impacts resulting from climate change.

Urban areas are witnessing and will witness increased impacts from local and global climate change due to their morphological characteristics. Temperatures in cities are already higher than their periphery (and expected to increase further) because urban materials absorb the sun's energy and release it during nighttime (the urban heat island phenomenon). Increased runoff and flooding is expected due to the high percentage of impervious surfaces and the inability of grey infrastructure to handle the expected higher than usual magnitude and frequency of weather events. Cities along water bodies will witness storm surges and increase flooding, threatening coastal assets. By planning connected and multi-scalar systems of parks, corridors, street trees, green roofs, and green facades within cities, pervious surfaces and vegetated land cover (Stone, 2012) can be increased to elevate the capacity of cities to absorb impacts from climate events. What characterizes GI from other climate-proofing measures is that it is a no-regrets approach. Multiple benefits that are suitable for adaptation also provide co-benefits at no additional cost. Improving ecological performance and livability of cities are co-benefits that are worth attaining regardless when and how climate change hits.

As much as GI promises to support climate adaptation in cities, there are challenges for its implementation. At the physical planning and design level, allocating space within and around cities is not evident when land is primarily valued for its real estate value. At the policy level, uptake remains slow because of the long term benefits and planning required contrary to the short term agendas typically set by policy makers. Lastly, there is insufficient empirically-based research on the performance of different typologies of GI in the context of climate adaptation. While literature on GI and climate adaptation continues to develop, we have chosen four manuscripts to introduce the subject. The first by David Rouse and Ignacio Bunster-Ossa is theoretical, setting GI within the context of other infrastructural systems and articulating the contribution of GI to resilience and sustainability. The second by Yaser Abunnasr and Elisabeth M. Hamin Infield presents the Green Infrastructure Transect where climate change affects, urban context, and responsive GI measures are matched emphasizing mainstreaming adaptation in to current planning practices. The third, a quintessential article by Susannah E. Gill et al., integrates climate science, modelling, and planning scenarios to inform GI planning for city climate adaptation. The last manuscript by Robin M. Leichenko and William D. Solecki provides a discussion on climate impacts in suburbs, a less addressed topic.

REFERENCES

Benedict, M.A. and McMahon, E.T. (2006). *Green Infrastructure: Linking Landscapes and Communities*. Washington, DC: Island Press.

Eisenman, T.S. (2016). Greening Cities in an Urbanizing Age: The Human Health Basis in the Nineteenth and Early Twentieth century. *Change Over Time* 6(2), Fall.

Fabos, J.G. and Ryan, R.L. (2006). An Introduction to Greenway Planning around the World. *Landscape and Urban Planning* 76(1–4):1–6.

Forman, Richard T.T. and Godron, Michel (1986). *Landscape Ecology*. New York: Wiley.

McHarg, I.L. (1971). *Design with Nature*. New York: American Museum of Natural History.

MEA (2005). The Millennium Ecosystem Assessment Report.

President's Council on Sustainable Development (1999). *Towards a Sustainable America: Advancing Prosperity, Opportunity, and a Healthy Environment for the 21st Century*, May 1999. The President's Council on Sustainable Development.

Spirn, A.W. (1984). *The Granite Garden: Urban Nature and Human Design*. New York: Basic Books.

Stone, Brian (2012). *The City and the Coming Climate: Climate Change in the Places We Live*. New York: Cambridge University Press.

16 Landscape Planning, Design, and Green Infrastructure

David Rouse and Ignacio Bunster-Ossa

EDITOR'S INTRODUCTION

Like many key concepts used in the language of climate change planning, green infrastructure (GI) often suffers from definition confusion. As this article clarifies, there are two approaches to green infrastructure that are not interchangeable. The first approach, defined in this article by the U.S. Environmental Protection Agency (EPA), refers to "systems and practices that use or mimic natural processes to infiltrate, evapotranspirate (the return of water to the atmosphere either through evaporation or by plants), or reuse stormwater or runoff on the site where it is generated." This approach is usually implemented at the site scale, through design solutions like bioswales, rain gardens, green roofs, or other relatively small installations.

The second approach to green infrastructure is conceptually larger than the first. Defined here by the Conservation Fund, this version of green infrastructure encompasses a landscape's entire network of natural areas and includes places like "wilderness, parks, greenways," conservation areas, and farms. It even exists within urban areas of dense development as the landscape itself on which the development is built, affecting the ecological patterns that suffuse urban settings—like temperature, water movement, and common vegetation.

The authors aim to unify these definitions to create a cross-scale conception of green infrastructure that is viewed through the "lens of landscape." This version of green infrastructure is a "physical manifestation of processes that connect the built and natural environments, performing multiple functions and yielding associated benefits for the health and well-being of people and wildlife."

From this definition, they break down the many "ecosystem services" that green infrastructure provides to society. They also detail how it can support the popular goal of sustainability and its emphasis on the three "Es": environment, economy, and equity. To measure GI's contribution to these goals, they list key indicators (means of tracking progress) under each E, which is an important means of translating abstract definitions to actual planning and landscape architecture projects. In addition to GI's role within sustainability, public health is also discussed as a thematic area within which green infrastructure can play a major part.

To accomplish these aims, however, GI must be implemented comprehensively and strategically, as it exists in a complex interrelationship of environmental, economic, and social systems. Implementation therefore requires systems thinking, a design approach that is "coherently organized or interconnected in a pattern or structure that produces . . . a 'function' or 'purpose.'" Systems thinking is a means of ensuring that green infrastructure crosses spatial scales and addresses multiple sustainability problems, an essential goal of climate change planning and design.

David Rouse is a principal with Philadelphia-based Wallace Roberts & Todd. Ignacio Bunster-Ossa, also a principal with WRT, is a pioneer in landscape urbanism and a Loeb Fellow at Harvard University's Graduate School of Design.

(2013) GREEN INFRASTRUCTURE: A LANDSCAPE APPROACH

What is a "landscape" approach to green infrastructure? How is it more than just implementing green infrastructure measures at various scales, from green roofs and rain gardens to regional greenways and open space? The answer lies in conceiving of landscape as an integrated whole, as the "scene" across the land that encapsulates the adaptation and manipulation of natural form and processes for the purpose of human habitation. A landscape approach to green infrastructure entails a design vision that translates planning strategy into physical reality while heeding the ecological and cultural characteristics of a particular locale—whether a region or an individual building site. It is, by necessity, an approach that involves esthetics: what a place should look like as informed by the people who live on the land, their past, and their aspirations.

In this context, green infrastructure becomes both "effective" as an agent of environmental quality and "affective" as an expression of local conditions. A landscape approach to green infrastructure requires considering not only how infrastructure could improve water or air quality but also how, say, a rain garden, constructed wetland, or greenway might engender a sense of community identity. It raises the question: How and where should green infrastructure be placed on the land? It is more than a strictly functional question, as it both enriches and complicates practice.

[. . .]

DEFINITIONS OF LANDSCAPE AND GREEN INFRASTRUCTURE

Landscape has traditionally been defined as an esthetic resource, such as an expanse of scenery, or as the overall geography of a region. In the words of the American Society of Landscape Architects (ASLA):

landscape architects design the built environment of neighborhoods, towns, and cities while also protecting and managing the natural environment, from its forests and fields to rivers and coasts. Members of the profession have a special commitment to improving the quality of life through the best design of places for people and other living things.

(www.asla.org/nonmembers/What_is_Asla.cfm)

Green infrastructure is relatively new to the lexicon of urban planning and landscape design. According to Firehock (2010), the term was first used in a 1994 report on land conservation strategies by the Florida Greenways Commission. The intent was to elevate the societal value and functions of natural lands and systems to the same level of importance as gray infrastructure:

> The Commission's vision for Florida represents a new way of looking at conservation, an approach that emphasizes the interconnectedness of both our natural systems and our common goals and recognizes that the state's "green infrastructure" is just as important to conserve and manage as our built infrastructure.
>
> (Florida Greenways Commission 1994)

Mark Benedict and Ed McMahon (2006) of the Conservation Fund defined green infrastructure as:

> a strategically planned and managed network of wilderness, parks, green-ways, conservation easements, and working lands with conservation value that supports native species, maintains natural ecological processes, sustains air and water re- sources, and contributes to the health and quality of life for America's communities and people.

More recently, a second definition of green infrastructure evolved from the need to address the water quality impacts of urban stormwater runoff in response to the Clean Water Act and related regulatory mandates. According to the U.S. Environmental Protection Agency (EPA; www.epa.gov/owow/NPS/lid), green infrastructure refers to "systems and practices that use or mimic natural processes to infiltrate, evapotranspirate (the return of water to the atmosphere either through evaporation or by plants), or reuse stormwater or runoff on the site where it is generated." While the Florida Greenways Commission and Conservation Fund definitions emphasize large landscape elements such as parks, natural areas, greenways, and working (agricultural and forest) lands, the EPA identifies smaller-scale features in urban contexts—green roofs, trees, rain gardens, vegetated swales, pocket wetlands, infiltration planters, vegetated median strips, and so on—as typical components of green infrastructure.

This report seeks to bring these two definitions together and enrich them by viewing green infrastructure through the lens of landscape—the physical manifestation of processes that connect the built and natural environments, performing multiple functions and yielding associated benefits for the health and well-being of people and wildlife. This perspective links physical form and esthetics with function and outcomes (benefits), natural habitats with landscapes managed by humans for specific purposes, and green infrastructure with gray infrastructure. It envisions green infrastructure as a three-dimensional "envelope" that surrounds, connects, and infuses buildings, streets, utilities, and the like. As such, it is not separate from gray infrastructure, but forms the ground on which it exists. In other words, there is no fixed boundary between the two. The erasure of boundaries compels a holistic and interdisciplinary approach to the planning and design of infrastructure.

[. . .]

KEY CONCEPTS

This report is intended for planners, landscape architects, architects, civil engineers, scientists, and others interested in the spatial structure, functions, and values (environmental, economic, and social) of natural and built landscapes. In traditional practice, these professionals have tended to operate independently of one another. The concept of landscape as green infrastructure provides a potent platform for integrating the work of physical designers, policy planners, and others and leveraging this collaboration to achieve larger societal goals.

[. . .]

A related concept is ecosystem services (i.e., the benefits that natural ecosystems provide for people). These services can be broken down into provisioning services (e.g., food and water production), regulating services (e.g., improved air and water quality, carbon sequestration), supporting services (e.g., nutrient cycling, crop pollination), and cultural services (e.g., recreation, community bonding, and spiritual inspiration). Chapter 24 explicates an emerging practice model designed to promote an integrated process for making green infrastructure a reality. Several overarching concepts thread through it, including:

- the importance of green infrastructure to the "triple bottom line" of sustainability;
- the contributions green infrastructure can make to public health, broadly conceived; and
- the performance of green infrastructure as a system, interacting with other systems in ways that shape and connect the natural and built environments.

Sustainability: Realizing the Multiple Benefits of Green Infrastructure

Central to the concept of green infrastructure is that it provides a wide suite of benefits. The three "Es" of sustainability (environment, economy, and equity)—also referred to as the triple bottom line (people, prosperity, and planet)—offer a useful framework for characterizing these benefits.

Environment
- Green infrastructure can absorb stormwater, reducing runoff and associated impacts such as flooding and erosion.
- It can improve environmental quality by removing harmful pollutants from the air and water.
- It can moderate the local climate and lessens the urban heat island effect, contributing to energy conservation.
- It can preserve and restore natural ecosystems and provide habitats for native fauna and flora.
- It can mitigate climate change by reducing fossil fuel emissions from vehicles, lessening energy consumption by buildings, and sequestering and storing carbon.

Economy
- Green infrastructure can create job and business opportunities in fields such as landscape management, recreation, and tourism.
- Studies have shown that it can stimulate retail sales and other economic activity in local business districts (Wolf 1998 and 1999).
- It can increase property values (Neelay 1988; Economy League of Greater Philadelphia 2010).
- It can attract visitors, residents, and businesses to a community (Campos 2009).
- It can reduce energy, healthcare, and gray infrastructure costs, making more funds available for other purposes (Heisler 1986; Simpson and McPherson 1996; Economy League of Greater Philadelphia 2010).

Community
- Green infrastructure can promote healthy lifestyles by providing outdoor recreation opportunities and enabling people to walk or bike as part of their daily routines.
- It can improve environmental conditions (e.g., air and water quality) and their effects on public health.
- It can promote environmental justice, equity, and access for underserved populations.
- It can provide places for people to gather, socialize, and build community spirit.
- It can improve the aesthetic quality of urban and suburban development.
- It can provide opportunities for public art and expression of cultural values.
- It can connect people to nature. Studies have shown that better health outcomes, improved educational performance, and reduced violence can be among the resulting benefits (Ulrich 1984; Kaplan 1995; Berman et al. 2008; Kuo and Sullivan 2001a, and 2001b).
- It can yield locally produced resources (food, fiber, and water).

A key question for planners and designers is: how can we measure these benefits to demonstrate the value green infrastructure brings to society? Indicators are quantitative or qualitative measurement tools that track progress toward goals and objectives. They are useful in characterizing complex system changes over time in relatively simple terms. Early indicator systems were developed largely to address human impacts on natural ecosystems, but their scope has broadened to encompass other dimensions of sustainability, often structured around the triple bottom line. Many of the previously listed benefits lend themselves to quantitative measurement; for example:

- *Environmental Indicators*: stormwater volume reduction, harmful pollutants removed from the air, tree canopy coverage, carbon storage and sequestration, etc.
- *Economic Indicators*: jobs created, property values increased, reductions in building energy use, etc.
- *Social (Community) Indicators*: parks and open space access (typically measured in terms of walking distance to the nearest resource), parks and open space equity (typically measured in terms of distribution relative to demographics), public health outcomes, etc.

Other benefits, such as improved esthetic quality, support of public art, and facilitation of cultural expression, are harder to measure, though they are central to the practice of landscape architects and other design professionals. Thus, an important challenge is to develop meaningful ways to define the qualitative benefits provided by landscape as green infrastructure.

[. . .]

Public Health: Expanding the Scope of Green Infrastructure

Public health is an overarching concern that cuts across the triple bottom line of sustainability. It has become an increasingly important issue for society as health care costs have escalated and awareness has grown of the broader impacts of environment, lifestyle, and community conditions on health. Marya Morris (2006) refers to the "social"—as opposed to the "medical"—model of health, under which public health addresses the health of the community as a whole, rather than focusing on symptoms and diseases suffered by individuals. The health of a community is inextricably linked to the health of its environment as reflected in the landscape, and green infrastructure can bring important public health benefits. Examples of these benefits include:

- Green infrastructure can improve environmental conditions such as air and water quality and their associated impacts on human health (exposure to hazardous substances, asthma, etc.).
- It can encourage walking, biking, and other forms of outdoor activity.[1]

- It can improve health by bringing people into contact with nature. Richard Louv (2011) proposes a "Natural Health Care System" to capitalize on the restorative effects of such experiences on physical and mental health. For example, many health care professionals are issuing "park" or "nature" prescriptions for their patients to exercise outdoors in parks or on trails. Another example is the Medical Mile greenway trail in downtown Little Rock, Arkansas. Created through a collaboration among parks, recreation, and public health organizations, it is both a walking/biking trail and an outdoor "health museum" designed to encourage people to make healthy living choices.
- It can provide a safer environment for outdoor activity through design, thus counterbalancing crime, traffic, and other deterrents.
- It can improve conditions in poor and marginalized communities that too often bear a disproportionate burden from environmental and health hazards (thus addressing the equity component of the three "Es"). Green infrastructure can provide a range of health benefits for the residents of such communities, including improved water quality, reduced air pollution, increased opportunities for physical exercise, and access to locally grown food (Dunn 2010).

Green Infrastructure and Systems Thinking

Green infrastructure lends itself to an integrated, systems thinking approach, one that overcomes the limitations of more specialized or "silo" methods of problem solving. Whereas traditional, mechanistic analysis dissects a system into individual pieces, systems analysis focuses on how the pieces interact to produce the behavior of a system (Aronson 1996–1998). A particular system can, in turn, be both influenced by the behavior of smaller subsystems and nested within a larger system (a concept referred to as "systems hierarchy"). From this perspective, systems defined by separate structures, functions, and processes intersect in the landscape, working together to determine its overall behavior as green infrastructure.

But how does such an approach apply in practice and what are its implications for planners and designers? Recognizing the boundary of the system in question—the sphere of influence of a specific problem—is the first step in a systems thinking approach. Next, tracing connections to other systems inevitably widens the context of the problem. It is this focus on interactions that defines a systems approach.

To delve further into the topic, it is useful to understand the basic characteristics of systems. Noted scientist, author, and systems analyst Donella Meadows defined a system as "A set of elements or parts that is coherently organized or interconnected in a pattern or structure that produces a characteristic set of behaviors, often classified as its 'function' or 'purpose'" (Meadows 2008, 188). Applying this definition, green infrastructure is a system that comprises constituent parts (e.g., trees, soil, and constructed infrastructure); that is organized into a *pattern* (the landscape); and that performs *functions* (e.g., stormwater management and the removal of air and water pollutants) that have a *purpose* (the benefits described above). Moreover, green infrastructure is part of a *hierarchy*: it incorporates multiple subsystems (e.g., hydrology, vegetation, and movement) and in turn is a sub- system within a larger system (e.g., region, city, or neighborhood), where it interacts with other systems (e.g., transportation, economy, and governance).

The following are additional attributes of systems:

- *Interconnections* are relationships that hold the parts of a system together. Examples include flows of resources (e.g., water or energy); flows of information (e.g., the communication of knowledge); and interactions among functional subsystems (e.g., intermodal connections among forms of transportation such as walking, biking, driving, and transit).
- A *stock* is the material or information that has accumulated over time from flows through the system (e.g., the biomass within a mature forest).
- A *feedback loop* is a circular (as opposed to linear) pathway formed by an effect returning to its cause and generating either more or less of the same effect. A *balancing* feedback loop tends to counteract or resist any small change in system behavior (e.g., by keeping the system's stock within a stable range, thus maintaining its equilibrium over time). A *reinforcing* feedback loop tends to enhance or augment any small change in system behavior in a positive or negative direction (e.g., a disturbance that causes the system to cross a critical "threshold" beyond which it is unable to return to its previous condition).
- A *leverage point* occurs when a targeted intervention results in a significant change in the behavior of the system. For green infrastructure, this implies that a solution that addresses multiple problems and "leverages" improvement throughout a system can be more effective than one dealing with a problem in isolation (e.g., maintaining or restoring the natural hydrologic processes of a river and floodplain system rather than piecemeal construction of flood protection devices).
- *Resilience* is the ability of a system to recover from or adapt to disturbance or change. (See Walker and Salt 2006.) First developed by ecologists to help understand the dynamics of natural ecosystems, this concept has broad implications for planning practice. For example, a city with a diverse economic base is less vulnerable to a sudden economic downturn than one that relies on a single large employer or industry cluster, just as a diverse plant community is more resistant to insects and disease than a monoculture.

Figure 16.1 conceptualizes how green infrastructure operates as part of a hierarchy of nested systems, each of which contains stocks of assets held together by interconnections (flows and interactions between systems). In this diagram, green and gray infrastructure are shown as subsystems that together make up the urban landscape. Landscape is a system that bridges multiple levels of scale across higher-level systems: environment, community, and economy.

Flows of resources (e.g., energy, materials, and information) are drawn from the higher-level systems into interactions that generate the various stocks of assets that make up the landscape (green infrastructure components such as trees and

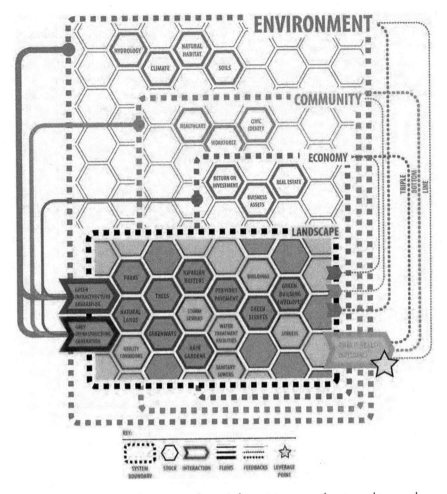

Figure 16.1 (2.6 in original) Green and gray infrastructure are subsystems that together make up the urban landscape.

Source: David Witham, WRT

rain gardens; gray infrastructure components such as buildings and streets). While for diagrammatic purposes, green and gray infrastructure are shown as separate, interlocking systems, in reality they can overlap in design elements such as green buildings and green streets.

Figure 16.1 shows the generation of green and gray infrastructure as parallel processes. Systems at similar (parallel) levels will often compete for limited resources (e.g., funding from the economic system), but cooperation is also possible. Systems thinking can help identify opportunities for cooperation (i.e., sharing of resources) rather than competition among parallel systems.

The green and gray infrastructure assets in the urban landscape produce feedback loops that have positive or negative impacts on higher-level systems. Public health is shown as a leverage point that can yield triple-bottom-line improvement in the community, economy, and environment systems. This underscores the potential of connecting green infrastructure to public health.

Application of the three key concepts—the "triple bottom line" of sustainability, the connection to public health, and systems thinking—can enrich the practice of green infrastructure. Chapter 24 further explores how they can be used to inform the work of urban planners, landscape architects, engineers, and others involved in planning and design of green infrastructure.

[. . .]

NOTE

1. Frank, Engelke, and Schmid (2003) differentiate between "recreational" and "utilitarian" exercise: "Recreational forms of exercise are those undertaken for discretionary reasons on someone's leisure time. . . . Utilitarian forms of physical activity are those that are worked into one's daily habits" (56–88). They hold that utilitarian physical activity (e.g., walking or biking to work or to shop) is likely to more significantly affect a person's health than recreational activity.

REFERENCES

Aronson, Daniel. 1996–1998. "Introduction to Systems Thinking." Available at www. thinking.net/Systems_Thinking/Intro_to_ST/intro_to_st.html.

Benedict, Mark, and Ed McMahon. 2006. *Green Infrastructure: Linking Landscapes and Communities*. Washington, D.C.: Island Press.

Berman, Marc G., John Jonides, and Stephen Kaplan. 2008. "The Cognitive Benefits of Interacting with Nature." *Psychological Science* 19(12).

Campos. 2009. *The Great Allegheny Passage Economic Impact Study (2007–2008)*. Prepared for the Progress Fund's Trail Town Program, Laurel Highlands Visitors Bureau, and Allegheny Trail Alliance. August 7. Available at www.atatrail.org/docs/ GAPeconomicImpactStudy200809.pdf.

Dunn, Alexandra Dapolita. 2010. *Siting Green Infrastructure: Legal and Policy Solutions to Alleviate Urban Poverty and Promote Healthy Communities*. Pace University Law Faculty Publications Paper no. 559. New York: Pace University.

Economy League of Greater Philadelphia et al. 2011. *Return on Environment: The Economic Value of Protected Open Space in Southeastern Pennsylvania*. November. Available at http://economyleague.org/files/Protected_Open_Space_SEPA_2-11.pdf.

Firehock, Karen. 2010. "A Short History of the Term Green Infrastructure and Selected Literature." January. A vailable at www.gicinc.org/PDFs/GI%20History.pdf.

Florida Greenways Commission. 1994. *Creating a Statewide Greenways System: for People . . . for Wildlife . . . for Florida*. Report to the governor.

Heisler, G. M. 1986. "Energy Savings with Trees." *Journal of Arboriculture* 12(5): 113–25.

Kaplan, Stephen. 1995. "The Restorative Benefits of Nature: Toward an Integrative Framework." *Journal of Environmental Psychology* 15.

Kuo, F. E., and W. C. Sullivan. 2001a. "Aggression and Violence in the Inner City: Effects of Environment vs. Mental Fatigue." *Environment and Behavior* 33(4): 543–71.

———. 2001b. "Environment and Crime in the Inner City: Does Vegetation Reduce Crime?" *Environment and Behavior* 33(3): 343–67.

Louv, Richard. 2011. *The Nature Principle*. Chapel Hill, N.C.: Algonquin Books.

Meadows, Donella H. 2008. *Thinking in Systems: A Primer*, ed. Diana Wright. White River Junction, Vt.: Chelsea Green.

Morris, Marya, ed. 2006. *Integrating Planning and Public Health: Tools and Strategies to Create Healthy Places*. PAS Report no. 539/540. Chicago: American Planning Association.

Neelay, D., ed. 1988. *Valuation of Landscape Trees, Shrubs, and Other Plants*, 7th ed. Council of Tree and Landscape Appraisers, International Society of Arboriculture.

Simpson, J. R., and E. G. McPherson. 1996. "Potential of Tree Shade for Reducing Residential Energy Use in California." *Journal of Arboriculture* 22(1): 10–18.

Ulrich, R. 1984. "View through Window May Influence Recovery from Surgery." *Science* 224: 420–21.

Walker, Brian, and David Salt. 2006. *Resilience Thinking: Sustaining Ecosystems and People in a Changing World*. Washington, D.C.: Island Press.

Wolf, K. L. 1998. "Trees in Business Districts: Positive Effects on Consumer Behavior!" Fact Sheet no. 5. Seattle: University of Washington, College of Forest Resources, Center for Urban Horticulture.

———. 1999. "Nature and Commerce: Human Ecology in Business Districts." In *Building Cities of Green: Proceedings of the Ninth National Urban Forest Conference*, ed. C. Kollin. Washington, D.C.: American Forests.

17 The Green Infrastructure Transect

An Organizational Framework for Mainstreaming Adaptation Planning Policies

Yaser Abunnasr and Elisabeth M. Hamin Infield

EDITOR'S INTRODUCTION

In the previous article, Rouse and Bunster-Ossa established green infrastructure as a broad, multi-scale approach to planning how people and natural spaces can support each other. We now build on this concept to explore its implementation, as green infrastructure (like any design strategy) should be context-dependent and adaptable to different settings. Understanding how GI can be applied to an array of development circumstances will help integration into mainstream planning practice.

Some readers may be familiar with the New Urbanist idea of 'urban transects': a spectrum of the character and intensity of development, with zones ranging from natural environments to dense urban cores. These zones specify a suitable "mix of uses, transportation options, and traditional architectural styles and housing diversity", but do not include the types and purposes of green infrastructure appropriate to each zone. The Green Infrastructure Transect fills this gap.

The GI Transect uses zones similar to the urban transect—coastal (if present), urban core, urban, transition (the middle ground), suburban, and peri-urban—to determine which elements of green infrastructure are most suitable to each zone. To implement the concept and plan for green infrastructure, each zone within an area of study is mapped, and green infrastructure relevant to each zone is assessed against several criteria (most notably, relevant climate impacts and vulnerabilities) to determine its suitability. To ensure that the existing strengths of the area are

considered, the green infrastructure already present in each zone is also characterized, with attention paid both to public GI (parks, for example) and private
GI (residential backyards, which can perform many ecosystem functions). These
assessments are then analyzed to produce recommendations, which can include
new forms of GI or protections and expansions of existing green infrastructure.
We are particularly interested in recommendations that make places more resilient
to climate change, a key function of green infrastructure.

Similar to Rouse and Bunster-Ossa, we argue that success in GI planning
depends on horizontal integration (coordination between zones and types of green
infrastructure) and vertical integration (coordination across spatial scales, from
neighborhood to city to region). To explore how these principles could take effect
in real settings, we use a case study of the Boston metropolitan area, and find that
the transect could be an effective climate adaptation strategy.

(2012) THE GREEN INFRASTRUCTURE TRANSECT: AN ORGANIZATIONAL FRAMEWORK FOR MAINSTREAMING ADAPTATION PLANNING POLICIES

INTRODUCTION

One of the primary principles of green infrastructure (GI) planning is to reconnect
communities in urban regions to natural environments (Lewis 1964; McHarg
1969; Noss and Harris 1986; Benedict and McMahon 2002, 2006; Jongman
1995; Jongman et al. 2004; Fábos 2004). This is achieved through practices
within and around cities that identify, protect, and create spatial elements that
provide ecosystem services that communities depend on (Benedict and McMahon
2006; Forman 2008). Development of community parks and recreation trails,
greenways, ecological networks, restored streams, natural reserves, gardens, engineered natural systems, green roofs and facades, and conserved agricultural land
are all within the scope of GI. Furthermore, the same spatial areas also provide
urban cooling, stormwater management, floodwater storage, flora and fauna
habitat, and biking and walking routes. All of these urban functions must be
increased to build resilience to climate change. By connecting ecosystem benefits
to community well-being (Nassauer 2006) and adaptation needs, GI planning
may be mainstreamed to become an integral part of adaptation planning policies.

A key advantage of the GI approach to adaptation is that it is already becoming an accepted practice (Benedict and McMahon 2002; Ahern 2008). GI has
become part of current sustainable planning and design practices in many cities
(EPA 2011; Newman and Jennings 2008; Farr 2008). These initiatives function at
multiple scales to improve urban living conditions. These may include retention
ponds and swales (at the parcel scale), green streets and parks (at the neighborhood scale), increased tree canopies (at the urban scale), and greenways (at the
regional scale). As an accepted practice, GI is also a 'no-regrets approach' (Bedsworth and Hanak 2010) when considered as an adaptation measure. As we move
into the future, investment in GI policies will prove to be beneficial regardless
of whether climate change scenarios materialize. For example, urban greening

results in cleaner air and cooler temperatures that would address current problems (pollution and urban island heat effect) as well as ameliorate future increasing temperatures. As a result, fairly minor changes to the technical specifications for GI could, quite effectively, bring adaptation into mainstream practice. As GI is implemented to accommodate increased flooding, ameliorate rising temperatures, or address the rise in sea levels, communities can take advantage of the cultural, social, and health benefits of cleaner and greener environments, regardless of the future magnitude of climate change impacts. Furthermore, the same characteristics that qualify GI as a spatial adaptation tool within urban regions (notably GI's multifunctional and multi-scalar properties) make it difficult to mainstream GI into adaptation planning. These characteristics create problems in organizing intervention areas, jurisdictional coordination and implementation, and tradeoffs in economic benefits and urban quality.

THE GREEN INFRASTRUCTURE TRANSECT

To address these problems, we propose the green infrastructure transect (GI transect) as a framework to utilize GI as an adaptation policy and to mainstream adaptation into current planning practices. The GI transect is a conceptual tool that integrates GI measures across varying urban contexts and across planning scales. It builds on transect concepts from ecology, landscape planning, and urban planning. We specifically use the urban transect as a stepping stone to develop this framework.

The urban transect (Duany and Talen 2002) was devised as an urban planning tool to plan and design physical environments according to peoples' preferences of where to live and work. The urban transect identifies as units of study six zones (urban core, urban center, general urban, suburban, rural, and natural) with distinct physical boundaries. These zones form a planning model applicable within many urban contexts. The zones provide the basis for a neighborhood structure based on walkable streets, mix of uses, transportation options, and traditional architectural styles and housing diversity. The strength of the urban transect is in describing the appropriate built forms and identifying interventions within each urban zone in a simple and comprehensible manner. The concept falls short of specifying the respective open spaces and natural functions that respond to the specific urban contexts and needs within each transect zone.

In contrast, the natural transect used by ecologists and biologists is a scientific method of assessment of habitat. It is based on the fundamental principles of relationships and interdependencies between ecozones and used to assess the physical, biological, and natural processes within and across ecozones. Contrary to the urban transect, it does not specify distinct spatial zones. Rather, the characteristics of different local ecosystems define different habitat zones and the relationship between them. This same principle is later adopted within landscape and regional planning to assess and understand relationships between land and natural and human systems in order to plan and manage natural resources within urban regions (McHarg 1969; Picket 2004; Berger 2006).

Overall, the GI transect combines the general principles of urban and natural transects into a single assessment model. The primary characteristics are three: (1) the simultaneous consideration of human and natural systems as a mutual cause-and-effect relationship affecting the functional capability of GI (pervious and impervious surfaces as indicators), (2) the designation of urban zones as unique spatial contexts that may impact the adaptive capacity of communities within, and (3) the explicit consideration that GI is an interconnected system that transcends administrative and political boundaries.

This interconnectedness of GI serves as an impetus and analogy to integrate adaptation policies across the GI zones, increasing the local capacity for adaption. We qualify this level of policy integration as 'horizontal integration'. The term is meant to generate targeted GI recommendations specific to each GI zone and coordinate them across boundaries (within scales). This is achieved by mapping and assessing each GI zone against a set of criteria to be able to recommend targeted GI measures. Six GI zones are identified and are intended to represent an alternative model (to the urban transect) of contemporary urban regions. These include coastal (if present), urban core, urban, transition (the middle ground), suburban, and peri-urban zones. In addition, we use the following criteria to assess each GI zone: vulnerability assessment using spatial data (physical and social), identifying the primary climate change impact based on spatial configuration and character, identifying the spatial character of each GI zone, determining the spatial configuration of pervious and impervious surfaces (existing and potential GI), determining GI typology relevant to each zone, and recommending appropriate GI measures within each GI zone (Figure 17.1). The sequential process of assessment begins with vulnerability assessment and concludes with recommendations providing a specific policy focus to local communities for adaptation and the possible responses through GI.

Furthermore, several existing GI recommendations relevant to adaptation policies call for the protection of forest stands and wetlands or increasing tree canopy or engineering swales and rain garden systems. These GI spatial elements are not restricted to regional, city, town, or property boundaries, as they are subject to conditions (i.e. topography, geology, and hydrology) beyond the control of governing bodies. Therefore, analysis and assessment should consider recommendations within each zone and the outward extensions of GI. By mapping adjacent spatial configurations, horizontal integration is attained. This enhances the adaptation capacity of local communities through coordination of policies. Yet, it does not account for coordination across jurisdictional boundaries and planning scales necessary for regional resiliency.

Developing a network of GI increases the resiliency of a region. It provides alternative evacuation routes, species migration routes, CO_2 sinks, floodwater storage, buffer zones against rising sea water, and reduction in regional temperatures. To achieve a coordinated regional network requires the integration of planning scales (neighborhood, urban, regional) into a single regional planning framework providing a platform for communication and coordination across jurisdictions. We term this integration across scales as 'vertical integration'.

Vertical integration provides the means to respond to the multi-scalar and hierarchal nature of GI by considering current planning processes. GI networks are hierarchal especially when planned within urban contexts. When considering GI for stormwater management, connectivity of GI elements should be considered across the hierarchy of urban planning scales (street or parcel neighborhood, city,

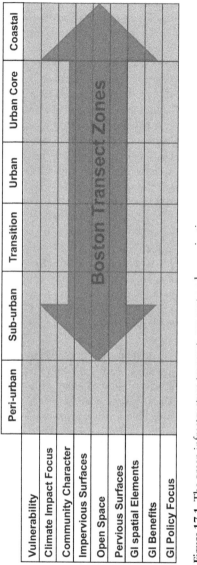

Figure 17.1 The green infrastructure transect: concept and organization.

and urban region) (Kato 2010). For example [. . .], several streets with bioswales and retention ponds in residential yards at the neighborhood scale can constitute a green corridor at the city scale, which in turn with city parks, can be part of a regional park system (Jim and Chen 2003; Girling and Kellett 2005). But each individual GI element (parcel to regional scales) is planned and implemented differently, depending on the context, size, and planning process. Vertical integration provides a way to unify these processes under a hierarchal single framework that leads to a regional vision.

Integration across scales is necessary to increase the adaptive capacity at both the regional and local levels. The adaptive planning meta-model developed by Kato (2010), for a planning framework to manage GI, is an example of such a process. It is an iterative process designed for the US context. Similar to the GI hierarchy, neighborhood plans that are participatory in nature form the basis of an urban plan. The sum of the several urban plans could define a vision for a region. In the US context, a bottom-up approach (participatory) could lead to a regional vision. The reverse (top-down planning) may also hold true when considered within other planning and administrative contexts. Regardless of whether the vision (top-down) or local planning (bottom-up) comes first, the intention here is to advocate for a two-way and iterative approach that includes both and provides the flexibility and adaptability to respond as circumstances arise and change.

[. . .]

The underlying concepts behind the GI transect point to the spatial, contextual, and administrative interdependencies governing mainstreaming adaptation planning. Vertical and horizontal integration are the primary elements of the GI transect that integrate local and regional plans into a single and flexible adaptation planning framework. To make these ideas concrete, we apply the three-step approach of vulnerability assessment, characterization of existing GI, and GI policies recommendations to the Boston metropolitan region.

BOSTON METROPOLITAN REGION

The metropolitan region of Boston occupies the eastern shoreline of the state of Massachusetts in the USA. It covers a land area of approximately 12,000 km^2, housing 4.5 million people with an average density of 366 persons per square kilometer (Census Bureau 2010). The metropolitan region incorporates 120 towns and eight regional jurisdictions within its boundary (Census Bureau 2010). It is characterized by an urban core (Boston) as the center of governance, business, and transportation. From the urban core to the periphery, residential sprawl of varying densities along transportation corridors and around commercial centers is interspersed by forest, wetlands, river basins, and, to lesser extent, agricultural land [. . .]. At the planning level, the state of Massachusetts (MA) has adopted and is implementing smart growth principles to control development and preserve natural and cultural assets. Part of the smart growth initiative is the Climate Action Plan (CAP 2010). The plan is focused on mitigation measures to reduce emissions from buildings, transportation, waste management, and land use. In the

2010 update of the plan, recommendations for adaptation were included as part of addressing causes and effects of climate change.

The NECIA (2007) report on climate change impacts within the New England region shows that Massachusetts climate will resemble the southern states of the Eastern Coast of the USA. Taking the year 2000 as the baseline, the report demonstrates that the metropolitan region of Boston will experience increase in temperatures by 4–7°C in the winter and 3–8°C in the summer, rising sea level of 25–60 cm, and increased precipitation by 20–30%. To address these impacts, the City of Boston identified guidelines for adaptation planning (CAP 2010) that include, in addition to economic and social measures, spatial measures that focus on GI.

The adaptation recommendations for Boston (CAP 2010) set priorities and define the required information and planning priorities and approaches. Many of the 13 recommendations focus on GI principles such as greening the city, green roofs, sustainable water management, and protection and increase of large tracts of vegetated surfaces. In addition, planning cross-jurisdictions and scales is identified as a priority to increase the adaptive capacity of the urban region.

[. . .]

In the process of transforming these adaptation recommendations into actions, we apply the GI transect to assess the applicability of the multi-tiered organizational framework to Boston. In the assessment stage, we map vulnerability, climate change impacts, and the physical environment across the GI zones (Figure 17.2). Vulnerability is mapped using the following spatial data layers from the state's MassGIS geographic information system: topography, open space, roads, location within the watershed, and socio-economic data for each location. Climate impact is mapped according to the NECIA (2007) report showing the magnitude and focus within each zone. Aerial images are used to map the urban character identifying the physical environment of work and housing.

We found that the coastal zone is predominantly impacted by rising sea level, the urban to transition zones are affected by a high magnitude of increased temperatures and flooding, and the peripheral zones are impacted, at a lower magnitude, by temperature rise and flooding. The exposure to physical risks is further exacerbated by the effect of the urban heat island (UHI) effect and the gradation of impervious and pervious surfaces across the GI transect. The compounded impacts of climate change and the physical characteristics of the urban region of Boston are grounds to consider different adaptation planning focuses for communities across the GI transect. To be able to devise and recommend GI policies within existing pervious surfaces, which address the variation of vulnerability, we map the existing distribution of GI across the zones.

To map the spatial distribution of GI across the zones, we also use MassGIS data. We overlay the following layers: impervious surfaces, digital terrain, open space layers (public domain), waterways, forests, roads, and administrative boundaries.

[. . .]

We find that open space and unbuilt land increases in area as we move towards the periphery [. . .]. What significantly increases, and is not usually included in the inventory of GI, are unbuilt spaces within the private domain (yards, gardens, and school grounds). Since ecosystem benefits are not bounded by administrative

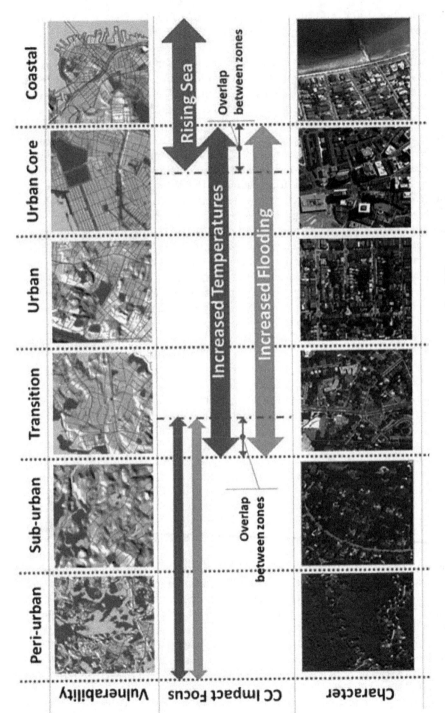

Figure 17.2 Green infrastructure transect application to Boston region, step one: vulnerability assessment.

limits (Fábos 2004) and increase proportionally with GI area, it is critical to ensure that GI policies simultaneously address land within the private and public domains.

The final step is to identify and recommend appropriate GI policies across the GI transect zones. We distinguish clear complementarities between GI benefits, community needs, and vulnerability requirements. We list the typologies of GI elements that already exist within each zone, and those that could potentially be introduced or enhanced. Ecosystem benefits that are complementary to community needs and climate impacts are also listed, in accordance with the spatial typology. By overlaying information from steps one and two, we begin to identify the potential GI policies. For example, the coastal area will benefit from planned retreat—where vulnerable built areas across the coast may gradually be transformed into landscapes for recreation. The resulting coastal landscapes become non-structural defenses incorporated as recreational and ecological landscape features. Therefore, the policy here would focus on preserving and intensifying all existing GI elements and to define a long-term plan to allow time for legal procedures and financial compensation to take place for the coastal zone transformation. Within the urban zone of the GI transect, policies should address increased temperatures (compounded by UHI) and retention of water runoff. Existing parks and open space, green roofs, green facades, and street planting are spatial elements that should be increased through revisions to building regulations, open space plans, and environmental policies. Through the Biotope Area factor, the city of Berlin is an example where zoning and financial incentives result in an increase in tree canopy and 'at-the-source' water management. Towards the periphery, policies that enhance connectivity and preserve, conserve, and increase forests, large parks, natural reserves, and biospheres are integral for runoff storage, species migration, temperature control, and water infiltration to ensure ecosystem services at the regional scale.

To ensure consistency across local GI policies with the Boston region, vertical and horizontal integration of policies [. . .] is utilized to coordinate and implement planning projects across town jurisdictions. Planning in Massachusetts is predominantly participatory and happens at the local (town) scale. This means that parcel- and neighborhood-scale plans should build up to form an overall town plan that explicitly considers GI measures for adaptation. The open space plans that are mandatory to US towns could be extended beyond recreation to incorporate ecological and adaptation plans. Town plans, then, need to build the overall regional vision. This may be achieved by expanding the mandate of regional planning bodies beyond transportation and economic development towards a more active role to coordinate and integrate local plans. Even more, regional bodies should be responsible to monitor and develop regional climate projections that help in providing the vision for regional and local adaptation plans. A hierarchal organizational structure that works in both directions (from local to regional or from regional to local) ensures that all constituents and measures serve an intended local role within a larger regional approach. The proposed structure that we have presented may be a first step in integrating local adaptation planning across scales and jurisdictions using current and accepted knowledge.

CONCLUSION

Adaptation policies run the risk of a piecemeal, systematized approach. It is easy to prescribe a green roof here and a rain garden there and hope that they will add up to a proper systematic approach. However, the challenges of adaptation are too significant for this to be effective. Framing GI planning through the transect approach provides a way to conceptualize a whole system of GI spatial elements, identify coming climate challenges, and plan to integrate local policies at site scale with adaptation needs at the neighborhood, city, and regional scales. In this chapter, we briefly used Boston as a case study to demonstrate how the GI transect may be applied and how it can assist in interpreting and framing overall GI for adaptation. We conclude that GI will be an effective adaptation policy when it is matched to the physical character of urban environments (urban, suburban, and rural) and the needs of communities they are intended to serve. This approach is a first step in mainstreaming adaptation planning using current GI practices.

REFERENCES

Ahern, J. (2008). Green infrastructure for cities: The spatial dimension. In V. Novotny & P. Brown (Eds.), *Cities of the future* (p. 2). London: IWA Publishing.

Bedsworth, L. W., & Hanak, E. (2010). Adaptation to climate change: A review of challenges and tradeoffs in six areas. *JAPA, 76*(4), 477–495.

Benedict, M. A., & McMahon, M. T. (2002). *Green infrastructure: Smart conservation for the 21st century. Renewable Resources Journal, 20,* 12–17.

Benedict, M. A., & McMahon, M. T. (2006). *Green infrastructure: Linking landscape and communities.* Washington, DC: Island Press.

Berger, A. (2006). *Drosscape: Wasting land in urban America.* New York: Princeton Architectural Press.

CAP. (2010). *The city of Boston's climate action plan.* City of Boston. December 2007. http://www.abettercity.org/environment/bostoncap.html. Accessed 18 June 2011.

Duany, A., & Talen, E. (2002). Transect planning. *Journal of American Planning Association, 68*(3), 245–266.

EPA. (2011). US Environmental Protection Agency. http://www.epa.gov/. Accessed 20 June 2011.

Fábos, J. G. (2004). Greenway planning in the United States: Its origins and recent case studies. *Landscape and Urban Planning, 68,* 321–342.

Farr, D. (2008). *Sustainable urbanism: Urban design with nature.* Hoboken: Wiley.

Forman, R. T. T. (2008). *Urban regions: Ecology and planning beyond the city.* Cambridge: Cambridge University Press.

Girling, C., & Kellett, R. (2005). *Skinny streets and green neighborhoods: Design for environment and community.* Washington, DC: Island Press.

Jim, C. Y., & Chen, S. S. (2003). Comprehensive greenspace planning based on landscape ecology principles in compact Nanjing city, China. *Landscape and Urban Planning, 65*(3), 95–116.

Jongman, R. H. G., Külvik, M., & Kristiansen, I. (2004). European ecological networks and greenways. *Landscape and Urban Planning, 68,* 305–319.

Kato, S. (2010). *Green space conservation planning framework for urban regions based on a forest bird-habitat relationship study and the resilience thinking.* Ph.D. dissertation, Umass, Amherst, AAT 3409604.

Lewis, P. H., Jr. (1964). Quality corridors for Wisconsin. *Landscape Architecture, 54,* 100–107.

McHarg, I. (1969). *Design with nature.* Garden City: The Natural History Press.

Nassauer, J. (2006). Landscape planning and conservation biology: Systems thinking revisited. *Conservation Biology, 20,* 677–678.

NECIA. (2007). *Confronting climate change in the U.S. Northeast: Science, impacts, and solutions: A report of the Northeast climate impacts assessment.* Union of Concerned Scientists. http://www.climatechoices.org/ne/resources ne/nereport.html. Accessed 19 June 2011.

Newman, P., & Jennings, I. (2008). *Cities as sustainable ecosystems: Principles and practices.* Washington, DC: Island Press.

Noss, R. F., & Harris, L. D. (1986). Nodes, networks, and mums: Preserving diversity at all scales. *Environmental Management, 10*(3), 299–309.

Pickett, S. T. A., Cadenasso, M. L., & Grove, J. M. (2004). Resilient cities: Meaning, models, and metaphor for integrating the ecological, socio-economic, and planning realms. *Landscape and Urban Planning, 69*(4), 369–384.

United States Census Bureau, Data Section, http://2010.census.gov/2010census/. Accessed 18 June 2011.

18 Adapting Cities for Climate Change

The Role of the Green Infrastructure

Susannah E. Gill, John F. Handley,
Adrian R. Ennos and Stephan Pauleit

EDITOR'S INTRODUCTION

Green infrastructure strategies for improving the places we live and work, like those covered in the previous articles of this section, are a great stride ahead of the low density, car-centered policies of the twentieth century. However, how do we know if these new (or old, depending on perspective), nature-based designs are effective? What services do they really provide, and how can we measure them? How much green infrastructure do we need to make a difference against climate change? These questions form the focus of this article.

Focusing on Britain, and the Greater Manchester area specifically, the authors cover regional climate change projections before examining the potential adaptation impact of green infrastructure. They begin by mapping various 'urban morphologies', or UMTs—distinct categories of land use and physical form, related to the urban transect but differentiated by its focus on usage over form—and surface covers. They find that 60 per cent of Greater Manchester is urbanized, half of which is residential. However, nearly 60 per cent of the total urban area still consists of vegetated or water surfaces, which increase urban cooling through evaporation. Significantly, 40 per cent of these surfaces occur in residential areas, highlighting the importance of including small, private spaces in green infrastructure planning.

The article then moves on to modelling the impact of increasing green infrastructure on climate impacts. Strikingly, results determined that a 10% increase in green space "kept maximum surface temperatures at or below 1961–1990 baseline levels" until projected 2080s high-emissions climate conditions. Conversely, removing 10% of the area's green space increased temperatures by 7–8.2% by the 2080s.

Further, the authors advise a greater focus on GI that includes trees and water surfaces, given that grass loses its cooling capacity if it dries out during droughts. Mature trees are especially important, as their shade was found to cool surface temperatures by as much as 15.6°C. The article also explores a key difference between green space in general and GI designed specifically for stormwater management (bioswales, retention ponds, etc), noting that conventional green space may not always be capable of mitigating runoff, but the latter has a significant role to play in doing so.

When promoting, planning and implementing green infrastructure, planners and designers must be knowledgeable and realistic about the degree of climate adaptation that can be achieved. This will help keep the expectations of policymakers and the public reasonable, which is key to long-term support for the concept. Remaining based in evidence of the kind found in this article is therefore critical to broadening green infrastructure's role in responding to climate change.

Susannah E. Gill was at the Centre for Urban Regional Ecology (CURE) in the University of Manchester, United Kingdom. John F. Handley is professor at the University of Manchester, United Kingdom. Adrian R. Ennos is professor of ecology and biomechanics at the University of Hull, United Kingdom. Stephan Pauleit is the Chair for Strategic Landscape Planning and Management Department at the Technische Universität München, Germany.

ADAPTING CITIES FOR CLIMATE CHANGE: THE ROLE OF THE GREEN INFRASTRUCTURE

INTRODUCTION

Much of the emphasis in planning for climate change is, quite properly, focused on reducing or mitigating greenhouse gas emissions. Present day emissions will impact on the severity of climate change in future years (Hulme et al., 2002). However, climate change is already with us. The World Wide Fund for Nature, for example, has recently drawn attention to the significant warming of capital cities across Europe (WWF, 2005). Due to the long shelf-life of carbon dioxide in the atmosphere, much of the climate change over the next 30–40 years has already been determined by historic emissions (Hulme et al., 2002). Thus, there is a need to prepare for climate change that will occur, whatever the trajectory of future greenhouse gas emissions.

[. . .]

In 1991, 90 per cent of people in Great Britain lived in urban areas (Denham and White, 1998), and it is here that climate change impacts will be felt. Urban areas have distinctive biophysical features in comparison with surrounding rural areas (Bridgman et al., 1995). For example, energy exchanges are modified to create an urban heat island, where air temperatures may be several degrees warmer than in the countryside (Wilby, 2003; Graves et al., 2001). The magnitude of the urban heat island effect varies in time and space as a result of meteorological, locational and urban characteristics (Oke, 1987). Hydrological processes are also altered such that there is an increase in the rate and volume of surface runoff of rainwater (Mansell, 2003; Whitford et al., 2001).

Such biophysical changes are, in part, a result of the altered surface cover of the urban area (Whitford et al., 2001). Urbanization replaces vegetated surfaces, which provide shading, evaporative cooling, rainwater interception and storage and infiltration functions, with impervious built surfaces. However, urban green spaces provide areas within the built environment where such processes can take place (Whitford et al., 2001). These ecosystem services (Daily, 1997) provided by urban green space are often overlooked and undervalued. For example, trees are felled for the perceived threat they pose near highways and buildings (Biddle, 1998), infill development takes place on former gardens, front gardens are paved over to provide parking spaces for cars and biodiverse urban 'wasteland' is earmarked for redevelopment (e.g. Duckworth, 2005; GLA, 2005; Pauleit et al., 2005).

In a changing climate, the functionality provided by urban green space becomes increasingly important. In the UK, climate change scenarios (UKCIP02) suggest average annual temperatures may increase by between 1°C and 5°C by the 2080s, with summer temperatures expected to increase more than winter temperatures. There will also be a change in the seasonality of precipitation, with winters up to 30 per cent wetter by the 2080s and summers up to 50 per cent drier. These figures are dependent on both the region and emissions scenario (Hulme et al., 2002). Precipitation intensity also increases, especially in winter, and the number of very hot days increases, especially in summer and autumn (Hulme et al., 2002). It should be noted that these climate change scenarios do not take urban surfaces into account. There is likely to be significant urban warming over and above that expected for rural areas (Wilby and Perry, 2006; Wilby, 2003).

Climate change will impact the urban environment, and these impacts will be felt by both people and the built infrastructure. For example, it is estimated that the European summer heat wave in 2003 claimed 35,000 lives (Larsen, 2003). Incidents of flooding also result in both physical and psychological illnesses (e.g. Reacher et al., 2004; Baxter et al., 2002; Shackley et al., 2001). In addition, buildings are vulnerable to flooding depending on their location (Graves and Phillipson, 2000).

The biophysical features of green space in urban areas, through the provision of cooler microclimates and reduction of surface water runoff, therefore offer potential to help adapt cities for climate change. However, little is known about the quantity and quality of green space required. The green infrastructure is 'an interconnected network of green space that conserves natural ecosystem values and functions and provides associated benefits to human populations' (Benedict and McMahon, 2002, p. 12). The green infrastructure should operate at all spatial scales from urban centres to the surrounding countryside (URBED, 2004).

The aim of this paper is to explore the potential of green infrastructure in adapting cities for climate change. This will be achieved through a characterization of the case study site, and quantifying its environmental functions under both current and future climate scenarios, as well as with differing patterns of green cover.

CASE STUDY SITE

Greater Manchester, selected as the case study site, is representative of a large conurbation (population 2.5 million) in Britain and Northern Europe. The Metropolitan County of Greater Manchester, located in northwest England, is administered
by ten local authorities: Bolton, Bury, Manchester, Oldham, Rochdale, Salford,
Stockport, Tameside, Trafford and Wigan. There is some coordination at the conurbation level through the Association of Greater Manchester Authorities, but
planning powers at the larger scale are vested in the North West Regional Assembly (NWRA). The NWRA prepares a Regional Spatial Strategy (NWRA, 2006),
which is the broad planning framework for the region, whilst the municipalities
each prepare a Local Development Framework which provides a more detailed
template for development.

Greater Manchester covers an area of approximately 1300 km^2 and has developed on a river basin flanked by the Pennine hills. The altitudinal range is between
10 m and 540 m above sea level. Greater Manchester offers sufficient size for full
expression of urban environmental character, contrasting soil types, a range of
neighbourhood and land use types (including restructuring and urban extension
areas with substantial scope for climate change adaptation), as well as a range of
built forms.

[. . .]

URBAN CHARACTERIZATION

The first stage of the research was to characterize the urban environment. This
involved the mapping of urban morphology types (UMTs) (LUC, 1993) followed
by a surface cover analysis. The UMTs effectively serve as integrating spatial units
linking human activities and natural processes. The assumption is that UMTs have
characteristic physical features and are distinctive according to the human activities that they accommodate (i.e. land uses). Greater Manchester was stratified
into 29 distinctive UMTs, digitized in ArcView GIS from 1997 aerial photographs
(resolution: 0.25 m, source: Cities Revealed). These were grouped into 12 primary
UMT categories.

[. . .]

Some 506 km^2, or just under 40 per cent, of Greater Manchester is farmland,
with the remaining 60 per cent (793 km^2) representing the 'urbanized' area. Residential areas account for just under half of the urbanized area, or 29 per cent of
Greater Manchester, and can thus be viewed from a landscape ecology perspective
as the 'matrix' representing the dominant landscape category in the urban mosaic
(Forman and Godron, 1986).

Whilst the UMT categories provide an initial indication of where patches of
green may be expected, e.g. in formal and informal open spaces, and where green
corridors may be found, e.g. alongside roads, railways, rivers and canals, they do
not reveal the extent of green cover within the built matrix of the conurbation.
Thus, the surface cover of each of the 29 UMT categories was then estimated by
aerial photograph interpretation of random points (Akbari et al., 2003). This is

very important as the surface cover affects the environmental performance of the conurbation (Pauleit et al., 2005; Nowak et al., 2001; Whitford et al., 2001; Pauleit and Duhme, 2000). Nine surface cover types were used: building, other impervious, tree, shrub, mown grass, rough grass, cultivated, water and bare soil/ gravel.

[. . .]

The results indicate that on average 72 per cent of Greater Manchester, or 59 per cent of the 'urbanized' area, consists of evapotranspiring (i.e. vegetated and water) surfaces. All the UMT categories have, on average, more than 20 per cent evapotranspiring surfaces. However, there is considerable variation across the UMTs. Town centres have the lowest evapotranspiring cover of 20 per cent compared to woodlands with the highest cover of 98 per cent. In general, the proportion of tree cover is fairly low, covering on average 12 per cent over Greater Manchester and 16 per cent in 'urbanized' Greater Manchester. Whilst the woodland UMT category has 70 per cent trees, all other UMTs have below 30 per cent tree cover. Town centres have a tree cover of 5 per cent.

Particular attention must be given to the surface cover in residential areas, as these cover almost half of 'urbanized' Greater Manchester and therefore have a great impact on the environmental performance of the conurbation. Approximately 40 per cent of all the evapotranspiring surfaces in 'urbanized' Greater Manchester occur in residential areas, with medium-density residential areas accounting for the majority of such surfaces. The three types of residential area have different surface covers from each other. In high-density residential areas, built surfaces (i.e. building and other impervious surfaces) cover about two-thirds of the area, compared to about half in medium-density areas and one-third in low-density areas. Tree cover is 26 per cent in low-density areas, 13 per cent in medium-density areas, and 7 per cent in high-density areas.

QUANTIFYING THE ENVIRONMENTAL FUNCTIONS

The UMTs, with their distinctive surface covers, formed one of the inputs into energy exchange and surface runoff models (Whitford et al., 2001). The energy exchange model has maximum surface temperature as its output and is based on an energy balance equation (Whitford et al., 2001; Tso et al., 1990, 1991). The warming of the urban environment in summer is an important issue because of its implications for human comfort and wellbeing (e.g. Svensson and Eliasson, 2002; Eliasson, 2000). Whilst air temperature provides a simple estimator of human thermal comfort, it is less reliable outdoors owing to the variability of other factors such as humidity, radiation, wind and precipitation (Brown and Gillespie, 1995). In practice, the mean radiant temperature, which in essence is a measure of the combined effect of surface temperatures within a space, is a significant factor in determining human comfort, especially on hot days with little wind (Matzarakis et al., 1999). Whitford et al. (2001) therefore considered surface temperature to be an effective indicator for energy exchange in the urban environment. As well as requiring input of the proportional area covered by built and evapotranspiring (i.e. all vegetation and water) surfaces, the model also requires a building mass per unit of land, and various meteorological parameters including air temperature.

The surface runoff model uses the curve number approach of the US Soil Conservation Service (Whitford et al., 2001; USDA Natural Resources Conservation Service, 1986). Again, surface cover is required as an input along with precipitation, antecedent moisture conditions and hydrologic soil type.

[. . .]

CLIMATE ADAPTATION VIA THE GREEN INFRASTRUCTURE

The modelling work presented here suggests that the use of urban green space offers significant potential in moderating the increase in summer temperatures expected with climate change. Adding 10 per cent green in high-density residential areas and town centres kept maximum surface temperatures at or below 1961–1990 baseline levels up to, but not including, the 2080s High. Greening roofs in areas with a high proportion of buildings, for example in town centres, manufacturing, high-density residential, distribution and storage, and retail, also appeared to be an effective strategy to keep surface temperatures below the baseline level for all time periods and emissions scenarios. On the other hand, the modelling work highlights the dangers of removing green from the conurbation. For example, if green cover in high-density residential areas and town centres is reduced by 10 per cent, surface temperatures will be 7°C or 8.2°C warmer by the 2080s High in each, when compared to the 1961–1990 baseline case; or 3.3°C and 3.9°C when compared to the 2080s High case where green cover stays the same.

Thus, one possible adaptation strategy to increasing temperatures is to preserve existing areas of green space and to enhance it where possible, whether in private gardens, public spaces or streets. For example, in Housing Market Renewal Areas or in the Growth Areas, significant new green spaces should be created. These initiatives are part of the UK government's Sustainable Communities Programme. Nine Housing Market Renewal Areas have been identified by the government across the North of England and the Midlands, including Manchester/Salford and Oldham/Rochdale, with the objective of renewing failing housing markets through refurbishment, replacement and new build of houses. The Growth Areas are in South East England and will provide as many as 200,000 new homes to relieve housing pressures in the region (DCLG, no date). Given the long life time of buildings, from 20 to over 100 years (Graves and Phillipson, 2000), it is crucial to take opportunities for creating green spaces as they arise.

However, in many existing urban areas where the built form is already established, it is not feasible to create large new green spaces. Thus, green space will have to be added creatively by making the most of all opportunities, for example through the greening of roofs, building facades, and railway lines, street tree planting, and converting selected streets into greenways. Priority should be given to areas where the vulnerability of the population is highest. A study in Merseyside found that vegetation, and in particular tree cover, is lower in residential areas with higher levels of socio-economic deprivation (Pauleit et al., 2005). The socio-economic deprivation index used included variables relating to health deprivation. Such populations will therefore be more vulnerable to the impacts of climate change.

One caveat to the potential of green cover in moderating surface temperatures is the case of a drought, when grass dries out and loses its evaporative cooling function. Output from the daily weather generator used suggests that with climate change there will be more consecutive dry days and heat waves of longer duration in summer (BETWIXT, 2005; Watts et al., 2004a, 2004b). Similarly, research undertaken as part of the ASCCUE project to map drought risk through the combination of available water in the soils, precipitation and evapotranspiration suggests a significant increase in the duration of droughts with climate change. Thus, it is likely that there will be more cases in which the grass loses its evaporative cooling function unless counter measures are taken. In such situations the role of water surfaces in providing cooling and trees in providing shade become increasingly important. The modelling work presented here does not include the effect of shading on surface temperatures. A pilot study undertaken by the ASCCUE project suggests that the shade provided by mature trees can keep surfaces cooler by as much as 15.6°C.

One possible adaptation strategy would be drought-resistant plantings. In Greater Manchester, this would involve planting vegetation, such as trees, that is less sensitive to drought than grasslands. Trees are common in open spaces in the Mediterranean. Tree species which are less sensitive to drought can be chosen from temperate zones, such that they will still evapotranspire and provide shade. Site conditions for trees in streets may need improving so that there is sufficient rooting space. In addition, irrigation measures must be considered to ensure that they have an adequate water supply. This could be through rainwater harvesting, the re-use of greywater, making use of water in rising aquifers under cities where present, and floodwater storage. Unless adequate provision is made, there will be conflict as green space will require irrigating at the same time as water supplies are low and restrictions may be placed on its use. Ironically, measures which are currently in hand to reduce leakage in the water supply system may reduce available water for street trees, which are critically important for human comfort in the public realm.

There may be other potential conflicts arising from planting trees in proximity to buildings. On clay soils in particular, changes in soil moisture content, as may occur with climate change, result in dimensional changes in the soil (Percival, 2004). If changes occur below the foundation level of the buildings, this can result in damage. However, the persistence of a moisture deficit beyond seasonal fluctuations only occurs in extreme cases. Tree roots are involved in at least 80 per cent of subsidence claims on shrinkable clay soils, yet even on clay soils the risk of a tree causing damage is less than 1 per cent (Biddle, 1998). Biddle (1998) argues that, due to the importance of trees in urban environments, a proper understanding is required of the mechanism of damage, how this can be prevented, and of appropriate remedies if damage occurs. An approach which accepts that minor damage may sometimes occur, and then remedies the situation if it does, is the most appropriate. In addition, new buildings should include precautions in the design and construction of foundations to allow for tree growth near buildings (Biddle, 1998).

The modelling work suggests that green space on its own is less effective at moderating the volume of surface runoff under climate change. While green space helps to reduce surface runoff, especially at a local level, the increase in winter precipitation brought by climate change is such that runoff increases regardless of changes to surface cover. Thus, in order to adapt to the increased winter precipitation expected with climate change, green space provision will need to be considered alongside increased storage. There is significant potential to utilize sustainable urban drainage (SUDS) techniques, such as creating swales, infiltration, detention and retention ponds in parks (Mansell, 2003; CIRIA, 2000). There is also an opportunity to store this excess water and make use of it for irrigating green spaces in times of drought.

Another way of exploring possible climatic adaptations is to consider the green infrastructure of the conurbation from the perspective of landscape ecology. The modelling work has concentrated on the environmental performance of the UMTs regardless of their spatial context. However, the functionality of the green infrastructure will be dependent on its location. Thus, the green infrastructure can be viewed as consisting of corridors, patches and the overall matrix (Forman and Godron, 1986).

These components of the green infrastructure play different roles in terms of climatic adaptation. For example, flood storage is especially important in corridors, but also has some importance as SUDS in the patches. In Greater Manchester, for example, green spaces such as golf courses and nature reserves alongside the River Mersey are used as flood storage basins at times of high river flow (Sale Community Web, no date). On the other hand, the matrix is especially important when it comes to rainwater infiltration, as are patches. Green space is most effective at reducing surface runoff on sandy, faster infiltrating soils. There may be a case for adapting to climate change through preserving and enhancing vegetated surfaces on such soils; for example, through the creation of Conservation Areas. Infill development could be restricted in lower density residential areas where soils have a high infiltration capacity. Evaporative cooling is very important in the patches which provide green oases with cooler microclimates and also in the matrix where people live. Green spaces develop a distinctive microclimate when they are greater than 1 hectare (von Stülpnagel et al., 1990). Similarly, shading is required in the matrix and patches, especially within residential areas.

In addition to providing climate adaptation, the green infrastructure offers a range of other benefits in urban areas (e.g. URBED, 2004; Givoni, 1991). The combination of these functions makes the use of green infrastructure an attractive climate adaptation strategy. Moreover, the use of green infrastructure may help in reducing greenhouse gas emissions, or in mitigating climate change. For example, vegetation can reduce solar heat gain in buildings and can thus reduce the demand for mechanical cooling through air conditioning, which contributes both the greenhouse gas emissions as well as the intensification of the urban heat island through waste heat (e.g. Niachou et al., 2001; Onmura et al., 2001; Papadakis et al., 2001).

CONCLUSION

The research findings presented here are significant because they begin to quantify the potential of the green infrastructure to moderate climate change impacts in towns and cities. Such claims are often made for urban green space (e.g. Hough,

2004), but the introduction of a modelling approach clarifies the magnitude of the effect and allows adaptation strategies to be tested. We do not suggest that the model outputs can be directly translated in practice; for example, it would be quite unrealistic to green all roofs in city centres and high-density residential areas. However, the model runs indicate which type of actions are likely to be most beneficial and in which locations. Urban green spaces, from street trees to private gardens to city parks, provide vital ecosystem services which will become even more critical under climate change.

Within urban centres, green spaces therefore constitute critical environmental capital that, once developed, is difficult to replace. This green space needs to be strategically planned. The priorities for planners and green space managers is to ensure that the functionality of green space is properly understood and that what exists is conserved. Then it should be possible to enrich the green cover in critical locations; for example, the planting of shade trees in city centres, schools and hospitals. Opportunities to enhance the green cover should also be taken where structural change is taking place, for example, in urban regeneration projects and new development. The combination of the UMT-based modelling approach with the patch-corridor-matrix model may help in the development of spatial strategies for the green infrastructure to preserve existing green space and create new green space such that a functional network is formed. This approach, however, requires further exploration.

Mature trees will be very important for the roles they play in providing shade and intercepting rainfall. Also, in times of drought they may provide a cooling function for longer than grass, which will dry out faster. At present, those areas experiencing highest surface temperatures and socio-economic disadvantage also have the lowest tree population and here urban forestry initiatives, such as the Green Streets project of the Red Rose Forest of Greater Manchester (Red Rose Forest, no date), are beginning to redress the balance. During periods of water shortages, as for example in South East England at the time of writing, urban vegetation is often the first target of a 'drought order'. The research suggests that the benefits of green space go well beyond consideration of amenity, and that opportunities will have to be taken to ensure an adequate water supply to vegetation in times of drought.

[. . .]

REFERENCES

Akbari, H., Rose, L.S. and Taha, H. (2003) Analyzing the land cover of an urban environment using high-resolution orthophotos. *Landscape and Urban Planning*, 63(1), pp. 1–14.

Baxter, P.J., Moller, I., Spencer, T., Spence, R.J. and Tapsell, S. (2002) Flooding and climate change, in Baxter, P., Haines, A., Hulme, M., Kovats, R.S., Maynard, R., Rogers, D.J. and Wilkinson, P. (eds.) *Health Effects of Climate Change in the UK*. London: Department of Health.

Benedict, M.A. and McMahon, E.T. (2002) Green infrastructure: Smart conservation for the 21st century. *Renewable Resources Journal*, 20(3), pp. 12–17.

BETWIXT (2005) Built Environment: Weather scenarios for investigation of Impacts and eXTremes. *Daily time-series output and figures from the CRU weather generator* [online]. Available from: http: //www.cru.uea.ac.uk/cru/projects/betwixt/ cruwg_daily/ [Accessed 2005].

Biddle, P.G. (1998) *Tree Root Damage to Buildings. Volume 1: Causes, Diagnosis and Remedy*. Wantage: Willowmead.

Bridgman, H., Warner, R. and Dodson, J. (1995) *Urban Biophysical Environments*. Oxford: Oxford University Press.

Brown, R.D. and Gillespie, T.J. (1995) *Microclimate Landscape Design: Creating Thermal Comfort and Energy Efficiency*. Chichester: John Wiley & Sons.

CIRIA (2000) *Sustainable Drainage Systems: Design Manual for England and Wales*. London: Construction Industry Research and Information Association.

Daily, G.C. (ed.) (1997) *Nature's Services: Societal Dependence on Natural Ecosystems*. Washington, DC: Island Press.

Denham, C. and White, I. (1998) Differences in urban and rural Britain. *Population Trends*, 91(Spring), pp. 23–34.

Duckworth, C. (2005) Assessment of Urban Creep Rates for House Types in Keighley and the Capacity for Future Urban Creep. Unpublished MA thesis, University of Manchester.

Eliasson, I. (2000) The use of climate knowledge in urban planning. *Landscape and Urban Planning*, 48(1–2), pp. 31–44.

Forman, R.T.T. and Godron, M. (1986) *Landscape Ecology*. New York: John Wiley & Sons.

Givoni, B. (1991) Impact of planted areas on urban environmental quality: A review. *Atmospheric Environment*, 25B(3), pp. 289–299.

GLA (2005) *Crazy Paving: The Environmental Importance of London's Front Gardens*. London: Greater London Authority.

Graves, H., Watkins, R., Westbury, R. and Littlefair, P. (2001) *Cooling Buildings in London: Overcoming the Heat Island*. London: BRE and DETR.

Graves, H.M. and Phillipson, M.C. (2000) *Potential Implications of Climate Change in the Built Environment*. East Kilbride: BRE, Centre for Environmental Engineering.

Hough, M. (2004) *Cities and Natural Process*. London: Routledge.

Hulme, M., Jenkins, G., Lu, X., Turnpenny, J., Mitchell, T., Jones, R., Lowe, J., Murphy, J., Hassell, D., Boorman, P., McDonald, R. and Hill, S. (2002) *Climate Change Scenarios for the United Kingdom: The UKCIP02 Scientific Report*. Norwich: Tyndall Centre for Climate Change Research, School of Environmental Sciences, University of East Anglia.

Larsen, J. (2003) *Record Heat Wave in Europe Takes 35,000 Lives*. Eco-Economy Update. Washington DC: Earth Policy Institute.

LUC (1993) *Trees in Towns: Report to the Department of the Environment*. London: Land Use Consultants.

Mansell, M.G. (2003) *Rural and Urban Hydrology*. London: Thomas Telford.

Matzarakis, A., Mayer, H. and Iziomon, M. (1999) Applications of a universal thermal index: physiological equivalent temperature. *International Journal of Biometeorology*, 43, pp. 76–84.

Niachou, A., Papakonstantinou, K., Santamouris, M., Tsangrassoulis, A. and Mihalakakou, G. (2001) Analysis of the green roof thermal properties and investigation of its energy performance. *Energy and Buildings*, 33(7), pp. 719–729.

Nowak, D.J., Noble, M.H., Sisinni, S.M. and Dwyer, J.F. (2001) People and trees: Assessing the US urban forest resource. *Journal of Forestry*, 99(3), pp. 37–42.

NWRA (2006) *The North West Plan: Submitted Draft Regional Spatial Strategy for the North West of England*. Wigan: North West Regional Assembly.

Oke, T.R. (1987) *Boundary Layer Climates*. London: Routledge

Onmura, S., Matsumoto, M. and Hokoi, S. (2001) Study on evaporative cooling effect of roof lawn gardens. *Energy and Buildings*, 33(7), pp. 653–666.

Papadakis, G., Tsamis, P. and Kyritsis, S. (2001) An experimental investigation of the effect of shading with plants for solar control of buildings. *Energy and Buildings*, 33(8), pp. 831–836.

Pauleit, S. and Duhme, F. (2000) Assessing the environmental performance of land cover types for urban planning. *Landscape and Urban Planning*, 52(1), pp. 1–20.

Pauleit, S., Ennos, R. and Golding, Y. (2005) Modeling the environmental impacts of urban land use and land cover change: A study in Merseyside, UK. *Landscape and Urban Planning*, 71(2–4), pp. 295–310.

Percival, G. (2004) Tree roots and buildings, in Hitchmough, J. and Fieldhouse, K. (eds.) *Plant User Handbook: A Guide to Effective Specifying*. Oxford: Blackwell Science.

Reacher, M., McKenzie, K., Lane, C., Nichols, T., Kedge, I., Iversen, A., Hepple, P., Walter, T., Laxton, C. and Simpson, J. (2004) Health impacts of flooding in Lewes: A comparison of reported gastrointestinal and other illness and mental health in flooded and non-flooded households. *Communicable Disease and Public Health*, 7(1), pp. 1–8.

Red Rose Forest (no date) Green Streets [online]. Available from: http://www.redroseforest.co.uk/forestproI greenstreets.html [Accessed 30th June 2006].

Sale Community Web (no date) The River Mersey [online]. Available from: http://www.salecommunityweb.co.uk/rivermersey.htm [Accessed 2006].

Shackley, S., Kersey, J., Wilby, R. and Fleming, P. (2001) *Changing by Degrees: The Potential Impacts of Climate Change in the East Midlands*. Aldershot: Ashgate.

Svensson, M.K. and Eliasson, I. (2002) Diurnal air temperatures in built-up areas in relation to urban planning. *Landscape and Urban Planning*, 61(1), pp. 37–54.

Tso, C.P., Chan, B.K. and Hashim, M.A. (1990) An improvement to the basic energy balance model for urban thermal environment analysis. *Energy and Buildings*, 14(2), pp. 143–152.

Tso, C.P., Chan, B.K. and Hashim, M.A. (1991) Analytical solutions to the near-neutral atmospheric surface energy balance with and without heat storage for urban climatological studies. *Journal of Applied Meteorology*, 30(4), pp. 413–424.

URBED (2004) *Biodiversity by Design: A Guide for Sustainable Communities*. London: Town and Country Planning Association.

USDA Natural Resources Conservation Service (1986) *Urban Hydrology for Small Watersheds*. Washington, DC: United States Department of Agriculture.

von Stülpnagel, A., Horbert, M. and Sukopp, H. (1990) The importance of vegetation for the urban climate, in Sukopp, H. (ed.) *Urban Ecology*. The Hague: SPB Academic Publishing.

Watts, M., Goodess, C.M. and Jones, P.D. (2004a) *The CRU Daily Weather Generator*. Norwich: Climatic Research Unit, University of East Anglia.

Watts, M., Goodess, C.M. and Jones, P.D. (2004b) *Validation of the CRU Daily Weather Generator*. Norwich: Climatic Research Unit, University of East Anglia.

Whitford, V., Ennos, A.R. and Handley, J.F. (2001) 'City form and natural process': Indicators for the ecological performance of urban areas and their application to Merseyside, UK. *Landscape and Urban Planning*, 57(2), pp. 91–103.

Wilby, R.L. (2003) Past and projected trends in London's urban heat island. *Weather*, 58(7), pp. 251–260.

Wilby, R.L. and Perry, G.L.W. (2006) Climate change, biodiversity and the urban environment: A critical review based on London, UK. *Progress in Physical Geography*, 30(1), pp. 73–98.

WWF (2005) *Europe Feels the Heat: The Power Sector and Extreme Weather*. Gland, Switzerland: WWF International.

19 Climate Change in Suburbs

An Exploration of Key Impacts and Vulnerabilities

Robin M. Leichenko and William D. Solecki

EDITOR'S INTRODUCTION

As many have pointed out, global populations are increasingly concentrated in cities. However, not everyone is moving into the densest cores of those cities. As Leichenko and Solecki clarify in this article, "Within the United States, suburban communities within metropolitan regions are where the majority of residents already live . . . and suburban areas are among the most rapidly growing population zones worldwide." Despite this trend, most climate vulnerability studies focus on dense urban settings, leaving a research gap on the impacts of climate change on suburban areas and their inhabitants. This article provides a comprehensive list of those impacts, clarifying the distinct challenges suburban regions face.

Using the state of New Jersey as a case study, the authors characterize climate change effects and vulnerabilities by high-, medium-, and low-density suburbs, each possessing slightly different ecologies, development pressures, and socio-economic conditions, thus differing in vulnerability. What unifies these suburb types is that their climate threats and contexts interact to "create synergistic, additive, and secondary impacts." In other words, different climate change effects will multiply each other (flooding and sea level rise, or heat and drought) and exacerbate existing stresses (population growth and increasing social vulnerability), creating ripple effects through many social and environmental systems. In addition to the breakdown of suburban vulnerability, the idea of interacting primary and secondary effects is a key takeaway from this article and should inform climate planning in all sectors and geographies.

Dr. Robin Leichenko is a Professor and Chair of the Department of Geography at Rutgers University, focusing on economic geography and human dimensions of global environmental change. She also served as Review Editor for the IPCC Fifth Assessment Report. Dr. William Solecki is a Professor in the Department of Geography at Hunter College, in the City University of New York (CUNY). His research focuses on urban environmental change, resilience, and adaptation transitions. He served as Founding Director of the CUNY Institute for Sustainable Cities from 2006–2014, and as lead author of the IPCC Working Group II, Urban Areas chapter (Chapter 8).

[. . .]

(2013) CLIMATE CHANGE IN SUBURBS: AN EXPLORATION OF KEY IMPACTS AND VULNERABILITIES

INTRODUCTION

Within the climate change literature, attention to suburban areas generally focuses on their contributions to land use change and global greenhouse gas emissions (Lindsey et al., 2011; Kennedy et al., 2011; Norman et al., 2006). The expansion of low-density, automobile-centric communities in cities throughout the world is widely recognized as a major driver of local environmental change and degradation, as well as having implications for global greenhouse emissions forcing (Davoudi et al., 2009; Leichenko and Solecki, 2005). Far less attention, however, has been directed to issues of vulnerability, impacts, and adaptation (VIA) in suburban areas. Although there is an expanding body of literature that examines how climate change could impact cities (Hunt et al., 2007; Hunt and Watkiss, 2011; Romero-Lankao and Dodman, 2011; Hallegatte et al., 2011), this literature generally focuses on impacts, risks, and vulnerabilities in densely settled urban core areas, particularly in larger cities such as London and New York (London Climate Change Partnership, 2006; Rosenzweig et al., 2011; Rosenzweig and Solecki, 2001, 2010). Studies in this vein typically pay limited attention to vulnerabilities across broader metropolitan regions, and particularly lower-density suburban and urban-rural fringe areas.

Given these conditions, the objective of this paper is to provide an initial exploration of the effects of climate change on suburban areas. Within the United States, suburban communities within metropolitan regions are where the majority of residents already live (Mather et al., 2011), and suburban areas are among the most rapidly growing population zones worldwide (Seto et al., 2010). Settlement patterns in U.S. suburban areas are highly diverse, ranging from classic "bedroom" residential areas, to significant regional employment and commercial centers (i.e., edge cities), to old industrial mill or mining towns, to newly suburbanizing communities where agricultural production is still economically viable. While suburban communities are interdependent and functionally linked via transportation networks, commuting patterns, and economic activities, they each face a variety of development pressures and tensions. The nature and magnitude of these pressures and tensions vary across the different types of suburbs. Within high-density suburban areas close to an urban core, for example, aging infrastructure, rapid in-and-out population migration, and declining tax bases combine to create continuous socio-economic challenges. By contrast, in exurban and urban fringe areas, important tensions more typically emerge from new housing development, population growth and transition, and inadequate infrastructure capacity to meet changing demands. These fringe communities, by definition, are experiencing ongoing land use conversion from agricultural, forest, or open space to residential, commercial, and industrial land uses and often face significant environmental stresses associated with loss of pervious surface, hydrologic alteration, ecosystem service decline, and increased water and air pollution.

In the paper, we examine how climate change vulnerabilities and impacts vary across a diversity of suburban community types, and we identify critical issues for further research on climate change in suburban regions. With the notable exceptions of Williams et al. (2012, 2010) and Smith and Hopkins (2010), each of which focus on defining different types of suburbs and on the need to improve suburban adaptive capacity, few studies to date have specifically examined climate change vulnerability and impact issues in suburban areas. Building on the widely accepted premise that vulnerability and impacts to climate change must be understood within the context of multiple stresses, we demonstrate how climate change issues "overlay" onto development stresses that are already present in many large metropolitan regions to create synergistic, additive, and secondary impacts of significance. By focusing on climate change in suburban regions, this study also inserts consideration of vulnerability and impacts of climate change into the growing body of literature on socio-ecological understanding of suburbs that has started to emerge in the past decade (Harris et al., 2012; Roy et al., 2011; Robbins, 2007).

The paper draws, in part, from an investigation of economic vulnerabilities to climate change within the U.S. state of New Jersey (Solecki et al., 2012). New Jersey encompasses the wide variety of metropolitan conditions present in the United States and can be characterized as a "quintessential" American suburban landscape. While insights from New Jersey are most directly applicable to coastal metropolitan regions of the United States, many of the findings also apply to large metropolitan regions within both developed and emerging economies where suburban landscapes are becoming an increasingly important settlement form (Leichenko and Solecki, 2005).

[. . .]

VULNERABILITIES AND IMPACTS IN SUBURBAN NEW JERSEY

In this section, we highlight and illustrate how key vulnerabilities and impacts associated with climate change vary across different types of suburban settlement zones. These impacts and vulnerabilities are summarized in Table 19.1 by major sector type (infrastructure, natural resources, public health) and by category of suburban zone (low-, medium-, high-density). Some of the major contextual conditions that contribute to this variation include elements such as settlement

Table 19.1 Key sectoral climate change vulnerabilities and impacts for different types of suburban communities.

Sector	Suburban communities		
	High-density, pre-World War II	Medium-density, post-World War II	Low-density, exurban
Infrastructure	Highway, railway, and airport flooding; drinking water and sewerage facility flooding	Flooding of industrial sites, residences, and key transport corridors; water supply and quality stress; long-lasting power outages	Water supply stress; flooding of key transport corridors
Ecological/natural resources	Degradation of remnant ecosystems	Damage to high-value natural amenities such as beaches; damage to trees and loss of protective ecosystem services	Diminished water access for wetlands; loss of critical wildlife habitats; forest fire risk; agricultural production stress; outdoor recreation amenity decline
Public health	Heat stress on sensitive populations; heat-related exacerbation of respiratory diseases	Difficulty of evacuation of large numbers of vulnerable residents (e.g., elderly); flooding of toxic waste sites	Isolation of elderly/disabled residents during extreme storm events

pattern and development pressures within each zone, differing age and purpose of infrastructure, and legacy effects of past economic activities.

[. . .]

Key Vulnerabilities and Impacts in High-Density Suburbs

For many of New Jersey's municipalities, the flooding of transportation infrastructure, especially roads, is a well-known vulnerability, especially for towns along waterways and coastlines. Yet climate change-related flooding from extreme rain events and from sea level rise and coastal storm surge presents a significantly heightened risk to New Jersey's high-density suburban communities because many are located in vulnerable coastal zone areas. In public transit-dependent northeast New Jersey, many of the railroad corridors and tracks, as well as hub facilities, are located at or near sea level and are already subject to flooding. With climate change, more frequent occurrence of extreme rainfall events, such as those experienced during Tropical Storm Floyd in 1999, Hurricane Irene in 2011, and Hurricane Sandy in 2012, is expected to result in increased flooding of transportation routes and short-term disruption of other critical transportation infrastructure, such as airport and seaport facilities. Hurricane Sandy's impact graphically illustrates this point. Many rail lines and rail yards were inundated and severely damaged during the storm surge. The transport disruptions were aggravated by the decision of the state's public transit company, New Jersey Transit, to store a large portion of its electric locomotives and passenger cars in suburban rail yards that were located within the projected storm surge zone. The yards were severely impacted, resulting in significant flooding damage and pushing resumption of normal train service to almost a month after the storm. The direct costs of the damage to the trains and rail infrastructure were estimated to be close to $400 million, including more than $100 million for water-damaged trains and equipment (Frassinelli, 2012). Economic consequences were aggravated by extended, multi-week, closure of these transportation systems, which had secondary effects throughout all other sectors and zones.

Climate-related disruption of airport and seaport facilities also illustrates the intricate relationship between different infrastructure features and economic activities, and between cities and older suburban areas. For example, the largest airport and seaport facilities in New Jersey (as well as the greater New York metropolitan region) are located in the cities of Newark and adjacent Elizabeth. In many of the surrounding suburban towns, warehousing and light manufacturing facilities have been sited on former tidal wetland areas that comprise the Hackensack Meadowlands region. These facilities are involved in the processing of materials shipped into the port or delivered as air cargo freight, and as a result, flooding of these sites can result in significant local and regional economic disruption. For example, substantial losses were incurred on products in storage near the port area as a result of Hurricane Sandy; the 16,000 automobiles that were being stored at the Newark Terminal incurred damage estimated at approximately $400 million (Newman, 2012). Furthermore, temporary closure of these facilities meant that delivery of products to local and regional outlets had to be suspended.

Critical water-related infrastructure located in older suburban communities also is highly vulnerable to climate risks such as extreme precipitation events or droughts. This infrastructure includes drinking water supply facilities (e.g., freshwater intake sites, water purification plants) and sewage treatment facilities. Many of the older suburban areas of New Jersey are dependent for their water supply on small-scale reservoir systems or systems with groundwater well fields. During Tropical Storm Floyd in 1999, many of the water supply facilities in older suburban areas of the state were compromised because of flooding and contamination. In the aftermath of Hurricane Irene in 2011, many of same or similar community water supply systems again were fouled. Flooding in older suburban areas of the state often results in CSO—combined sewer overflow—discharges. During high-volume stormwater events, typical sewage base flow is combined in the same pipe with rapid street runoff, which together exceeds the treatment capacity of sewerage facilities resulting in the outflow of untreated waste water to local water bodies. CSO events during which municipal water supply reservoirs can become contaminated are especially likely during short-term intense rain events those flush large volumes of waste and other surface pollutants in reservoirs. Within New Jersey, there are 280 CSO outfalls (i.e., locations where overflows are discharged in rivers or other waterways), most of which are located in urban or high-density suburban areas near New York City or Philadelphia (New Jersey Department of Environmental Protection, 2006).

Public health impacts of climate change represent another key hazard for New Jersey's older suburban communities, many of which have higher concentrations of low-income residents and at-risk populations (i.e., elderly, very young, health compromised). Climate change will exacerbate health problems in these communities as hazards are made worse and new ones are introduced (e.g., novel disease vectors that thrive in a warmer climate). Increased risk of illness will translate into higher costs to prevent disease, promote healthy lifestyles and treat the sick. This dynamic is illustrated by the threat of increased asthma rates that will come with higher temperatures, and changes in seasonal temperature regimes and variability (e.g., more heat waves) and worsening air quality (all else being equal). Asthma is already a major public health issue in New Jersey. In 2006, there were approximately 15,665 hospital admissions in New Jersey as the result of asthma-related illness (New Jersey Department of Health and Senior Services, 2008), accounting for 1 in 100 hospitalizations in the state. Asthma is geographically concentrated in that state's high-density communities with the highest rates of asthma hospitalization in Camden, Essex, Hudson, and Passaic counties [. . .] (New Jersey Department of Health and Senior Services, 2008). More frequent summer heat waves may increase the incidence of heat-related morbidity and mortality. Elderly, lower-income residents in older, high-density suburbs are particularly vulnerable to heat-stress. Lower-income high-density suburbs, many of which include substantial minority populations, are more subject to intense urban heat island effects due to a lack of shade trees and green space, presence of extensive impervious surfaces, and lack of access to home air conditioning.

While ecosystem services in older suburban areas are limited because of the intense levels of urbanized development and environmental degradation, they nonetheless play a critical role in local environmental quality and amenity provision. Woodland lots, open space, and street trees provide value for property owners and other users in these communities via active and passive recreation, stormwater management, species habitat and heat island mitigation. In many situations, these systems are already stressed because of reduced municipal street tree budgets and the presence of diseases and other pathogens. The most recent published survey completed in 1999 found a significant decrease in the number of trees in good health in New Jersey (from 69% to 34%) despite a slight increase in the number of street trees during the study period (2.0–2.1 million from 1994–1999) (Dwyer et al., 2000).

Climate change shifts, particularly increased heat and growing season droughts, are expected to create conditions for additive and synergistic stress on these systems. For example, urban forest patches (e.g., areas less than 3–4 acres) typically have limited resilience to any added stress from climate perturbations because they face non-optimal growing conditions including poor soil quality, exposure to damage or vandalism, competition from alien and invasive species, and air and water pollution. The significant degradation of these woodland parcels under conditions of climate change, though less important from an ecological standpoint (they represent only a small percentage state's ecosystems and wildlife habitat), will have significant local impacts because of their relative scarcity in these communities and high local amenity value.

[. . .]

Key Vulnerabilities and Impacts in Medium-Density Suburbs

Climate vulnerabilities within medium-density suburbs are deeply intertwined with settlement patterns and with the long-term pressures they place on ecosystem services. Inland and coastal flooding represent a significant threat to infrastructure and property in medium-density communities, and past extreme flooding events have resulted in significant costs. The magnitude of potential inland flood damages is suggested by the $80 million in losses from flooding in the Green Brook sub-basin of the Raritan River in 1999 and the $729 million in flood damage in the Passaic River basin in 2007 (Solecki et al., 2012). Dozens of similar high impact flooding events have occurred in New Jersey since 1900 (Mitchell, 2006). Inland flooding risks in suburban communities increase as forest and wetlands are lost to development and impervious surface becomes greater. The combination of increased impervious surface extent and heightened probability of extreme rain events under climate change creates conditions for a highly dynamic hydrology and a likelihood of more frequent flooding and more flood damage in the future.

For medium-density suburbs in coastal areas, storm surge flooding can have catastrophic impacts. In New Jersey, coastal suburbs that initially started as vacation sites have transitioned from seasonal, relatively low-density resort towns to year-round residential communities. Extensive development, particularly since the 1970s, has brought tens of thousands of new residents into former vacation communities, and has also led to substantial new property development in the potential storm surge zone, especially along the waterfront and in areas with beach access. Ocean County, an Atlantic coastal county in the central part of the state, was one of the counties in the U.S. with the most rapid population growth during the last quarter of the 20th century. In addition to putting a greater number of people at risk, this concentrated coastal development has created significant property exposure to sea level rise. Government and private expenditures tend to increase this exposure through infrastructure development, commercial investment, and market incentives including property insurance (Thomas and Leichenko, 2011; Leichenko et al., 2013). Within Ocean County alone, more than $89 billion in property is estimated to be at risk to sea level rise (Neumann et al., 2010).

Hurricane Sandy brought this risk profile into sharp relief. Extensive damage to critical infrastructure, including roads, bridges, gas lines, and electric and water utilities, on barrier islands and other coastal sites took place as the result of the storm surge. Given the increasing probability of future storms and the decline of local, state, and national revenues available for augmentation of flood and erosion control features, property owners of high-amenity and high-vulnerability sites face the prospect of taking on more of the cost of property protection, relative loss of property value, or reduced access to the property. This condition raises the possibility that lower- and middle-income households will relocate away from the coastal zone because they do not have the resources to rebuild and insure damaged homes. This outcome is already recognized as an emerging possibility in the lower-income suburban areas of both New Jersey and New York that were most impacted by Hurricane Sandy (Halbfinger, 2012).

Provision of drinking water supply is another sector where vulnerability coupled with declining public service capacity provides conditions for significant climate impacts in medium-density suburbs. These towns have populations beyond which private wells could supply drinking water for all the residents and business enterprises, but typically are not connected to a large and extensive water supply system such as those available for higher-density suburbs and central cities. Mid-sized communities in suburban New Jersey most often maintain small water supply systems either separately or in conjunction with other surrounding towns. In the northern part of New Jersey, the municipal systems are composed of small reservoirs or relatively shallow well fields that generally have low resilience to drought or other supply disruptions. These suburban water supply systems are some of the first to experience water restrictions during periods of decreased rainfall and droughtiness. For example, on August 5, 2010 the state of New Jersey declared a drought watch for five northeast counties (New Jersey Department of Environmental Protection, 2012), affecting hundreds of suburban communities in this area. The enhanced precipitation variability, along with lower runoff from reduced snowpack and increased evaporation from warmer temperatures that come with climate change, increases the probability of drought conditions and potential water shortages.

In more distant from the urban core, post-war suburbs, transportation generally and commuting specifically is highly automobile dependent. Because of relatively low development density, few highways and major access roads exist, and as a result, there is less redundancy within the transport network than observed in cities or higher-density suburbs. This condition creates vulnerabilities in the context of climate change because if one transportation corridor is compromised by flooding or similar disruption, there are few meaningful alternatives. During Hurricane Irene, for example, the most extensive transportation disruptions occurred in medium-density suburbs where traffic volume and the disruption and damage to key highway arteries produced massive delays and severe disruptions until highways were repaired.

The spatially dispersed, lower-density infrastructure, coupled with the sylvan character of medium-density communities, also creates significant vulnerabilities for energy infrastructure. Communities with extensive tree canopies are at risk of widespread, multi-day electrical power disruption during extreme wind events. Electric utility crews in New Jersey have had to respond repeatedly in recent years to extensive tree damage and power loss across a wide swath of territory, and these types of wind events are likely to become more common in the future because of climate change.

While infrastructure-related vulnerabilities are perhaps most apparent for medium-density suburbs, several characteristics of these communities are associated with specific challenges for public health. Large numbers of retirement communities are present in these areas, particularly in the coastal and other high amenity locations. Many elderly residents of these communities have health or mobility constraints and require extra attention to ensure their safety during extreme storm events. Similarly, lower-income international immigrants are increasingly concentrated in areas where riverine flood hazards are present. Land prices and housing costs in these areas are substantially lower than other locations, and many new immigrants are less aware of the flood hazards that long-term residents know to avoid. Because transportation corridors are limited, evacuation during flood events or other emergencies is a particular challenge for these communities.

The presence of toxic waste sites in New Jersey's coastal zone, including solid waste disposal areas, industrial and Superfund sites, and brownfield areas, also pose direct threats to public health in medium-density suburbs. These sites, which already represent a public health concern, may be increasingly subject to inundation as the result of sea level rise and coastal storm surge. The association of these types of sites with concentrations of lower-income people of color has been a longstanding concern within the environmental justice community (Sze and London, 2008). Climate conditions that increase toxic runoff and raise the potential for brownfield or Superfund site flooding bring additional urgency to addressing these concerns.

[. . .]

Key Vulnerabilities and Impacts in Low-Density Suburbs

Although the agriculture economy that remains in urban-rural fringe areas of New Jersey is quite adaptive to change—if the historical record is a guide, farmers will adopt new crop varieties that are more consistent with emerging climate trends or choose to replace a crop facing declining production with another crop—the situation becomes more complex when production of specific, high-value crops makes up a large percentage of an exurban community's local economy. For example, blueberry and cranberry production, which accounts for more than $110 million/ year in the state, is highly concentrated in a few exurban municipalities in the southern coastal plain of New Jersey. The production process, particularly for cranberries, is dependent on large supplies of freshwater. Shifts in freshwater availability resulting from climate change could alter local berry production capacity, which would have additive and synergistic economic impacts on these communities, affecting both production and processing facilities. Adaptive capacity also is limited when specific agricultural production systems are already stressed and where alternative production options are limited (Solecki et al., 2012). Such is the case for the New Jersey dairy industry, which has witnessed closure of more than half of the state's dairy farms during the past decade (New Jersey Department of Agriculture, 2012).

In addition to agricultural production, the exurban region in New Jersey includes several other types of ecosystems and native habitats such as freshwater wetlands, and ridge-line forests which are home to many of the state's endangered and threatened species. These systems increasingly will be stressed with climate change, especially as a result of shifts in precipitation regimes and increased frequency of drought conditions. These stresses will be compounded by ever-rising pressure for residential development, which results in further habitat loss. Wildlife and plant species found in exurban New Jersey communities are likely to face significant declines because they occupy climate-sensitive habitats or because their vulnerability to pests and associated blights will be exacerbated with climate change. Climate change-related blights such as the pine bark beetle in the western U.S. forests and the white wooly adelgid (*Adelges tsugae*) on the Canadian Hemlock (*Tsuga canadensis*) trees in the northeastern U.S. already are impacting exurban wildlands and communities.

While exurban communities may not experience a net decline of forest cover because of climate change during this century, tree species that are better adapted to new warming climates will become more common, while less adaptive species will decline. Exurban communities also will experience forest-related costs associated with potential increased forest fire risk. Exurban fire management has become a critical issue of concern for these communities throughout the United States. The recent fires in the metropolitan region of Colorado Springs, Colorado during the early summer 2012 illustrate the risk and vulnerability of exurban communities to forest fire. Known as the "Waldo Canyon fire," the Colorado Springs blaze burned almost 19,000 acres of exurban woodland, destroyed approximately 400 homes, and is associated with property insurance claims of more than $352 million (Coffman, 2012; Wineke, 2012). Within southern New Jersey's pineland ecosystem areas, forest fires are a perennial risk during the spring season. Expansion of suburban settlement in these areas has led to a number of fire-related incidents in recent years, whereby residents needed to be evacuated and property and homes were destroyed (Osborne, 2011).

Climate change also could impact lucrative ecotourism and outdoor winter recreation businesses present in exurban communities. For example, New Jersey has significant birding sites in the shore wetland areas. These sites are especially popular for birders during bird migration periods. A loss of these habitats might reduce the attractiveness of New Jersey as a birding destination, and may thus jeopardize this segment of the tourism industry. Other facets of the state's outdoor recreation industries that could be affected by climate change include sportfishing, especially for trout, which are threatened by higher water temperatures in rivers and lakes, and skiing and snowboarding, which are threatened by higher winter temperatures and lack of snowfall. The warm winter temperatures in 2011–2012, for example, resulted in many exurban ski resorts in the state opening later in the season and closing earlier, leading to greatly reduced revenue (Capuzzo, 2012; Portlock, 2012).

While impacts and vulnerabilities associated with land use and ecosystem services dominate in the exurban and fringe areas, interrelated infrastructure and public health concerns also emerge. For example, many exurban communities have limited water supply infrastructure and largely are dependent on private wells or small municipal water systems. Climate change will place increased stress on local water supplies because increased doughtiness potential will accentuate the already mounting water resources conflicts between residential/commercial, agricultural, and ecosystem demands. Infrastructure issues include pressures and competition for water supply in exurban communities, particularly if agricultural users need to expand irrigation capacity to cope with drought and increased variability. Limited density of transportation networks and the possibility of significant loss of access following a major disruption create risks for emergency management as well as economic activities. Regarding public health, when fringe areas lose power during a storm, they may be the last restored because higher-density areas typically receive first priority for restoration (Jacob et al., 2011). This has significant implications for elderly and disabled residents who might have weak or compromised immune systems or mobility, rely on electrically powered health care devises, or need to communicate with emergency assistance.

[. . .]

REFERENCES

Capuzzo, J.P., 2012. Warm winter, cool sales. *N. Y. Times.* Available from: http://www.nytimes.com/2012/03/11/realestate/new-jersey-in-the-region-mild-winter-shifted-sales-pitch-at-ski-resort.html?_r=1#.

Coffman, K., 2012. Update 2: Colorado Springs fire ranks as state's most destructive on record. Reuters Available from: http://www.reuters.com/article/2012/06/28/usa-wildfires-colorado-idUSL2E8HS9UF20120628.

Davoudi, S., Crawford, J., Mehmood, A., 2009. *Planning for Climate Change: Strategies for Mitigation and Adaptation for Spatial Planners.* Earthscan, London.

Dwyer, J.F., Nowak, D., Noble, J., Heather, M., Sisinni, S.M., 2000. Connecting people with ecosystems in the 21st century: An assessment of our nation's urban forests. Gen. Tech. Rep. PNW-GTR-490, Portland, OR: U.S. Department of Agriculture, Forest Service, Pacific Northwest Research Station 483.

Frassinelli, M., 2012. NJ Transit head puts Sandy damage estimate at $400M. *The Star-Ledger.* Available from: http://www.nj.com/news/index.ssf/2012/12/nj_transit_head_puts_sandy_dam.html.

Halbfinger, D.M., 2012. Post-storm cost may force many from coast life. *N. Y. Times.* Available from: http://www.nytimes.com/2012/11/29/nyregion/cost-of-coastal-living-to-climb-under-new-flood-rules.html.

Hallegatte, S. et al., 2011. The economics of climate change impacts and policy benefits at city scale: A conceptual framework. *Clim. Chang.* 104, 51–87.

Harris, E.M. et al., 2012. Heterogeneity in residential yard care: Evidence from Boston, Miami, and Phoenix. *Hum. Ecol.* 40, 1–15.

Hunt, A., Watkiss, P., 2011. Climate change impacts and adaptation in cities: A review of the literature. *Clim. Chang.* 104, 13–49.

Hunt, J. et al., 2007. Introduction, climate change and urban areas: Research dialogue in a policy framework. *Philos. Trans. R. Soc. A Math. Phys. Eng. Sci.* 365, 2615.

Jacob, K. et al., 2011. Telecommunications. *Ann. N. Y. Acad. Sci.* 1244, 363–396.

Kennedy, C., Ramaswami, A., Carney, S., Dhakal, S., 2011. Greenhouse gas emission baselines for global cities and metropolitan areas. In: Hoornweg, D., Freire, M., Lee, M.J., Bhada-Tata, P., Yuen, B. (Eds.), *Cities and Climate Change: Responding to an Urgent Agenda.* World Bank Publications, Washington, DC, pp. 15–54.

Leichenko, M., McDermott, M., Bezborodko, E., Namendorf, E., Kirby, T., Brady, M., Matusewicz, B., 2013. Economic Vulnerability and Adaptation to Climate Hazards and Climate Change: Building Resilience in the Barnegat Bay Region, Report submitted to the Barnegat Bay Partnership. Available from: http://bbp.ocean.edu/Reports/Leichenko-March2013_FinalReport%20with%20logos.pdf.

Leichenko, R., Solecki, W., 2005. Exporting the American dream: The globalization of suburban consumption landscapes. *Reg. Stud.* 39, 241–253.

Lindsey, M., Schofer, J.L., Durango-Cohen, P., Gray, K.A., 2011. The effect of residential location on vehicle miles of travel, energy consumption and greenhouse gas emissions: Chicago case study. *Transp. Res. D* 16, 1–9.

London Climate Change Partnership, 2006. *Adapting to Climate Change: Lessons from London.* Greater London Authority, London.

Mather, M., Pollard, K., Jacobsen, L., 2011. *Reports on America: First Results from the 2010 U.S.* Population Reference Bureau, Washington, DC.

Mitchell, J.K., 2006. A century of natural disasters in a state of changing vulnerability. In: Maher, N. (Ed.), *New Jersey's Environments: Past, Present, and Future.* Rutgers University Press, New Brunswick, pp. 164–198.

Neumann, J.E., Hudgens, D.E., Herter, J., Martinich, J., 2010. Assessing sea-level rise impacts: A GIS-based frame-work and application to coastal New Jersey. *Coastal Manage.* 38, 433–455.

New Jersey Department of Agriculture, 2012. Garden State Dairy Alliance. Available from: http://www.nj.gov/agriculture/news/hottopics/Topics050104.html.

New Jersey Department of Environmental Protection, 2006. New Jersey Combined Sewer Overflow Program, Presentation to Citizen Advisory Committee, NY–NJ Harbor Estuary Program. Available from: http://www.harborestuary.org/pdf/CAC/NJDEP-HEPCAC-Oct112006.pdf.

New Jersey Department of Environmental Protection, 2012. Drought Watch Issued for Five Northeast Counties with Residents asked to Voluntarily Conserve Water. News Release. Available from: http://www.nj.gov/dep/newsrel/2010/10_0075.htm.

New Jersey Department of Health and Senior Services, 2008. Asthma Strategic Plan 2008–2013. Available from: http://www.nj.gov/health/fhs/asthma/index.shtml.

New Jersey Office of the State Climatologist, 2012. NJ Precipitation and Temperature Departures Over the Past 12 Months. Available from: http://climate.rutgers.edu/stateclim/.

Newman, R., 2012. 16,000 Vehicles Damaged by Sandy at NJ Port. *The Bergen Record*, November 13. Available from: http://www.northjersey.com/news/179089621_16_000_vehicles_damaged_by_Sandy_at_NJ_port.html.

Norman, J., MacLean, H., Kennedy, C., 2006. Comparing high and low residential density: Life-cycle analysis of energy use and greenhouse gas emissions. *J. Urban Plan. Dev.* 132, 10–21.

Osborne, J., 2011. New Jersey Wardens Keep Watch over Fire-Prone Pine Barrens. *Philadelphia Inquirer.* Available from: http://articles.philly.com/2011-08-01/news/29838910_1_fire-service-forest-fires-fires-spread.

Portlock, S., 2012. Making Do with Man-Made Snow, NJ's Ski Resorts Endure a Mild Winter. *The Star-Ledger.* Available from: http://www.nj.com/business/index.ssf/2012/03/making_do_with_man-made_snow_n.html.

Robbins, P., 2007. *Lawn People: How Grasses, Weeds and Chemicals Make Us Who We Are.* Temple University Press, Philadelphia.

Romero-Lankao, P., Dodman, D., 2011. Human settlements and industrial systems. *Curr. Opin. Environ. Sust.* 3 (special issue).

Rosenzweig, C., Solecki, W.D. (Eds.), 2001. *Climate Change and a Global City: The Potential Consequences of Climate Variability and Change, Metropolitan East Coast.* Report for the U.S. Global Change Research Program. Columbia Earth Institute, New York, NY.

Rosenzweig, C., Solecki, W.D. (Eds.), 2010. *Climate Change Adaptation in New York City: Building a Risk Management Response.* New York Academy of Sciences, New York, NY.

Rosenzweig, C. et al., 2011. Developing coastal adaptation to climate change in the New York City infrastructure-shed: Process, approach, tools, and strategies. *Clim. Chang.* 106, 93–127.

Roy, C. et al., 2011. A multi-scalar approach to theorizing socio-ecological dynamics of urban residential. *Landsc. Cities Environ.* 4, 6.

Seto, K.C., Sanchez-Rodriguez, R., Fragkias, M., 2010. The new geography of contemporary urbanization and the environment. *Annu. Rev. Environ. Resour.* 35, 167–194.

Smith, I., Hopkins, D., 2010. Adapting the English Suburbs for Climate Change: A Conceptual Model of Local Adaptive Capacity, 24th AESOP Annual Conference, Finland.

Solecki, W. et al., 2012. *Assessment of Climate Change Vulnerabilities in New Jersey: An Economic Perspective*. New Jersey Department of Environmental Protection, Office of Economic Analysis, Trenton, NJ.

Sze, J., London, J.K., 2008. Environmental justice at the crossroads. *Soc. Compass* 2, 1331–1354.

Thomas, A., Leichenko, R., 2011. Adaptation through insurance: Lessons from the U.S. national flood insurance program. *Int. J. Climate Change Strateg. Manage.* 3, 250–263.

Williams, K., Joynt, J.L.R., Hopkins, D., 2010. Adapting to climate change in the compact city: The suburban challenge. *Built Environ.* 36, 105–115.

Williams, K., Joynt, J.L.R., Payne, C., Hopkins, D., Smith, I., 2012. The conditions for, and challenges of, adapting England's suburbs for climate change. *Build. Environ.* 55, 131–140.

Wineke, A., 2012. Waldo Canyon Fire Most Expensive in State History. *Colorado Springs Gazette*. Available from: http://www.gazette.com/articles/insurance-141783-expensive-fire.html.

Section V

Green Infrastructure for Urban Heat and Stormwater

Introduction

Robert L. Ryan

For many inland cities, the primary challenges climate change will bring are managing water and heat. Many regions will see more intense precipitation events with overall less precipitation. Climate-resilient stormwater management both prevents flooding and can improve aquifer recharge and thus provision of water in dry periods. In this section, we move to the site scale and introduce specific ways to reduce urban heat mortality and morbidity, improve stormwater management, and provide co-benefits in overall improved or protected public health. The section discusses how to choose among a range of potential practices and prioritize interventions, and how they can and should fit into the overall open space plans for a region.

URBAN HEAT

Excess heat days have very significant public health implications. Heat waves are among the deadliest weather-related natural disasters; killing upwards of 70,000 people in Europe in 2003 (Patz et al., 2014; Robine et al., 2008). Climate change models point to an increase in excessive heat days in many inland cities (Patz et al., 2014). The public health challenge is that high temperatures affect the most vulnerable populations including elderly, low-income, and children. Climate change planners need to understand the causes and strategies to address excessive temperatures and its impacts on those with the least socio-economic resources to escape the heat.

Increased temperatures due to climate change are exacerbated by the urban heat island (UHI) effect. Urban areas with concentration of buildings and paved surfaces absorb more heat during the day and are slower to release heat at night than surrounding rural areas. Thus, cities are often 1–12°Celsius hotter than nearby rural areas (EPA, 2014). Urban form described in Section IV has an impact on microclimates. Lower-density suburban areas with more trees and vegetation are cooler than more densely developed areas. Nature's green infrastructure of trees and other vegetation, un-paved surfaces (soil), and water bodies moderate temperatures. Trees and vegetation shade the paved and unpaved surfaces, lowering surface temperatures, as well as cool the area through evapotranspiration. When rainwater is allowed to infiltrate unpaved areas, the moist soil cools the air through evaporation. Open water bodies, such as ponds and lakes, are slower to heat up than the surrounding air and moderate both surface and air temperatures through evaporation as well. This section will give readers a more detailed understanding of the urban heat island and the green infrastructure strategies to fight its effects.

Landscape architect Robert Brown describes how city parks act as urban cooling islands (UCI). "At the neighborhood or community scale landscape elements can modify not only the wind and the radiation, but also the air temperature and humidity" (Brown, 2011, p. 373). The challenge for climate change planners is determining where to locate these green spaces to make the most impact for the greatest number of people.

Brown describes the need to "ameliorate the effects of extreme climatic conditions" through "microclimatic planning and design" (Brown, 2011, p. 272). Microclimates are the site-scale climate (temperature, humidity, wind, etc.) that are more easily influenced by modifications, such as tree plantings, changes in surface material, and other well-known strategies. The site-scale microclimates agglomerate into neighborhood-, city-, and regional-level microclimates, requiring a multi-scalar planning approach.

Three readings in this section addressing climate change and the urban heat island present such a multi-scalar approach. The first article by U.S. planner Brian Stone and his collaborators takes a metropolitan-scale approach to study three U.S. urban areas, Atlanta, Georgia; Philadelphia, Pennsylvania; and Phoenix, Arizona. These urban areas are in different climate zones, yet each have diverse urban populations that are threatened by rising temperatures. This article illustrates the application of climate change models to determine "heat-related" mortalities that are associated with rising temperatures. The study then models the degree to which microclimatic planning and design using green infrastructure (i.e., urban greening on public and private land) and modifying surface materials on building roofs and paved areas to increase albedo rate (i.e., painting roofs white, etc.) can lower temperatures and "heat-related" deaths. This paper is important in illustrating how a regional approach can help identify which neighborhoods will have the most impact from rising temperatures and the most potential benefits from green infrastructure. Additionally, the study illustrates how these microclimate strategies will vary in their efficacy (or influence) across different climate zones from hot desert (Phoenix) to temperate (Philadelphia).

Building on the theme of multi-scalar approaches to climate adaptation, the second reading by Australian Briony Norton (and colleagues) focuses on the city and neighborhood-scales, describing a planning framework for prioritizing green infrastructure strategies to address the urban heat island effect. While applicable in many climate zones, this article highlights the particular challenges to planning in Mediterranean climates, where planners grapple with tradeoffs between conserving water and irrigating trees and other green infrastructure for microclimate benefits.

As a counterpoint, Dutch researcher Laura Kleerekoper and colleagues at the Delft University of Technology in the Netherlands provide a northern European example of "addressing the urban heat island effect." This article illustrates how many northern European cities that traditionally had cool moderate summers are now experiencing extreme heat events, but are unprepared as these high-density cities often lack air-conditioning or other cooling areas. This reading describes very detailed urban design strategies at the smaller scale (street and block-level) and then applies them to a neighborhood in Utrecht (Netherlands).

STORMWATER MANAGEMENT

While so far, this book has discussed mitigation and adaptation as it refers to climate change, these same terms can be applied to natural hazards, such as flooding. In the fourth article in this section, Irish geographer and planner, Mick Lennon and colleagues (2014, p. 746) write about "*mitigating* flood risk and *adaptation*, or increasing resilience to flooding events." Increased flooding is a worldwide phenomenon that is the result of climate change and subsequent increased intensity and duration of precipitation, which is magnified by development trends in cities worldwide. Catastrophic flood images of many inland cities have increased efforts to adapt to this changing new normal.

Urban flooding is caused by a combination of forces, including the predominance of impervious surfaces in cities (i.e., buildings and pavement); changes in the hydrologic system from natural rivers, floodplains, and wetlands to hard-surfaced channelized rivers; and underground drainage pipes of the modern engineered stormwater system. In addition, demand for development along riverfronts and other water bodies has led to urban development in floodplains and other flood-prone landscapes. In fact, the majority of major cities worldwide are either located along coastlines or rivers (or both).

The colossal failure of many engineered flood-protection systems in cities across the world have led to both great losses in life and economic losses. Planners and engineers have called for re-thinking the paradigm of the "hard" engineered solution, including the "dangers of 'false precision' when calculating flood risk" (Lennon et al., 2014 c.f. White, 2013). In other words, the magnitude of climate change and the actual devastation of flood events, point to a hubris predicting a static flood-level prediction or event. Instead, there is need to accommodate a much larger margin of error and adapt to changing climate by creating green infrastructure systems that can adapt to increasing flooding and storm events. Lennon et al. (2014) discuss the need to develop flood management systems that use "evolutionary resilience" as the guiding principle. Using the work of Scott (2013) and applying it to urban stormwater, this approach does not take a steady-state viewpoint, but suggests an ongoing, transformative approach that adapts and responds to landscape and hydrologic changes and allows the natural and human-built systems to evolve using natural processes. For example, building enough room along a river to allow the flood channel to move, or the natural forces of erosion and deposition to occur, which acknowledges the vital role of floodplain wetlands for flood storage.

Landscape architect Jack Ahern and others (Ahern, 2013; Novotny et al., 2010) write about the "non-equilibrium" paradigm as a key guiding principle for sustainable urban design for water that embraces change and disturbance as the norm rather than the exception. Resilience to flood disturbance, therefore, views stormwater as an asset to be capitalized on to recharge urban aquifers, restore hydrologic systems, and benefit both humans and biodiversity (or other species). The articles in this section describe green infrastructure solutions that are adaptive responses that use ideas such as bio-mimicry (i.e., designed using natural forms/ processes) to create multi-functional urban landscapes that not only accommodate the increased runoff from urban areas, but create places of beauty and biodiversity.

Like microclimate planning, accommodating increased stormwater requires a nested, multi-scalar approach that responds to hydrologic units or watersheds. A regional approach is needed to understand and plan for the natural and human forces at work in river basins, such as increased impervious surfaces, that can exacerbate flooding in downstream locations.

In the last reading in this section, planner David C. Rouse and landscape architect, Ignacio Bunster-Ossa (2013) describe a landscape approach to planning and designing green infrastructure that is relevant to climate change adaptation and mitigation. They describe the importance of creating a design vision that is based on the ecological and cultural aspects of the place, and incorporates the full range of human desires, including esthetics and identity. The theme of multi-functionality is key along with connectivity and resiliency. A case study from Philadelphia illustrates this landscape approach to implement a green infrastructure plan to handle urban stormwater runoff that is exacerbated by a combined-sewer system. The project is a model of an integrative, site-sensitive approach to stormwater management that is needed as cities adapt to increased flooding risk from climate change.

REFERENCES

Ahern, J. 2013. Urban landscape sustainability and resilience: The promise and challenges of integrating ecology with urban planning and design. *Landscape Ecology* 28(6): 1203–1212.

Brown, R.D. 2011. Ameliorating the effects of climate change: Modifying microclimates through design. *Landscape and Urban Planning*, 100: 372–374.

Lennon, M., Scott, M. and O'Neill, E. 2014. Urban Design and Adapting to Flood Risk: The Role of Green Infrastructure. *Journal of Urban Design*. 19 (5):645–758. doi:10.10 80/13574809.2014.944113?journalCode=cjud20#.VHBsqsmsnK0.

Novotny, V., Ahern, J., and Brown, P. 2010. *Water Centric Sustainable Communities: Planning, Retrofitting and Building the Next Urban Environment*. Hoboken, NJ: Wiley.

Patz, J.A., Frumkin, H., Holloway, T., Vimont, D.J., & Haines, A. 2014. Climate change: Challenges and opportunities for global health. *Journal of American Medical Association*, 312(15): 1565–1580. doi:10.1001/jama.2014.13186

Robine, J.-M., Cheung, S.L.K., Le Roy, S., et al. 2008. Death toll exceeded 70,000 in Europe during the summer of 2003. *C R Biol.*, 331(2): 171–178.

Rouse, D. C., AICP & Bunster-Ossa, I. 2013. *Green Infrastructure: A Landscape Approach* (PAS Report 571). Chicago: American Planning Association.

U.S. Environmental Protection Agency (EPA). 2014. Fact Sheet: Keeping Your Cool: How Communities Can Reduce the Heat Island Effect. Publication Number: 430F14041 Washington, DC. Available on line at: www.epa.gov/sites/production/files/2016-09/ documents/heat_island_4-page_brochure_508_120413.pdf

White, I. 2013. The more we know, the more we know we don't know: Reflections on a decade of planning, flood risk management and false precision. *Planning Theory and Practice* 14: 106–114.

20 Avoided Heat-Related Mortality Through Climate Adaptation Strategies in Three US Cities

Brian Stone Jr., Jason Vargo, Peng Liu, Dana Habeeb, Anthony DeLucia, Marcus Trail, Yongtao Hu, and Armistead Russell

EDITOR'S INTRODUCTION

Brian Stone Jr. is a Professor in the School of City and Regional Planning at the Georgia Institute of Technology where he is the Director of the Urban Climate Lab. He is the leader of a multi-disciplinary research team that focused on modeling the urban heat island effect in three US metropolitan areas over a 40-year time period (2010–2050). This study is unique in that not only did the researchers model the impacts of increased temperatures due to climate change, they also studied these urban areas as dynamic systems to understand how land use change would increase the urban heat island effect. Each of these urban areas, Atlanta, Georgia; Philadelphia, Pennsylvania; and Phoenix, Arizona is expected to have increased population and development, particularly on the suburban fringe. The researchers show that if no changes are made in climate change adaptation, heat-related deaths will increase from 40–99%. This article illustrates how deadly the urban heat island effect is when coupled with rising temperatures, especially in central city neighborhoods with higher density development dominated by pavement and buildings.

These researchers explore how green infrastructure can be a tool for micro-climate planning by developing a series of scenarios that simulate a range of heat management strategies including tree plantings for increased shade, green roofs, and converting paved areas to grass and shrubs. Since it is easier for municipal governments to implement greening strategies on public land, the scenarios differentiated public and private greening by land use. They also looked at increasing the albedo rate of impervious surfaces on building and roads, such as using light-colored paving and roofing materials. Their exploration of the benefits of combining different strategies is very relevant for planners determining the tradeoffs for different approaches.

The good news from this study is that green infrastructure strategies modeled in this study significantly decreased the likelihood of heat-related mortalities due to increased temperatures and urban sprawl in the three study regions. In addition, the study found that vegetative strategies, such as tree plantings and green roofs were more effective than albedo enhancements in Atlanta and Philadelphia, while the albedo enhancements alone were more effective in hot, dry Phoenix. This study shows the need to tailor climate change adaptation strategies by region for the most efficient and effective outcomes.

(Note: Details on this study's complex modeling approach have been edited for brevity, so readers are encouraged to look at the full article and related data links for more information.)

AVOIDED HEAT-RELATED MORTALITY THROUGH CLIMATE ADAPTATION STRATEGIES IN THREE US CITIES

INTRODUCTION

Human health effects associated with rising temperatures are expected to increase significantly by mid- to late century. A large body of work now estimates an increase in mean global temperature from pre-industrial averages of more than 2°C by late century under mid-range emissions scenarios. A smaller but growing body of work has sought to estimate the effects of projected warming on heat-related mortality. Employing health impact functions derived from epidemiological studies of historical warm season mortality rates, recent work projects an increase in annual heat-related mortality of between 3,500 and 27,000 deaths in the United States by mid-century. Studies focused on individual cities estimate an increase in annual heat-related mortality by a factor of 2–7 by the mid-to-late 21st century.

The urban heat island effect compounds the potential effects of global-scale climate change on heat-related mortality among urban populations. Time series analyses of climatic trends in cities find large urbanized regions to be warming at a higher rate than proximate rural areas, with many cities warming at more than twice the mean global rate. The combined effects of urban heat island formation and the global greenhouse effect are projected to significantly increase the number of extreme heat events in urbanized regions. At present, the extent to which the urban heat island effect may further increase heat-related mortality is not well established.

Here we examine the potential for urban heat island mitigation as a climate adaptation strategy to reduce projected heat-related mortality in three large US cities by mid-century. Future year climate and seasonal mortality are modeled across the metropolitan statistical areas (MSAs) of Atlanta, Georgia; Philadelphia, Pennsylvania; and Phoenix, Arizona to capture a wide continuum of climatic, geographic, and demographic characteristics known to underlie population vulnerability to extreme heat. Using coupled global- and regional-scale climate models together with an environmental health effects model, we project the number of heat-related deaths expected for these regions in 2050 in response to a "business-as-usual" (BAU) trajectory and an array of urban heat management scenarios characterized by variable land cover modifications. Employing separate health impact functions responsive to temperature change and derived from prior epidemiological studies, referred to herein as "heat response functions" (HRFs), we find different combinations of heat management strategies to offset projected increases in heat-related mortality across the three MSAs by a range of 40–99%.

Our work builds on previous studies of climate change and heat-related mortality in three respects. First, we develop a set of climate projections responsive not only to future changes in atmospheric composition, but to changes in land cover characteristics as well, to capture the influence of heat island formation on heat-related health outcomes. Second, in addition to estimating changes in heat-related mortality resulting from future year climatic conditions, we further model the influence of alternative heat management strategies on health outcomes. Third, we introduce a modeling approach that enables health outcomes resulting from mean warm season temperatures and shorter-term heat wave events to be estimated by employing multiple HRFs.

METHODS

Land Cover Modeling

The influence of local climate modification on heat-related mortality was estimated through the integration of separate land cover, climate, and human health effects models. To account for separate global and regional climate forcings on future climate, our approach made use of a land cover modeling routine responsive to historical rates of land cover change. As presented in an earlier paper (Vargo et al., 2013), historical land cover change rates by urbanization class were developed for each metropolitan region from the National Land Cover Database and projected forward based on population projections for each decade from 2010–2050. [. . .]

County level population data were obtained for all counties in the Atlanta, Philadelphia, and Phoenix MSAs from the economic forecasting firm Woods & Poole for the years 2010–2040 and then extrapolated to 2050 with a statistical routine employing ordinary least squares. [. . .] These maps project Atlanta and

Phoenix to grow more rapidly than Philadelphia, and for expected growth to continue to largely occur in suburban zones. [. . .]

Global and Regional Climate Modeling

Future year climatic conditions were simulated though the coupling of the Weather Research Forecasting (WRF) mesoscale meteorological model to the Goddard Institute for Space Studies (GISS) Global Atmosphere-Ocean ModelE (the GISS-WRF model system). [. . .]

The influence of alternative heat management scenarios was assessed through separate WRF runs parameterized around variable land cover assumptions. These WRF runs included two scenarios focused on vegetation enhancement differentiated by property type (private vs. public land parcels), two scenarios focused on albedo enhancement differentiated by material type (roofing vs. surface paving), and three scenarios employing varying combinations of these heat management strategies. [. . .]

To date, numerous observational and modeling studies have found vegetative cover and high albedo roofing and paving materials—referred to generally as "cool materials"—to be associated with lower surface and near-surface air temperatures than sparsely vegetated areas with low albedo impervious materials. In some studies, the cooling benefits of vegetative and high albedo materials are shown to extend beyond the zones in which these materials are found (Taha et al., 1991). The climatic benefits of these land cover types result from either an increase in local rates of evapotranspiration, which offsets sensible heating at the surface, or through an increase in shortwave reflection, reducing the absorption of solar energy. Consistent with environmental zoning policies recently adopted in Seattle, Washington and Washington, District of Columbia, several of our scenarios set minimum green area targets per parcel to bring about land cover changes associated with urban heat island mitigation.

To assess the potential for municipal governments to reduce urban temperatures through strategies focused on publicly managed land alone, we further stratify our vegetation and albedo enhancement scenarios by land ownership class. As such, the Public Greening (PUG) and Road Albedo Enhancement (RAE) scenarios modify the land cover characteristics of publicly owned street surfaces, parks, and other publicly owned parcels, while the Private Greening (PRG) and Building Albedo Enhancement (BAE) scenarios modify the land cover characteristics of privately owned parcels across each region. The combined scenarios of GREEN, ALBEDO, and ALL enable the assessment of vegetation and albedo enhancement alone or in combination across all land ownership types. [. . .]

Health Effects Modeling

The implications of each land cover change scenario for heat- related mortality were assessed with an environmental health effects model developed by the US Environmental Protection Agency, the Environmental Benefits Mapping and Analysis Program (BenMAP). [. . .] [Figure 20.1]

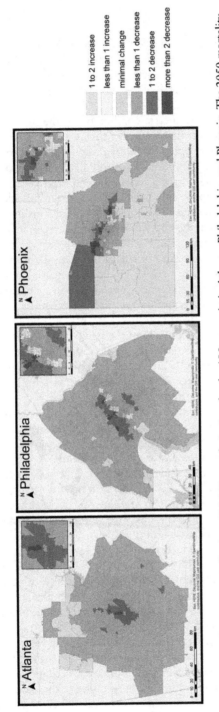

Figure 20.1 Change in mortality (per 100,000 population) under the ALL scenario in Atlanta, Philadelphia, and Phoenix. The 2050 mortality changes are estimated in response to the Medina-Ramon/Anderson HRFs and are based on the difference in mortality between the BAU and ALL scenarios.

Source doi:10.1371/journal.pone.0100852.g005

RESULTS

Temperature change was first modeled for the 2050 BAU scenario in reference to base year (2010) conditions in each metropolitan region. [. . .] Under the BAU scenario, warm season temperatures increase from base year temperatures by an average of 1.2°C in the Atlanta and Philadelphia MSAs, and by an average 2.2°C in the Phoenix MSA. [. . .]

Across the MSA-temperature metric combinations, the influence of variable heat management strategies on BAU temperatures was found to range from an increase in mean warm season apparent temperature of 0.06°C to a reduction in minimum temperature of 0.57°C. In Atlanta and Philadelphia, maximum temperature reductions were achieved through either vegetation enhancement or a combination of vegetation and albedo enhancement. By contrast, albedo enhancement alone was associated with the greatest temperature reductions in Phoenix. [. . .]

The variable effectiveness of the heat management strategies in lowering metrowide, average warm season temperatures is driven in large part by differences in the area of land conversions and rates of soil moisture availability. In the eastern US, where annual precipitation rates are high, both the spatial extent and species mix of vegetation are conducive to higher rates of evapotranspiration than found in the arid climate of Phoenix, promoting in these areas more regional cooling through the latent heat flux. In Atlanta and Phoenix, albedo enhancement, on average, is found to be more effective than the combined green strategies due to the fact that more land area is available for modification. In these cities, the total area of land converted to high albedo materials is about one-third greater than that total land area subject to vegetation enhancement, yielding a greater cooling effect in most scenario/temperature metric combinations.

Consistent with reported temperature change, trends in heat-related mortality are reported [. . .] as differences in the number of deaths relative to the BAU scenario (deaths under BAU scenario minus deaths under heat management scenario). The total number of avoided (or increased) deaths reported for each scenario accounts for non-heat wave and episodic heat wave periods during the 2050 warm season in each region. The "BASE" scenario reports the projected number of deaths resulting from changes in climate between the base year of 2010 and the 2050 BAU scenario, holding regional population characteristics constant at 2050 levels. The projected increase in annual heat-related mortality in response to warming over this 40-year period ranges from a low of 53 additional deaths in Philadelphia to a high of 132 additional deaths in Phoenix. Relative to base year levels, these 2050 projections represent an increase in heat-related mortality of 55% in Phoenix, 77% in Atlanta, and 319% in Philadelphia.

Heat management strategies offset projected increases in heat-related mortality within a 95% confidence level in 37 of 42 scenario runs. Mirroring the temperature change results, vegetation enhancement or a combination of vegetation and albedo enhancement resulted in the greatest reductions in BAU mortality in Atlanta and Philadelphia, while albedo enhancement in Phoenix was found to have the most significant effect on heat-related mortality in response to the Zanobetti/Anderson HRFs. The most effective heat management strategies in each region were found to offset projected increases in heat-related mortality by between a low of 40% in

Atlanta and Philadelphia (Zanobetti/ Anderson HRFs) to a high of 99% in Atlanta (Medina-Ramon/ Anderson HRFs), with an average reduction across all MSA and HRF combinations of 57%. We find vegetation and albedo enhancement in the Atlanta region to almost fully offset the projected increase in heat-related mortality associated with changes in minimum temperature between 2010 and 2050.

[. . .] The greatest concentration of avoided mortality is seen in the urban core of each metropolitan region, where population densities are high and the proportion of the land surface impacted by either albedo or vegetation enhancement is greatest. Heat-related mortality is shown to marginally increase in a small number of zones in the central districts of Philadelphia and Phoenix, an outcome attributed to the mixed thermal effects of tree planting along roadways and in public parks, as discussed in the next section.

DISCUSSION

The results of our study support climate adaptation strategies designed to lessen the risk of heat exposure through mitigation of the urban heat island effect. Heat management strategies were found to be effective in offsetting mortality during both heat wave and non-heat wave conditions. Our results suggest that measures of relative risk for heat-related mortality based on average warm season temperatures only may significantly underestimate the potential for heat deaths during extreme heat events spanning two or more days. When accounting for both average warm season and heat wave conditions, the estimated number of avoided deaths due to the various heat management strategies was found to be 33% higher, on average, than model runs responsive to average warm season temperatures only.

The additional health benefits found to result from heat island mitigation during periods of extreme temperatures highlights the potential for established climate modeling protocols to systematically underestimate health risks associated with climate change. [. . .]

The heat management strategies most effective in offsetting mortality vary by region. Accounting for both warm season and heat wave deaths, vegetative strategies were found to have protective benefits greater than or comparable to albedo enhancement in Atlanta and Philadelphia, while albedo enhancement was found to be more protective in Phoenix. While the combined vegetation and albedo enhancement scenario (ALL) was generally found to be more effective in offsetting heat-related mortality, albedo strategies alone were found to be most protective of health in Phoenix in response to the apparent temperature response function (Zanobetti/Anderson HRF). The greater effectiveness of albedo strategies in arid climates reflects the limitations of vegetation enhancement in regions characterized by low soil moisture availability. The variable effect of heat management strategies by region demonstrates the need for heat abatement approaches to be tailored to the unique climatic conditions of different urban environments. Our findings further demonstrate the need to associate heat management strategies with a health endpoint directly, as some strategies found to be highly effective in reducing temperatures were less effective in offsetting heat-related mortality. [. . .]

CONCLUSIONS

We examined the potential for urban heat management strategies to offset projected increases in heat-related mortality in three large US metropolitan regions by mid-century, using a set of global/regional climate and human health effects models. Variable combinations of heat management strategies involving vegetation and albedo enhancement were estimated to offset projected heat-related mortality by a range of 40–99%, depending on the metropolitan region and health impact function applied. These results highlight the potential for extensive land surface changes in cities to provide adaptive benefits to urban populations at risk for rising heat exposure with climate change.

We believe the study findings can inform the development of urban heat adaptation plans through which municipal governments can moderate the extremity of ambient temperatures during heat wave events, in concert with the implementation of emergency operations plans designed to protect public health once such events are underway. In selecting among alternative heat management strategies, urban planners and public health officials will want to consider the extent to which vegetation and albedo enhancement are consistent with a range of other climate adaptation objectives—including stormwater and air quality management—as well as other stakeholder preferences [30]. Future work will estimate the air quality implications of the modeled land cover change in Atlanta, Philadelphia, and Phoenix, as well as the economic costs and benefits of the various heat management strategies evaluated herein.

REFERENCES

Taha, H., Akbari, H., Rosenfeld, A. 1991. Heat island and oasis effects of vegetative canopies: Mecor-meteorological field-measurements. *Th. App. Clim.* 44: 123–138.
Vargo, J., Habeeb, D., Stone B.Jr. 2013. The importance of land cover change across urban-rural typologies for climate modeling. *J. Environ. Manage.* 114: 243–252.

21 Planning for Cooler Cities

A Framework to Prioritise Green Infrastructure to Mitigate High Temperatures in Urban Landscapes

Briony A. Norton, Andrew M. Coutts,
Stephen J. Livesley, Richard J. Harris,
Annie M. Hunter and Nicholas S.G. Williams

EDITOR'S INTRODUCTION

This article by Briony Norton (University of Melbourne) and her Australian colleagues including Dr. Andrew M. Coutts, urban climatologist at the Monash University, Centre for Water Sensitive Cities and School of Geography and Environmental Science, introduces a framework for planners to prioritise green infrastructure to address the urban heat island effect. Whilst the focus of this article is on Mediterranean climates, the basic hierarchical approach is very transferrable. For example, the first step, prioritising neighbourhoods in a city based on heat exposure, vulnerability and behaviour exposure is critical in any planning process. Analysis of existing neighbourhoods, including existing green infrastructure and the characteristics of urban form and street geometry, is essential. Some of the unique applications are maximising existing green infrastructure; for example, using irrigation of plant material as a cooling strategy. Choosing particular green infrastructure strategies is done at the micro-scale (site), where street geometry and building massing effects choices of trees, urban green spaces, green roofs, and facades.

PLANNING FOR COOLER CITIES: A FRAMEWORK TO PRIORITISE GREEN INFRASTRUCTURE TO MITIGATE HIGH TEMPERATURES IN URBAN LANDSCAPES

ABSTRACT

Warming associated with urban development will be exacerbated in future years by temperature increases due to climate change. The strategic implementation of urban green infrastructure (UGI), e.g. street trees, parks, green roofs and facades, can help achieve temperature reductions in urban areas whilst delivering diverse additional benefits such as pollution reduction and biodiversity habitat. Although the greatest thermal benefits of UGI are achieved in climates with hot, dry summers, there is comparatively little information available for land managers to determine an appropriate strategy for UGI implementation under these climatic conditions. We present a framework for prioritisation and selection of UGI for cooling. The framework is supported by a review of the scientific literature examining the relationships between urban geometry, UGI and temperature mitigation which we used to develop guidelines for UGI implementation that maximises urban surface temperature cooling. We focus particularly on quantifying the cooling benefits of four types of UGI: green open spaces (primarily public parks), shade trees, green roofs and vertical greening systems (green walls and facades), and demonstrate how the framework can be applied using a case study from Melbourne, Australia.

INTRODUCTION

Globally, extreme heat events (EHE) have led to particularly high rates of mortality and morbidity in cities as urban populations are pushed beyond their adaptive capacities. Recent EHE examples include: Chicago, USA (1995; 31% mortality increase) (Whitman et al., 1997); Paris, France (2003; 130% mortality increase) (Dhainaut, Claessens, Ginsburg, & Riou, 2003); Moscow, Russia (2010; 60% mortality increase) (Revich, 2011) and Melbourne, Australia (2009; 62% mortality increase) (Department of Human Services, 2009). Many cities expect catastrophic EHEs more often, as the frequency, intensity and duration of EHEs are projected to increase with climate change (Alexander & Arblaster, 2009).

There is evidence that increased mortality and morbidity from EHE are exacerbated in urban populations by the urban heat island (UHI) effect (e.g. Gabriel & Endlicher, 2011). Modified land surfaces from urbanisation lead to the formation of distinct urban climates (Coutts, Beringer, & Tapper, 2007). Natural surfaces and vegetation are replaced with a complex, three-dimensional impervious surface that absorbs large amounts of solar radiation during the day, and this energy is then slowly released at night, keeping urban areas warmer than the surrounding rural countryside and leading to the UHI (Oke, 1982). Rainfall is rapidly drained via stormwater pipes, leaving little moisture in the urban landscape, which reduces evapotranspiration and increases sensible heating of the local atmosphere (Coutts et al., 2007). Several studies have shown that higher night time temperatures limit people's recovery from daytime heat stress (Clarke & Bach, 1971). Consequently, many urban populations must adapt to the compounding effects of the UHI, climate change and EHE (Bi et al., 2011).

Many governments are now strategically planning for EHE (O'Neill et al., 2009), often with a focus on short-term preparation and prevention; for example, warning systems, promoting behavioural change and preparing emergency services (Kovats & Hajat, 2008; Queensland University of Technology, 2010). Increasing the amount of vegetation, or green infrastructure, in a city is one way to help address the root cause of the problem, by reducing urban air and surface temperature maxima and variation (Bowler, Buyung-Ali, Knight, & Pullin, 2010). However, to substantially reduce the UHI, widespread implementation of green infrastructure is required. For example, measurements during an EHE in Melbourne, Australia, suggested a 10% increase in vegetation cover could reduce daytime urban surface temperatures by approximately 1°C (Coutts & Harris, 2013).

Urban green infrastructure (UGI) can be defined as the network of planned and unplanned green spaces, spanning both the public and private realms, and managed as an integrated system to provide a range of benefits (Lovell & Taylor, 2013; Tzoulas et al., 2007). UGI can include remnant native vegetation, parks, private gardens, golf courses, street trees and more engineered options such as green roofs, green walls, biofilters and raingardens. This paper focuses on the integration of UGI into the public realm to mitigate high urban temperatures and considers the various UGI types and possible locations.

UGI research is not well integrated with urban design and planning, which contributes to the lack of guidance on how best to implement UGI (Bowler et al., 2010; Erell, 2008). UGI is a particularly good option for temperature mitigation in Mediterranean or warm temperate climates, due to the greater relative cooling benefits in hot, dry climates (Ottelé, Perini, Fraaij, Haas, & Raiteri, 2011), particularly if water is available to maintain vegetation health and evapotranspiration. Yet, there is a dearth of empirical evidence regarding the benefits of UGI in cities experiencing a Mediterranean climate, or information on successful and cost effective UGI implementation strategies (Williams, Rayner, & Raynor, 2010). Clearly, a cross-disciplinary approach is required.

We present a framework, supported by relevant literature, for green space managers, planners and designers to most effectively integrate UGI into existing urban areas for the primary goal of improved urban climate. With the aid of thermal mapping, a decision framework was developed for local government authorities in Melbourne, Australia. A step-by-step case study implementing the framework is provided, drawing on high resolution, airborne thermal mapping as a tool within this framework. Melbourne (37° 49′ S; 144° 58′ E), on the southern coast of southeastern Australia, has a warm Maritime Temperate climate (Peel, Finlayson, & McMahon, 2007), but has long periods of summer drought and extreme heat. This framework can be applied to cities with classic Mediterranean climates (e.g. Perth, San Francisco, Seville, Beirut and Athens), and those that experience extended summer periods of hot, dry conditions, such as Adelaide and Melbourne. Cities in colder or more humid climates may have different considerations, for example in humid areas there can be a greater emphasis on maximising air flow (Emmanuel, 2005).

A FRAMEWORK FOR USING UGI TO MITIGATE EXCESS URBAN HEAT

We propose a hierarchical, five-step framework to prioritise urban public open space for microclimate cooling (Steps 1–4) using the most appropriate 'fit for place' UGI (Step 5) (Figure 21.1). The same principles will apply to privately owned outdoor space, although this may be complicated by issues of multiple ownership (Pandit, Polyakov, Tapsuwan, & Moran, 2013).

The framework operates firstly at the 'neighbourhood' scale, then the 'street' scale and finally the 'microscale' (Figure 21.1). Whilst the actual area would be defined by the organisation implementing the framework, a neighbourhood would encompass hundreds of houses and urban features such as a shopping precinct, a school, a railway station, parks and playing fields. The street scale is a smaller unit within a neighbourhood; for example, some houses and a strip of shops. The micro scale is an area within a street canyon, equivalent to one or more property frontages, perhaps. Integrating these three scales is central to this framework, and is important to the strategic integration of UGI for microclimate cooling (Düt-emeyer, Barlag, Kuttler, & Axt-Kittner, 2014). This framework is flexible and can be applied and adapted by green space mangers, planners and designers to meet their local circumstances. Local stakeholders can also be involved in the decision framework at any, or all, stages as determined by budget, time and engagement philosophy of the local government authority.

Step 1—Identify Priority Urban Neighbourhoods

Specific neighbourhoods are prioritised by identifying areas with the largest numbers of people who may be exposed and/or are vulnerable to excessive urban

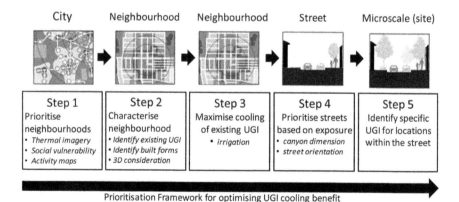

Figure 21.1 The steps in the prioritisation operate at the neighbourhood scale (Steps 1–3), where the physical environment and people's vulnerability are characterised for the area; and the street scale (Step 4) and microscale (Step 5), at which scales UGI that is fit for place is selected and implemented. See text for details.

heat. A risk of mortality and morbidity from excessive urban heat is based on a combination of heat exposure and vulnerability to extreme heat (Dütemeyer et al., 2014), as well as the behavioural exposure occurring, in terms of the number of people using public open spaces. When these three risk drivers intersect, a high priority neighbourhood has been identified. However, it is hard to predict the amount of behavioural exposure in public open spaces such as community health centres, so neighbourhoods where heat exposure and vulnerability intersect can also be regarded as a priority.

Heat Exposure

Areas within cities that experience extreme heat are not evenly distributed spatially, and 'hotspots' occur where there is intense urban development with little vegetation and/or water. Consequently, air temperatures predicted from coarse resolution models (e.g. 100–200 km) can frequently be exceeded in susceptible urban neighbourhoods or 'hotspots' (McCarthy, Best, & Betts, 2010). To adequately assess how exposed a neighbourhood population may be to high temperatures, temperature information that is specific to that location is important (Kovats & Hajat, 2008). Satellite or airborne remotely sensed thermal data can provide a snapshot in time of land surface temperature across a large spatial area, and can be used as a proxy for air temperature (Saaroni, Ben-Dor, Bitan, & Potchter, 2000), although the correlation may be poor under unstable (windy) conditions (Stoll & Brazel, 1992). Whilst land surface temperature and air temperatures are clearly different, mitigating high surface temperatures in cities is an appropriate target, as these reflect locations where both air temperature and absorbance of solar radiation is high, which impacts directly on human thermal comfort (Matzarakis, Rutz, & Mayer, 2007). Satellite remotely sensed data are low-resolution but often freely available, whereas airborne remotely sensed data can provide higher resolution (1–5 m), but can be costly and time-consuming to process (Coutts & Harris, 2013; Tomlinson, Chapman, Thornes, & Baker, 2011).

Vulnerability

A wide range of factors influences the vulnerability of urban populations to extreme heat. Socially disadvantaged neighbourhoods (those with lower household income and lower-quality parks, shops and transport) often experience greater negative health impacts from extreme heat. The elderly, those with pre-existing physical (i.e. heart disease, obesity) or mental illness, the very young and those living alone and in low socio-economic circumstances are particularly vulnerable (Bi et al., 2011). Prioritising neighbourhoods for high temperature mitigation is therefore a social justice issue, as well as a preventative health measure (Wolch, Byrne, & Newell, 2014). Assessing vulnerability of a population to high temperatures requires demographic information (e.g. Huang, Zhou, & Cadenasso, 2011; O'Neill et al., 2009). Loughnan, Tapper, Phan, Lynch, and McInnes (2013) have developed methods for assessing vulnerability in Australian cities primarily using Australian census information (Australian Bureau of Statistics, 2011) collected every five years, including a vulnerability index for all Australian capital cities.

Behavioural Exposure

Areas in a city where large numbers of the public are active outdoors should rate highly for heat mitigation, such as public transport interchanges, recreational spaces, outdoor shopping strips, schools and pedestrian thoroughfares. These areas may be prioritised to modify the human thermal comfort of large proportions of the population. For instance, during an extreme heat event, the public transport network can be interrupted, leaving commuters waiting in extreme heat for transport services. Furthermore, public areas of activity where vulnerable populations may be exposed should be identified, including outside aged care facilities, schools and community centres, health care centres, socio-economic support locations and social housing complexes. Such information can be sourced from census data, local planning schemes and other institutional resources.

Heat-related stress, stroke or death do not occur spontaneously or rapidly; it is prolonged exposure to higher than normal temperatures, often over several days, that causes heat-related illness (e.g. Harlan, Brazel, Prashad, Stefanov, & Larsen, 2006; Luber & McGeehin, 2008; McGeehin & Mirabelli, 2001). Hence, people are exposed to thermal stress throughout the day and night, and respond negatively after different periods of time, depending upon their vulnerability and the temperatures they experience. The aim of this framework to prioritise UGI implementation for heat mitigations is really an aim to reduce the overall outdoor exposure of vulnerable individuals (and all people) to high temperatures throughout the course of the day. Furthermore, this framework applies to public spaces where local governments can more easily intervene.

Step 2—Characterise UGI and Grey Infrastructure

Once priority neighbourhoods have been identified, it is important to characterise the built form (grey infrastructure) in a three-dimensional sense, and to identify existing UGI. Step 2 helps identify opportunities for microclimate improvements, and documents the landscape for later steps. The aim is to identify the location of existing, healthy vegetation, and where UGI is lacking, i.e. which parts of the current built environment could be retrofitted with UGI. If thermal mapping data (Step 1) are unavailable, this step increases in importance. Characterising street width and building height will determine street openness to solar radiation, and self-shading by buildings. This information can be gathered from a combination of visual surveys, aerial imagery, LiDAR data, GIS databases, etc.

Step 3—Maximise the Cooling Benefit from Existing UGI

Many cities already have well-established urban forests and other green infrastructure networks. Their cooling benefit is most important during very hot, dry periods; however, this is when urban vegetation can be most water stressed. Stress from low water availability during hot weather can lead to defoliation and possibly death. The impacts of this are most serious when large trees die due to the large reduction in cooling they provide and high replacement cost (Gill, Handley,

Ennos, & Pauleit, 2007). Vegetation that is water stressed has higher surface temperatures than irrigated vegetation (Coutts & Harris, 2013). Inadequate water availability will also lead to reduced plant transpiration when it is most desired (Leuzinger, Vogt, & Körner, 2010; Shashua-Bar, Pearlmutter, & Erell, 2011). Consequently, supplementary irrigation of UGI in cities that experience hot, dry summers is a wise investment to ensure long-term temperature mitigation, as well as other ecosystem services (May, Livesley, & Shears, 2013). However, some cities (e.g. Melbourne) introduce water use restrictions in response to extended drought, even though this approach immediately reduces and threatens the long-term temperature mitigation benefits from UGI (Coutts, Tapper, Beringer, Loughnan, & Demuzere, 2013; May et al., 2013). Some supplementary water can also be supplied through water sensitive urban design that utilises stormwater runoff rather than potable water (Coutts et al., 2013), but this will require increased investment in stormwater capture and storage within the urban landscape.

Step 4—Develop a Hierarchy of Streets for New UGI Integration

After selecting priority neighbourhoods for temperature mitigation, particular streets that are most vulnerable to high temperatures can be targeted. Urban streets can be viewed as canyons, with a floor (the road, walkway, verge and front yards) and two walls (the building frontages up to the top of the roof). Our five-step hierarchy focuses on street canyons because: (1) they occupy a large proportion of the public domain in cities, (2) a lot of urban climate research is based around street canyons, (3) street features relevant to assessing the thermal environment are relatively easy to measure and often already available to local government agencies, (4) street geometry and orientation are important determinants of surface and air temperatures in urban areas (Bourbia & Awbi, 2004a, 2004b) and (5) the principles for cooling based on canyon geometry can be usefully applied to other urban open spaces, e.g. car parks (Onishi, Cao, Ito, Shi, & Imura, 2010) and intersections (Chudnovsky, Ben-Dor, & Saaroni, 2004; Saaroni et al., 2000).

An important goal in using UGI to reduce surface temperature is to replace or shade impervious surfaces with vegetation (Oke, Crowther, McNaughton, Monteith, & Gardiner, 1989). Selection of UGI should therefore focus on the properties of the street canyon that determine level of solar exposure. These are building height (H), street width (W), height to width ratio (H:W), and orientation, but providing sufficient capacity for ventilation at night is also important. The street canyon H:W ratio determines the amount of shade cast by the buildings themselves across the canyon floor. Wide, open canyons (low H:W ratios) experience higher daytime temperatures due to high solar exposure, as compared to deep, narrow canyons (high H:W ratios) where buildings self-shade the canyon (Johansson, 2006). Canyon orientation influences the level of solar exposure, as east-west canyons receive more hours of direct solar radiation than north-south oriented canyons (Ali-Toudert & Mayer, 2006). If street H:W ratio is low (e.g. 0.5), an east-west oriented street will receive direct solar radiation whilst the sun is up, whereas north-south streets are solar exposed only in the middle hours of the day (Bourbia & Awbi, 2004a). The number of solar exposed hours is also related to a street canyon's H:W ratio and solar zenith angle, which changes predictably throughout the year. For Melbourne's latitude (37.8° S), a street canyon H:W ratio of 0.5–1.0 would provide some self-shading during the day, but be able to dissipate heat at night (Bourbia & Awbi, 2004b; Mills, 1997; Oke, 1988).

Implementing UGI is one of the easiest ways to modify street canyon microclimates, other than facade awnings and overhangs to shade footpaths (Ali-Toudert & Mayer, 2007). Ranking canyon geometry and orientation can help prioritise streets for tree planting or other UGI interventions. Using the RayMan model (Matzarakis, Rutz, & Mayer, 2010), we hierarchically prioritised streets of different geometry, based on self-shading by buildings at the summer solstice. For east-west oriented canyons, the proportion of the street canyon floor exposed to the sun is calculated at solar noon, and for north-south oriented canyons, the proportion of the day that the canyon floor is shaded is calculated. The amount of shading was then equally divided into four priority classes. It should be noted that these priorities are specific to Melbourne and will vary with geographic location. This hierarchical approach demonstrates that wide/very wide, east-west oriented streets should be prioritised for street trees because of high solar exposure. Street trees would provide less benefit in narrow street canyons with a high degree of self-shading. In an analysis of daytime thermal imagery, Coutts and Harris (2013) found that street trees in Melbourne were particularly effective at reducing surface temperatures in canyons with a H:W < 0.8, whilst above this H:W the effects of trees on surface temperature were reduced, which is consistent with our findings.

In narrow canyons, where there is adequate light, green walls and facades as well as ground level vegetation should be prioritised over trees due to reduced space, and because they allow better ventilation and long wave cooling at night. Appropriate plant selection is very important in these situations. As H:W increases, light levels drop and wind turbulence may increase, and few plant species are likely to tolerate these conditions. There is a paucity of empirical data on the performance of plants suitable for green walls and facades in deep, narrow urban canyons (Hunter et al., 2014; Rayner, Raynor, & Williams, 2010).

Step 5—Select New UGI Based on Site Characteristics and Cooling Potential

The final step selects and implements new UGI that is 'fit-for-place'. The order of UGI elements presented in this section reflects their priority given the goal of surface temperature reduction. The primary goal for new UGI implementation should be to maximise 'overhead' vegetation canopy cover, to reduce canyon surface temperatures as well as provide shading of pedestrian space and transpirative cooling. The secondary goal should be to implement either ground or wall 'surface' vegetation cover, also to reduce surface temperatures and provide transpirative cooling, but no (or little) shading. Surface vegetation cover includes vertical greening systems, green roofs and grassed ground surfaces.

Trees

In most cases, tree canopies are the optimal solution for shading both canyon surfaces and the pedestrian space, and they also provide evapotranspirative cooling (Rosenzweig et al., 2006; Spronken-Smith & Oke, 1999). The amount of shade trees provide depends on their architectural form and canopy density (Pataki, Carreiro, et al., 2011; Shashua-Bar, Potchter, Bitan, Boltansky, & Yaakov, 2010). Thick or dense canopy trees provide particularly good shade, meaning that broadleaf trees are generally more effective than needle-leaf trees (Leuzinger et al., 2010; Lin & Lin, 2010). However, trees that provide the greatest shade during hot summer days can also trap heat under their canopy at night (Spronken-Smith & Oke, 1999). To minimise heat trapping, street trees should not form a continuous canopy, thereby allowing ventilation and long-wave radiation to escape (Dimoudi & Nikolopoulou, 2003; Spronken-Smith & Oke, 1999). A mix of tree species, with different canopy architectures, could be considered for the same reason (Pauleit, 2003).

Urban Green Open Spaces

Urban green open spaces are primarily grassed areas with a relatively sparse (or absent) tree canopy, such as ornamental parks, sporting fields and golf courses. Depending on their design and irrigation regimes, urban green open spaces can potentially provide 'islands' of cool in hot urban areas, so it is important they be easily accessible to people (Giles-Corti et al., 2005). Depending on their size and the wind direction, they can also cool urban areas downwind (Dimoudi & Nikolopoulou, 2003; Spronken-Smith & Oke, 1998). Urban green open spaces cool more effectively if they contain scattered trees and receive irrigation (Spronken-Smith & Oke, 1998, 1999), and their spatial layout and vegetation structure will be important in determining their cooling potential (Lehmann, Mathey, Rößler, Bräuer, & Goldberg, 2014).

Greatly increasing the total area of green open space within a city may significantly reduce temperatures at the city scale (Bowler et al., 2010), but this is unlikely to be an option in most cities. Providing many small, distributed green open spaces could benefit a larger number of neighbourhoods (Coutts et al., 2013; Shashua-Bar & Hoffman, 2000), and the spatial prioritisation of green open space for urban cooling is an area of ongoing research (Chang, Li, & Chang, 2007; Connors, Galletti, & Chow, 2013). As cooling benefits are focussed downwind of any urban green open spaces, they would be best placed upwind of particularly hot areas or vulnerable populations.

Green Facades

Green facades are climbing plants grown up a wall directly or on a trellis or similar structure set away from the wall (Hunter et al., 2014). Green facades can be planted in the ground or in planter boxes at any height up the walls of a building. As well as preventing heat gain to building walls, green facades can provide cooling through evapotranspiration (Köhler, 2008). Unlike green walls, green facades

are a realistic option for widespread UGI implementation because of lower installation and maintenance costs (Ottelé et al., 2011).

Green facades are particularly beneficial on walls with high solar exposure and
where space at ground level is limited (Wong & Chen, 2010), or where aerial
obstructions limit tree growth. Dark-coloured walls should be prioritised for green
facade covering over light-coloured walls, which do not become as hot (Kontoleon & Eumorfopoulou, 2010). To benefit pedestrians, green facades should be
installed adjacent to walkways.

Green Roofs

During the day, roofs are some of the hottest surfaces in urban areas (Chudnovsky et al., 2004). Greening those roofs can greatly mitigate urban surface
temperatures, as well as reducing air-space cooling requirement inside those buildings. Green roofs may be extensive, with thin substrates (2–20 cm) and a limited
range of plants, or, where building structure is sufficiently strong, intensive, with
a thicker substrate layer that can support a wider range of plants (Oberndorfer
et al., 2007; Wilkinson & Reed, 2009).

Modelling suggests that green roofs can cool at a neighbourhood scale if they
cover a large area (Gill et al., 2007; Rosenzweig et al., 2006). To be effective,
green roofs need to be irrigated and maintain a high leaf area index before they
become comparable to the cooling provided by roofs painted with high albedo
paint (Santamouris, 2014), but their influence on cooling at street level will be low
(Ng, Chen, Wang, & Yuan, 2012). Green roofs reduce surface temperatures best
when they are covered in taller vegetation (Lundholm, MacIvor, MacDougall, &
Ranalli, 2010; Wong & Chen, 2010) and irrigated (Liu & Bass, 2005). Achieving a
balance between maximising cooling performance during hot summer conditions,
whilst keeping plants alive in shallow soils with minimal irrigation is an ongoing
research challenge (Williams et al., 2010). Green roofs have multiple benefits, but
for urban surface cooling that has human health benefits, we recommended adding green roofs to large, low buildings, or in areas with little ground level green
open space.

[. . .]

DISCUSSION

We have reviewed the potential of urban green infrastructure to mitigate high temperatures and integrated this information with census data and remotely sensed
thermal data to provide a decision framework that prioritises effective implementation of UGI. Although we make recommendations on what types of UGI will
be most suitable in different circumstances, the selection of appropriate UGI will
always depend on the local climate, soils and water availability, as well as community norms and cultural values (Bowler et al., 2010; Pataki, Carreiro, et al., 2011).

This framework enables prioritisation of placement and UGI type at the neigh-
bourhood-scale. Most existing studies have measured cooling effects from UGI

at the micro scale or modelled them at the city scale. More research is needed to understand the interactions between street canyon geometries, UGI placement and plant species selection to establish firm connections between UGI spatial arrangement and street-scale cooling. Increasingly, modelling tools are available to do this, and there are concerted efforts to improve the representation and simulation of vegetation in urban climate models (Grimmond et al., 2011). This is a complex problem and ultimately a combination of field measurements and modelling are likely required (Oke et al., 1989). Once a greater understanding is achieved, it might be possible to develop spatially explicit planning support tools similar to those used in conservation planning (e.g. Carsjens & Ligtenberg, 2007).

UGI should be part of any urban heat mitigation strategy, and the strengths and flexibility of the other components to this strategy, such as alternative surface materials and street design, should be similarly well understood to enable an informed and optimised response (Emmanuel, 2005). These need to run in conjunction with adaptation measures in the public health service and attempts to invoke behavioural change in the urban population to better cope with higher temperatures (Bi et al., 2011; O'Neill et al., 2009). Furthermore, UGI will rarely be installed exclusively to mitigate high temperatures, so there will likely be trade-offs and compromises when selecting the type of UGI and the plant species used.

There are two other major knowledge gaps that hinder successful implementation of UGI in hot or warm climates. The first is the horticultural limitations of UGI, which highlight a disconnect between some architectural and urban design 'visions' and what is biologically or physically possible (Hunter et al., 2014). There is an urgent need for species-specific (or functional type) data on plant ecophysiology, thermoregulation, water use and micro- climate cooling benefits in urban settings to inform UGI plant selection, substrate selection, placement and subsequent irrigation. Related to this is the other major knowledge gap: the lack of a quantitative understanding of the water requirements of different UGI systems and plant species. Trees have received greatest research attention, yet there is still little information regarding the water requirements of urban trees (May et al., 2013; McCarthy & Pataki, 2010; Pataki, Carreiro, et al., 2011; Pataki, McCarthy, Litvak, & Pincetl, 2011). Water use and transpiration by street trees varies greatly among species (McCarthy & Pataki, 2010; Pataki, McCarthy, et al., 2011), but providing supplementary irrigation can increase cooling benefits (Gober et al., 2009). Until more detailed information on plant water requirements is available, strategies to maintain and maximise water availability to UGI elements during drought periods would be prudent, especially so for street trees because of the direct and profound cooling benefits they provide to pedestrians and because of the many years 'invested' in their establishment and growth that can be lost if they die in one year of poor water management.

CONCLUSIONS

Mitigating extreme heat in urban climates will become increasingly important as climate change progresses and urban populations expand. UGI should be an important component of any urban climate change adaptation strategy because of the multiple benefits it provides to the community and local ecosystems. However, any UGI initiative should determine what the key objective(s) is/are at the outset. This study assumes that the key objective is temperature mitigation. As such, in a situation where a decision may negatively impact other ecosystem service benefits provided by UGI, the tradeoff would always be in favour of greatest temperature mitigation. If a UGI initiative has multiple objectives, this becomes more difficult and priorities will have to be ranked, or tradeoffs individually discussed with or without local community stakeholder engagement.

Despite the increasing amount of research on how UGI can prevent climatic extremes in urban areas, our understanding remains fragmented and the level of 'take up' by urban planners is low. We have presented, justified and applied a hierarchical decision framework that prioritises high-risk neighbourhoods and then selects the most appropriate UGI elements for various contexts. Much work remains to be done, especially in determining the optimal arrangement of UGI in a street canyon or the wider urban landscape, but there is sufficient information available for local governing bodies to take positive, preventive action and start mitigating high urban temperatures using UGI.

ACKNOWLEDGEMENTS

This paper arose from a project funded by the Victorian Centre for Climate Change Adaptation Research (VCCCAR). Sincere thanks to the City of Port Phillip for making available the thermal imagery data and supporting GIS layers. The manuscript has benefited from input during the project from Brod Street, all workshop participants, and Karyn Bosomworth and Alexei Trundle from RMIT University as well as from two anonymous reviewers. Andrew M. Coutts is funded by the Cooperative Research Centre for Water Sensitive Cities. Monash University provides research into the CRC for Water Sensitive Cities through the Monash Water for Liveability Centre.

REFERENCES

Alexander, L. V., & Arblaster, J. M. (2009). Assessing trends in observed and modelled climate extremes over Australia in relation to future projections. *International Journal of Climatology*, 29(3), 417–435. http://dx.doi.org/10.1002/joc.1730

Ali-Toudert, F., & Mayer, H. (2006). Numerical study on the effects of aspect ratio and orientation of anurban street canyon on outdoor thermal comfort in hot and dry climate. *Building and Environment*, 41(2), 94–108. http://dx.doi.org/10.1016/j.buildenv. 2005.01.013

Ali-Toudert, F., & Mayer, H. (2007). Effects of asymmetry, galleries, overhanging facades and vegetation on thermal comfort in urban street canyons. *Solar Energy*, 81(6), 742–754. http://dx.doi.org/10.1016Zj.solener.2006.10.007

Australian Bureau of Statistics. (2011). Data and analysis. Retrieved 8 April 2014, from http://www.abs.gov.au/websitedbs/censushome.nsf/home/data

Bi, P., Williams, S., Loughnan, M., Lloyd, G., Hansen, A., Kjellstrom, T., et al. (2011). The effects of extreme heat on human mortality and morbidity in Australia: Implications for public health. *Asia-Pacific Journal of Public Health*, 23(2 Suppl), 27S–36S. http://dx.doi.org/10.1177/1010539510391644

Bourbia, F., & Awbi, H. B. (2004a). Building cluster and shading in urban canyon for hot dry climate: Part 1: Air and surface temperature measurements. *Renewable Energy*, 29(2), 249–262. http://dx.doi.org/10.1016/S0960-1481(03)00170-8

Bourbia, F., & Awbi, H. B. (2004b). Building cluster and shading in urban canyon for hot dry climate: Part 2: Shading simulations. *Renewable Energy*, 29(2), 291–301. http://dx.doi.org/10.1016/S0960-1481(03)00171-X

Bowler, D. E., Buyung-Ali, L., Knight, T. M., & Pullin, A. S. (2010). Urban greening to cool towns and cities: A systematic review of the empirical evidence. *Landscape and Urban Planning*, 97(3), 147–155. http://dx.doi.org/10.1016/j.landurbplan.2010.05.006

Carsjens, G. J., & Ligtenberg, A. (2007). A GIS-based support tool for sustainable spatial planning in metropolitan areas. *Landscape and Urban Planning*, 80(1–2), 72–83. http://dx.doi.org/10.1016/j.landurbplan.2006.06.004

Chang, C.-R., Li, M.-H., & Chang, S.-D. (2007). A preliminary study on the local cool-island intensity of Taipei city parks. *Landscape and Urban Planning*, 80(4), 386–395. http://dx.doi.org/10.1016/j.landurbplan.2006.09.005

Clarke, J.F. & Bach, W. (1971). Comparison of the comfort conditions in different urban and suburban microenvironments. *International Journal of Biometeorology*, 15(1), 41–54. http://dx.doi.org/10.1007/s10980-012-9833-1

Chudnovsky, A., Ben-Dor, E., & Saaroni, H. (2004). Diurnal thermal behavior of selected urban objects using remote sensing measurements. *Energy and Buildings*, 36(11), 1063–1074. http://dx.doi.org/10.1016/j.enbuild.2004.01.052

Connors, J., Galletti, C., & Chow, W. L. (2013). Landscape configuration and urban heat island effects: Assessing the relationship between landscape characteristics and land surface temperature in Phoenix, Arizona. *Landscape Ecology*, 28(2), 271–283. http://dx.doi.org/10.1007/s10980-012-9833-1

Coutts, A. M., Beringer, J., & Tapper, N. J. (2007). Impact of increasing urban density on local climate: Spatial and temporal variations in the surface energy balance in Melbourne, Australia. *Journal of Applied Meteorology and Climatology*, 46(4), 477–493. http://dx.doi.org/10.1175/JAM2462.1

Coutts, A. M., & Harris, R. (2013). *A multi-scale assessment of urban heating in Melbourne during an extreme heat event and policy approaches for adaptation* (Technical Report, p. 64). Melbourne: Victorian Centre for Climate Change and Adaptation Research. http://www.vcccar.org.au/sites/default/files/publications/Multiscale%20assessment%20urban%20heating%20Technical%20Report.pdf

Coutts, A. M., Tapper, N. J., Beringer, J., Loughnan, M., & Demuzere, M. (2013). Watering our cities: The capacity for Water Sensitive Urban Design to support urban cooling and improve human thermal comfort in the Australian context. *Progress in Physical Geography*, 37(1), 2–28. http://dx.doi.org/10.1177/0309133312461032

Department of Human Services. (2009). *January 2009 heatwave in Victoria: An assessment of health impacts*. (State of Victoria Report, p. 24). Melbourne, Victoria: Victorian Government Department of Human Services. http://docs.health.vic.gov.au/docs/doc/F7EEA4050981101ACA257AD80074AE8B/$FILE/heat_health_impact_rpt_Vic2009.pdf

Dhainaut, J.-F., Claessens, Y.-E., Ginsburg, C., & Riou, B. (2003). Unprecedented heat-related deaths during the 2003 heat wave in Paris: Consequences on emergency departments. *Critical Care*, 8(1), 1–2. http://dx.doi.org/10.1186/cc2404

Dimoudi, A., & Nikolopoulou, M. (2003). Vegetation in the urban environment: Microclimatic analysis and benefits. *Energy and Buildings*, 35(1), 69–76. http://dx.doi.org/10.1016/S0378-7788(02)00081-6

Dütemeyer, D., Barlag, A.-B., Kuttler, W., & Axt-Kittner, U. (2014). Measures against heat stress in the city of Gelsenkirchen, Germany. *DIE ERDE-Journal of the Geographical Society of Berlin*, 144(3–4), 181–201. http://dx.doi.org/10.12854/erde-144-14

Emmanuel, M. R. (2005). *An urban approach to climate sensitive design: Strategies for the tropics.* Abingdon, Oxon: Spon Press.

Erell, E. (2008). The application of urban climate research in the design of cities. *Advances in Building Energy Research, 2*(1), 95–121. http://dx.doi.org/10.3763/aber.2008.0204

Gabriel, K. M. A., & Endlicher, W. R. (2011). Urban and rural mortality rates during heat waves in Berlin and Brandenburg, Germany. *Environmental Pollution, 159*(8–9), 2044–2050. http://dx.doi.org/10.1016/j.envpol.2011.01.016

Giles-Corti, B., Broomhall, M. H., Knuiman, M., Collins, C., Douglas, K., Ng, K., et al. (2005). Increasing walking: How important is distance to, attractiveness, and size of public open space? *American Journal of Preventive Medicine, 28*(2, Suppl 2), 169–176. http://dx.doi.org/10.1016/j.amepre.2004.10.018

Gill, S., Handley, J., Ennos, A., & Pauleit, S. (2007). Adapting cities for climate change: The role of the green infrastructure. *Built Environment, 33*(1), 115–133.

Gober, P., Brazel, A., Quay, R., Myint, S., Grossman-Clarke, S., Miller, A., et al. (2009). Using watered landscapes to manipulate Urban Heat Island effects: How much water will it take to cool Phoenix? *Journal of the American Planning Association, 76*(1), 109–121. http://dx.doi.org/10.1080/01944360903433113

Grimmond, C. S. B., Blackett, M., Best, M. J., Baik, J. J., Belcher, S. E., Beringer, J., et al. (2011). Initial results from Phase 2 of the international urban energy balance model comparison. *International Journal of Climatology, 31*(2), 244–272. http://dx.doi.org/10.1002/joc.2227

Harlan, S. L., Brazel, A. J., Prashad, L., Stefanov, W. L., & Larsen, L. (2006). Neighborhood microclimates and vulnerability to heat stress. *Social Science & Medicine, 63*(11), 2847–2863. http://dx.doi.org/10.1016/j.socscimed.2006.07.030

Huang, G., Zhou, W., & Cadenasso, M. L. (2011). Is everyone hot in the city? Spatial pattern of land surface temperatures, land cover and neighborhood socioeconomic characteristics in Baltimore, MD. *Journal of Environmental Management, 92*(7), 1753–1759. http://dx.doi.org/10.1016/j.jenvman.2011.02.006

Hunter, A. M., Williams, N. S. G., Rayner, J. P., Aye, L., Hes, D., & Livesley, S. J. (2014). Quantifying the thermal performance of green facades: A critical review. *Ecological Engineering, 63*, 102–113. http://dx.doi.org/10.1016/j.ecoleng.2013.12.021

Johansson, E. (2006). Influence of urban geometry on outdoor thermal comfort in a hot dry climate: A study in Fez, Morocco. *Building and Environment, 41*(10), 1326–1338. http://dx.doi.org/10.1016/j.buildenv.2005.05.022

Köhler, M. (2008). Green facades: A view back and some visions. *Urban Ecosystems, 11*(4), 423–436. http://dx.doi.org/10.1007/s11252-008-0063-x

Kontoleon, K. J., & Eumorfopoulou, E. A. (2010). The effect of the orientation and proportion of a plant-covered wall layer on the thermal performance of a building zone. *Building and Environment, 45*(5), 1287–1303. http://dx.doi.org/10.1016/j.buildenv.2009.11.013

Kovats, R. S., & Hajat, S. (2008). Heat stress and public health: A critical review. *Annual Review of Public Health, 29*, 41–55. http://dx.doi.org/10.1146/annurev.publhealth.29.020907.090843

Lehmann, I., Mathey, J., Rößler, S., Bräuer, A., & Goldberg, V. (2014). Urban vegetation structure types as a methodological approach for identifying ecosystem services: Application to the analysis of micro-climatic effects. *Ecological Indicators, 42*, 58–72. http://dx.doi.org/10.1016/j.ecolind.2014.02.036

Leuzinger, S., Vogt, R., & Körner, C. (2010). Tree surface temperature in an urban environment. *Agricultural and Forest Meteorology, 150*(1), 56–62. http://dx.doi.org/10.1016/j.agrformet.2009.08.006

Lin, B.-S., & Lin, Y.-J. (2010). Cooling effect of shade trees with different characteristics in a subtropical urban park. *HortScience, 45*(1), 83–86.

Liu, K., & Bass, B. (2005). Performance of green roof systems. *Paper Presented at the Cool Roofing Symposium.* Atlanta, GA, USA. http://nparc.cisti-icist.nrc-cnrc.gc.ca/npsi/ctrl?lang=en

Loughnan, M., Tapper, N., Phan, T., Lynch, K., & McInnes, J. (2013). *A spatial vulnerability analysis of urban populations during extreme heat events in Australian capital cities* (Final Report). Gold Coast: National Climate Change Adaptation Research Facility. http://www.nccarf.edu.au/publications/spatial-vulnerability-urban-extreme-heat-events

Lovell, S. T., & Taylor, J. R. (2013). Supplying urban ecosystem services through multifunctional green infrastructure in the United States. *Landscape Ecology, 28*(8), 1447–1463. http://dx.doi.org/10.1007/s10980-013-9912-y

Luber, G., & McGeehin, M. (2008). Climate change and extreme heat events. *American Journal of Preventive Medicine, 35*(5), 429–435. http://dx.doi.org/10.1016/j.amepre.2008.08.021

Lundholm, J., MacIvor, J. S., MacDougall, Z., & Ranalli, M. (2010). Plant species and functional group combinations affect green roof ecosystem functions. *PloS One, 5*, e9677. http://dx.doi.org/10.1371/journal.pone.0009677

Matzarakis, A., Rutz, F., & Mayer, H. (2007). Modelling radiation fluxes in simple and complex environments: Application of the RayMan model. *International Journal of Biometeorology, 51*(4), 323–334. http://dx.doi.org/10.1007/s00484-006-0061-8

Matzarakis, A., Rutz, F., & Mayer, H. (2010). Modelling radiation fluxes in simple and complex environments: Basics of the RayMan model. *International Journal of Biometeorology, 54*(2), 131–139. http://dx.doi.org/10.1007/s00484-009-0261-0

May, P. B., Livesley, S. J., & Shears, I. (2013). Managing and monitoring tree health and soil water status during extreme drought in Melbourne, Victoria. *Arboriculture & Urban Forestry, 39*(3), 136–145.

McCarthy, H. R., & Pataki, D. E. (2010). Drivers of variability in water use of native and non-native urban trees in the greater Los Angeles area. *Urban Ecosystems, 13*(4), 393–414. http://dx.doi.org/10.1007/s11252-010-0127-6

McCarthy, M. P., Best, M. J., & Betts, R. A. (2010). Climate change in cities due to global warming and urban effects. *Geophysical Research Letters, 37*(9), L09705. http://dx.doi.org/10.1029/2010gl042845

McGeehin, M. A., & Mirabelli, M. (2001). The potential impacts of climate variability and change on temperature-related morbidity and mortality in the United States. *Environmental Health Perspectives, 109*(Suppl 2), 185–189. http://dx.doi.org/10.2307/3435008

Mills, G. (1997). The radiative effects of building groups on single structures. *Energy and Buildings, 25*(1), 51–61. http://dx.doi.org/10.1016/S0378-7788(96)00989-9

Ng, E., Chen, L., Wang, Y., & Yuan, C. (2012). A study on the cooling effects of greening in a high-density city: An experience from Hong Kong. *Building and Environment, 47*, 256–271. http://dx.doi.org/10.1016Zj.buildenv.2011.07.014

Oberndorfer, E., Lundholm, J., Bass, B., Coffman, R. R., Doshi, H., Dunnett, F. N., et al. (2007). Green roofs as urban ecosystems: Ecological structures, functions, and services. *Bioscience, 57*(10), 823–833. http://dx.doi.org/10.1641/B571005

O'Neill, M. S., Carter, R., Kish, J. K., Gronlund, C. J., White-Newsome, J. L., Manarolla, X., et al. (2009). Preventing heat-related morbidity and mortality: New approaches in a changing climate. *Maturitas, 64*(2), 98–103. http://dx.doi.org/10.1016/j.maturitas.2009.08.005

Oke, T. R. (1982). The energetic basis of the urban heat island. *Quarterly Journal of the Royal Meteorological Society, 108*(455), 1–24. http://dx.doi.org/10.1002/qj.49710845502

Oke, T. R. (1988). Street design and urban canopy layer climate. *Energy and Buildings, 11*(1–3), 103–113. http://dx.doi.org/10.1016/0378-7788(88)90026-6

Oke, T. R., Crowther, J. M., McNaughton, K. G., Monteith, J. L., & Gardiner, B. (1989). The micrometeorology of the urban forest. *Philosophical Transactions of the Royal Society of London: Series B, Biological Sciences, 324*(1223), 335–349. http://dx.doi.org/10.1098/rstb.1989.0051

Onishi, A., Cao, X., Ito, T., Shi, F., & Imura, H. (2010). Evaluating the potential for urban heat-island mitigation by greening parking lots. *Urban Forestry & Urban Greening, 9*(4), 323–332. http://dx.doi.org/10.1016/j.ufug.2010.06.002

Ottelé, M., Perini, K., Fraaij, A. L. A., Haas, E. M., & Raiteri, R. (2011). Comparative life cycle analysis for green facades and living wall systems. *Energy and Buildings*, *43*(12), 3419–3429. http://dx.doi.org/10.1016/j.enbuild.2011.09.010

Pandit, R., Polyakov, M., Tapsuwan, S., & Moran, T. (2013). The effect of street trees on property value in Perth, Western Australia. *Landscape and Urban Planning*, *110*, 134–142. http://dx.doi.org/10.1016/j.landurbplan.2012.11.001

Pataki, D. E., Carreiro, M. M., Cherrier, J., Grulke, N. E., Jennings, V., Pincetl, S., et al. (2011). Coupling biogeochemical cycles in urban environments: Ecosystem services, green solutions, and misconceptions. *Frontiers in Ecology and the Environment*, *9*(1), 27–36. http://dx.doi.org/10.1890/090220

Pataki, D. E., McCarthy, H. R., Litvak, E., & Pincetl, S. (2011). Transpiration of urban forests in the Los Angeles metropolitan area. *Ecological Applications*, *21*(3), 661–677. http://dx.doi.org/10.1890/09-1717.1

Pauleit, S. (2003). Urban street tree plantings: Identifying the key requirements. *Municipal Engineer*, *156*(1), 43–50. http://dx.doi.org/10.1680/muen.2003.156.1.43

Peel, M. C., Finlayson, B. L., & McMahon, T. A. (2007). Updated world map of the Koppen-Geiger climate classification. *Hydrology and Earth System Sciences Discussion*, *4*, 439–473. http://dx.doi.org/10.5194/hessd-4-439-2007

Queensland University of Technology. (2010). Impacts and adaptation response of infrastructure and communities to heatwaves: The southern Australian experience of 2009. Historical Case Studies of Extreme Events (p. 163). Gold Coast, Australia. http://www.isr.qut.edu.au/downloads/heatwave_case_study_2010_isr.pdf

Rayner, J., Raynor, K., & Williams, N. (2010). Facade greening: A case study from Melbourne, Australia. *Acta Horticulturae (ISHS)*, *881*, 709–713. http://www.actahort.org/books/881/88K116.htm

Revich, B. (2011). Heat-wave, air quality and mortality in European Russia in summer 2010: Preliminary assessment. *Yekologiya Cheloveka/Human Ecology*, *7*, 3–9.

Rosenzweig, C., Solecki, W., Parshall, L., Gaffin, S., Lynn, B., Goldberg, R., et al. (2006). Mitigating New York City's heat island with urban forestry, living roofs, and light surfaces. *Paper Presented at the Proceedings of the Sixth Symposium on the Urban Environment*. Atlanta, GA, USA.

Saaroni, H., Ben-Dor, E., Bitan, A., & Potchter, O. (2000). Spatial distribution and microscale characteristics of the urban heat island in Tel-Aviv, Israel. *Landscape and Urban Planning*, *48*(1–2), 1–18. http://dx.doi.org/10.1016/S0169-2046(99)00075-4

Santamouris, M. (2014). Cooling the cities: A review of reflective and green roof mitigation technologies to fight heat island and improve comfort in urban environments. *Solar Energy*, *103*, 682–703. http://dx.doi.org/10.1016/j.solener.2012.07.003

Shashua-Bar, L., & Hoffman, M. (2000). Vegetation as a climatic component in the design of an urban street: An empirical model for predicting the cooling effect of urban green areas with trees. *Energy and Buildings*, *31*(3), 221–235.

Shashua-Bar, L., Pearlmutter, D., & Erell, E. (2011). The influence of trees and grass on outdoor thermal comfort in a hot-arid environment. *International Journal of Climatology*, *31*(10), 1498–1506. http://dx.doi.org/10.1002/joc.2177

Shashua-Bar, L., Potchter, O., Bitan, A., Boltansky, D., & Yaakov, Y. (2010). Microclimate modelling of street tree species effects within the varied urban morphology in the Mediterranean city of Tel Aviv, Israel. *International Journal of Climatology*, *30*, 44–57. http://dx.doi.org/10.1002/joc

Spronken-Smith, R., & Oke, T. (1998). The thermal regime of urban parks in two cities with different summer climates. *International Journal of Remote Sensing*, *19*(11), 2085–2104. http://dx.doi.org/10.1080/014311698214884

Spronken-Smith, R., & Oke, T. (1999). Scale modelling of nocturnal cooling in urban parks. *Boundary-Layer Meteorology*, *93*(2), 287–312. http://dx.doi.org/10.1023/A:1002001408973

Stoll, M. J., & Brazel, A. J. (1992). Surface-air temperature relationships in the urban environment of Phoenix, Arizona. *Physical Geography, 13*(2), 160–179. http://dx.doi.org/10.1080/02723646.1992.10642451

Tomlinson, C. J., Chapman, L., Thornes, J. E., & Baker, C. (2011). Remote sensing land surface temperature for meteorology and climatology: A review. *Meteorological Applications, 18*(3), 296–306. http://dx.doi.org/10.1002/met.287

Tzoulas, K., Korpela, K., Venn, S., Yli-Pelkonen, V., Kazmierczak, A., Niemela, J., et al. (2007). Promoting ecosystem and human health in urban areas using green infrastructure: A literature review. *Landscape and Urban Planning, 81*(3), 167–178. http://dx.doi.org/10.1016/j.landurbplan.2007.02.001

Whitman, S., Good, G., Donoghue, E. R., Benbow, N., Shou, W., & Mou, S. (1997). Mortality in Chicago attributed to the July 1995 heat wave. *American Journal of Public Health, 87*(9), 1515–1518. http://dx.doi.org/10.2105/AJPH.87.a1515

Wilkinson, S. J., & Reed, R. (2009). Green roof retrofit potential in the central business district. *Property Management, 27*(5), 284–301. http://dx.doi.org/10.1108/02637470910998456

Williams, N. S. G., Rayner, J. P., & Raynor, K. J. (2010). Green roofs for a wide brown land: Opportunities and barriers for rooftop greening in Australia. *Urban Forestry & Urban Greening, 9*(3), 245–251. http://dx.doi.org/10.1016/j.ufug.2010.01.005

Wolch, J. R., Byrne, J., & Newell, J. P. (2014). Urban green space, public health, and environmental justice: The challenge of making cities 'just green enough'. *Landscape and Urban Planning, 125*, 234–244. http://dx.doi.org/10.1016/j.landurbplan.2014.01.017

Wong, N.-H., & Chen, Y. (2010). The role of urban greenery in high-density cities. In E. Ng (Ed.), *Designing high-density cities for social and environmental sustainability* (pp. 227–262). London: Earthscan.

22 How to Make a City Climate-Proof

Addressing the Urban Heat Island Effect

Laura Kleerekoper, Marjolein van Esch and Tadeo Baldiri Salcedo

EDITOR'S INTRODUCTION

The urban heat island is especially challenging in the Netherlands and other northern European countries, which are experiencing higher temperatures due to climate change. The highly urbanized populations, unlike those in Australia, are unaccustomed to heat waves and the existing urban form does not provide the type of adaptations for this hotter weather resulting in increased heat-related mortalities. Researchers at the Delft University of Technology in the Netherlands led by Laura Kleerekoper explore implementation strategies for Dutch cities that are applicable in similar climate zones. The strategies are grouped into four broad categories: vegetation, water, built form, and materials. As illustrated in the previous study in Chapter 20 by Brian Stone Jr. and colleagues, urban greening is a key strategy to address the urban heat island effect. In the current article, the Dutch researchers discuss the importance of urban parks (cool islands), street trees, private greening (gardens and green roofs) and green facades, and use existing studies to illustrate the cooling effect of each strategy. The use of water, including ponds, canals and fountains, has not received as much attention and is especially relevant to the Dutch urban landscape with its canals. While urban form with narrow streets can provide summer shading, in winter it creates too much shading and increases heating demands in cold northern climates. The authors suggest that deciduous trees are a better solution than narrowing street canyons, which might be the approach in the hot Mediterranean climates. Architectural forms, such as slanted roofs, encourage air movement to dissipate heat in summer. Material choices including more pervious paving materials can allow infiltration and cooling due to evaporation.

This article uses a case study to apply these implementation strategies to redesign an existing neighbourhood in Utrecht that is vulnerable to higher temperatures. While this design includes traditional urban greening, it also includes more radical urban design approach that redevelops city blocks to create wider green swaths down key transportation corridors. Also unique is the incorporation of linear water systems to capture stormwater and urban greywater to use for watering street trees and increase cooling evapotranspiration. This case study illustrates how creative planning, as part of larger urban redevelopment initiatives, can help cities adapt existing neighbourhoods for hotter temperatures.

CITIES AND CLIMATE—CAUSES OF THE URBAN HEAT ISLAND EFFECT

[. . .] One of the best known effects of the influence of the urban environment on its climate is the urban heat island effect (UHI effect). This is the phenomenon that the urban air temperature is higher than that of the surrounding rural environment. The extent of the temperature differences vary in time and place as a result of meteorological, locational and urban characteristics. The urban heat island effect has the following causes (Oke, 1987; Santamouris, 2001):

1. Absorption of short-wave radiation from the sun in low albedo (reflection) materials and trapping by multiple reflections between buildings and street surface.
2. Air pollution in the urban atmosphere absorbs and re-emits long-wave radiation to the urban environment.
3. Obstruction of the sky by buildings results in a decreased long-wave radiative heat loss from street canyons. The heat is intercepted by the obstructing surfaces and absorbed or radiated back to the urban tissue.
4. Anthropogenic heat is released by combustion processes, such as traffic, space heating and industries.
5. Increased heat storage by building materials with large thermal admittance. Furthermore, cities have a larger surface area compared to rural areas, and therefore more heat can be stored.
6. The evaporation from urban areas is decreased because of 'waterproofed surfaces'—less permeable materials, and less vegetation compared to rural areas. As a consequence, more energy is put into sensible heat and less into latent heat.
7. The turbulent heat transport from within streets is decreased by a reduction of wind speed. [. . .]

This paper aims to explore the effects of climate change for the urban environment and aims to provide tools for urban design and strategies for implementation. First an introduction of the problem field and climate change effects is given, followed by a review of climate adaptation measures; these are categorized in four themes:

vegetation, water, built form and materials. The next section describes the transfer of scientific knowledge into practice. In the last section, the applicability of the climate adaptation measures from the second section are tested in a design for two existing Dutch neighbourhoods. The review is directed to the general field of climate adaptation, while the test designs have the specific context of the Netherlands and therefore provide insights for locations with similar climate, latitude and urban characteristics.

Health Effects of Heat Stress

Physical well-being can be significantly influenced by the meteorological climate in general and by the urban microclimate more specifically. [. . .]

Considering the climate predictions for the Netherlands, the largest threat lies in heat stress. [. . .] The optimal outdoor temperature related to the lowest mortality is 17°C (Hoyois et al., 2007).

HVAC (heating, ventilation and air-conditioning) systems make thermal stresses virtually obsolete indoors—with a substantial rise in energy consumption and anthropogenic waste heat as a result—but outdoors, they remain. Moreover, due to the predicted climate change, heat stresses will increase as a result of a global temperature rise, and an increase in hot extremes and heat waves. Combined with urban heat island effects, these conditions are likely to result in uncomfortable and unhealthy heat stresses, and more alarmingly, a significant increase in heat-related mortality. The heat wave in the summer of 2006 caused about a thousand heat-related deaths in The Netherlands and was rated the fifth natural disaster of that year (Hoyois et al., 2007).

Another harmful effect of higher temperatures is the stimulation of the formation of ground-level ozone in urban areas, which can lead to or aggravate cardio-respiratory diseases such as lung inflammation and decreased lung function (WHO, 2004).

Climate Change and Predicted Effects

[. . .] The Royal Dutch Meteorological Institute (KNMI) has made predictions for the climate in The Netherlands in 2050. They predict that the winters will be warmer and moister and that summers will be warmer and dryer. [. . .] The rise in temperature in the Netherlands is already higher than the mean global temperature rise, and this is thought to continue in the future [. . .] (KNMI, 2006). The best way to deal with these uncertainties regarding the future climate is to build new urban expansions, as well as to adapt existing urban environments in a robust way, dealing with all causes of urban warming.

TOOLS FOR URBAN DESIGN AND STRATEGIES FOR IMPLEMENTATION

By diminishing the accumulation of heat and applying cooling techniques, cities can mitigate their UHI effect. Here, design principles for Dutch cities are described in four categories: vegetation, water, built form and material.

Vegetation

Vegetation cools the environment actively by evaporation and transpiration (evapotranspiration[1]) and passively by shading surfaces that otherwise would have absorbed short-wave radiation. During the night, the high sky view factor of open fields allows heat to escape fast through long-wave radiation.

There are four different types of application of vegetation in urban areas: urban forests (parks), street trees, private green in gardens and green roofs or facades. Vegetation has an average cooling effect of 1–4.7°C that spreads 100–1000 m into an urban area, but is highly dependent on the amount of water the plant or tree has available (Schmidt, 2006).

An urban forest or a park is a green area within an urbanized environment. These areas have a lower air and surface temperature and thus form a PCI (park cool island). In numerous studies, it is shown that vegetated areas result in PCIs. A green area does not have to be particularly large in order to generate a cooling effect. According to a study in Tel Aviv, a park of only 0.15 hectares had an average cooling effect of 1.5°C and at noon reached a 3°C difference (Shashua-Bar and Hoffman, 2000). A study in Göteborg shows that a large green area does generate a large cooling effect. A maximum difference of 5.9°C in summer in a green area of 156 hectares was measured there (Upmanis et al., 1998).

When using PCI for cooling, the effect on the periphery is very important. The effect is variable, depending on airflow and other climatological circumstances. The studies just mentioned show an effect at 100 m distance from the PCI in Tel Aviv and an effect at 1100 m distance from Göteborg's PCI.

Street trees might seem to have a low impact on the temperature within the city because they are so dispersed, but since there are so many, they actually have a big impact. On a sunny day, the evapotranspiration of a tree alone cools with a power equal to 20–30 kW, a power comparable to that of more than 10 air-conditioning units (Kravčík et al., 2007).

Covering a roof or facade with vegetation has a cooling effect on the urban environment and the building itself. The responsible cooling mechanisms of a roof are: evapotranspiration of the leaves, converting heat into latent heat by evaporation from the soil and preventing the absorption of short-wave radiation by low albedo materials through shading. The indoor temperature also reduces because of the high insulation value of the green package, which will keep the heat outside in summer and inside in the winter.

[. . .] Other suggestions to improve the application of vegetation are: (1) Shading of windows and west-facing walls provides the most savings in cooling energy. (2) With regard to shading, the tree's crown shape can be more important than its crown density. (3) Energy and water rates determine the extent to which it is economical to substitute electric air-conditioning with cooling by vegetation. (4) Effects of tree shade on winter heating demand can be substantial with non-deciduous trees (McPherson, 1994).

Strategies for Implementation

Applying more green in public spaces has a relative low cost and high acceptance among citizens. The most effective green elements are street trees (Rosenzweig et al., 2006), therefore, the greening policies of different pioneer cities have had clear goals concerning the increase of the total number of trees and their hetero-geneity to assure resistance to vegetal diseases (ill trees rarely affect trees from different families). Examples of these policies are given by cities like Chicago (Ferkenhooff, 2006) and Edinburgh (The City of Edinburgh Council, 2001).

Even though greening public spaces is mainly a responsibility of the municipal-ity, it is feasible and recommendable to involve citizens in the initiative as this topic has a high public acceptance (Greenspace, 2005). This has been successfully achieved in different greening initiatives. In Paris, for example, where gardening around trees was encouraged. [. . .]

The promotion of green in private spaces has a higher relevance in the case of high-density cities, as the municipality is not the owner of the major part of the surface exposed to the solar radiation. In that case, initiatives like the one in Paris promoting green facades and green terraces (Mairie de Paris, 2009) and the subsidy programme of green roofs in Rotterdam are defining the future trend of adaptation strategies (Waterplan Rotterdam, 2008).

Water

Water can cool by evaporation, by absorbing heat when there is a large water mass—which functions as a heat buffer—or by transporting heat out of the area by moving, as in rivers. This is already happening in Dutch cities due to existing water applications.

Water has an average cooling effect of 1–3°C to an extent of about 30–35 m. Water applications in general are more effective when they have a large surface, or when the water is flowing or dispersed, like from a fountain. The effect of cooling by water evaporation depends on the airflow that replaces the cooled air through the city. [. . .]

While flowing water has a larger cooling effect than stagnant water, dispersed water like that from a fountain has the biggest cooling effect. A study in Japan shows air temperature measurements on the leeward side of a fountain with a reduction of approximately 3°C. The effect of the water system can be felt (from 14.00–15.00 h) up to 35 m distance (Nishimura et al., 1998).

Strategies for Implementation

From a strategic point of view, the promotion of the use of water infrastructures to benefit from the evapotranspiration effect is difficult due to the high costs involved. Only the implementation of fountains can be seen as a good cost-effective option in specific spaces with a high use, like commercial streets or squares. With a smart fountain design, it is possible to use the same space for other purposes in winter time.

In addition to the cooling effect from evaporation, water plays another crucial role in heat adaptation due its contribution to the increase of green infrastructure. More vegetation adds extra water buffering capacity, which is useful in case of heavy rainfall, and it increases the effectiveness of the evapotranspiration from the vegetation, which depends on the amount of water available. That is why the promotion of green infrastructure must go together with the promotion of better rainwater management.

Promoting the use of permeable pavement and storage infrastructure is a beneficial strategy in case of droughts and flooding. Water storage in public spaces is one of the proposals of the city of Rotterdam in the design of new development areas of the city. Some of the designs include multifunctional spaces as in the case of the 'water plaza'; a public space for storage of rainwater surplus that will be presented in the city pavilion of the World Expo 2010.

On a lower scale, several municipalities in the United States are creating reference guides about pavement options for low used traffic zones, like private paths, terraces and parking spaces (City of Portland, 2008).

Built Form

Building density and geometry are composition variables that influence the incidence of radiation on materials that can store heat, and the trapping of radiation by multiple reflections between buildings and street surfaces. Obstruction of the sky by buildings results in a decreased long-wave radiative heat loss from street canyons. The heat is intercepted by the obstructing surfaces, and absorbed or radiated back to the canyon.

Overheating by solar radiation in summer can be reduced with high ratios of street height to street width (Futcher, 2008). However, this may also reduce airflow, promote multiple solar reflections and lower the sky view factor which leads to the trapping of heat. These last negative effects may do more harm than the positive effects of the measure itself. Even if the measure would help in summer, in winter even more buildings will overshadow other buildings. In a cool winter climate, this leads to uncomfortable situations.

A better alternative to shade buildings are trees and green walls, which are green in summer and transparent in winter. Also, operable shading devices can be used in summer and can be easily removed in winter. [. . .]

Another way to improve ventilation is to generate a mix of the air in the canopy layer3 with the air from the boundary layer.4 One way to obtain this mix is to adjust the canopy layout. The best ventilation is acquired at a height-to-width ratio of around 0.5. At a height-to-width ratio of more than 2, there is almost no mix of the canopy and boundary layer (Xiaomin et al., 2006). The mix of the two layers also takes place with slanted roofs. These generate effective natural wind ventilation at the 'mouth' openings of urban street canyons. This is a much more effective means for improving natural ventilation than increasing building spacing (Rafailidis, 1997).

[. . .] Cities have a larger surface area compared to rural areas, and therefore more heat can be stored. Compact buildings have less external facades and therefore less heat storage.

Strategies for Implementation

Influencing the built form of a city from a policy standpoint is rather difficult and more using climatic parameters. Nevertheless, certain cities have included clear and rigorous spatial parameters in their urban planning guidelines. The city of Stuttgart has published an interesting booklet of climate change adaptation for urban planners (Baumüller, 2008). [. . .]

Material

The evaporation from urban areas is decreased because of 'waterproofed surfaces'—less permeable materials, and less vegetation compared to rural areas. As a consequence, more energy is put into sensible heat and less into latent heat.

While permeable materials allow cooling by evaporation, hard materials accumulate heat. Next to that, short-wave radiation is absorbed in low albedo materials. Results of increasing albedo were computed in a simulation model for Sacramento, California. By increasing the albedo city-wide from 25% to 40%, a temperature drop of 1–4°C can be achieved. Increasing the building albedo from 9% to 70% can reduce the annual cooling demand by 19%. Simulations showed a reduction of 62% in cooling energy demand when both the city-wide albedo and building albedo are increased (Taha et al., 1988).

The thermal admittance of materials also plays a significant role. Materials like brick store more heat, and radiate this heat into the air during nighttime until sunrise. Hollow block concrete has a smaller thermal admittance and therefore stores less heat. [. . .]

Strategies for Implementation

Changing the thermal property of the different surface materials of the city is the cheapest way to reduce the urban heat island effect. Even though the effects of this strategy are lower than the effects achieved using vegetation, the price and the technical feasibility allow covering bigger surfaces, achieving better results (Rosenzweig et al., 2006).

Even though all surfaces exposed to solar radiation have the potential to improve their thermal properties, the most common strategies carried by different municipalities are based mainly on the change of street pavement and roofs, commonly known as cool pavements and cool roofs.

Numerous research projects have been carried around the properties of the cool pavements. Several cities have introduced this strategy in their plans to mitigate the UHI effect, as in the case of Houston (Hitchcock, 2004). Unfortunately, there are no experiences yet of implementation on a large scale.

The pavement of spaces with a low use rate like parking spaces or private roads could be different to allow for a higher permeability; bricks instead of asphalt, or even bricks with holes allowing grass to grow in them. This strategy is mainly promoted among private users, individuals and companies. . . .

Applying cool roofs has been posited by several studies as a very good strategy to deal with the urban heat island effect; nevertheless, this strategy is not as popular among politicians as greening the city, which is the common trend at the moment. Nevertheless, in California, cool roofs have been introduced in the Building Energy Efficiency Standard regulation of the state, and will be in effect on the first of January 2010 (California Energy Commission, 2009).

TRANSFER OF KNOWLEDGE

As has been pointed out in the previous pages, there is already quite some knowledge available on the causes and effects of the UHI effect. Furthermore, several tools and strategies to counteract the UHI effect are available, and some of them have been already successfully implemented in several cities around the world. Nevertheless, one of the biggest problems faced is the transfer of this knowledge to the urban planning process.

[. . .] A good example of how to integrate climate knowledge in the urban planning process is given by the city of Stuttgart, Germany. Stuttgart has set up a set of guidelines that are used for the design and restructuring of the city.

Climate change is already a powerful leading force to implement spatial measures at governance level. A better transfer of knowledge from science to practice and a signal from the general public indicating they perceive the topic of UHI effects as important might make politicians decide to give priority to these matters.

CASE STUDY OF EXISTING URBAN FABRICS IN DEN HAAG AND UTRECHT

By assessing the amount of green and water, the amount and kinds of material and built form, neighbourhoods can be compared in their heat accumulation. Such an assessment of six neighbourhoods from different periods (the old city centre, 1930 and 1960) in Utrecht and Den Haag (three in each city), shows that the neighbourhoods from the 1930s have the highest probability of accumulating heat. These are not the neighbourhoods designed according to the 'garden' concept, which are usually based on a large green structure. In the analyzed neighbourhoods, green is actually lacking in both public space and private 'gardens'. Private yards are often paved or built. In addition to the large amount of paved surfaces, these neighbourhoods have relatively narrow streets where natural ventilation is low. For the neighbourhoods from the 1930s, a design proposition to diminish heat accumulation is made.

Based on the theories and measurements described, the following design criteria were formulated:

- All dwellings are to be situated within 200 m from a green area with a minimum size of 0.15 hectares.
- The preferred street orientation is perpendicular to green areas.
- Green filters are to be placed in streets with a high traffic pressure.

- New dwellings should replace an equal amount of dwellings or more, but with a larger dwelling surface.
- Combinations of green with water should be made where possible.
- A lack of greening possibilities in streets should be compensated with surface water, green facades and permeable pavements.
- Flat roofs should be transformed to green roofs or be covered with a reflecting light surface.
- Slanted roofs should have PV-T panels or a reflecting light surface.

The design plans for the neighbourhoods of Ondiep show how the design principles can be applied in a practical situation. For both neighbourhoods, a renovation plan is described in which demolition is kept to a minimum. The applied measures might not be the most effective ones with regard to minimizing heat accumulation, but the best in relation to the existing spatial situation and the impact on social and financial aspects.

Ondiep

Ondiep is situated 1.5 km from the city centre of Utrecht. It forms a transit area for inhabitants from Zuilen and commuters. There are three different routings: a commercial street connecting the area to the west side of Utrecht, a car and bus route connected to the ring road through Ondiep, and a route along the river Vecht.

Considering the criterion 'all dwellings are to be situated within 200 m from a green area', a large part in the middle of the neighbourhood does not meet this standard in the current situation as shown in Figure 22.2. Since there are very few (green) open spaces in this particular part, it will be difficult to create them without decreasing the amount of dwellings while preserving the characteristics of the neighbourhood.

The design plan for Ondiep is based on improving the routings described before with green zones in combination with other heat diminishing measures.

Building Plan

Implementing green in the form of green zones and routes demands space. The car and bus route has a width of 25–30 m and does not offer the amount of space that is needed. To create space for green, the dwellings along the North side of the street will be shifted backwards. The existing dwellings have two or three building layers; new dwellings with four layers have to compensate for the amount of demolished dwellings along this route.

When streets are widened and the amount of building layers is changed, the height-to-width ratio is influenced as well. The lowered height to width ratio improves natural ventilation which is extra stimulated by the slanted roofs.

Thanks to the favourable street orientation in Ondiep—every street receives solar radiation in the late morning or early afternoon—and the slanted roofs, the houses are very suitable for PV-T panels.

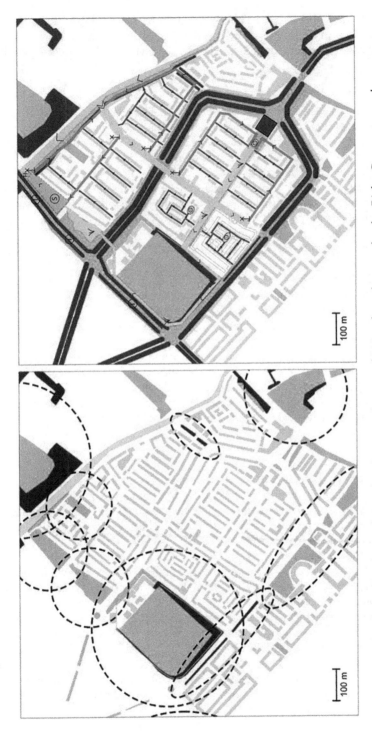

Figure 22.2 Left: Green in Ondiep with a circle indicating a distance of 200 m from the green border. Right: Green zones and water system. (For interpretation of the references to colour in this figure legend, refer to the web version of the article.)

100 m

100 m

In the 'Witte Wijk' (white neighbourhood), a recent developed white coating will be applied on the roofs. White roofs emphasize the image of this particular area. The coating reflects sunlight and keeps its high albedo because it repels dirt.

Green Plan

The green zones each have a different character. The green areas differ in usage, ambiance, combination with water, traffic frequency and kind of traffic.

A six-storey-high building with a green facade forms the entrance of the neighbourhood from the centre. The facade could look like the one Patrick Blanc designed for the Caixa Forum in Madrid.

The streets that form the car and bus route cut through the whole neighbourhood. The green added in this zone has an important cooling function, but also needs to filter out air pollution. The natural green filter in this zone is based on a research done by Alterra Wageningen UR.

In order to optimize the cooling capacity of the trees, a water storage system under the street supplies trees with enough water.

In the Netherlands, a street accompanied by coniferous (non-deciduous) trees is very unusual. On the busy car and bus route, these trees are however necessary, since the air needs to be filtered in both summer and winter.

Along the river Vecht, a quiet and recreational green zone forms a picturesque and pleasant route for cyclists, but also for locals to stroll, let the children play or the dog run. An extension of this green zone would improve the microclimate in Ondiep, offer more recreational space and stimulate bicycle use.

Another green zone is situated in between strips of single-family houses. Here *Malus* (apple) trees will create an intimate peaceful area. The street becomes a car-free zone with space for a water canal with one sloping edge and one hard quay to stroll along.

Water Plan

In the design for Ondiep, the main function of water applications is to supply trees with enough water to maximize their cooling capacity. Next to this, the water cools the outdoor environment. An integral water plan is also calculated to incorporate other aspects of a sustainable water system, like the re-use of water for household activities like toilet flushing. The dwellings discharge all wastewater except for toilet flushing onto the surface water, where helophyte plants clean it.

The water system has a fluctuation of 800 mm to deal with heavy rainfall. Seasonal storage and water for trees and households is all taken into account in the calculation for extra storage.

Water needs to circulate in order to preserve a good quality. Water also demands a lot of space, especially when the edges need to be natural slopes. In many streets this space is simply not available. However, there are other possibilities; instead of surface water, it is possible to lift the water up to street level. This so called 'shallow water' has to be pumped up from the surface water to a shallow canal that ensures a water circulation. Rainwater from roofs and pavement streams into a drain at surface level and is collected in the shallow canals.

[. . .]

CONCLUSION

The two design plans for Ondiep show that there are enough possibilities to apply the design principles to diminish the accumulation of heat. When a neighbourhood needs to be renovated anyway, measures against heat accumulation can be combined with other measures that are necessary to improve the social, physical or economical condition.

[. . .] A climate adaptation plan can only be successful when it is also addressing social, economical and spatial aspects. If an adaptation measure leads to a solution on various levels, we do not even need all the quantifications. If we take green as an example, besides cooling it has a positive effect on the human psyche in preventing depression, etc. Green also produces oxygen and filters particulate matter and ozone out of the air. With an increase of green routes through a city, bicycle use is stimulated and green forms a habitat for fauna and makes a city more attractive and improves its image.

NOTE

1. ET: Evaporation and transpiration of vegetation.

REFERENCES

Baumüller, J.A.A.V.V. *Climate booklet for urban development*. Stuttgart, Germany: Ministry of Economy Baden-Wuerttemberg; 2008.

California Energy Commission. Building energy efficiency standards, http://www.energy.ca.gov/title24/2005standards/index.html; 2009 [accessed 7.11.09].

City of Portland. Sustainable Stormwater management, http://www.portlandonline.com/BES/index.cfm?c=34598; 2008 [accessed 7.11.09].

Ferkenhooff, E. The greening of Chicago. *Time*, www.time.com/time/nation/article/0,8599,1193833,00.html; 2006 [accessed 7.11.09].

Futcher, J.A. 658-Ice Tea City. In: PLEA 2008 – 25th Conference on Passive and Low Energy Architecture, Dublin, Ireland; 2008.

Greenspace. Final Report, www.green-space.org; 2005.

Hitchcock, D. *Cool Houston! A plan for cooling the region*. Houston, US: Houston Advanced Research Centre; 2004.

Hoyois, P., Below, R., Scheuren, J.-M., Guha-Sapir, D. *Annual disaster statistical review: Numbers and trends 2006*. (Centre for Research on the Epidemiology of Disasters (CRED). Belgium, Brussels: School of Public Health, Catholic University of Louvain Brussels; 2007.

Kravčík, M., Pokorny, K.J., Kováč, M., Tóth, E. *Water for the recovery of the climate: A new water paradigm*. Publication from partner cooperation between the People and Water NGO, the Association of Towns and Municipalities of Slovakia, ENKI and the Foundation for the Support of Civic Activities; 2007.

KNMI. KNMI Climate Change Scenarios 2006 for the Netherlands. The Netherlands: De Bilt; 2006.

Mairie de Paris. Végétalisation des toitures-terrases, http://www.paris.fr/portail/Urbanisme/Portal.lut?pageid=6785&documenttypeid=5&document id=63491&portlet id=15473; 2009 [accessed 7.11.09].

McPherson, E. Cooling urban heat islands with sustainable landscapes. *The Ecological City: Preserving and Restoring Urban Biodiversity* 1994: 161–171.

Nishimura, N., Nomura, T., Iyota, H., Kimoto, S. Novel water facilities for creation of comfortable urban micrometeorology. *Solar Energy* 1998; 64:197–207.

Oke, T. *Boundary layer climates*. New York: Routledge; 1987.

Rafailidis, S. Influence of building areal density and roof shape on the wind characteristics above a town. *Boundary-Layer Meteorology* 1997; 85:255–271, Kluwer Academic Publishers.

Rosenzweig, C., Solecki, W.D., Slosberg, R.B. *Mitigating New York City's heat Island with urban forestry, living roofs and light surfaces*. New York, NY: New York State Energy Research and Development Authority; 2006.

Santamouris, M., editor. *Energy and climate in the urban built environment*. London: James and James; 2001.

Schmidt, M. *The contribution of rainwater harvesting against global warming*. London, UK: Technische Universität Berlin, IWA Publishing; 2006.

Shashua-Bar, L., Hoffman, M.E. Vegetation as a climatic component in the design of an urban street: An empirical model for predicting the cooling effect of urban green areas with trees. *Energy and Buildings* 2000; 31:221–235.

Taha, H., Rosenfeld, A., Akbari, H., Huang, J. Residential cooling loads and the urban heat islands-the effect of albedo. *Building and Environment* 1988; 23(4):271–283.

Upmanis, H., Eliasson, I., Lindqvist, S. The influence of green areas on nocturnal temperatures in a high latitude city (Goteborg, Sweden). *International Journal of Climatology* 1998; 18:681–700.

Waterplan Rotterdam. Groene Daken, http://www.waterplan.rotterdam.nl/smartsite1144. dws?Menu=700025&MainMenu=700025&channel=19500&goto=2169469; 2008 [accessed 7.11.09].

WHO. *Health and global environmental change*; Geneva: World Health Organization, 2004.

Xiaomin, X., Zhen, H., Jiasong, W. The impact of urban street layout on local atmospheric environment. *Building and Environment* 2006; 41:1352–1363.

23 Urban Design and Adapting to Flood Risk

The Role of Green Infrastructure

*Mick Lennon, Mark Scott
and Eoin O'Neill*

EDITOR'S INTRODUCTION

Planner Mick Lennon, along with faculty colleagues Mark Scott and Eoin O'Neill at University College Dublin, Ireland, explore the challenges and opportunities of adapting to increased stormwater due to climate change and urbanization. They propose that urban design strategies be integrated with stormwater planning as a response to the traditional, hard-engineered approaches of the past. In addition to the human cost of flood damage, these authors note the growing economic cost associated with catastrophic flooding. The authors call for a multi-disciplinary approach to addressing flooding that brings urban design and planning to the forefront of adaptation. The theme of nested spatial units discussed in the micro-climate planning articles is relevant in this article as well with the urban watershed as the unit of analysis that is nested in a larger watershed. The contribution of each watershed to the overall water balance is a key concept for more holistic stormwater planning.

The authors call for a transformative approach to stormwater management that goes beyond simply accommodating flooding or trying to manage it with hard structures. Instead, stormwater is an asset to be incorporated in a manner that increases ecological functioning, recreational opportunities, and urban fabric using green infrastructure. The authors illustrate this approach using examples from Europe and North America that show these multiple benefits. In addition, they give policy examples of cities that have promoted green infrastructure through a variety of planning regulations and incentive systems. The evolutionary approach proposed in this article is akin to the adaptive gradients proposed earlier in this book by Hamin Infield and colleagues. The idea is that using urban design as a frame creates more holistic green infrastructure projects that can evolve and change over time to respond to changing hydrologic conditions and societal needs.

URBAN DESIGN AND ADAPTING TO FLOOD RISK: THE ROLE OF GREEN INFRASTRUCTURE

INTRODUCTION

Recent severe flooding events in the United Kingdom and Ireland have once again highlighted the vulnerability of urban settlements to the ever-more-prevalent effects of climate change. [. . .] While the initial debate in the aftermath of such flooding events often centres on the immediate recovery efforts, increasingly flood risk (and the potential for increased risk from climate change impacts) raises more fundamental questions concerning how urban places should prepare or transform to cope with increased exposure to flooding events. This Practice Paper seeks to position urban design as central to flood risk management strategies, advancing an evolutionary resilience framework and design principles, operationalized through green infrastructure (GI) at the urban scale.

International literature on flooding has, until recent years, tended to focus on flood defence measures to reduce the probability of flooding. Of particular note within the recent crisis is how a legacy of past 'hard' engineering interventions that sought to constrain rivers and channel runoff failed in the face of exceptional rainfall. Moreover, as Harries and Penning-Rowsell (2011) identify, institutional cultures and public perceptions formed when structural, engineered approaches were the norm tend to hamper the ability of government policies to implement a broader range of adaptation measures. However, the potential costs of flooding have driven a renewed interest in flood risk management around the globe. For example, a recent study published in *Nature Climate Change* (Jongman et al. 2014) suggests that the costs of flooding throughout Europe (to homes, businesses, infrastructure, etc.) are likely to rise from an annual cost of €4.5 billion at present to €23 billion per year by 2050 under anticipated climate change impacts and current trends in socio-economic development. Both the scale of vulnerability and the complexity of flooding causes undermines the efficacy of traditional 'keep floodwater out' approaches. [. . .] The benefits (damages avoided) of this approach may be very large. Again, taking account of anticipated climate change impacts and current trends in socio-economic development, Feyen and Watkiss (2011) suggest the annual benefits of adaptation to river flooding across Europe will increase from about €1.3 billion today to €8.3 billion in the 2020s, and may be up to €50 billion by the 2080s. [. . .] Within this context, urban design has the potential to move centre stage as part of a 'whole catchment' framework to risk management, particularly relating to encouraging more ecologically sensitive development.

The causes of flooding are complex, requiring multidimensional management approaches. For example, White (2013) outlines the nature of flood risk to include not only fluvial, tidal and coastal flooding, but also exposure to flood risk from surface water, including urban runoff and local drainage failure. Climate change adds a further layer of complexity, with the impact of climate change processes likely to increase flooding vulnerability, both inland and coastal, e.g. caused by sea level rise and storm surges in coastal locations, and increased frequency of extreme precipitation events is expected to increase risks associated with surface, fluvial and groundwater flooding, with consequences for property, livelihoods, infrastructure, agricultural production and ecosystems (EEA 2008). In this context, White argues that the lessons of flood risk management in England over the last decade highlight the dangers of 'false precision' when calculating flood risk and translating these risks into spatial plans. Instead, White calls for a more critical stance towards flood risk data and for empowering urban policy-makers to intervene on a more precautionary basis.

The costly, and at times irreparable, damage left in the wake of traditional flood defences being overwhelmed or failing highlights the lack of critical attention to 'resilience' in approaches to urban flood risk management. Here, resilience denotes a heuristic for conceptualizing change management. The term has an inherent normative dimension that seeks to shift thinking towards design approaches that are more responsive to disturbance (Barr and Devine-Wright 2012; Plieninger and Bieling 2012). Much contemporary debate concerning the use of the concept centres on the distinction between 'equilibrium' and 'evolutionary' interpretations of resilience (Scott 2013). The former understanding has its roots in disaster management and concerns a 'survival discourse' that focuses on the ability of a system to 'bounce back' towards 'business as usual' following a catastrophe (Shaw and Maythorne 2013). In contrast, 'evolutionary' resilience challenges the desire for a single-state equilibrium or a 'return to normal'. Instead, it emphasizes an ongoing evolutionary change process (Scott 2013). This interpretation focuses on resilience as enabling transformation such that disturbance delivers the spur for re-invention and thereby ensures strength through continuing reflection (Erixon, Borgström, and Andersson 2013). Therefore, 'evolutionary' resilience entails a more radical and optimistic perspective that embraces the opportunity to 'bounce forward' (Shaw and Maythorne 2013). It seeks to supplant a desire for stability with the acceptance of inevitable change such that it inverts conventional modes of thought by 'assuming change and explaining stability, instead of assuming stability and explaining change' (Folke, Colding, and Berkes 2003, 352).

This Practice Paper seeks to outline the benefit of advancing evolutionary resilience in urban design for flood risk management. It identifies and critically examines three alternative approaches and associated design philosophies in response to the problem of urban flooding. [. . .] The paper then examines the potential of the GI approach as a means to realize evolutionary resilience in designing urban environments for enhanced drainage management. [. . .]

DESIGNING FOR FLOOD RISK MANAGEMENT

Designing for flood risk management is a complex endeavour often involving many variables, uncertainty, large temporal and spatial scales, and a multitude of agents. Nevertheless, it is possible to identify three broad approaches and the design philosophies associated with each. These approaches are characterized by different functional objectives, namely: persistence, adaptation and transformation.

Persistence

The fabric of urban areas was largely produced without much consideration for flood risk (White 2008). Where regard was had to flooding, this most frequently involved the construction of expensive 'hard' solutions such as levees, flood barriers and the underground piping of historic drainage channels. Consequently, the accumulated legacy of design interventions has often interrupted natural flooding processes by removing vegetation, paving extensive areas with artificial impermeable surfaces, eliminating natural water storage capacity and disrupting flow paths (O'Neill 2013). The consequence has been a divorcing of urban areas and their populations from environmental constraints (White 2008), and, compounded by the trust people place in technical experts and structural solutions (Terpstra 2011), an embedding of urban areas with a vulnerability to flood risk. Such traditional approaches to flood risk management persist. In essence, these approaches are characterized by a design philosophy focused on resisting the perceived capriciousness of nature and are typified by modes of intervention wherein the functional objective is exclusively directed at flood 'defence'. [. . .] [T]he enduring failure of such a 'hard' approach to address urban flooding issues effectively has undermined its authority and prompted alternative perspectives on managing flood risk. One such perspective concerns a greater focus on adapting urban environments to the inevitability of flooding.

Adaptation

The turn to adapting urban environments for flood risk management reflects broader societal concerns with the inevitability of some degree of climate change. It is a design response to a projected increase in the frequency and severity of flooding events (Bulkeley 2013). This perspective seeks to complement rather than challenge traditional 'hard' approaches focused on flood defence through recalibrating design to facilitate a more flood adapted urban environment. In this sense, urban design initiatives focused on adaptation signal a desire to promote a 'bounce back' form of resilience. Such an approach is characterized by a design philosophy concerned with accommodating the unavoidability of flooding events through modifications to architectural detailing and design of the public realm. For example, this approach is evident in raised plinths to 'flood proof' new developments, the allocation of attenuation areas in car parks and sequential methods of land-use allocation that aim to steer developments away from identified flood plains (Roaf, Crichton, and Nicol 2009; Smith 2009). As a departure from traditional governance approaches, a focus on adaptation encompasses a broader skill set and therefore involves the cooperation of a variety of construction-related disciplines. In the case of municipal authorities, this is reflected in efforts to promote greater cooperation between engineers, architects, urban designers, emergence planners and landscape architects.

However, there is an increasing focus on moving beyond urban design adaptation. Such interest echoes wider concern with the appropriateness of current approaches to flood risk management and calls for a more profound re-evaluation of how flooding issues are considered in urban environments. [. . .]

Transformation

As with approaches focused on adaptation, those advocating transformative approaches to flood risk management view a measure of climate change as inevitable. However, calls for a transformation in urban design involves moving beyond a focus on construction-based interventions or simple sequential land-use modes of governance aimed at flood risk 'defence' and/or 'accommodation'. Instead, it entails a holistic reassessment of the relationship between the built and non-built components of urban environments (O'Neill and Scott 2011). In this way, a transformation demands seeing the urban environment as a hydrological unit embedded within a larger or series of larger hydrological units, rather than as a collection of various built elements adversely affected by flooding. This approach advances a design philosophy focused on biomimicry and working with water rather than concentrating solely on controlling or avoiding it (Grant 2012; Novotny, Ahern, and Brown 2010), reducing the hydrological impact of the built environment, thereby transforming the urban footprint of the city (O'Neill 2013). In this sense, a transformative perspective seeks to orientate urban design towards an 'evolutionary' form of resilience thinking. In desiring greater holism in the consideration of flooding, such an approach necessitates broadening the skill set of those involved in flood risk management beyond disciplines primarily concerned with construction. Hence, it involves new working arrangements with an array of professionals not normally associated with flooding-related design issues, such as ecologists, recreation and transport planners, and more conventional participants such as engineers, architects, urban designers, emergency planners and landscape architects. Furthermore, a transformative and holistic approach to flooding would require full collaboration in interdisciplinary partnerships as opposed to cooperation between different disciplines that remain largely isolated beyond the requirements of occasional association during flood risk design exercises (Lennon 2014). This begs the question: what form could such a transformation in urban design take? An answer to this may be found in the increasing popularity of the GI approach to planning, design and management.

THE GREEN INFRASTRUCTURE (GI) APPROACH

The theory and application of GI has grown in depth and breadth over the past decade [. . .] Although there remains an array of interpretations as to what exactly it entails (Cameron et al. 2012; EC 2012; Ellis 2013), most understandings resonate with the explanation offered by Benedict and McMahon (2006, 1) as: 'an interconnected network of natural areas and other open spaces that conserves natural ecosystem values and functions [. . .] and provides a wide array of benefits for people and wildlife'. Prominent among these 'benefits' is the retention of water so that drainage into watercourses is more protracted and the peaks in flow associated with flood events are avoided. A GI approach seeks to realize such benefits by giving greater consideration to multifunctionality in the design process. [. . .]

Attention to enhancing the multifunctional potential of sites is a key attribute differentiating the GI design philosophy from more conventional approaches focused solely on flood 'defence' or 'accommodation'. [. . .] Indeed, advocates of a GI design approach contend that the multifunctional potential of the wider urban environment can be maximized by combining the need for temporary flood storage with other ongoing functional, recreational and ecological uses (White 2008).

The city of Portland, Oregon, in the northwestern United States presents an example of how a GI design approach to flood risk management can provide an array of benefits for the local community at the site and neighbourhood scales. Prompted by an excessive burden on the city's drainage system, resulting in an average of 50 combined sewer overflows (about 6 billion gallons) to the Willamette River in 1990, Hoyer, Dickhaut, and Weber (2011) note how Portland's municipal authority has employed a suite of GI design initiatives to alleviate the pressure on the sewer system and reduce adverse impacts to urban watercourses. Such measures have included financial incentives for downpipe disconnection (with stormwater redirected to lawns, gardens and infiltration into the ground), the construction of green roofs that enhance local biodiversity and the provision of a green space recreational network that simultaneously serves to slow rainwater runoff into the Willamette. [. . .] The cumulative effect of numerous local small-scale GI measures [. . .] has helped to reactivate the local hydrological cycle, thereby easing pressure on the city's combined sewer system by over 2.1 billion gallons annually and consequently reducing flood events generated by under-capacity in the urban drainage system. [. . .] Indeed, 'soft' design initiatives undertaking by the municipal authority to reduce the quantum of impervious surfaces in the urban area have improved the appearance and experience of the urban landscape. Such initiatives include roadside tree planting, increasing the number of publically accessible green spaces and the construction of attractive swales and rain gardens in residential streets which are specifically designed to supplement a decentralized approach to drainage management, enhance streetscape appearance and boost local biodiversity. [. . .]

At the city scale, guidance on how a GI design approach may be advanced is provided by points-based planning regulations in Berlin (Kazmierczak and Carter 2010), Malmö (Kruuse 2011) and Seattle in Washington state (Beatley 2010). The objective of such schemes is to increase the quantum and quality of permeable surface area in a move towards achieving water infiltration rates experienced in natural ground cover. This is promoted through increased planting to deliver a combination of reduced water runoff rates, enhanced biodiversity and an improved aesthetic experience of urban spaces. These schemes enable designers to integrate landscaping elements flexibly into developments by allowing them to propose designs that respond to the particular opportunities and constraints of a specific site. The 'Biotope Area Factor' (Berlin) and 'Green Factor' (Malmö and Seattle) operate by allocating different scores to different design elements. The developer must ensure that the proposed design exceeds a certain minimum threshold to proceed with construction on site. [. . .] Prominent in these scoring mechanisms are issues concerning drainage management, ecological enhancement, recreational space provision and aesthetic benefit. In Berlin, focus is placed on the use of planting schemes in private properties to increase on-site water retention.

In Malmö, greater emphasis has been placed on improving user experience of semi-private residential courtyards by constructing new water retention areas that provide ecologically rich habitats and offer recreational opportunities for local residents. These private and semi-private space issues are also addressed in the Seattle Green Factor scheme, although here considerable stress has also been given to public spaces. In this scheme, applicants to the municipal authority are permitted to include landscape-enhancing elements in public areas adjacent to the development site. This has increased the permeable surface cover in public areas by incentivizing developers to improve the quality of the public realm by investing in the streetscape. [. . .]

Successfully implementing these initiatives involves the acquisition of new design skills and knowledge concerning less interventionist, yet innovative approaches to maintenance. For example, Portland has attempted to reconcile aesthetic appeal with a low-cost approach by 'refining the planting plans for green streets to ensure they are both attractive and low-maintenance' (Hoyer, Dickhaut, and Weber 2011, 44). This approach has been synergized with community development initiatives by supporting local residents in helping maintain the appearance and functionality of green street initiatives. [. . .] In this sense, city-wide GI initiatives can have a direct positive impact on urban design at a range of scales and cater for a variety of functions. These different approaches also reflect different design traditions, property rights and regulatory approaches, and environmental contexts. However, the key principle is transferable across these contexts: the enhancement, creation and the integration of multifunctional green networks and spaces into ecologically sensitive urban development. Uniting these approaches is a holistic and optimistic perspective to forging positive synergies between the complex abiotic, biotic and cultural dimensions of the urban environment (Ahern 2013). Each of the examples outlined here thereby advances evolutionary resilience by promoting a future-orientated stance that elevates innovation through continuing reflection in a desire to 'bounce forward' in response to an assumption of ongoing change [. . .].

CONCLUSIONS

[. . .] This paper advances the GI approach as a means for realizing evolutionary resilience in urban flood risk management. It does not oppose the application of traditional or adaptation-focused approaches to flooding, as these are likely to be the most appropriate modes of action in certain circumstances. However, the paper does challenge the dominance of traditional 'hard' solutions to issues of flood risk management, while concurrently suggesting that an adaptation-focused approach is often limited in scope and ambition. Thus, in seeking to complement these two approaches, this paper advances an alternative design perspective that advocates 'working with' as opposed to 'dominating' or 'adapting to' nature. Such an approach necessitates a broader skill set than that which is currently deployed in addressing urban flooding issues. For example, a challenge arising is to advance urban design that 'works with' nature by creating a more 'permeable landscape' which provides for water absorption and storage, habitat connectivity, recreational access, and the requirements of emergency response (legible evacuation route to safety). Consequently, it requires greater collaboration between an array of different specialisms. However, it is contended that the hard work of producing these new interdisciplinary working arrangements will ultimately result in an aesthetically and functionally enhanced urban public realm.

This paper focused on the role of GI in adapting and transforming urban places in the context of increased flood risk. In a Northern European context, anticipated climate change will increase flooding risk with increased frequency of precipitation events. Within this context, a tension potentially arises between GI measures to adapt to climate change and policies designed to mitigate climate change. For example, over the last two decades urban planning orthodoxy has promoted compact urban form and higher densities to reduce energy consumption and the ecological footprint of cities (Howley, Scott, and Redmond 2009). However, as McEvoy, Lindley, and Handley (2006) outline, densification efforts often pose problems for urban drainage systems, while brownfield sites targeted for development may actually serve more important functions in terms of water retention, recreational uses and urban cooling. At the same time, a GI approach may undermine compact city policies through a greater emphasis on multifunctional green space provision and less intensive urban development patterns. Within the context of mitigation/adaptation tensions, the role of urban design is to reconcile these competing demands within the design process. For example, a GI approach may suggest promoting higher density development within key nodes or public transport corridors (reducing the need for car travel) intermeshed with multifunctional green corridors, or promoting green roofs and green walls to promote water retention within densely developed areas.

REFERENCES

Ahern, J. 2013. "Urban Landscape Sustainability and Resilience: The Promise and Challenges of Integrating Ecology with Urban Planning and Design." *Landscape Ecology* 28 (6): 1203–1212.

Barr, S., and P. Devine-Wright. 2012. "Resilient Communities: Sustainabilities in Transition." *Local Environment* 17 (5): 525–532.

Beatley, T. 2010. *Biophilic Cities: Integrating Nature Into Urban Design and Planning.* London: Island Press.

Benedict, M., and E. McMahon. 2006. *Green Infrastructure: Linking Landscapes and Communities.* London: Island Press.

Bulkeley, H. 2013. *Cities and Climate Change.* London: Routledge.

Cameron, R. W. F., T. Blanuša, J. E. Taylor, A. Salisbury, A. J. Halstead, B. Henricot, and K. Thompson. 2012. "The Domestic Garden: Its Contribution to Urban Green Infrastructure." *Urban Forestry & Urban Greening* 11 (2): 129–137.

EC. 2012. *The Multifunctionality of Green Infrastructure.* Brussels: European Commission.

EEA. 2008. *Impacts of Europe's Changing Climate: 2008 Indicator based Assessment (EEA Report No. 5/2008).* Copenhagen: European Environment Agency (EEA).

Ellis, J. B. 2013. "Sustainable Surface Water Management and Green Infrastructure in UK Urban Catchment Planning." *Journal of Environmental Planning and Management* 56 (1): 24–41.

Erixon, H., S. Borgström, and E. Andersson. 2013. "Challenging Dichotomies: Exploring Resilience as an Integrative and Operative Conceptual Framework for Large-Scale Urban Green Structures." *Planning Theory & Practice* 14 (3): 349–372.

Feyen, L., and P. Watkiss. 2011. "Technical Policy Briefing Note 3: The Impacts and Economic Costs of River Floods in Europe, and the Costs and Benefits of Adaptation: Results from the EC RTD Climate Cost Project." In *The Climate Cost Project: Final report*, edited by P. Watkiss. Stockholm: Stockholm Environment Institute.

Folke, C., J. Colding, and F. Berkes. 2003. "Synthesis: Building Resilience and Adaptive Capacity in Social-Ecological Systems." In *Navigating Social-Ecological Systems: Building Resilience for Complexity and Change*, edited by F. Berkes, J. Colding, and C. Folke. Cambridge: Cambridge University Press.

Grant, G. 2012. *Ecosystem Services Come to Town: Greening Cities by Working with Nature*. Chichester: Wiley.

Harries, T., and E. Penning-Rowsell. 2011. "Victim Pressure, Institutional Inertia and Climate Change Adaptation: The Case of Flood Risk." *Global Environmental Change* 21 (1): 188–197.

Howley, P., M. Scott, and D. Redmond. 2009. "Sustainability Versus Liveability: An Investigation of Neighbourhood Satisfaction." *Journal of Environmental Planning and Management* 52 (6): 847–864.

Hoyer, J., W. Dickhaut, and B. Weber. 2011. *Water Sensitive Urban Design: Principles and Inspiration for Sustainable Stormwater Management in the City of the Future*. Hamburg: Hafen City Universität.

Jongman, B., S. Hochrainer-Stigler, L. Feyen, J. C. J. H., Aerts, R. Mechler, W. J. W. Botzen, L. M. Bouwer, G. Pflug, R. Rojas, and P. J. Ward. 2014. "Increasing Stress on Disaster-Risk Finance Due to Large Floods." *Nature Climate Change* 4: 264–268. doi:10.1038/nclimate2124.

Kazmierczak, A., and J. Carter. 2010. "Adaptation to Climate Change Using Green and Blue Infrastructure." In *A Database of Case Studies*. Manchester: University of Manchester.

Kruuse, A. 2011. "The Green Space Factor and Green Points." *Town & Country Planning* 80: 287–290.

Lennon, M. 2014. "Green Infrastructure and Planning Policy: A Critical Assessment." *Local Environment* 20 (8): 957–980. http://dx.doi.org/10.1080/13549839.2014.880411

McEvoy, D., S. Lindley, and J. Handley. 2006. "Adaptation and Mitigation in Urban Areas: Synergies and Conflicts." In *Proceedings of the Institution of Civil Engineers-Municipal Engineer*, 185–192. London: Published for the Institution of Civil Engineers by Thomas Telford Services, c1992-.

Novotny, V., J. Ahern, and P. Brown. 2010. *Water Centric Sustainable Communities: Planning, Retrofitting and Building the Next Urban Environment*. Hoboken, NJ: Wiley.

O'Neill, E. 2013. "Neighbourhood Design Considerations in Flood Risk Management." *Planning Theory and Practice* 14: 129–134.

O'Neill, E., and M. Scott. 2011. "Policy & Planning Brief." *Planning Theory and Practice* 12 (2): 312–317.

Plieninger, T., and C. Bieling. 2012. "Connecting Cultural Landscapes to Resilience." In *Resilience and the Cultural Landscape: Understanding and Managing Change in Human-Shaped Environments*, edited by T. Plieninger and C. Bieling. Cambridge: Cambridge University Press.

Roaf, S., D. Crichton, and F. Nicol. 2009. *Adapting Buildings and Cities for Climate Change: A 21st Century Survival Guide*. Oxford: Elsevier.

Scott, M. 2013. "Resilience: A Conceptual Lens for Rural Studies?" *Geography Compass* 7 (9): 597–610.

Shaw, K., and L. Maythorne. 2013. "Managing for Local Resilience: Towards a Strategic Approach." *Public Policy and Administration* 28 (1): 43–65.

Smith, P. F. 2009. *Building for a Changing Climate: The Challenge for Construction, Planning and Energy*. London: Earthscan

Terpstra, T. 2011. "Emotions, Trust, and Perceived Risk: Affective and Cognitive Routes to Flood Preparedness Behavior." *Risk Analysis* 31 (10): 1658–1675.

White, I. 2008. "The Absorbent City: Urban form and Flood Risk Management." *Proceedings of the ICE—Urban Design Planning* 161 (4): 151–161.

White, I. 2013. "The More We Know, the More We Know We Don't Know: Reflections on a Decade of Planning, Flood Risk Management and False Precision." *Planning Theory and Practice* 14: 106–114.

24 Green Infrastructure
A Landscape Approach

David C. Rouse and Ignacio Bunster-Ossa

EDITOR'S INTRODUCTION

This excerpt from the American Planning Association (APA)'s publication on green infrastructure proposes a landscape approach that incorporates the full range of human desires for the places they live. The authors, planner David C. Rouse and landscape architect Ignacio Bunster-Ossa (WRT Philadelphia), describe six principles for the planning and design of green infrastructure. The first principle, multi-functionality, is theme that runs through many of the articles in this reader. Climate change adaptation is one function alongside many including flood mitigation, stormwater management, and recreation. Connectivity is a hallmark of integrated green infrastructure projects and is often overlooked in some site-scale adaptation projects. Habitability means that the green infrastructure should provide a place for people as well as other forms of life. Resiliency, discussed previously in this book, is a key aspect of green infrastructure that applies to stormwater management. Identity is about creating a "sense of place" that is based in the unique local characteristics, esthetics, and culture. Finally, return on investment is the notion that green infrastructure must demonstrate that is it an economically efficient solution, as compared to traditional gray infrastructure.

The authors use the Green City, Clean Waters program from the City of Philadelphia (US) to demonstrate the integration of sustainable principles. Like the Portland example in Mick Lennon and colleagues article in Chapter 23, the impetus for Philadelphia was federal environmental mandates to retrofit an outdated combined sewer system. In lieu of costly gray infrastructure, Philadelphia embarked on an innovative, holistic green infrastructure solution that addressed energy, environment, equity, economy, and engagement. The project used an integrated approach that benefits local residents through new parks and open space, green streets, green roofs, and other strategies. The authors conclude with key lessons for planners that can be transferred to many other settings.

What is a "landscape" approach to green infrastructure? How is it more than just implementing green infrastructure measures at various scales, from green roofs and rain gardens to regional greenways and open space? The answer lies in conceiving of landscape as an integrated whole, as the "scene" across the land that encapsulates the adaptation and manipulation of natural form and processes for the purpose of human habitation. A landscape approach to green infrastructure entails a design vision that translates planning strategy into physical reality while heeding the ecological and cultural characteristics of a particular locale—whether a region or an individual building site. It is, by necessity, an approach that involves esthetics: what a place should look like as informed by the people who live on the land, their past, and their aspirations.

[. . .] So what, specifically, can planners do to promote green infrastructure? [. . .]

The key is to find common interests across disciplinary and organizational boundaries to make green infrastructure a vital part of the fabric of our communities and landscapes. This chapter defines a set of unifying principles intended to accomplish this. It indicates how green infrastructure can be woven into the established missions, services, and methods of planning and other professions.

GREEN INFRASTRUCTURE: A LANDSCAPE APPROACH

PLANNING AND DESIGN PRINCIPLES

Six principles inform the planning and design of green infrastructure across different disciplines and scales of professional practice:

1. Multi-functionality
2. Connectivity
3. Habitability
4. Resiliency
5. Identity
6. Return on investment

Multi-Functionality

This principle builds on the concept of the triple bottom line—the environmental, economic, and community benefits provided by green infrastructure. Also called ecosystem services, these benefits derive from the multiple and overlapping functions provided across the different systems—hydrology, transportation, energy, economy, and so on—that can intersect in green infrastructure. The multi-functionality principle calls on planners and designers to maximize value for the communities they serve by using green infrastructure to achieve seemingly disparate goals such as flood control, reduced dependence on imported energy, and improved public health outcomes. [. . .]

Connectivity

This principle means that green infrastructure is most effective in providing services and benefits when it is part of a physically connected system across the landscape (e.g., a natural reserve or a park). For example, a natural reserve that is connected to others by a corridor of native vegetation (e.g., along a river or stream) is more valuable (all other factors being equal) than one surrounded by urban development, because it allows for wildlife movement between different habitat areas. [. . .]

Habitability

The habitability principle positions green infrastructure as visible space that provides outdoor habitat for people, flora, and fauna. The mission of the public health profession—to foster conditions in which people can be healthy—is central to the idea of habitable green infrastructure. Examples of green infrastructure planning and design outcomes that advance this principle include improved air and water quality (resulting in improved health of humans and ecosystems), increased opportunity for outdoor recreation and exercise, and restoration of native habitats.

Resiliency

Defined as the ability to recover from or adapt to disturbance and change, resiliency is particularly relevant in a time when natural and human ecosystems are experiencing accelerating change and instability, ranging from higher energy prices to economic shocks to the projected effects of climate change. [. . .]

Green infrastructure can increase community resiliency over short and long timeframes (e.g., reduced damage and faster recovery from natural disasters, increased ability to adapt to climate change). One study concluded that green infrastructure treatments (increased tree cover, green roofs, etc.) could significantly reduce the stormwater runoff and surface temperature increases projected in the 2080s as a result of greenhouse gas emissions (Gill et al. 2007).

Identity

Design of landscape elements to create a perceptible identity and sense of place is a central motivation of landscape architects. Planners often use the term "community character" to express the special and valued attributes that make a place desirable to live in or visit. The identity principle addresses the potential of green infrastructure to contribute to the visual definition of a place. [. . .]

In this context, the integration of art within the public sphere becomes a relevant consideration. In recent decades Ecological Art or "Eco-Art" has emerged as a distinctive genre within the field of public art. [. . .] Thinking across scales, could a recurring motif expressed through stormwater or other forms of green infrastructure help visually define a neighborhood, city, or region? [. . .]

Return on Investment

In a time of scarce financial resources, this principle calls on planners and designers to demonstrate how green infrastructure can reduce costs and yield positive financial outcomes for governments, institutions, businesses, and citizens. Examples of ways that green infrastructure can generate monetary value include increasing land values, providing a catalyst for economic development, lessening energy consumption, and reducing gray infrastructure costs. Planners and designers should use cost-benefit analyses to justify green infrastructure approaches, to plan and design green infrastructure components to achieve goals such as reduced energy use and increased revenue, and to establish targets and indicators to monitor whether these goals are being met in implementation. [. . .]

In his inaugural address, Philadelphia Mayor Michael Nutter put forth a vision to make Philadelphia the greenest city in America. To make this vision a reality, the mayor appointed a director of sustainability who embarked on a process to create an action plan for sustainability. This plan, Greenworks Philadelphia, elevated and integrated the multiple sustainability efforts that were already underway and set 15 sustainability targets in the areas of energy, environment, equity, economy, and engagement.

[. . .]

GREEN INFRASTRUCTURE IN PHILADELPHIA

There is no single definition of sustainability or green infrastructure in Philadelphia, although there are overlapping definitions that are used concurrently. [. . .]

"Green infrastructure" is used broadly, as in the city's comprehensive open space plan, GreenPlan Philadelphia, to refer to the entirety of the city's open space network. The term is also used as shorthand in Philadelphia for green stormwater infrastructure, which is designed to capture and manage stormwater at the source. Greenworks Philadelphia recommends that "the natural links between land and water be reconnected and that green infrastructure—trees, vegetation, and soil—become the City's preferred stormwater management system" (Philadelphia, City of. 2009). The Philadelphia Water Department is currently working to promote and implement green stormwater infrastructure as part of its Green City, Clean Waters program to reduce combined sewer overflows (CSOs). This case study will examine GreenPlan Philadelphia and Green City, Clean Waters in more detail.

Making the Case for Green Infrastructure: GreenPlan Philadelphia

GreenPlan Philadelphia, the city's guide to creating sustainable open space, takes an approach to open space planning that sets it apart from typical open space plans [. . .]. Typically, open space plans focus on specific elements (parks) or specific issues (recreation). GreenPlan Philadelphia makes the case for investment in open space by highlighting the necessary and irreplaceable benefits it provides to the city's environment, economy, and quality of life. [. . .]

Since GreenPlan Philadelphia's completion, the city has taken a number of steps toward implementing the plan's recommendations. Philadelphia's Department of Parks and Recreation used those recommendations in developing Green 2015, a short-term action plan for adding 500 acres of open space to the city by 2015. The Philadelphia Water Department developed its Green City, Clean Waters strategy—discussed in detail ahead—pioneering the use of green infrastructure on public and private property as the primary means of expanding stormwater management capacity and improving water quality. [. . .]

Stormwater Management: GreenPlan Meets Green City, Clean Waters

[. . .]

Federal and state mandates related to clean waterways have required that the city, through the Philadelphia Water Department (PWD), develop a strategy to better manage the discharge of pollutants into streams via stormwater. PWD has embraced this challenge and is striving to become America's model of a 21st-century urban water utility. Clean water is the goal, but PWD realizes that greening the city's streets and lands is the key to fishable, swimmable, safe, attractive, and accessible rivers and streams. Green City, Clean Waters is PWD's strategy for managing stormwater primarily through the expanded implementation of green stormwater infrastructure.

Like many older cities in the United States, 60 percent of Philadelphia is served by combined sewers, which carry both sanitary waste and stormwater in the same pipes during rainfall events. The other 40 percent of the city is served by a separate storm sewer system. Both storm sewers and combined sewers can create problems on both ends of the pipe. If inlets are clogged or pipes are at capacity, stormwater trying to enter backed-up sewers can cause street and basement flooding. And, as stormwater rushes into the city's creeks and rivers, water levels rise, flooding adjacent land, scouring stream banks, and eroding valuable aquatic and riparian habitat. Stormwater, and especially CSOs, threaten the water quality in the city's two main rivers—the Delaware and the Schuylkill—which also happen to be the sources of the city's drinking water.

A Green Stormwater Management Approach

The National Combined Sewer Overflow Control Policy requires that every city with combined sewer overflows must create a Long Term Control Plan to comply with the Clean Water Act. To reduce CSOs, cities must better manage stormwater flowing into combined sewers. The conventional approach to CSO stormwater management is to build additional sewer infrastructure with greater capacity to collect larger volumes of stormwater and then pipe it to deep tanks and tunnels during the storm event. After the storm is over and combined sewer flows return to normal, the sewage that was stored during the storm is then pumped back into the sewer system for treatment at the wastewater treatment plant. Because of the high amount of impervious surface in most cities, and the tremendous volume of runoff that occurs during rainfall events, underground tanks and tunnels to store such runoff temporarily are huge, both in size and cost.

PWD's Green City, Clean Waters approach proposes to rely primarily on a citywide green stormwater infrastructure system with urban streets and lands designed to allow rainfall to infiltrate, evaporate, and be reused where it falls. Managing stormwater at the source keeps it out of the combined sewer system, eliminating the need to increase the system's storage and treatment capacity.

Green Infrastructure Benefits

There are numerous major advantages of the Green City, Clean Waters strategy. The large centralized tunnels and tanks needed with the traditional infrastructure approach require a long time to construct and are unavailable until they are complete. Hence, the city's rivers continue to experience CSOs during the long construction period. Further, the underground tanks and tunnels require significant energy to construct as well as to pump the stored wastewater back to the treatment plant. Because the green stormwater infrastructure approach is distributed throughout the city, there are immediate improvements as smaller, individual projects are implemented and less energy is required long-term for operation.

Traditional "gray" infrastructure succeeds at piping stormwater from city streets to rivers (or storage tunnels), but that is the only function it provides. The green infrastructure approach manages and improves the water quality of stormwater while contributing to the economic, environmental, and social sustainability of the city through a greener city landscape. PWD is looking to receive the greatest return on investment for its stormwater management investment dollars by choosing to invest in infrastructure that both manages stormwater and provides many corollary sustainable benefits.

These benefits are economic, social, and environmental. Green stormwater infrastructure reduces the social cost of poverty by creating jobs that require limited experience and are therefore suitable for individuals who might be otherwise unemployed and living in poverty. It manages stormwater runoff naturally without the cost of expensive pumping and wastewater treatment investments. Green stormwater infrastructure enhancements improve visual amenity, reduce heat island effects, provide cleaner water quality, and provide opportunities to create more desirable outdoor spaces for the public. Trees and parks can transform neighborhoods into exciting and more comfortable places to live, work, and play. Green stormwater infrastructure also reduces the severity of extreme heat events by creating shade, reducing the amount of heat-absorbing pavement and rooftops, and emitting water vapor—all of which cool hot air. Through these cooling effects, and by reducing the volume of water that needs to be stored, piped, and treated, green stormwater infrastructure reduces energy use, fuel use, and carbon emissions.

Infiltrating rainfall on site and directing it along greenways to the city's rivers and streams helps restore the water cycle and reduce the large fluctuations in flows. Last, but not least, green stormwater significantly improves the quality of the stormwater runoff to city streams.

Implementation

PWD has already implemented a number of projects on public property across the city that demonstrate the feasibility of constructing green stormwater infrastructure. The long-term success of the overall green infrastructure approach will require the implementation of green stormwater infrastructure on both public and private property in the future. This is being achieved through projects on public property, a new rate structure for stormwater runoff, and developer and landowner incentives for good stormwater management on private property.

Stormwater regulations adopted by Philadelphia in 2006 require that new development and redevelopment projects address water quality and quantity through stormwater management plans and site designs. Regulations describe the volume of rainfall that must be managed on site, as well as the rate at which stormwater can be released from the site. A development review process has been established for PWD to ensure that development follows these regulations.

PWD also modified the way it charges customers for stormwater management. Traditionally, stormwater management fees were based on the size of the site's water meter (a historical convenience). Under this system, 40,000 stormwater customers, including, for example, parking lots, were not billed because many didn't have a water meter. With PWD's rate reallocation, stormwater charges are based on the amount of runoff from the property, using the gross size of the property and the imperviousness of the land cover—directly tying the amount of runoff produced on a property to the stormwater charge it pays. By implementing green stormwater infrastructure, a landowner can reduce the stormwater fee.

Measuring Progress

The two primary metrics for measuring the success of Green City, Clean Waters implementation are the volume of combined sewer overflows that continue to occur, and the number of "greened acres," a measure of the stormwater volume managed by green stormwater infrastructure. [. . .]

Since 2006, stormwater regulations have reduced runoff by over 1.5 billion gallons per year. As the pace of construction of green infrastructure increases in the upcoming years, Philadelphia anticipates fully managing combined sewer overflows and achieving considerable improvement in the water quality of its streams and rivers, with correspondent benefits to the esthetics, economy, health, and quality of life in the city.

LESSONS LEARNED

Leadership and Vision Are Key

This is particularly important in creating essential change in city workflow and fostering interaction among city departments. Though efforts to plan for and implement green infrastructure started before Mayor Nutter took office, with his leadership on sustainability and the development of Greenworks Philadelphia there has been greater motivation to pursue green infrastructure and sustainability goals.

Green Infrastructure Requires Partnerships

Because green infrastructure, to be effective, needs to be geographically distributed, it is necessary for city departments to work with one another, and for planners, landscape architects, engineers, business owners, developers, and the community to gain buy-in for including green infrastructure in public and private projects.

Multiple Benefits Are a Plus

One of green infrastructure's greatest selling points is that it provides multiple benefits. At a time when budgets are tight, it is important that infrastructure investments can serve multiple benefits. The economic, environmental, and social advantages of green infrastructure are numerous, and those benefits must be communicated.

Passion and Patience Are Needed

Managing change can be challenging. Green infrastructure practices must be fully integrated into day-to-day business processes and work activities. They need to become "business as usual." When embarking on a program that diverges from traditional paths and changes established standards, the reasons for change must be constantly reinforced, and change cannot be expected to occur immediately.

Allow Flexible Approaches

Changes in regulatory review processes and new workflows among city departments may take time, so flexibility is needed to accommodate innovation. Examples include identifying multiple implementation pathways to meet green infrastructure goals and being flexible about pursuing and shifting these pathways. It is very difficult to anticipate all the possible impediments to green infrastructure planning and implementation; having alternative program elements lets you move forward on some program elements, while conflict resolution occurs for other program elements.

Back It Up With Research and Data

There are many intuitive and qualitative benefits to green infrastructure, but getting people to choose green infrastructure over traditional infrastructure can hinge on demonstrating quantitative benefits and the advantages of a green infrastructure approach.—*Andrew Dobshinsky*, AICP, *and Bill Cesanek*, AICP

REFERENCES

Gill, S. E., J. F. Handley, A. R. Ennos, and S. Pauleit. 2007. "Adapting Cities for Climate Change: The Role of the Green Infrastructure." *Built Environment* 33(1): 115–133.

Philadelphia, City of. 2009. *Greenworks Philadelphia*. Mayor's Office of Sustainability. Available at www.phila.gov/green/greenworks/pdf/Greenworks_OnlinePDF_FINAL.pdf.

Introduction to Green Infrastructure for Rising Sea Levels and Coastal Risks

Introduction

Elisabeth M. Hamin Infield

This section of the Reader focuses on challenges and solutions unique to coastal cities, with particular attention to reducing vulnerability to storms and sea level rise. We explore principles for better adapted coastal land use and infrastructure, the challenges for developing countries and tourism locations, and the interconnectedness of urban systems. Students will gain a solid understanding of green as well as hybrid systems for coastal protection, organizational and regulatory approaches such as planned retreat and coastal zone management, and learn by example how scenario analysis can be used to test different outcomes of coastal interventions.

Climate change is affecting urban areas in many different geographies, but coastal cities are certainly among the most vulnerable. Sea level rise will be a gradual but constant pressure on coastal areas, particularly those that are also subsiding (sinking) from natural geological forces or the withdrawal of water from underlying water tables. Coastal storms are likely to intensify, with more frequent hurricanes and other severe events coming in from the ocean. Storms will, on average, drop more rain in inland areas, increasing flooding to the coast as water from inland areas flows to the ocean. At the same time, coastal populations are growing globally and more land is being converted from ecosystems to urban uses, increasing the assets—people, buildings, economic activity—at risk from climate change. Some global urbanization context will help. The UN forecasts that 5 billion people will live in cities by 2030, fully 60% of the world's population (UN, 2012). Roughly 1 in 10 persons currently live in low-elevation coastal zones; in Bangladesh, for instance, 46% of the population lives within 10 meters of the average sea level. A 2015 article by Güneralp, Güneralp and Liu modeled changing urbanization of land and the exposure of infrastructure globally to floods and droughts. They found that by 2030, 40% of urban land will be in high-frequency flood zones, and that the percent of global land that lies within low elevation coastal zones will increase by 230% by 2030. Most of that increase will be in coastal metropolitan areas of Africa and Asia (Güneralp, Güneralp, & Liu, 2015). The problem, in short, is huge, but these newly urbanizing areas also create a potential to use greener and more socially informed approaches to vulnerability reduction, as will be explored in this section.

The traditional approach to protecting coasts has been to 'harden' them—to build concrete seawalls along shores, for instance. These traditional gray approaches provide immediate storm protection and can be quite effective in large storm events. In addition, the engineering and cost estimating for gray approaches is well understood, making these the easy choice for storm protection. But seawalls and other structures often have negative longer-range impacts because they do not respond to changing conditions at the shore, often leading to disappearing beaches in front of seawalls and increased wave intensity. They may also interfere with the touristic benefits of visual and physical access to a sandy beach; for tourism-dependent areas, this can be a significant problem.

An alternative approach is to focus on supporting natural or green infrastructure protections. Natural ecosystem protection for coastal areas includes marshes, mangroves, coral and oyster reefs, sand beaches, dunes and barrier islands. When severe storm events (hurricanes, for example) occur, the marshes, dunes, reefs and barrier islands tend to absorb much of the energy of the waves. Damage happens to these natural shorelines, with sand being scoured away in some areas and thrust ashore into others. But as long as the shoreline has room to move, the basic protective function does not change after a storm event, and the beach rebuilds itself often pretty quickly after a severe storm. As climate change increases and results in rising seas, the shoreline needs to be able to shift inland and upland to accommodate sea level rise. As humans build structures on the beach, natural ecosystem protections are reduced, and the ability of the shore to naturally shift is squeezed, leaving the coastal areas near our cities more vulnerable to storm events. A third approach focuses on managing property rights, zoning, building codes and location of development, or what can be called non-structural approaches. The idea here is to prevent development or redevelopment in vulnerable locations, or to make buildings 'flood-proof' if they will be in a flooding zone.

One widely used way to conceptualize the options for coastal communities is 'protect, accommodate or retreat.' Protection prevents floodwater from coming ashore or reduces wave energy; accommodation reduces the impact of floodwater; retreat moves structures out of harm's way. For example, living shorelines and/or seawalls can provide protection in case of a storm, elevating homes and putting mechanical systems on second floors can provide accommodation that keeps people with power during a flood, and buying out owners of property that repeatedly gets flooded and then demolishing the building is a retreat strategy. New, innovative solutions are combining a variety of approaches into 'hybrid' approaches, representing a portfolio of steps that together provide greater safety from risk while also achieving other goals such as ecosystem health (Sutton-Grier, Wowka, & Bamford, 2015). The image below from Sutton-Grier, Wowka and Bamford demonstrates a range of physical interventions that could be applied in an urban coastal area is shown below. An even broader understanding of hybrid would include more social practices and regulatory approaches.

In the first article in the section, Kousky reviews some of the challenges that working with private coastal property brings. Actions of great benefit to individuals, like seawalls, can be harmful for the broader population and the ecosystem. Theoretically, it might make ecological and economic sense for homeowners to move away from flood zones, but it rarely happens. As she notes, in some areas

Minimal Defense
Many communities have developed
right along the ocean with only minimal
natural defenses from a small strip of
beach between them and the ocean.

Natural
Natural habitats that can provide storm
protection include salt marsh, oyster and
coral reefs, mangroves, seagrasses,
dunes, and barrier islands. A
combination of natural habitats can be
used to provide more protection, as seen
in this figure. Communities could
restore or create a barrier island,
followed by oyster reefs and salt marsh.
Temporary infrastructure (such as a
removable sea wall) can protect natural
infrastructure as it gets established.

Managed Realignment
Natural infrastructure can be used to
protect built infrastructure in order to
help the built infrastructure have a
longer lifetime and to provide more
storm protection benefits. In managed
realignment, communities are moving
sea walls farther away from the ocean
edge, closer to the community and
allowing natural infrastructure to recruit
between the ocean edge and the sea
wall.

Hybrid
In the hybrid approach, specific built
infrastructure, such as removable sea
walls or openable flood gates (as shown
here) are installed simultaneously with
restored or created natural
infrastructure, such as salt marsh and
oyster reefs. Other options include
moving houses away from the water and
raising them on stilts. The natural
infrastructure provides key storm
protection benefits for small to medium
storms and then when a large storm is
expected, the built infrastructure is used
for additional protection.

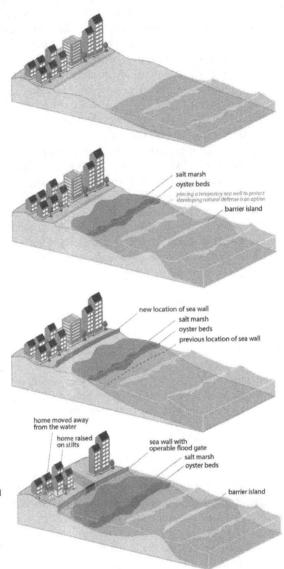

Figure VI.1 Examples of coastal defenses including natural infrastructure, managed realignment, and hybrid approaches.

Source: Sutton-Grier, Ariana & Wowk, Kateryna & Bamford, Holly. (2015). Future of our coasts: The potential for natural and hybrid infrastructure to enhance the resilience of our coastal communities, economies and ecosystems. Environmental Science & Policy. 51. 137–148.

with very high property values, protective measures are likely to be built. In others, it may be possible to accommodate sea level rise through changes to buildings. Still, in some places it may make the most sense to move away—to retreat. She outlines these options and avenues for their implementation.

In the second article, Popkin introduces 'living shorelines.' This is a policy and design model that uses natural protections rather than gray structural approaches. In an innovative program in Maryland, living shorelines are the default choice for protecting shorelines, in effect the plan A; coastal hardening is a Plan B to be used only where living shorelines are shown to be infeasible. Popkin shows ways that ecological solutions provide cost-effective protection during smaller storms along with a wide range of co-benefits.

Highly urbanized coastal environments require integrated consideration of a wide variety of infrastructural systems, and may be an appropriate place for structural solutions that require less urban space. Kirshen et al. in this section demonstrate one approach to the complexity of understanding the likely impacts of climate change on urban infrastructure. The authors create analytic scenarios for metropolitan Boston, Massachusetts, based on demographic change and two different climate change scenarios in addition to the present climate. They use these to test the outcomes from three types of responses to climate change. One scenario is to do no adaptation and just ride out future conditions; another is to utilize highly anticipatory, largely non-structural and green infrastructure solutions—most falling under the 'accommodate or retreat' categories previously described. The third approach is to protect—to harden shorelines and undertake other structural solutions as systems fail. Their analysis finds that in most cases, the best solutions are taken before full climate impacts are experienced, and that many of these are 'no-regrets' actions. The article demonstrates the interactions of systems on each other, which provides an important lesson in the importance of systems thinking and holistically understanding urban environments. Analyzing individual systems as stand-alone entities results in less overall urban efficiency and effectiveness.

For many economies, the unique amenities of coastal areas are their bread and butter, and protecting coasts is central to sustaining livelihoods and achieving sustainable development goals. In the final article in this section, Mycoos provides a holistic view of what climate change means for tourism-based economies in what are called 'small island developing states' or SIDS, and the implications are quite serious. Studies suggest that the potential for economic loss to the Caribbean region as a whole, for example, could amount to 22% of GDP by 2100 (Bueno et al., 2008). Governments in many SIDS demonstrate considerable skill in managing their coasts. In Barbados, as Mycoos reports, the use of Integrated Coastal Zone Management and town planning, requiring setbacks and assuring public access to beaches have helped mitigate the relentless pressure for mass tourism and near-shore beach development. Still, coral reefs are significantly degraded, sewage and water challenges remain, and institutional capacity to enforce good policy is challenged. And, as Mycoos notes:

> SIDS are concerned about the financial costs of climate change adaptation, especially given their small carbon footprints. The question of who will pay

and who will benefit from adaptation measures is controversial and should be the subject of policy debate among Governments, investors and communities.

Taken together, these articles demonstrate that there are significant challenges to coastal protection, but significant innovation and experimentation is underway to improve greener approaches and to document outcomes. Selection of interventions needs to be based on careful analysis of sites and likely future conditions. Green infrastructure along with non-structural approaches will be increasingly important in achieving climate protection while maintaining ecological, esthetic, cultural and economic values of coastal areas. To keep the section manageable, we do not go into technical information on specific interventions. Readers who would like an introduction to the types of interventions being used (e.g., jetties, levees, etc.) can see these in the US Army Corps of Engineers guide to coastal risk reduction (US Army Corps of Engineers, 2013), or other similar guides from their home countries.

REFERENCES

Bueno, R., Herzfeld, C. A., Stanton, E., & Ackerman, F. (2008). *The Caribbean and Climate Change: The Costs of Inaction.* Boston, MA: Stockholm Environment Institute.

Güneralp, B., Güneralp, İ., & Liu, Y. (2015). Changing global patterns of urban exposure to flood and drought hazards. *Global Environmental Change, 31,* 217–225. Doi: https://doi.org/10.1016/j.gloenvcha.2015.01.002

Sutton-Grier, A. E., Wowka, K., & Bamford, H. (2015). Future of our coasts: The potential for natural and hybrid infrastructure to enhance the resilience of our coastal communities, economies and ecosystems. *Environmental Science & Policy, 51*(August), 137–148.

United Nations (2012). *World Urbanization Prospects: The 2011 Revision Highlights.* New York, NY: United Nations Department of Economic and Social Affairs/Population Division, p. 33.

US Army Corps of Engineers. (2013). *Coastal Risk Reduction and Resilience.* CWTS 2013-3. Washington, DC: Directorate of Civil Works, US Army Corps of Engineers.

25 Managing Shoreline Retreat

A US Perspective

Carolyn Kousky

EDITOR'S INTRODUCTION

Across the globe, cities tend to be located at ocean harbors as well as major inland rivers, because one of the first roles of Western-style cities is to serve as a trade hub, and waterways have always provided effective transportation. This has always required some acceptance of flooding, since throughout history, big storms happen. But with climate change's increased frequency and intensity of storms combined with rising seas, the new risk profile of cities is changing. To address this new risk universe, cities, and populations may have to make some hard choices. One of the key choices is whether and when to retreat from the shore, when to try to accommodate coastal risks, and when to protect shorelines. In this article, Kousky describes some of the background on these practices and suggests general principles for how to implement policy changes.

Carolyn Kousky is a University Fellow with Resources for the Future's Land, Water, and Nature Program. She holds a Ph.D. in Public Policy from Harvard University and a B.S. in Earth Systems from Stanford, and is currently affiliated as a Visiting Scholar with the Wharton School of University of Pennsylvania. Her main research areas are the economics and policy of natural disasters and disaster insurance markets. She has examined the demand for natural disaster insurance, the functioning of the National Flood Insurance Program, the incentive effects of disaster aid, and policy responses to potential changes in extreme events with climate change. Kousky is the recipient of the 2013 Tartufari International Prize from the Accademia Nazionale dei Lincei, and was a member of the National Research Council Committee on Analysis of Costs and Benefits of Reforms to the National Flood Insurance Program.

MANAGING SHORELINE RETREAT:
A US PERSPECTIVE

INTRODUCTION

Sea level rise (SLR) projections vary considerably, from 30–180 cm by 2100 (Nicholls and Cazenave 2010). The amount of encroachment will also vary substantially across localities (Pilkey and Cooper 2004), depending on such factors as rates of local subsidence and topography. Adaptation to SLR generally falls into three categories: protect (build infrastructure to protect development), accommodate (build with the water, such as elevating houses), or retreat (move people away from the shore). Hardening the shore will make economic sense for highly developed coastal areas, particularly commercial and population centers. In a few places, accommodation will be a viable option, often for facilities that benefit from being on the coast. But for many coastal areas, or portions of them, retreat will be either preferred or required.

This paper focuses on managing retreat in the United States, although the discussion will be more broadly applicable. Retreat could be left to the market. As inundation occurs, property values should decrease, and people should move inland regardless of government policy. For at least four reasons, however, the market is unlikely to lead to optimal levels or types of retreat in all locations.

First, facing inundation, many coastal property owners and communities may unilaterally invest in seawalls or other structural protection. These structures may protect the property behind them, but will lead to loss of the beach as the sea rises to meet the wall and increase erosion on adjacent properties. The beach provides public benefits, and in many states, the public has legal access to the shore, such that loss of the beach due to unilateral protection may not be economically optimal, legal, or equitable.

Second, coastal ecosystems provide a range of public goods to surrounding communities, such as storm surge mitigation, water quality improvements, habitat, recreational opportunities, and esthetic improvements, which will be underprovided by the market. Such ecosystems will also not be able to migrate inland if they bump up against development or protective infrastructure and could consequently be lost.

Third, coastal property owners may not optimally invest in development, protection, or divestment of coastal areas if they do not bear the full costs of their decisions. Coastal development is often subsidized by public dollars for infrastructure (both initial construction and maintenance or repair). The costs of storm surge events are also not borne fully by communities or private property owners because of federal disaster aid. Finally, and relatedly, private owners may overinvest in risky locations or not optimally time development and divestment decisions because they lack information about the risks or are biased when evaluating risks.

Thus, if adjustments to rising sea levels are reactive and autonomous (Smith 1997; Smithers and Smit 1997)—that is to say, undertaken by individuals as the changes occur—there are likely to be costs for society as a whole. Some form of managed retreat may thus be preferred. Several researchers have predicted areas of protection versus retreat or undertaken a first-order calculation of benefits and costs of different options. This paper does not attempt a cost-benefit analysis of different approaches, but instead considers how retreat can be undertaken in the least costly and least socially disruptive way, if it is the chosen strategy.

This paper proposes a three-part strategy for managing retreat: (1) reduce new development in the highest-risk areas (Section 2); (2) adopt policies that allow for expected and orderly removal or modification of development as inundation occurs (Section 3); and (3) take advantage of disasters to implement retreat strategies (Section 4). Section 5 concludes by discussing the challenges of institutional change, broadly defined, drawing on theories of the policy process. It offers suggestions on when and how institutional change may be achieved.

REDUCING OR RESTRICTING NEW DEVELOPMENT IN HIGH-RISK AREAS

Coastal areas often have higher concentrations of people and capital. A recent analysis finds that 3.7 million Americans live within 1 m of high tide and 22.9 million live within 6 m of high tide (Strauss et al. 2012). Even more people visit coastal areas. Shore locations offer enormous benefits; these may exceed potential disaster damage or generate benefits that exceed eventual loss from SLR. In some situations, however, there are reasons to preclude new development in the highest-risk areas.

The first reason is preventing a squeeze on ecosystems and beaches. Some coastal ecosystems threatened with inundation or flooding provide valuable services that will be lost unless the ecosystems can migrate inland. The benefits are likely to be greatest in areas of higher population density (there are fewer substitutes for the service and more beneficiaries), yet these are the very areas where migration could be hindered by development. Along the Atlantic coast, one analysis found roughly 60% of land below 1 m will likely be developed, preventing inland migration of ecosystems (Titus et al. 2009).

For the most valuable ecosystems and/or where land conservation is less expensive, preventing development to allow for ecosystem migration could be desirable. Land acquisition could be in fee, or development could be restricted by easements or regulatory tools. Although protecting suitable lands now to allow for ecosystem migration in the future may make sense if they would otherwise be lost, this strategy, on a large scale, would likely cost substantially more than the benefits provided, and uncertainties would make acquisition targeting difficult (Titus 1990). A less costly alternative is to integrate managed retreat into the guidelines of established land acquisition programs. For instance, the Maryland Department of Natural Resources modeled SLR impacts to inform ongoing conservation. Targeting to allow for ecosystem migration could also be done by private conservation groups.

A larger question is whether ecosystems can migrate even if the land is set aside. Wetlands can accrete vertically and migrate inland for low rates of SLR but are unlikely to be able to keep pace with rates approaching 7 mm per year (US Climate Change Science Program 2009). Interventions, such as increasing the supply of sediment, may assist migration. Given the uncertainty surrounding SLR rates, there is some value to preserving land to have the option of migration, should it be ecologically feasible, but it would need to be compared to the opportunity costs.

Another possible justification for restrictions on development in high-risk areas is that development is a lumpy investment and can be difficult to undo. It may be optimal to have land in developed uses until a certain time, but converting it back to open space may not be practical. Or it may be desirable to have only a small level of less dense development, but that is politically difficult, particularly if agglomeration effects are operating. Thus realistically, the actual choice may be allowing development to occur and persist past the optimal time or at a greater intensity versus preventing it altogether.

Relatedly, as pointed out by Kydland and Prescott (1977), because economic actors have expectations about how government will respond, implementing policies that tie the hands of policymakers can sometimes be preferred to discretionary policy. They offer a relevant example: the optimal policy at a given time may be to not develop a floodplain, but if development is already there, to protect it. Knowing this, however, developers will build in floodplains, expecting protection. (Indeed, there are many cases of development responding to government-provided protection and vice versa; see Kousky et al. [2006]). Many observers have noted that the benefits of living on the coast will ensure that development behind coastal infrastructure continues (Cooper and McKenna 2008); it may therefore be preferable to have regulations preventing development or strict requirements against investments in shore protection (see Section 3).

Limiting new development in high-risk areas may also be appropriate if those making decisions about development do not have accurate information about climate risks or if they are not bearing all the costs of their decisions. Whether addressing these two issues would actually change development patterns remains to be seen, however, as they may not be influential enough to alter investments. Still, removing these barriers should lead to more efficient decisions.

[. . .]

Designated high-risk areas could also be used to more closely align the benefits and costs of coastal development to promote more economically efficient decision-making. Many costs of coastal development are borne by the government; subsidies for coastal development, such as public funding of roads, water, and sewerage, could be eliminated in the highest-risk areas. The federal government could adopt a policy of not funding major infrastructure or building in these areas. The Coastal Barrier Resources System (CBRS) offers precedent: federal funds are not available for coastal barrier lands designated by Congress. Development in these areas is allowed but not at taxpayer expense. CBRS does not restrict state funds, however; Platt et al. (2002) discuss how a North Carolina barrier island in the CBRS was intensely developed with state and local support. The idea, however, would not be to prevent all development, but to put the costs on property owners so that they can weigh the benefits of their location choice against the full costs. Still, it would be more effective if states enacted complementary policies. Some states, such as Maine, Florida, and Massachusetts, are taking similar steps, limiting public expenditures in certain coastal areas or barrier islands (Godschalk et al. 2000).

As another example of the disassociation of costs and benefits, lower-priced insurance in coastal areas, such as certain flood policies from the National Flood Insurance Program (NFIP) and homeowners policies from state-run programs such as Florida's Citizens, have been blamed with encouraging excess development in high-risk areas, although empirical evidence is limited. Discounted flood insurance premiums in the NFIP had been scheduled to phase out due to 2012 legislation. That reform raised difficult questions about affordability for low- and middle-income households and how much of the cost of locating in risky locations should be borne by those who choose to live there. Under political pressure, Congress reinstated many of the discounted rates in March 2014. Explicitly means-tested programs would offer a better solution (Kousky and Kunreuther 2013).

To guide NFIP rate setting, the Federal Emergency Management Agency (FEMA) maps flood risk, including storm surge risk. [. . .]

The contentious question, of course, is how to define those highest-risk areas. [. . .]

Local governments could be more aggressive in limiting future development through tools such as zoning, transferable development rights programs, density restrictions, and setback requirements. Whether these tools will be economically attractive and politically feasible will depend on local conditions, but a common challenge may be potential loss of tax revenue. Local governments also may be less concerned about benefits and costs accruing in the future, a common political economy challenge.

BACKING AWAY FROM THE SHORE

As the sea rises, inundated property and infrastructure will have to be abandoned. Relocating infrastructure inland in advance of any inundation is being considered in several locations that are less developed and largely recreational. At Ocean Beach in San Francisco, for example, the plan involves moving a highway and parking lot inland, along with restoration activities, recreational enhancement, and limited protection of certain infrastructure (SPUR 2012). The full plan is not cheap, with estimates at $350 million, but supporters say the costs of inaction could be even higher.

Relocating development and infrastructure can often be contentious. A plan for Goleta Beach in Santa Barbara that would remove parking spaces, move buried lines, and eliminate rock revetments that currently provide erosion protection has sparked resistance from some, as has a plan to halt renourishment undertaken to protect a parking lot in the Chincoteague National Wildlife Refuge.

The retreat option is even more challenging when private homes are targeted. Communities or property owners may build seawalls and other measures to hold back the rising waters and protect their investments rather than relocate. Structural protection will eventually result in beach and ecosystem loss, however, so there may be a public interest in preventing hardening of the shore. Thus, SLR will likely present a conflict between the property rights of homeowners and public ownership of intertidal wetlands and beaches.

Rolling easements could address that dilemma (Titus 1998): when the sea rises to the level of the property, the land is automatically turned over to the state to be held as open space. This allows for inward migration of the shore. The easements could be purchased from property owners by the state or conservation groups or imposed on owners through statute. [. . .]

The costs of moving structures could be made the responsibility of the property owners. It may be more practical, however, for the state or federal government to fund removal of structures and also any restoration of the newly public land. This will prevent degradation of the shoreline and maintain public recreational opportunities. Funds for such projects could come from a dedicated tax. One option that may be politically palatable is a tax on coastal tourists. Florida, for example, has a tax on rentals and accommodations of six months or less. Revenues from such a tax could be earmarked for the purchase of rolling easements or fund the restoration of abandoned land. In this way, those who come to enjoy the beach will also help fund the necessary adaptation to preserve the coastline.

[. . .]

As observed by McGuire (2013, p. 114), managing retreat is about "managing human expectations rather than on managing the forces of nature." For retreat to succeed, members of the community need to understand and support the policy; those building near the shore must fully internalize in their decisions that they will have to leave eventually. Expectations about change are inherently more difficult as preference for the status quo is strong (see Section 5).

USING DISASTERS AS OPPORTUNITIES

Severe storms and hurricanes are inevitable along much of the US coastline. Hurricanes may increase in intensity, and extreme rainfall events may be more frequent as the climate warms (IPCC 2012). Even absent changes in storm patterns, storm surge will reach farther inland and damage homes and businesses. If planned for in advance, rebuilding can be done in accordance with a strategy of managed retreat.

In most cases, absent planning, property owners will rebuild in the same locations despite the increasing risks. Rebuilding, not relocation, has been the dominant response to date. Some unplanned, voluntary relocation could nevertheless occur, once residents and firms start to perceive the risk as too great and the government cannot take satisfactory protective measures fast enough or everywhere (Tol et al. 2006). For instance, the population of New Orleans is less than 75% what it was before Hurricane Katrina. Catastrophic post-flood abandonment, however, is a costly response—in both dollars and human suffering.

Storm events can be windows of opportunity for change because they create a forced turnover in capital stock and a chance to rebuild differently. Decisions about such changes, however, should not be taken in the immediate aftermath (see Abel et al. 2011), when lengthy negotiations could leave disaster victims in an unacceptable limbo. Predisaster planning can also lock in socially beneficial decisions that are unlikely to be adopted in the hasty and contentious environment after a storm. Local governments should begin such discussions now, with extensive community input, so that policies and contracts are in place before the next storm (Lewis 2012).

Post-disaster managed retreat policies could take several forms. The first is a decision about where to rebuild and where to abandon. Buyouts of flood-prone properties, a tool already used around the country, could be adapted to areas at high-risk of SLR. Local governments have drawn on multiple sources of federal funds for buyouts. For example, after the devastating 1993 floods on the Missouri and Mississippi rivers, Missouri began a buyout program, drawing on federal and state funds, and more than 4,000 properties have now been converted to open space, reducing damages from subsequent floods (FEMA 2008). [. . .]

The buyout of entire blocks or neighborhoods would deliver greater benefits. If scattered properties are converted to open space, infrastructure will need to be maintained for the remaining homes, but now with a more limited tax base. Bonus payments for groups of properties could help. The power of eminent domain may allow a community to force the sale of holdouts, although political opposition is almost certain to prevent its use. Another proposal is to give a bonus payment to homeowners who relocate in the same county, just farther from the shore, to maintain the tax base.

More limited restrictions on rebuilding could also be undertaken. In South Carolina, when an oceanfront building is more than two-thirds damaged by a storm, if it is rebuilt, it must be moved as far landward on the lot as possible and cannot be enlarged (Grannis 2011). Many states have setback lines along the shore and could institute automatic updating of setback requirements after major storm events.

[. . .]

Finally, the public sector could limit its rebuilding in damaged, high-risk areas, even if private landowners can rebuild. Publicly owned buildings in these areas would be relocated. For infrastructure such as roads and water pipes, clear statements about what would be rebuilt and the implications for private property would be needed. For instance, poststorm sewer lines could be replaced with septic tanks for the remaining homeowners, if sewer lines would not be rebuilt. Some compensation might be required or the necessary adjustments (such as installation of the septic systems) might be covered by public funds if otherwise a takings issue would materialize. Firm adherence to clear plans would allow property owners to prepare and the market to capitalize the changes.

DISCUSSION: ACHIEVING INSTITUTIONAL CHANGE

The policy approaches discussed in this paper comprise two types of activities. The first improve the market's efficiency in responding to SLR—by providing information, removing government subsidies for development and infrastructure in high-risk areas, and altering property rights, such as through rolling easements. Second are regulations or expenditures of public funds to provide public goods or achieve outcomes that benefit society but may not be provided by the market—to fund land acquisition, for example, or restrict shore armoring.

Adopting any of these policies is no easy task, given the barriers to adaptation (e.g., see Moser and Ekstrom 2010). [. . .]

Retreat will not be optimal everywhere—economically, socially, or politically—and once population and development cross certain thresholds, retreat will be exceedingly unlikely (Abel et al. 2011). For places where retreat is desirable, however, this paper has outlined what managed retreat could look like in the United States, based on: (1) limiting new investment in high-risk areas; (2) providing for abandonment of property as inundation occurs; and (3) taking advantage of disasters to allow for retreat. Enacting policies in these three areas will be difficult, slow, and likely piecemeal. It will require stakeholders to agree on the future of the shore, and multiple levels of government to work together and determine responsibilities and synergistic policies. Developing institutions that allow for change and the dynamic nature of shorelines will take creativity and perseverance, as students of the policy process are aware.

REFERENCES

Abel, N., Gorddard, R., Harman, B., Leitch, A., Langridge, J., Ryan, A., Heyenga, S. (2011) Sea level rise, coastal development and planned retreat: Analytical framework, governance principles, and an Australian case study. *Environ Sci Policy* 14: 279–288.

Cooper, J.A.G., McKenna, J. (2008) Social justice in coastal erosion management: The temporal and spatial dimensions. *Geoforum* 39(1): 294–306.

FEMA (2008) *Missouri flood buyouts save lives, heartache and money.* Federal Emergency Management Agency, Washington, DC, September 1.

Godschalk, D.R., Norton, R., Richardson, C., Salvesen, D. (2000) Avoiding coastal hazard areas: Best state mitigation practices. *Environ Geosci* 7(1): 13–22.

Grannis, J. (2011) *Adaptation tool kit: Sea-level rise and coastal land use.* Georgetown Climate Center, Washington, DC.

IPCC (2012) *Managing the Risks of Extreme Events and Disasters to Advance Climate Change Adaptation. A Special Report of Working Groups I and II of the Intergovernmental Panel on Climate Change* [Field, C.B., Barros, V., Stocker, T.F., Qin, D., Dokken, D.J., Ebi, K.L., Mastrandrea, M.D., Mach, K.J., Plattner, G.-K., Allen, S.K., Tignor, M., and P.M. Midgley (eds.)]. Cambridge University Press, Cambridge.

Kousky, C., Kunreuther, H. (2013) *Addressing affordability in the National Flood Insurance Program.* RFF Issue Brief 13–02. Resources for the Future, Washington, DC, and Risk Management and Decision Processes Center, Wharton School, University of Pennsylvania.

Kousky, C., Luttmer, E., Zeckhauser, R. (2006) Private investment and government protection. *J Risk Uncertain* 33(1): 73–100.

Kydland, F.E., Prescott, E.C. (1977) Rules rather than discretion: The inconsistency of optimal plans. *J Polit Econ* 85(3): 473–491.

Lewis, D.A. (2012) The relocation of development from coastal hazards through publicly funded acquisition programs: Examples and lessons from the Gulf coast. *Sea Grant Law Policy J* 5(1): 98–139.

McGuire, C.J. (2013) *Adapting to sea level rise in the coastal zone.* Taylor & Francis Group, Boca Raton, FL.

Moser, S.C., Ekstrom, J.A. (2010) A framework to diagnose barriers to climate change adaptation. *Proc Natl Acad Sci U S A* 107(51): 22026–22031.

Nicholls, R.J., Cazenave, A. (2010) Sea-level rise and its impact on coastal zones. *Science* 328(5985): 1517–1520.

Pilkey, O.H., Cooper, J.A.G. (2004) Society and sea level rise. *Science* 303(5665): 1781–1782.

Platt, R.H., Salvesen, D., Baldwin, G.H.I. (2002) Rebuilding the North Carolina coast after Hurricane Fran: Did public regulations matter? *Coast Manag* 30: 249–269.

Smith, J.B. (1997) Setting priorities for adapting to climate change. *Glob Environ Chang* 7(3): 251–265.

Smithers, J., Smit, B. (1997) Human adaptation to climatic variability and change. *Glob Environ Chang* 7(2): 129–146.

SPUR (2012) *Ocean beach master plan.* San Francisco Planning and Urban Research Association, San Francisco.

Strauss, B.H., Ziemlinski, R., Weiss, J.L., Overpeck, J.T. (2012) Tidally adjusted estimates of topographic vulnerability to sea level rise and flooding for the contiguous United States. *Environ Res Lett* 7(1): 014033.

Titus, J.G. (1990) Strategies for adapting to the greenhouse effect. *J Am Planning Assoc* Summer 56(3): 311–323.

Titus, J.G. (1998) Rising seas, coastal erosion, and the takings clause: How to save wetlands and beaches without hurting property owners. *Maryland Law Rev* 57(4): 1279–1399.

Titus, J.G., Hudgens, D.E., Trescott, D.L., Craghan, M., Nuckols, W.H., Hershner, C.H., Kassakian, J.M., Linn, C.J., Merritt, P.G., McCue, T.M., O'Connell, J.F., Tanski, J., Wang, J. (2009) State and local governments plan for development of most land vulnerable to rising sea level along the US Atlantic coast. *Environ Res Lett* 4: 044008.

Tol, R.S.J., Bohn, M., Downing, T.E., Guillerminet, M.-L., Hizsnyik, E., Kasperson, R., Lonsdale, K., Mays, C., Nicholls, R.J., Olsthoorn, A.A., Pfeifle, G., Poumadere, M., Toth, F.L., Vafeidis, A., van der Werff, P.E., Yetkiner, I.H. (2006) Adaptation to five metres of sea level rise. *J Risk Res* 9(5): 467–482.

U.S. Climate Change Science Program (2009) *Coastal sensitivity to sea-level rise: A focus on the Mid-Atlantic region.* Synthesis and Assessment Product 4.1, Washington, DC.

26 Breaking the Waves

Gabriel Popkin

EDITOR'S INTRODUCTION

In "Breaking the Waves," journalist Gabriel Popkin describes new approaches to coastal protection that build on ecosystem services. He begins by giving examples of similar areas with different infrastructures, where the results of storms are different. In areas hard-hut by Hurricane Irene, those with marsh grass or barrier beaches experienced very little erosion or damage, while up to three-quarters of seawalls and bulkheads were damaged. He describes Maryland's pioneering law requiring that landowners who want to protect their shoreline build a "living shoreline" as the first option, and are only permitted to do coastal hardening if they prove that a living shoreline will not work at that particular site. These living shorelines have multiple co-benefits, including storing carbon, supporting more diverse and abundant marine life, and potentially providing oyster and other shellfish habitat and thus not only shoreline protection but jobs for local fisherfolk. Living shorelines can grow and move as sea levels rise, making them highly adaptable to change. Popkin identifies a key point in implementation—because the shore in the United States and many countries is owned by private parties, creating better but sustainable protection will come about through the cumulative action of millions of landowners. But the permitting bodies for construction will influence those decisions. Making greener infrastructure the standard permitted option and coastal hardening the second choice would go a long way toward assuring the resilience and ecological integrity of many shoreline areas. Popkin is a frequent contributor to a wide range of scientific and public interest media, including *Nature*, National Public Radio, the *Smithsonian*, and the *New York Times*.

BREAKING THE WAVES

When Hurricane Irene hit North Carolina's coast in 2011, waves 2 meters high began pounding the shore. Two properties on Pine Knoll Shores, a community on one of the state's many barrier islands, provided a study in contrasts. One homeowner had installed a concrete bulkhead to protect his yard from the sea. But the churning waves overtopped and ultimately toppled the wall, washing away tons of sediment and leaving a denuded mud flat.

Less than 200 meters away, another owner had installed a "living shoreline"—a planted carpet of marsh grass that gently sloped into the water, held in place by a rock sill placed a few meters offshore. The onrushing water bent the marsh grasses almost flat, but their flexing stalks dampened the waves and their deep roots held the soil. After the hurricane passed, the grasses sprang back; the property weathered the storm largely intact.

The contrast highlights how defenses inspired by nature, rather than concrete armor, can protect coastlines from battering storms, says ecologist Rachel Gittman of Northeastern University's Marine Science Center in Nahant, Massachusetts. In a study of Irene's effects, Gittman found that in hard-hit areas along the North Carolina coast, the storm destroyed or damaged three-quarters of the seawalls and bulkheads, and washed away valuable soil. Yet, shores fringed by marsh grasses experienced almost no erosion, and damaged vegetation bounced back within a year. "Plants are really good at handling big storms," Gittman says. "Bulkheads are really not."

Such findings are getting more attention as researchers and coastal planners confront rising seas—and possibly more powerful storms—caused by global warming. That double punch, they say, threatens hundreds of millions of coastal residents around the world and infrastructure worth trillions of dollars.

To be better prepared, many researchers are calling on coastal nations to rethink traditional approaches to shoreline defense, which rely largely on massive earthen dikes, rock barriers, and concrete walls. Such "gray" infrastructure damages coastal ecosystems, researchers argue, and can be difficult and expensive to adapt to changing environmental circumstances. Gittman and others argue that softer, "greener," approaches inspired by marshes, oyster reefs, and other natural features (see Figure 26.1) can do better. With clever engineering, they say, such features can provide not only cost-effective storm protection, but also healthier ecosystems able to adapt to rising seas. "When you put in a marsh," says environmental scientist Bhaskar Subramanian of the Maryland Department of Natural Resources (DNR) in Annapolis, "you're doing good by nature."

Not everyone is enthusiastic. Many people feel safer behind concrete, and—given the potentially high stakes—policymakers and regulators have been reluctant to shelve time-honored engineering techniques in favor of less familiar approaches. Some researchers also worry that even supposedly green designs could harm marine ecosystems by introducing exotic species and foreign materials into underwater habitats.

Despite the skeptics, the push to green traditionally gray coastal defenses is gaining traction. Prompted by the devastation caused by Hurricanes Katrina and Sandy, the U.S. government is bolstering research into nature-inspired coastal engineering. And a growing number of researchers around the world are evaluating which green techniques might work best—and how gray and green engineering might be combined to create layered defenses.

"There is so much happening on this right now," says ecologist Ariana Sutton-Grier of the University of Maryland (UMD), College Park, and the National Oceanic and Atmospheric Administration (NOAA). "We probably are at a sea change in the way we approach coastal protection."

Gray structures
A. Flood gates
B. Seawalls
C. Rock groins

Green structures
D. Oyster reefs
E. Marshes
F. Coral reefs
G. Barrier islands

Figure 26.1 Defending against rising seas, in gray and green

Some researchers are urging a move away from so-called gray coastal defense structures, such as seawalls, flood gates, and rock groins. They say greener structures—including natural or built marshes, oyster and coral reefs, and sandy barrier islands—can provide protection with less ecological damage, and a greater ability to adapt to rising seas. Combining green and gray structures could create hybrid, layered defenses that offer both ecological and economic benefits.

For millennia, humans have tried to hold back the sea. In China and along the Mediterranean, archeologists have found evidence of seawalls and other shoreline structures some 2,000 years old. And as human populations have grown, so have coastal defenses. In the United States, nearly 23,000 kilometers of shoreline—some 14% of the total—is armored, Gittman and colleagues estimated in August (2015) in *Frontiers in Ecology and the Environment*. That proportion could grow to one-third by the end of the century, they add, if coastal development continues at its current pace. Armoring can have devastating ecological consequences. Rock and concrete barriers reflect rather than dissipate wave energy, causing fast-moving waters to scour the sea floor, destroying marsh and underwater grasses that nurture fish, crabs, and other sea life. Hard structures can also cut off critical flows of sediments from uplands to the coast, starving and obliterating beaches and marshes. And as global sea levels have risen by an estimated 20 cm over the past century, many marshes and beaches have become squeezed between the higher water and unmoving concrete.

The squeeze will worsen if global greenhouse gas emissions continue unabated. Under some scenarios, modelers warn, sea level rise could accelerate to as much as 9 mm per year, driven by melting ice sheets and the expansion of warming seawater. At the same time, warming could catalyze more powerful storms, heightening the threat of wave damage and coastal flooding. Many point to the flooding that occurred in New Orleans, Louisiana, and along the Gulf of Mexico after Hurricane Katrina in 2005, and the devastation wrought by Hurricane Sandy in 2012, as examples of what the future may hold.

The shores of the Chesapeake Bay in Maryland are among the most vulnerable in the United States: Land subsidence there is causing local sea level rise to greatly exceed the global average, making coastal areas more vulnerable to storms. In 2003, a powerful hurricane, Isabel, swept up the coast and across the Chesapeake Bay area, killing 16 people and causing $7 billion worth of damage. It also amplified one of the nation's most prominent efforts to promote living shorelines.

Not long after the storm passed, calls began coming in from distraught landowners, recalls Subramanian of the Maryland DNR, which provides coastal protection assistance to landowners. "All the calls were: 'My bulkhead is floating in the neighbor's property,'" he says.

In contrast, the agency received no complaints from landowners who had installed living shorelines with the agency's help. The constructed marshes had dampened the storm waves and reduced damage, he says, just as they would in North Carolina nearly a decade later. Soon, landowners once wedded to concrete were lining up to get help building their own protective marshes.

Today, Maryland is considered a pioneer in green coastal infrastructure. In 2008, it adopted the nation's first law requiring landowners who want to protect their waterfront to use a living shoreline unless they can prove that only a hard structure will do the trick. The state has issued permits for more than 1000 living shorelines, almost all around the Chesapeake Bay and its tributaries. Many have not only survived but thrived through storms likely to have overwhelmed traditional gray structures.

Other states, however, have been slow to follow suit, in part because of lingering questions about the environmental impact, effectiveness, and life span of living shore- lines and other nature-inspired features.

One researcher trying to answer those questions is ecologist Carolyn Currin of NOAA's Beaufort, North Carolina, laboratory. The lab sits on Pivers Island, a spit of land near Pine Knolls Shore. In 2000, when lab officials had to replace a failed seawall on the island, Currin persuaded them to install a living shoreline, turning an otherwise humdrum construction job into an experiment. NOAA worked with local partners and volunteers to install bags of oyster shells off the island's shore and plant marsh grasses on a graded sand slope.

The new marsh—along with a second one built on the other side of Pivers Island using a rock sill—has allowed researchers to gain new insights into the capabilities and behavior of living shorelines. One finding is that they appear to keep pace with local sea level rise, building up soil that keeps the marsh's surface above the low tide line.

They also have potentially valuable "co-benefits." The artificial marshes pack away relatively large quantities of carbon, Davis et al. (2015) reported in *PLOS One*. And, as suspected, the rock and oyster-shell sills used to anchor such marshes support more abundant and diverse communities of fish and crustaceans—including economically important species—than do traditional concrete structures, a team led by Gittman et al. (2016) concludes in a paper in press at *Ecological Applications*.

Currin, Gittman, and colleagues also are assessing whether shorelines colonized by living oysters can provide an additional layer of defense in shellfish habitat such as North Carolina and the Gulf of Mexico. In one experiment, they have used thousands of bushels of shells to build three artificial oyster reefs off a rapidly eroding beach on Carrot Island in the Rachel Carson Reserve, not far from Pivers Island.

On a visit to the site, ecologist Joel Fodrie waded through quiet water to the reefs. The shell piles, now about three years old, were already protecting the beach, trapping sediment and helping it reverse past erosion losses. Better yet, the reef was coming to life, says Fodrie, who works at the University of North Carolina's Institute of Marine Sciences in Morehead City. Tiny crabs scurried across his hands as he examined shells covered with baby oysters. The youngsters should help the reef grow both vertically and horizontally, he noted, improving its protective effects. And properly placed oyster reefs have the capacity to grow in concert with even rapidly rising seas, Fodrie, the institute's Antonio Rodriguez et al. (2014) reported last year in *Nature Climate Change*.

The reef project faces challenges, however, Fodrie noted. Waves have pushed some of the oyster sills toward shore and washed away some grasses that researchers had planted. But that's OK, he says. "We planned to have some things fail, so we can see where the boundaries are."

Although some see living shorelines as a return to nature, others see them as coastal hardening by another name. Retired earth scientist Orrin Pilkey of Duke University in Durham, North Carolina, who has called for limiting coastal development, has criticized many living shoreline projects along the Atlantic coast because they make heavy use of offshore rock sills to shelter the planted grasses from wave action. The sills, he says, can bury native sea grasses and make it more difficult for fish and crabs to reach intertidal marshes.

Pilkey also complains that a lack of regulatory oversight and scientific monitoring makes it hard to figure out what works and what doesn't. "To me the living shoreline thing is the Wild West," he wrote in an email. "No standards, no enforcement, no real studies especially long term and an aura of environmental holiness."

Even living shoreline promoters acknowledge that projects can come with ecological tradeoffs. Newly constructed marshes in the Chesapeake Bay, for example, can bury sandy, near-shore habitats. "Everyone devalues flat, non-structural bottoms," says ecologist Donna Bilkovic of the Virginia Institute of Marine Science in Gloucester Point. "But there are lots of animals that live in those sediments."

Green defenses also face substantial regulatory and political hurdles. In the United States, it can often take just a few days to obtain the needed federal and state permits to build a new bulkhead, for instance, but the paperwork for nature-inspired projects can take much longer, in part because they may involve underwater components that bury shallow-water habitats and stretch into shipping lanes. Large projects can also trigger complicated mandatory cost-benefit analyzes. For gray projects, economists and engineers have long known how to calculate life span and financial return, but the task can be trickier for green projects, for which the calculus includes benefits such as carbon storage or improved fish habitat.

Some coastal experts have concluded that combining green and gray approaches promises the best payoff, because of their complementary strengths and weaknesses: Green infrastructure is dynamic and adaptable, but can take several years to become fully established, whereas concrete works on day one. Such hybrid defenses might involve building an oyster reef or marsh in front of a concrete seawall or dike, to provide both ecological benefits and multiple layers of storm protection.

The U.S. Army Corps of Engineers has embraced such "gray-green" thinking, and is promoting it in concert with NOAA and other institutions through an initiative called the Systems Approach to Geomorphic Engineering. The hope, says UMD's Sutton-Grier, is to "capitalize on the strengths of both approaches—you can use gray to protect green as it establishes, or green to protect gray so that [its] lifetime is longer."

The idea is also catching on internationally, with Korea, China, and Australia recently considering or installing combinations of marshes and hard structures. In the Netherlands, where coastal defenses are a matter of national existence, planners are introducing salt marshes and shellfish beds to help lessen storm impacts on seawalls and dikes. (Japan also considered greening its shoreline protection arsenal after the devastating 2011 tsunami, but has so far opted for even larger seawalls.)

The success of green infrastructure, however, may ultimately depend less on governments than on the willingness of millions of individual landowners to try something new, because so much coastline is in private hands. Persuading risk-averse homeowners can be a frustrating process, Gittman says. After Hurricane Irene, she showed the landowner with the toppled bulkhead how much better his neighbor's living shoreline had performed.

But the landowner opted to build a new concrete bulkhead instead, and then put his house up for sale. "People are stubborn," Gittman says.

REFERENCES

Davis, J. L., C. A. Currin, C. O'Brien, C. Raffenburg and A. Davis (2015) "Living shore-lines: Coastal resilience with a blue carbon benefit." *PLoS ONE* **10**(11): e0142595. https://doi.org/10.1371/journal.pone.0142595

Gittman, R. K., F. J. Fodrie, A. M. Popowich, D. A. Keller, J. F. Bruno, C. A. Currin, C. H. Peterson and M. F. Piehler (2015). "Engineering away our natural defenses: An analysis of shoreline hardening in the US." *Frontiers in Ecology and the Environment* **13**(6): 301–307.

Gittman, R. K., S. B. Scyphers, C. S. Smith, I. P. Neylan and J. H. Grabowski (2016). "Ecological consequences of shoreline hardening: A meta-analysis." *BioScience* **66**(9): 763–773.

Rodriguez, A. B., F. J. Fodrie, J. T. Ridge, N. L. Lindquist, E. J. Theuerkauf, S. E. Coleman, J. H. Grabowski, M. C. Brodeur, R. K. Gittman, D. A. Keller and M. D. Kenworthy (2014). "Oyster reefs can outpace sea-level rise." *Nature Climate Change* **4**: 493.

27 Interdependencies of Urban Climate Change Impacts and Adaptation Strategies

A Case Study of Metropolitan Boston, USA

Paul Kirshen, Matthias Ruth, and William Anderson

EDITOR'S INTRODUCTION

In this article Kirshen, Ruth, and Anderson outline an interesting and manageable approach to analysis of infrastructure options, using a limited range of climate scenarios and demographic trends to consider different approaches to future investment. In these we can see the basic policy approaches that are widely available. One approach is "Ride It Out," which could also be called a business-as-usual approach, in which no change to current infrastructure is made in response to coming climate change. A second approach is based on structural choices, called the "build your way out" approach, and includes seawalls and similar built forms. A third is the less structural or green option which includes more accommodation and retreat, as well as ecosystem-based interventions. The article goes on to explore the interdependencies among systems. Just one example is that water quality is connected to water quantity, and both can affect provision of energy for systems that use water for cooling or steam distribution. Interruptions in energy during heat waves can bring increased mortality and morbidity—etc. Based on this analysis, they find that the Ride It Out approach brings negative impacts in one system which in many cases leads to negative impacts in the performance of other infrastructure systems. The integration of infrastructure means that analyses need to consider infrastructure as a whole, rather than just focusing on individual parts. Generally, the study finds that anticipatory action taken well before 2050 results in less total adaptation and impact costs to the region than taking no action.

Paul Kirshen is a Professor in the School for the Environment at University of Massachusetts Boston and director of its Sustainable Solutions Lab. He is a civil engineer focusing on water resources engineering and climate change vulnerability assessment and planning. He is a distinguished researcher and leads complex interdisciplinary collaborative investigations into resilient infrastructure. His co-author Matthias Ruth is Professor and Director of the School of Public Policy and Urban Affairs at Northeastern University. William P. Anderson is the Director of the Cross-Border Institute and Ontario Research Chair in Cross-Border Transportation Policy in the Department of Political Science at University of Windsor.

INTERDEPENDENCIES OF URBAN CLIMATE CHANGE IMPACTS AND ADAPTATION STRATEGIES

INTRODUCTION

Only recently have researchers started to investigate potential impacts of climate change and adaptation strategies in urban areas (here we include suburban land use within our definition of urban)—the places of much economic and social activity. Moreover, most of these urban studies are sector or system specific; concentrating, for examples, on implications of climate change for water supply, coastal flooding, or air quality. Urban areas rely upon a complex set of infrastructure systems to provide human, environmental, and economic services. Examples include flood control, water supply, drainage, wastewater management, solid and hazardous waste management, energy, transportation, and constructed facilities for residential, commercial, and industrial activities. One of the features of urban areas is that the different infrastructure systems are physically close to each other and have the potential to positively interact with each other. For example, in urban areas, it is possible to economically use reclaimed wastewater for industrial cooling, use waste heat from power plants for district heating, install dual quality water supply systems, and manage storm runoff and improve low flows by recharging runoff. The interdependencies and physical proximities of systems in urban areas, however, can have negative consequences, as well. For example, failures in wastewater treatment systems can increase requirements for water supply treatment, increase flood losses because of contaminated floodwaters, and decrease availability of cooling water for power plants because of inadequate quality. These cumulative impacts can cause disruption of commercial, industrial, and domestic activities and have major ripple effects upon a region's economy. Here, in the context of the metropolitan Boston region, we analyze the interdependencies of the impacts of climate change and adaptation strategies upon infrastructure systems in urban areas.

[. . .]

THE CLIMB PROJECT

[. . .]

The CLIMB project was conducted from 1999–2004 by a multidisciplinary research team from Tufts University, University of Maryland, and Boston University with assistance from the Metropolitan Area Planning Council and a Stakeholder Advisory Committee composed of representatives of government and other interest groups and infrastructure and planning experts. The methodology and results are summarized in Ruth and Kirshen (2001) and Kirshen et al. (2006), and are available in full in Kirshen et al. (2004).

Metro Boston, which is located in the northeastern United States, is shown in Figure 27.1 and includes the major cities of Boston and Cambridge and the other 99 municipalities within approximately 20 miles of Boston. The area is bordered on the east by Boston Harbor (the confluence of three major rivers) and on the south, west, and north approximately by the circumferential Route 495, covering an area of 3,683 km². Metro Boston's population is approximately 3.2 million, and is expected to increase to 4.0 million by 2050. Land use varies from densely populated urban areas in the east, suburbs in the center, and undeveloped farmland and some urban "sprawl" on the fringes. It is the heart of the New England economy, and provides its major airport and seaport facilities. The region is currently experiencing pressure on most of its infrastructure systems and severe development pressure in the municipalities just outside of the core city areas. It is characterized by a climate with four distinct seasons with annual precipitation of [about] 1,000 mm relatively evenly distributed throughout the year; some as snow in the winter. The average monthly temperature is approximately 10°C.

METHODOLOGY

Potential changes in infrastructure performance play themselves out across space and time, owing to differences in infrastructure densities and use, differences in environmental conditions, and the long-term nature of climate change as well as the long-lived nature of the various infrastructure systems. To capture spatial variations in climate change impacts on Metro Boston, seven subregions or zones are distinguished (Figure 27.1) such that:

- Coastal regions are treated separately from regions inland.
- Areas north of the city of Boston, which have different coastal properties and socio-economic features, are delineated from southern parts of the MAPC region.
- Highly urbanized areas are dealt with separately from suburbs.
- Rapidly growing suburbs are distinguished from already highly developed and densely populated ones.

In most cases, annual impacts from 2000–2100 were examined under one set of demographic projections, two climate change scenarios in addition to the present climate, and three possible adaptations responses to climate change.

[. . .]

Zone 1 = South Coastal Urban, Zone 2 = North Coastal Urban, Zone 3 = North Coastal Suburban, Zone 4 = South Coastal Suburban, Zone 5 = Developed Suburbs, Zone 6 = Developing Suburbs South, Zone 7 = Developing Suburbs North

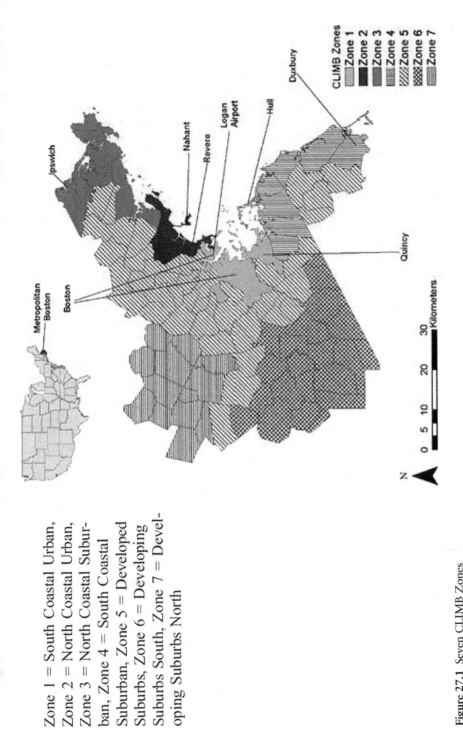

Figure 27.1 Seven CLIMB Zones

The adaptation scenarios included:

- The "Ride It Out" (RIO) scenario in essence assumes that no adaptation to climate change occurs and that damages and benefits continue to occur with no attempts by society to minimize damages or maximize benefits.
- The "Green" scenario assumes conscious, sustainable responses to observed trends, as well as proactive or anticipatory implementation of policies and technologies in efforts to counteract, and prepare for, adverse climate impacts. Some of the practices might be put in place before impacts are felt (for example, moving occupants out of flood plains), after impacts occur, or at the end of lifecycles of infrastructure systems.
- The "Build Your Way Out" (BYWO) scenario assumes that replacement of failed systems is undertaken and susceptible systems are protected by structural measures.

[. . .]

Regional systems analyzed included Energy Use, Sea Level Rise, River Flooding, Surface Vehicle Transportation, Water Supply, and Public Health (heat stress mortality). Localized Case Studies were carried out for Water Quality, Tall Buildings, and Bridge Scour.

[. . .]

Effects of the alternative assumptions about future climate, socio-economic characteristics and technological potentials in the region were assessed with respect to various impacts to the region. As appropriate within each system, three broad categories of impacts were distinguished:

- Loss of service: directly associated with a loss of service, such as number of lost days at work due to disruption of transportation services, loss of lives due to heat stress, decrease in reliability.
- Repair/replacement: costs associated with restoring infrastructure systems and services to their pre-impact level.
- Adaptation: cost of adjusting infrastructure systems and services to higher standards at which the experienced impact would have been avoided.

We did not discount any of the impacts. Implicitly, this assumes that property values and adaptation costs appreciated at the same rate and helps to avoid the ethical arguments surrounding the choice and magnitude of a discount rate.

A Stakeholder Advisory Group (SAG) made up of approximately 30 multi-level government officials, members of non-governmental organizations, and representatives from private industry was formed in the early stages of the project and used throughout the research to identify issues of regional concern, provide data sources, and, most importantly, ground-truth results [informally review findings to see if they match to the stakeholders' experiences]. Interaction with the SAG took place several times each year through meetings of the entire group, public workshops, sectoral specific workshops, and individual contact.

[. . .]

Generally, five themes emerge from these analyses. Either structural (BYWO scenario) or less structural (Green scenario) actions taken before full climate change impacts occur will result in less expected total infrastructure negative impacts to the region. The second is that under many scenarios, an effective adaptation action taken soon will result in less total future negative impacts in a system even if climate change does not occur. For example, this was found in the analyses of river and coastal flooding impacts and adaptation. The third theme is that climate change will significantly add to the negative impacts of demographic changes upon infrastructure services in the region. Another theme is the interactions upon each other of the climate change impacts of various infrastructure systems and their adaptation actions. The fifth theme is that adaptation of infrastructure to climate change must also consider integration with land use management, environmental, and socio-economic impacts, and various institutions. These final two themes are the focus of this paper and present additional considerations in adaptation planning.

INTERDEPENDENCIES OF IMPACTS AND ADAPTATION ACTIONS

Impacts: The emphasis of the CLIMB project was on the integration of climate and demographic changes upon infrastructure in Metro Boston and on examining these impacts with a common framework. Based upon the results of this research, it was possible to examine how impacts in one sector will impact another sector. While it was not possible in all cases to make quantitative estimates of the magnitude of interaction effects, we were able to identify a comprehensive set of such effects and indicate which are the most important. [. . .]

Table 27.1 identifies the most important interaction effects. It is based on the Ride It Out (RIO) scenario, which means no major policy interventions are assumed. System-specific RIO impacts are summarized in the gray cells of the table. Reading the table horizontally shows the impacts of one system upon another. Reading the table vertically shows possible impacts upon that system from all the systems we analyzed.

Table 27.1 indicates that the RIO negative impacts of climate change on one infrastructure system will, in most cases, also negatively impact the performances of other infrastructure systems. River flooding is a good example. Loss of land and land activity during flood events has negative impacts on all other infrastructure systems and generally negative impacts on the environment, economy, and society. Sea level rise also has widespread negative impacts. In general, energy, river flooding, and sea level rise are the systems whose negative impacts from climate change have the greatest secondary impacts on other systems. Water supply and water quality systems impacts are also transmitted to other systems.

Reading the table vertically indicates that health followed by water supply and water quality are the systems most impacted by impacts that occur directly to other systems. These interactions are important because they have the potential to magnify any negative impacts caused by climate change in any one system.

[. . .]

Table 27.1 Integration of infrastructure impacts

	Energy	Health	Transport	River Flooding	Sea Level Rise	Water Supply	Water Quality
Energy	N/A	*Summer* Also decrease in air quality; higher morbidity and mortality. *Winter* Also air quality improvement.	*Summer* Also if energy shortages; loss of rail service, loss of traffic signals, disruption of air traffic.	Not Applicable (N/A)	N/A	*Summer* Also increased cooling water needs.	*Summer* Also more cooling water will impact water quality (heat and blowdown).
Health	*Summer* More electricity demand. Also more brownouts and more local emissions. *Winter* Less gas and heating oil demand.	*Summer* Slightly higher heat-related mortality until about 2010. Also increased emission-related illness.	N/A	N/A	N/A	N/A	N/A
Transport Impacts Due to River and Coastal Flooding	Increased energy demand due to more miles traveled.	Also reduced public safety.	Increased travel time. Loss of trips. More miles. More hours.	N/A	N/A	N/A	N/A

River Flooding	Possible disruption in local deliveries.	Increased pathogens in water supply.	Lost trips and increased traffic delay (see Transportation Sector).	Temporary loss of land and land activity.	Also will increase flooding impacts.	Also could floodwater treatment plants and wells.	Also could flood wastewater treatment plants. More non-point source pollution.
Sea Level Rise	N/A	N/A	Lost trips and increased traffic delay (see Transportation Sector).	Also could increase river flood losses.	Permanent loss of some coastal land. Temporary loss of land and land activities.	Also salt water intrusion into coastal wells.	Also could flood wastewater treatment plants and may impact any new desalination plants.
Water Supply	Also possible loss of local energy supply because of lack of cooling water.	Less reliable local supply could result in hydration and water quality problems.	N/A	N/A	N/A	Less reliable local supply.	Times when more water withdrawal and thus less dilution.
Water Quality	Also warmer waters could result in loss of local energy production.	Also increased illness due to exposure to water-borne diseases.	N/A	N/A	N/A	More treatment necessary.	Less Dissolved Oxygen. More non-point source pollution. Warmer water.

(Horizontal row is the system impacted by the system in the first column. System-specific RIO impacts are summarized in the gray cells of the table. Additional information is preceded by "also.")

CONCLUSIONS

The CLIMB study is based upon the hypothesis that the operation and services provided by urban infrastructure will be impacted by climate change as they are sensitive to climate. Using various indicators, our research has shown that compared to conditions of just population growth, climate change impacts are significant on many infrastructure systems. What is more, the impacts on each infrastructure system give rise to secondary impacts on other systems. Since these secondary impacts tend to be mutually reinforcing (negative impacts on one system create negative impacts on other systems), impacts measured for a single system in isolation will tend to be underestimated. An ideal analysis would be of a single, diversified infrastructure system to provide for all the needs of the urban area. In the absence of such an analysis, however, the second-best option is to carefully identify interaction effects among systems.

We have identified some specific actions and policies that can be taken in the near-term future to lessen some of the negative impacts. These adaptation actions are not intended to be optimal in terms of timing, location, or even action, but they do show that taking anticipatory actions well before 2050 results in less total adaptation and impact costs to the region than taking no action. Similar results for other sectors of the US economy have been reported by Easterling et al. (2004). Because of the interrelations among infrastructure systems, we have found that it is critical to take account of the effect that an adaptation action designed to lessen the effect of climate change on one system has on other systems. For the most part these cross-system effects are complementary in nature. But there are important exceptions, so an integrated approach to adaptation policy formulation is needed. Furthermore, adaptation efforts must be chosen and implemented so as not to confound mitigation efforts.

28 Sustainable Tourism, Climate Change and Sea Level Rise Adaptation Policies in Barbados

Michelle Mycoo

EDITOR'S INTRODUCTION

Michelle Mycoo turns our attention to the institutional setting for coastal infrastructure decision-making. This article explores the implications of climate change for small island developing states, and in particular those like Barbados that rely heavily on beach tourism for their economic health. She reports on a study that found that up to 22% of the gross domestic product of the Caribbean region as a whole could be lost due to climate change by 2100 (Bueno et al., 2008). The pressure in coastal areas for development is already intense, as countries and regions have to balance long-term protection of ecology and aesthetics to maintain their touristic attractiveness with the current benefits of jobs and tax revenues from large tourism projects. Adding in the costs from more severe and frequent storm events and rising seas and the considerations become quite remarkably complex. In the abstract to her article presented here, Mycoo notes, "The vulnerability of tourism-dependent communities, coastal tourism facilities, and beaches to climate change demands the use of measures that can urgently minimise vulnerability and in the long-term achieve sustainable development." Barbados, which is ranked as a "developed" country by the UN, has responded to these challenges by implementing integrated coastal zone management, physical planning policies and infrastructure projects. One example is the redevelopment along Accra/Rockley beach, a new south-coast ecologically informed boardwalk that enabled natural rebuilding of coastal conditions while providing public space for tourists and residents alike. This article is particularly helpful in the way it clearly explains some of the regulatory approaches supporting resilient green infrastructure, such as integrated coastal zone management and zoning setbacks. The article demonstrates some of the ways that small island countries are finding their own solutions to climate change adaptation, but also the challenges they face that may impair their ability to sustain a good standard of living for residents.

Michelle Mycoo is a tenured Lecturer and Coordinator of the MSc Planning and Development Programme in the University of the West Indies, St. Augustine. Prior to joining academia, Mycoo worked as a Chartered Town Planner in the Town and Country Planning Division of Trinidad and Tobago, was author of the Chaguanas Land Use Plan and team member for the National Physical Development Plan review. After doctoral studies, she worked at the World Bank as a consultant in the Urban Division of the Environmentally Sustainable Development Department.

SUSTAINABLE TOURISM, CLIMATE CHANGE AND SEA LEVEL RISE ADAPTATION POLICIES IN BARBADOS

INTRODUCTION

The degraded natural environment of the small island developing states (SIDS) of the Caribbean is due to multiple drivers of change and is now further vulnerable to climate change and its associated sea level rise (SLR). SIDS' vulnerability to these phenomena is of concern to the region's policymakers because they endanger the livelihood of communities and tourism investors that are located in the coastal zone. Hall (2011) predicts that Caribbean SIDS will be among the most at-risk tourism destinations between 2025 and the mid-21st century. More than ever before, there is a need to ensure that the "possible effects of climate change are effectively factored into relevant tourism policies and development and management plans" (Scott and Becken, 2010:287). In the post-Rio+20 period, greater attention needs to be paid to the links between climate change and impacts on sustainable development, especially in SIDS that are dependent on natural resource-based tourism. Two geographic peculiarities make SIDS highly susceptible to SLR: they have long coastlines relative to land area, and large proportions of their land area are low-lying (Belle and Bramwell, 2005). Many islands are therefore susceptible to inundation of low-lying coastal land, beach and shoreline erosion, and saltwater intrusion in coastal aquifers (Cambers et al., 2008). Researchers such as Nicholls (2004) and Nicholls and Tol (2006) have noted that while the absolute impacts in small islands are quite small at a global scale, in relative terms the impacts are the highest. [. . .] Recent studies conducted by UNECLAC (2010) revealed that unless there is meaningful adaptation to and mitigation of climate change, the potential economic loss to the Caribbean region would be 2–3% of its gross domestic product (GDP) annually. Furthermore, the total loss due to inaction will amount to 22% of GDP for the Caribbean as a whole by 2100 (Bueno et al., 2008).

The issue of becoming climate ready is not a new one for Caribbean SIDS. Almost two decades ago, the region became proactive in dealing with climate change because of threats posed to the rich biodiversity and fragility of their island ecosystems. [. . .]

Limited research exists on climate change and SLR adaptation policies in Caribbean SIDS. For this reason, a study using Barbados as a case study was conducted to analyse existing policy measures and projects implemented to address problems associated with earlier unsustainable tourism practices, as well as adaptation to new challenges placed on coastal tourism by climate change. Ultimately, the paper seeks to provide policy recommendations on ways of advancing sustainable tourism that are consistent with adapting to climate change and the associated SLR.

RESEARCH METHODS

Data was collected from face-to-face semi-structured in-depth interviews, site visits, government policy documents and scientific studies conducted by academicians. [. . .]

BACKGROUND ON BARBADOS TOURISM SECTOR

[. . .] Barbados is one of the SIDS located in the Caribbean Sea, and many of its hotels are concentrated along beaches on the southwest and west coasts. Climate change and rising sea levels will significantly influence Barbados' tourism industry, which is vital to its economic survival. The CZMU (Coastal Zone Management Unit), using a flood model with a probability of a return period of one flood in every 100 years, projects that 70% of the hotels located on the west coast of Barbados will suffer from flooding and related damage by such an event (Government of Barbados (GOB), 2010; Fish et al., 2008). Research points to mounting evidence of a relationship between climate change and beach erosion (Cambers et al., 2008). In 1999, the project on Caribbean Planning for Adaptation to Climate Change (CPACC) projected that elevated sea levels were likely to increase beach erosion in Barbados because most beaches were very narrow averaging 12–15 metres. Since then, new studies have revealed shoreline erosion rates of 15 metres per 100 years for the entire coastline (GOB, 2010). These changes may have deleterious consequences for Barbados, according to Uyarra et al. (2005), who found that approximately 80% of the tourists they interviewed had indicated an unwillingness to return to Barbados for the same price if SLR and erosion caused the loss of beach area.

While climate change poses threats to the island, earlier unsustainable land management practices with a bias towards mass tourism, high-density beach accommodation and past failures of plans and policies to protect its key tourism assets, were major factors in the destruction of the island's fragile ecosystems (Weaver, 2001). Only 1 hectare of coastal mangrove remained, giving way to hotel development (GOB, 2001). Coral reef degradation was reported in two studies spanning 20 years. [. . .] GOB (2001) reported that the main causes of coral reef destruction were careless diving near the shore, disposal of solid waste and indiscriminate alterations to the coastal topography mainly from tourism development, destructive fishing practices and anchoring boats over reefs. [. . .] Approximately 80% of Barbados' fringing reefs were seriously degraded, and bank reefs decreased from 37% to 23% over a decade (GOB, 2010). Furthermore, severe coral bleaching associated with climate change in late August 2005 affected all reef habitats and nearly all coral taxa and an average of 71% of all colonies experienced bleaching (Oxenford et al., 2008).

[. . .] In recent times, a major concern of the island's policymakers is that losses to coastal ecosystem services, infrastructure damage and threats to livelihoods due to climate change can undermine economic resiliency (GOB, 2010). [. . .]

So far, the contextualisation of tourism in Barbados points to a clear juxtaposition and paradox emerging between tourism's many undesirable impacts on the coastal zone and climate changes threatening to adversely affect coastal tourism infrastructure, ultimately threatening the very nature, character and socio-economic well-being of this coastal tourist destination. Coastal ecosystem degradation and the challenges of climate change require policy shifts and innovative practices in sustainable tourism and climate change adaptation. The following sections of this paper analyse policy reform and practices used in Barbados' tourism industry to confront these challenges.

SUSTAINABLE TOURISM, PHYSICAL PLANNING POLICY AND PRACTICE AND CLIMATE CHANGE ADAPTATION

Sustainable tourism in Barbados is unattainable if coral reefs, one of its most important coastal assets, are vulnerable. In the context of SLR and coastal erosion, reefs play a key role in ecosystem-based adaptation to climate change because they serve as natural breakwaters. Barbados' existing physical planning policy minimises soil erosion and sedimentation given that coral reefs require clear water conditions to survive. [. . .] In practice, built development is disallowed on erosion-prone lands and sediment control and management plans are mandatory for all building and engineering operations, including hotels and other related facilities located in coastal areas.

Over the past 30 years, coastal setbacks have been used to regulate development in Barbados. A coastal setback distance is a prescribed distance to a coastal feature within which all or certain types of development are prohibited. The TCPD applies a coastal setback policy because it eliminates the need for sea walls and other engineering structures that reduce beach erosion and flooding, but which may also affect coastal property. In islands such as Barbados, setbacks also provide buffer zones between the ocean and coastal infrastructure, where the beach zone may expand or contract naturally, as observed by French (2006). Additionally, setbacks enhance the probability that artificial light will not shine directly on the beach to disturb turtle nesting.

[. . .]

New evidence on climate change projections highlights the importance of revisiting the setback policy for Barbados. Fish et al. (2008) found that beach area was lost from all of Barbados' beaches under all SLR scenarios with a 10-metre and 30-metre setback. They argued that whereas the benefits of long-term beach maintenance accrued from adequate setback regulations are clear, consideration must also be given to issues that can hinder the implementation or effectiveness of setbacks. [. . .]

INTEGRATED COASTAL ZONE MANAGEMENT POLICIES AND PROJECTS, SUSTAINABLE TOURISM AND CLIMATE CHANGE ADAPTATION

Integrated coastal zone management (ICZM) can assist in planning for adaptation to climate change because it provides an anticipatory and predictive approach to facilitate a response to medium and long-term concerns such as SLR, as well as responds to short-term needs (Belle and Bramwell, 2005; Tobey et al., 2010). Tobey et al. (2010) have argued that the process and best practices of ICZM are not radically changed by applying a climate lens. From their perspective, the best practices of planning and implementation of coastal management measures apply equally to climate change as they do to other coastal issues.

[. . .]

Among the three generic climate change adaptation strategies that exist, Barbados has focused on protection and accommodation as opposed to retreat. The accommodation, or "do nothing", approach has been applied to undeveloped locations on the east coast of the island. Measures for beach protection and enhancement have been implemented on the more highly developed southwest and west coasts (Brewster, 2007; Fish et al., 2008). These include "hard options" such as sea walls, revetments, groyne fields, gabions and breakwaters, which absorb wave energy and stimulate beach nourishment (See Figure 28.1).

Figure 28.1 Protective measures used along the southwest coast of Barbados to minimise beach erosion.

Source: Author's elaboration

Protection Measures

The CZMU has taken into account that "hold the line" measures intended to reinforce coastal lands should be designed to the highest standards; otherwise, they
would temporarily mitigate erosion and be costly to maintain if poorly designed.
But these "hard" structures are also aesthetically unpleasing, as they visually
impair the natural ambience of beaches (Mycoo and Chadwick, 2012). However,
the CZMU has "softened" the vista of a highly engineered shoreline by integrating landscaping to help the beaches look more natural in appearance. As part of
the promotion of sustainable tourism, the design of visually pleasing boardwalks
and landscaping has helped dilute the harsh concrete vistas that would otherwise
encircle the coast.

[. . .]

Planned Retreat

Planned retreat is a controversial, untenable option for dealing with climate
change and SLR because the coast of Barbados is highly developed. [. . .] Cambers et al. (2003) have found that planned strategic retreat using setback distances
for hotels takes a long time because these buildings have an economic life span
of 25–30 years before they need to be extensively renovated, converted or demolished. They argue that it is at the end of this life span when there is the opportunity
for rebuilding further back from the water. Fish et al. (2008) argue that although
it is an expensive option, moving buildings back could minimise the likelihood of
paying out considerable amounts in the future.

Beach Nourishment

Another popular approach is the use of "soft" measures such as beach nourishment. Restoration occurs by bringing sand to the beach from inland sites or
adjoining beach segments, or by hydraulically pumping sand onshore from an offshore site. With climate change, beaches will seek to re-establish their equilibrium
by shifting landward in response to rising seas. [. . .]

Ecosystem-Based Adaptation

Ecosystem-based measures are used in Barbados to address reef damage and
coastal erosion arising from SLR and storm surges. Given coral reef damage over
the years, the CZMU has embarked on a coral reef transplantation project because
corals are an essential constituent of Barbados' beaches and a major asset for
sustainable tourism. [. . .]

The CZMU uses several adaptation measures in response to erosion and flooding in coastal areas, but the right balance between "hard" and "soft" options needs
to be achieved over the long term, and cost-benefit analysis will be of tremendous

help as a decision-making tool. Striking the right balance of adaptation measures is especially important in economic, ecological, social and political terms.
[. . .]

POLICY RECOMMENDATIONS FOR SIDS

SIDS policymakers can learn from sustainable tourism policies implemented in Barbados that are doubling as pre-emptive measures for adaptation to climate change and SLR.

Physical Planning Policies, Risk Assessment and Hazard Mapping

In SIDS where coastal erosion is severe, physical planning policies should be implemented to control sediment loss and minimise beach erosion. Failure to do so will result in coral reef damage, beach loss, and erosion of beachfront tourism accommodations. Coastal setbacks are recommended to minimise these impacts, but some flexibility in applying setbacks would be needed. A place-based approach to coastal tourism management is essential, and therefore these setbacks should be based on the merits of the specific proposed coastal development. [. . .]

ICZM, Sustainable Tourism and Climate Change Adaptation Strategies

SIDS should adopt ICZM because it has proven to be a successful strategy for addressing past failures in the promotion of coastal-oriented mass tourism and has become important in the context of climate change adaptation, as the Barbados case study highlights. Moreover, as the Barbados study has revealed, and as noted by Nicholls (2011), SIDS require an integrated coastal management philosophy that incorporates climate change adaptation strategies with wider societal and sustainable development objectives. [. . .]

SIDS have three strategies to select from: protection, accommodation and retreat. However, a stand-alone strategy is ill-advised, because it may compromise successful adaptation to climate change. In practice, many real-world responses are hybrid, combining elements of more than one approach.

[. . .]

One of the lessons for SIDS is that not all three strategies can be easily implemented, and each will need to be considered over the short, medium and long terms. SIDS policymakers should be aware that protection and accommodation strategies are short- to medium-term measures and less contentious to implement. In contrast, relocating built development is a long-term costly measure, especially if the overwhelming majority of hotels are already located in the coastal zone. Moreover, policymakers should be sensitised to the possibility that stakeholders will resist the abandonment of high value real estate to the sea unless cost-benefit analysis is conducted.

SIDS that are economically dependent on erosion-prone beaches should consider the use of coastal structures in the short term if they are affordable. Barbados has successfully used protective coastal infrastructure to arrest severe beach erosion on the southwest and west coasts, where most of its hotels and popular beaches are concentrated.

In addition, ecosystem-based measures such as maintaining existing vegetation, re-vegetation where loss has occurred and coral reef replanting should be incorporated into climate change adaptation strategies, and the costs of doing so should be weighed against long-term benefits.

SIDS are concerned about the financial costs of climate change adaptation, especially given their small carbon footprints. The question of who will pay and who will benefit from adaptation measures is controversial and should be the subject of policy debate among governments, investors and communities. Barbados has secured loans from international financial institutions to address severe coastal erosion where its hotels are spatially concentrated. [. . .]

Infrastructure Policies and Projects

Infrastructure policies and projects that promote sustainable tourism are useful adaptation measures to climate change. An important policy reform for SIDS is increased investment in central sewage treatment projects with the appropriate level of treatment to minimise coastal ecosystem degradation. As Barbados has found, without effective sewage treatment, coral reefs will be degraded. Coral reefs are essential to beach sand production, snorkeling, diving and fisheries, as well as to minimising the coastal erosion associated with climate change and SLR, as they function as natural breakwaters. In SIDS where no central sewerage system exists and hotels located on the coast use private sewage treatment plants, these plants should be carefully monitored by certified inspectors trained by academic institutions to ensure compliance with waste disposal regulations. Additionally, tax incentives should be offered to hoteliers for improving their wastewater disposal system.

Water Conservation

Climate change models predict that water scarcity will result from drought or saline intrusion of freshwater resources associated with climate change. The construction of desalination plants can cause severe environmental damage of the sensitive coastal ecosystems found in SIDS. Water conservation policies, therefore, should be given high priority. [. . .]

Capacity-Building and Institutional Reform

Although there is no national coastal tourism policy to support sustainable development, Barbados has shown that this policy gap can be managed when there is clear responsibility and delegation of powers between government agencies such as the TCPD and CZMU. SIDS need to ensure that there is strong collaboration among their physical planning and environmental management agencies as well as CZMUs where these have been established. The success of policy implementation depends on strong institutional capacity for monitoring and enforcement, reliable databases for decision-making and sensitisation of policymakers on how critical governance is to sustainable natural resources management in the face of climate change challenges. [. . .] Table 28.1 provides a summary of the policies, practices and projects used by Barbados to support sustainable tourism and adaptation to climate change.

Table 28.1 Barbados' policies, practices and projects to support sustainable tourism, green economy and climate change adaptation

Policy measures	Sustainable tourism	Adaptation to climate change
TCPD policy		
Sediment control plan mandatory for all building and engineering operations	Coral reef protection	Natural breakwater against SLR and coastal erosion
Coastal setbacks applied over 30 years	Protection of tourism facilities	Protects property and population from SLR and storm surges that may cause coastal flooding and erosion
		Can eliminate use of engineering structures to reduce beach erosion and flooding
ICZMU policies and practices		
"Hard" options implemented (sea walls, revetments, groyne fields, gabions and breakwaters) to protect developed southwest and west coasts	Absorb wave energy and stimulate beach nourishment; important in protecting beach-based tourism product	CZMU is focussing on incorporation of climate change adaptation in engineering designs
"Soft" options used, e.g. beach nourishment	Projects located in areas of high investments in tourism facilities and beach supports economic activities	An adaptation response to climate change, e.g. erosion and SLR
Coral reef transplant	Supports beach and diving tourism	Reduces coastal erosion from SLR and storm surges
Infrastructure policy and projects		
Water conservation	Desalination plant (1999)	Adaptation to drought and water scarcity
	Water recycling and water storage mandatory for hotels	Tax rebates for new hotels
Central sewerage system	On tourism-intensive southwest and west coasts	Reef health maintained and coastal protection promoted

Source: Author's elaboration

CONCLUSION

Climate change adaptation for most SIDS will require policy reform in the areas of building construction, coastal management, water resources management, waste management, physical planning and sustainable land management, all of which are components of sustainable tourism. Policies should be linked to market mechanisms that offer incentives for adoption, including subsidies and rebates. Furthermore, these policies should be an integral part of SIDS' national sustainable development policies.

Much work still needs to be done among SIDS, including conducting rigorous research, prioritising and costing measures that will achieve climate change adaptation and sustainable tourism, weighing the benefits to society, building adaptive capacity among all stakeholders and exercising vigilance in systematically monitoring and evaluating the effectiveness of these measures in adapting to climate change. What remains to be answered is who will pay and who will benefit from the policies and projects implemented. This matter calls for stakeholder input informed by an awareness of the philosophy of equity, economic efficiency and environmental sustainability.

REFERENCES

Belle, N., Bramwell, B., 2005. Climate change and small island tourism: Policy maker and industry perspectives in Barbados. *Journal of Travel Research*, 44(1): 32–41.

Brewster, L., 2007. Coastal erosion risk mitigation strategies in small island developing states: The Barbados model. Presented at the United Nations Framework for the Convention on Climate Change Expert Meeting on SIDS Adaptation to Climate Change, Kingston.

Bueno, R., Herzfeld, C., Stanton, E.A., Ackerman, F., 2008. *The Caribbean and climate change: The costs of inaction.* Stockholm Environment Institute and Global Development and Environment Institute, Tufts University.

Cambers, G., Claro, R., Juman, R., Scott, S., 2008. *Climate change impacts on coastal and marine biodiversity in the insular Caribbean.* Caribbean Natural Resources Institute, Technical Report 382.

Cambers, G., Muehlig-Hofmann, A., Troost, D., 2003. *Coastal land tenure: A Small islands' perspective.* UNESCO, CSI Info. 15, Paris.

Easterling, W., Hurd, B., Smith, J. 2004. *Coping with climate change. The role of adaptation in the United States.* Washington, DC: Pew Center in Global Climate Change.

Fish, M.R., Côté, I., Horrocks, M., Mulligan, J.A., Watkinson, B., Jones, A.P., 2008. Construction setback regulations and sea level rise: Mitigating sea turtle nesting beach loss. *Ocean and Coastal Management*, 5(3): 330–334.

French, P.W., 2006. Managed realignment: The developing story of a comparatively new approach to soft engineering. *Estuarine, Coastal and Shelf Science*, 67(3): 409–423.

Government of Barbados, 2001. *Barbados' first national communications to the United Nations.* GOB, Bridgetown.

Government of Barbados, 2010. *National assessment report.* GOB, Bridgetown.

Hall, C.M., 2011. Climate change and its impact on tourism: Regional assessments, knowledge gaps and issues. In: Jones, P., Phillips, M. (Eds.), *Disappearing destinations: Climate change and future challenges for coastal tourism.* CABI Publishing, Oxford, pp. 10–29.

Kirshen, P., Ruth, M., Anderson, W., 2006. Climate's long-term impacts on urban infrastructures and services: The case of Metro Boston, chapter 7. In: Ruth, M., Donaghy, K.,

Kirshen, P.H. (Eds.) *Climate change and variability: Local impacts and responses.* Edward Elgar, Cheltenham, England.

Kirshen, P., Ruth, M., Anderson, W., Lakshmanan, T.R., 2004. *Infrastructure systems, services and climate change: Integrated impacts and response strategies for the Boston Metropolitan area.* Final Report to US EPA ORD, EPA grant number: R.827450-01.

Mycoo, M., Chadwick, A., 2012. Adaptation to climate change: The coastal zone of Barbados. *Maritime Engineering,* 165(4): 159–168.

Nicholls, R., 2004. Coastal flooding and wetland loss in the 21st century: Changes under the SRES climate and socio-economic scenarios, *Global Environmental Change,* 14(1): 69–86.

Nicholls, R., 2011. Planning for the impacts of sea level rise. *Oceanography,* 24(2): 144–157.

Nicholls, R., Tol, R.S.J., 2006. Impacts and responses to sea level rise: A global analysis of the SRES scenarios over the twenty first century. *Philosophical Transactions of the Royal Society A,* 364(1841): 1073–1095.

Oxenford, H.A., Roach, R., Brathwaite, A., Nurse, L., Goodridge, R., Hinds, F., Finney, C., 2008. Quantitative observations of a major coral bleaching. *Climatic Change,* 87(3): 435–449.

Ruth, M., Kirshen, P., 2001. Integrated impacts of climate change upon infrastructure systems and services in the Boston Metropolitan area. *World Resources Review,* 13(1): 106–122.

Scott, D., Becken, S., 2010. Adapting to climate change and climate policy: Progress, problems and potentials. *Journal of Sustainable Tourism,* 18(3): 283–295.

Tobey, J.P., Rubinoff, D., Robadue, G., Ricci, R., Volk, R., Furlow, J., Anderson, G., 2010. Practicing coastal adaptation to climate change: Lessons from integrated coastal management. *Coastal Management,* 38(3): 317–335.

United Nations Economic Commission for Latin America and the Caribbean (UNECLAC), 2010. *Review of the economics of climate change in the Caribbean project: Phase 1 climate change profiles in select Caribbean countries.* UNECLAC, Port of Spain.

Uyarra, M., Côté, I., Gill, J., Tinch, R., Viner, D., Watkinson, A., 2005. Island-specific preferences of tourists for environmental features: Implications of climate change for tourism-dependent states. *Environmental Conservation,* 32(1): 11–19.

Weaver, D.B., 2001. Mass and alternative tourism in the Caribbean. In: Harrison, D. (Ed.), *Tourism and the less developed world: Issues and case studies.* CABI Publishing, Oxford, pp. 161–174.

Section VII
Implementing the Vision

Introduction

Robert L. Ryan

The plans and designs discussed in the previous sections have to be implemented through local decision making and supported by regional and national policy. The initial articles in this section present the current status of adaptation, identify innovations in climate planning and the ways that climate-smart planning can both support and be supported by current best practice. The overall balance between mitigation and adaptation is explored, along with policies that achieve both. Community engagement is essential to the planning and implementation of these policies. The last article (by Sheppard) explores the importance of visualization as a catalyst for public engagement, particularly the role of landscape professionals in helping communities create a vision for climate change adaptation.

The first article explores the challenge of adapting to climate change while balancing climate change mitigation. This seminal work, a review of climate change plans in the United States and Australia, found that in about half the cases, climate change adaptation plans potentially conflicted with mitigation efforts. In many instances, climate change adaptation plans, such as those described earlier in this volume, use open space for flood storage, biodiversity protection and natural buffers to rising sea levels. The authors point out the inherent conflicts when these green space solutions that protect large blocks of open space inadvertently encourage disbursed, lower-density development, which is more carbon intensive than higher-density, compact urban forms. Thus, urban form is essential in considering plans to implement climate change adaptation. In addition, evaluating potential plans for their adaptation and mitigation benefits is an important criteria for landscape planners. The theme of balancing climate change adaptation and mitigation is also illustrated in Sheppard's article that uses examples from the Vancouver urban region.

The articles in this section illustrate key themes about implementing climate change adaptation plans. The first theme is that local governments, especially, cities are taking the lead in climate change planning. As described by Sheppard (2015), the public is much more motivated to be engaged in plans that directly affect their neighborhood. Shi et al. (2015) note that in the United States where climate change planning policies at the state and national level are weak or non-existent, cities and urban regions have found themselves addressing this issue with a range of creative and innovative solutions. However, the challenge of local implementation is that the lack of a regional- or large-scale plan can lead to a scattered, uncoordinated approach when layered upon the larger landscape at the county, state (provincial) and national levels.

The next theme which emerges in the articles (Shi et al., 2015) is the important role of local leadership among government officials to engage in climate change planning. More than community wealth or other factors, leadership is key to climate change planning. Sheppard (2015) also talks about using visualizations to engage and motivate local advocacy, aiding and fostering leadership amongst local citizens as well. Kithiia and Lyth (2010) discuss how leadership in developing nations where governments are ill-equipped to deal with climate change can come from the private sector. They use an East African case study in which a multi-national corporation transformed a cement quarry into an urban green space.

Another theme is the importance of first-hand experience with climate change. Cities that had experienced the direct effects of changing climate (i.e., increased precipitation, higher temperatures, and coastal impacts) were more likely to engage in climate change adaptation planning (Shi et al., 2015). In his article, Sheppard (2015) talks about the need to make climate change more visible in the local landscape as a catalyst for action. He talks about using markers to show higher sea level rise and tides along publically accessible coastal areas, such as parks and boardwalks. Embedding these visible references to climate change in new infrastructure is one method to create "experiential learning" about climate change in the local, everyday landscape.

Another important theme is to keep it keep climate change planning local and grounded in place (Sheppard, 2015). People have a strong connection to local places, and that can be a motivation to take action, especially when local residents observe climate change impacts, such as flooding, that are affecting places they cherish. In addition, local projects can have tangible co-benefits for residents.

Larger-scale climate change planning, however, is also needed. Nesting local initiatives into a larger-scale adaptation and mitigation framework as has been done in several metropolitan regions (i.e., Vancouver, San Francisco Bay area, and New York City) is critical to making changes at the regional scale. Sheppard talks about using local examples as demonstration projects that can be scaled up across a watershed or region, while being adapted to local conditions.

Public participation is another important consideration for climate change planning, but detailed strategies are beyond the scope of this volume. Readers are encouraged to look at the extensive body of literature on public participation (e.g., Arnstein (1969), Sanoff (2000) and others). The role of the planner includes both technical expert and facilitator. Empowering vulnerable populations that are often most impacted by climate change is an important role for planners that builds on the social advocacy role of today's planner. Climate change requires planners to be able to interpret scientific information into understandable, compelling and relevant information for local residents about the impacts of climate change and articulating the range of potential planning responses (Sheppard, 2015).

Several authors in this section discuss the need for climate change adaptation that is holistic and achieves multiple benefits. Mainstreaming climate change into overall master planning makes it another consideration alongside traditional topics such as transportation and land use. As discussed by Hamin and Gurran (2009), a more balanced approach is needed whereby strategies to mitigate climate change, such as preserving more green space in urban areas, are balanced with higher density urban form that is low-carbon and less car dependent. Climate change adaptation projects should increase the beauty and livability of our cities rather than be simply utilitarian, engineered solutions. The examples from Philadelphia earlier in this book, as well as those found in the case studies (digital resources) help to illustrate the type of transformative, creative and future-looking plans and projects that improve community resiliency to climate change while achieve multiple community objectives.

REFERENCES

Arnstein, S. R. (1969). "A Ladder of Citizen Participation." *Journal of the American Institute of Planners*, 35(4): 216–224.

Hamin, E., & Gurran, N. (2009). "Urban Form and Climate Change: Balancing Adaptation and Mitigation in the U.S. and Australia." *Habitat International*, 33: 238–245.

Kithiia, J., & Lyth, A. (2010). "Urban Wildscapes and Green Spaces in Mombasa and Their Potential to Address the Impacts of Climate Change in Kenya: The Case of Mombasa." *Environment and Urbanization*, 23 (1): 251–265.

Sanoff, H. (2000). *Community Participation Methods in Design and Planning*. New York: Wiley.

Sheppard, S. R. J. (2015). "Making Climate Change Visible: A Critical Role for Landscape Professionals." *Landscape and Urban Planning*, 142: 95–105.

Shi, L., Chu, E., & Debats, J. (2015). "Explaining Progress in Climate Adaptation Planning Across 156 U.S. Municipalities." *Journal of the American Planning Association*: 1–12.

29 Urban Form and Climate Change

Balancing Adaptation and Mitigation in the U.S. and Australia

Elisabeth M. Hamin Infield and Nicole Gurran

EDITOR'S INTRODUCTION

This study explores the question: how do policies designed to adapt to changing climates support policies to mitigate climate change? This study reviewed adaptation case studies in the United States and Australia. Half of the plans/policies that were reviewed had conflicting outcomes/goals. For example, habitat protection solutions that promote green space create lower density residential patterns that are more car dependent and energy consumptive, conflicting with mitigation goals. The challenge is that green infrastructure using natural solutions to adapt to new climate regimes including higher tides and flooding often propose large areas of "natural" open space that create lower density development. In order to address these inherent contradictions in many climate adaptation plans, the authors propose urban form that maximizes multiple benefits and efficiently uses ribbons of open space, while creating compact areas of higher density development.

URBAN FORM AND CLIMATE CHANGE: BALANCING ADAPTATION AND MITIGATION IN THE U.S. AND AUSTRALIA

INTRODUCTION

[. . .] [T]he issue of adaptation, alongside mitigation, is emerging as one of the most pressing issues nations and cities face. While mitigation planning works to reduce current and future greenhouse gas emissions, including emissions that are generated through the built environment and transportation sectors, adaptation seeks to adjust the built and social environment to minimize the negative outcomes of now-unavoidable climate change. Thus, mitigation and adaptation must be treated as twin issues. [. . .]

RESEARCH QUESTION AND METHOD

A key challenge in achieving the dual goals of climate change planning is that the land-use policy options to address adaptation and mitigation may conflict. Preliminary testing of whether there are and of what sort those conflicts might be, and any clear ways to reduce them, is the topic of this paper. Despite clear recognition by the IPCC of the need to ensure that adaptation actions do not undermine mitigation attempts, let alone broader sustainability goals (IPCC, 2007a, 2007b), surprisingly little research exists on the types of conflicts that might arise in practice. This is understandable, given the institutional divergences that have arisen between adaptation and mitigation responses at national, regional, and local levels, reflecting the different scales at which these responses operate and take effect (McEvoy & Handley, 2006). Mitigation strategies seek to reduce global warming over the long term, while adaptation strategies protect local communities from sudden and immediate dangers. It is certainly possible to conceptualize ways for mitigation and adaptation strategies to complement one another. For instance, shifting to decentralized low-carbon forms of energy generation reduces greenhouse gas emissions. Shifting to wind, solar or wave energy is also a key adaptation strategy as smaller, more decentralized forms of power generation reduce the risks associated with widespread power loss through severe storm events, or from peak power loads under temperature extremes.

However, it is equally possible to conceptualize scenarios in which mitigation and adaptation goals are in conflict with each other. For instance, urban containment through higher density often results in a loss of permeable surfaces and tree cover, intensifying stormwater and flood risks associated with changed climatic scenarios, and in some climatic conditions exacerbating the discomfort and health impacts of hotter summers. Strategic planning processes are intended to provide a way of resolving competing goals, so it is likely that once identified, ways to overcome or offset many of the latent conflicts between mitigation and adaptation approaches will be developed. However, at the present time, very little of the existing guidance on planning for climate change mitigation or adaptation identifies areas of potential conflict in urban policy decisions, let alone ways to resolve such dilemmas.

Our research used an international comparison approach to maximize the broad relevance of our findings and increase the pool of examples, which was needed given the early adoption stage of local or regional climate change/land-use policies. We focus on coastal communities largely beyond the metropolitan areas, where potential tensions between adaptation and mitigation actions may arise [. . .]

While such issues affect socially disadvantaged metropolitan areas too, what is interesting about natural amenity communities is their need to ensure that vulnerable natural systems—species, habitat, and the ecological processes on which they depend—are also able to adapt to climatic change.

Examining local level policy responses is important because it is the specific qualities of particular urban settings and climatic zones that determine relative vulnerability to particular climate change impacts and it is at this scale that most adaptation actions should be defined. In turn, it is at this level that particular decisions regarding mitigation responses might conflict with or exacerbate climatic exposure, thus undermining adaptation attempts or vice versa.

The research methods involved:

1. International, U.S. and Australian literature on climate change was reviewed, to identify impacts for coastal or amenity communities, and to establish leading practice principles and approaches in planning to reduce settlement contributions to greenhouse gas emissions, and to adapt to climatic changes already under way.
2. A targeted review of local planning practices relating to climate change mitigation or adaptation was undertaken. The review focused on recent work undertaken by coastal amenity communities in Australia and the United States, but also includes a limited group of leading practice examples from other local government areas internationally. The review includes planning approaches directly or indirectly relevant to both mitigation and adaptation. [. . .]
3. Based on the principles explained ahead, the identified practices were categorized as adaptive or mitigating, and a determination was made as to whether in most cases the action could create a negative outcome for the alternative goal—adaptation or mitigation. These actions were identified as potential conflict actions. We then theorize about ways in which these potential conflicts could be avoided.

There are significant limitations to these findings. Two key ones are that while we spent a great deal of time on literature search to find our case studies [. . .], we will certainly have missed some and thus do not claim that th[is review] [. . .] represents the universe of mitigation or adaptation actions; and, the specifics of how any one place or project is built will ultimately determine whether our generalized finding of conflict or not is correct. Further, our focus on amenity communities brings certain tensions between mitigation and adaptation into sharp relief, particularly in relation to biodiversity. Parallel empirical analyses of adaptation/mitigation tensions emerging in major city regions will likely reveal several other dilemmas. We view this paper as the start of investigations, rather than the end, and anticipate that we and other writers will revise these as the basic premises are tested in more detail.

In the following sections, we first discuss key concepts and approaches underlying mitigation planning, then the responses increasingly advocated for climate change adaptation, before highlighting areas of potential conflict.

MITIGATION POLICY GOALS

The perceived appropriate and necessary policy actions on local land-use toward greenhouse gas mitigation can be gleaned from both literature and practice. For example, a book by Ewing et al. (2008) argues that we need to build more compactly to reduce vehicle miles traveled (VMT) [. . .]

The message of the book is that smart growth—as it has been commonly defined—is an essential step toward achieving climate change mitigation goals.

The authors of the study make a number of recommendations on local land-use policy. In relation to process, these include undertaking a local climate action plan, revising building codes for altered climate scenarios, and investing in civic education and engagement. Specific physical planning recommendations include favoring smart growth projects which situate denser housing and services near transit stations and contain urban growth boundaries, ensuring a jobs/housing balance, so that workforce housing is near jobs, and adopting pedestrian friendly site and building design standards (the provided examples suggest maximum setbacks of 20 feet, with a small amount of parking allowed only in the back of the building; see Ewing et al., 2008: pp. 150–153).

Other works connects urban form to non-transport related energy use (Ewing & Rong, 2008; Randolph, 2008). The premise is that lower density and detached housing tends to be larger than multi-unit developments or attached housing, requiring more energy to heat and cool, and additional energy output to establish and maintain electricity transmission and distribution (Ewing & Rong, 2008; Randolph, 2008). The significance of urban form and household energy use aside from transportation impacts is underscored by the fact that that the residential sector in the United States consumes more than one-fifth of total energy use in that nation (Ewing & Rong, 2008). The relationship of household energy use and urban form thus reinforces the need for more compact cities and housing types, both to reduce carbon dioxide generation from vehicle miles and to reduce local domestic emissions. [. . .]

In summary, the consensus in greenhouse gas mitigation is that the appropriate local land-use policies must limit sprawl and create denser built forms, while maintaining urban forests if at all possible.

ADAPTATION

Research and policy action on planning for adaptation of cities and towns is just now emerging (IPCC, 2007a). Because so much of Australia is quite vulnerable to natural disasters, there has been more work there than in the United States, although it remains quite preliminary. [. . .]

Some of the key actions that communities are undertaking for adaptation include changing infrastructure and disaster plans to include forecasts for climate change (for instance, the State of South Australia requires local plans to include provisions for potential climate-induced sea level rise), planning for larger river floodplains and protecting wetlands in areas likely to see increased severe storm events from climate change (as undertaken by Noosa Shire in Australia's southeast), providing corridors for species movement as climate changes and species ranges need to change (Port Stephens Shire in New South Wales [NSW] has proclaimed a koala habitat plan of management for this purpose), and changing building codes to reflect the need for more natural cooling/less contribution to the heat island effect.

Within the United States, there have been only very preliminary steps taken on planning for or implementing adaptation. Three notable efforts include the pilot study of adaptation planning by ICLEI for Keene, New Hampshire (City of Keene,

2007); the water infrastructure planning being undertaken by the New York City Department of Environmental Protection (NYC Department of Environmental Protection Climate Change Program, 2008; Rosenzweig et al., 2007), and the specific work by King County, Washington (2007). [. . .] A point that stands out for many of the noted actions is that they require significant land to undertake, often through the provision of open space used for instance for stormwater management, sea level rise planning, or for migration corridors.

MITIGATION, ADAPTATION, AND LAND-USE CONFLICT

To summarize, the key land-use pattern implication of climate change mitigation is concentrating development so that car travel and building energy use is reduced; it brings a strong new impetus to the existing anti-sprawl/smart growth campaign. Alongside land-use densification, however, we see the importance of maintaining an urban forest to cool buildings and sidewalks, as well as to sequester carbon. [. . .]

A key point of adaptation is that many actions, although certainly not all, require more land left in open space, and/or a less dense built environment. Current approaches to floodwater management suggest less piping and more natural infiltration; bioswales require space that pipes do not. More water to manage often means more space needed to manage it. Similarly, adding (or not removing) space-using greenery is an important step in preventing or treating urban heat island effects (Stone, 2005). Buildings that are more moderate in height and placed to enable ventilation between individual dwellings provide adaptation to higher temperatures, but tend to reduce density. While there is little adaptation benefit from low density, sprawling development, under adaptation it appears that moderate density with significant fingers of green infrastructure running through the city may be the most effective form.

To provide an initial test of this problem of where mitigation and adaptation conflict and correspond, we prepared [a] table [. . .] which lists the actions that we have been able to identify towns and cities as undertaking to address the land-use implications of climate change. We grouped these by sector affected, and then judged whether they achieved the goals of mitigation (reduction of greenhouse gas), adaptation (adjusting the built or social environment to have greater resilience in the face of climate changes), or both. [. . .] [W]e find that 22 out of 50 of the actions being undertaken or recommended for implementation have the potential to create conflicts between adaptation and mitigation.

TWO EXAMPLES OF CONFLICTS BETWEEN ADAPTATION AND MITIGATION

To illustrate these issues, we provide two indicative examples from our review of local climate change responses. Byron Shire in the far north coast of Australia's New South Wales has adopted specific climate change parameters for temperature increases, sea level rises, rainfall intensities, cyclone intensities, and storm surges (Gurran et al., 2008). Its Strategic Planning and Climate Change approach includes a 100-year planning period for proposals or issues that may be affected by climate change, and undertakes to incorporate climate change planning scenarios into all relevant plans and responsibilities (including infrastructure, land-use planning, and development assessment). The planning parameters are designed to change following subsequent IPCC information or recommendations from Australia's Commonwealth Scientific and Industrial Research Organization (CSIRO) and the New South Wales Department of Environment and Climate Change.

However, applying the parameters in practice implies a dramatic reduction in available areas for new development and redevelopment within the existing Byron village centre, potentially competing with the Shire's other sustainability and climate change mitigation objectives, such as reducing local vehicle miles traveled by promoting walking and cycling. The issue has come to the forefront with decisions regarding the siting and construction of the new council library. The current site, acquired prior to the determination of the climate change planning parameters in late 2007, is centrally located in the Shire but now falls within the expanded flood zone, necessitating very extensive adaptation works if the site is to be used at all. Ironically, one of the solutions is to use the ground level of the site as a car park, elevating the building to a level beyond predicted flood waters. The alternative would relocate the library to higher ground beyond the city centre, meaning that most users would need to drive to access it.

This example highlights the difficulties in practice of retrofitting adaptation strategies over existing settlement, while continuing to promote forms of development within these areas that reduce, rather than exacerbate, greenhouse gas emissions.

The second example demonstrates some of the dilemmas that arise in designing new residential development. The case in point, Port Stephens, on the mid-northern New South Wales coast, has an established planning policy whereby new housing areas must maintain sufficient Eucalypt cover and other environmental features to preserve the habitat of the local koala population (Gurran et al., 2008). The policy (known as the Port Stephens Council Comprehensive Koala Plan of Management) provides a good model of how areas of endogenous vegetation must be protected and expanded to assist native plants and animals to adapt to increasing pressures under changed climatic conditions. However, the model results in very low density, car-dependent housing. Even if some of the household energy needs associated with these koala conservation estates can be satisfied in the future through locally generated renewable sources, they will remain car dependent and situated at some distance from centres of services and employment. Nesting the housing within natural bushland also increases exposure to other dangers likely to extend to the coastal zone under climate change scenarios—such as increased frequency and intensity of forest fires.

SIGNIFICANCE

To us, the table and these examples suggest that climate change creates a "density conundrum." Mitigating climate change requires a denser urban environment to reduce vehicle miles traveled and building energy use, while adapting to climate change requires open space available for stormwater management of severe storm events, species migration, and urban cooling, among other goals. The answer here is not that we must do one or the other, but that we need to seek urban form answers that allow communities to minimize the conflicts. The likely best urban form, we argue, must bring green space within settlements focused along green transportation routes and floodplains (ribbons and corridors) rather than large expanses. Those open spaces must also be designed to achieve multiple goals— urban agriculture and floodplain protection, for instance. Larger blocks of open space are limited to peripheries—beach foreshores where open space provides recreation and leisure, as well as space to adapt to changes in sea level; greenbelts or foodbelts, where they are able to reinforce internal settlement containment. The urban form which will respond best to the needs of both adaptation and mitigation will be the one whereby available resources achieve multiple goals. Buildings will need to provide more natural cooling potential, solar power, and moderate density so as to enable transit options. Open space, in particular, will need to be very carefully planned to maximize its multiple benefits while minimizing its reductions in density of development. While heroic responses to biodiversity conservation, such as Port Stephen's iconic koala habitat plan of management, seek to balance settlement aspirations with wildlife needs, the correct response may be to avoid such sensitive locations altogether. Rather than creating dispersed, car-dependent housing, genuine wildlife protection in an era of increasing climate volatility likely preserves and extends remaining habitat and provides connected corridors for species migration, resulting in contained, denser, discrete, and multifunctional human settlements. While not embedded within the bush, as envisaged by the koala habitat plan and other innovative tools like it, such places would be selectively greened and cooled by corridors of low-fire-risk vegetation and networked via high-speed rapid transit to other settlements. Actions like these with careful design have the potential to mitigate the space requirements of adaptation, and adapt the density needs of mitigation to create resilient, lower carbon, and potentially quite beautiful urban forms.

REFERENCES

City of Keene, NH. (2007). Adapting to climate change: Planning a climate resilient community. Keene, NH: City of Keene.

Ewing, R., Bartholomew, K., Winkelman, S., Walters, J., & Chen, D. (2008). *Growing cooler: The evidence on urban development and climate change*. Washington, DC: Urban Land Institute.

Ewing, R., & Rong, F. (2008). The impact of urban form on U.S. residential energy use. *Housing Policy Debate*, 19(1), 1.

Gurran, N., Hamin, E., & Norman, B. (2008). *Planning for climate change: Leading practice principles and models for sea change communities in coastal Australia*. Sydney: University of Sydney, Faculty of Architecture and the Sea Change Task Force.

Intergovernmental Panel on Climate Change (IPCC). (2007a). *Climate change 2007: Climate change impacts, adaptation and vulnerability*. Summary for Policy Makers, April 6 2007.

Intergovernmental Panel on Climate Change (IPCC). (2007b). Contribution of working group III to the fourth assessment report of the intergovernment panel on climate change.

In B. Mertz, O. R. Davidson, P. R. Bosch, R. Dave, & L. A. Meyer (Eds.), *Climate change 2007: Mitigation*. Cambridge: Cambridge University Press.

King County, Washington. (2007). *2007 King County climate plan*. http://www.metrokc. gov/exec/news/2007/pdf/ClimatePlan.pdf. Accessed 26.06.08.

McEvoy, D., & Handley, L. (2006). Adaptation and mitigation in urban areas: Synergies and conflicts. *Municipal Engineer, 159*(4), 185–191.

NYC Department of Environmental Protection Climate Change Program. (2008). *The NYC DEP climate change program assessment and action plan, report 1*. http://www. nyc.gov/html/dep/. Accessed 20.06.08.

Randolph, J. (2008). Comment on Reid Ewing and Fan Rong's "The impact of urban form on U.S. residential energy use". *Housing Policy Debate, 19*(1), 45.

Rosenzweig, C., Major, D., Demong, K., Stanton, C., Horton, R., & Stults, M. (2007). Managing climate change risks in New York city's water system: Assessment and adaptation planning. *Mitigation and Adaptation Strategies for Global Change, 12*(8), 1391–1409.

Stone, B. (2005). Urban heat and air pollution: An emerging role for planners in the climate change debate. *Journal of the American Planning Association, 71*(1), 13.

30 Explaining Progress in Climate Adaptation Planning Across 156 U.S. Municipalities

Linda Shi, Eric Chu, and Jessica Debats Garrison

EDITOR'S INTRODUCTION

This survey of climate change adaptation in U.S. cities found that over half (60%) are planning for climate change. Significant predictors of engaging in planning were elected officials' commitment, wealth (more municipal expenditures per capita), and awareness that climate is already changing. State policies did not have an impact on engaging in climate change, suggesting that these policies are not strong enough to create change. This study illustrates that the more disbursed nature of U.S. governance (vis-à-vis planning) creates a more heterogeneous response, whereby individual cities are "leading the way" when it comes to climate change planning. However, this heterogeneity creates an uneven response when taken at a national scale. The study also points to the challenges for less wealthy cities and those where climate change effects are still not recognized as having impacts. It should be noted that this study was written during the Obama administration when climate change policies promoted adaptation. In the current political climate in the United States, adaptation leadership is even more focused on state and local governments rather than at the federal level.

EXPLAINING PROGRESS IN CLIMATE ADAPTATION PLANNING ACROSS 156 U.S. MUNICIPALITIES

Local governments around the country are beginning to adapt to the negative impacts of climate change, such as increasingly erratic and extreme natural hazards. [. . .]

Many local governments, however, find it difficult to understand climate science or to alter historic development and planning practices in response to projected impacts (Bassett & Shandas, 2010; Cutter et al., 2014; While & Whitehead, 2013). The conditions that prevent or enable cities to adapt to climate change are collectively known as their *adaptive capacity* (IPCC, 2014). Studies find that cities with high adaptive capacity can overcome barriers to adaptation planning because they possess administrative and financial resources, strong local leadership, the ability to obtain and communicate climate information to others, cultural values that support institutional responses, and strong state policies (Aylett, 2014; Carmin, Nadkarni, & Rhie, 2012; Hamin, Gurran, & Emlinger, 2014; Moser & Ekstrom, 2012). However, no study has systematically analyzed the importance of different determinants of adaptive capacity across a large number of cities, as has been done for climate mitigation and sustainability policy (Bedsworth & Hanak, 2013; Krause, 2010, 2012; Lubell, Feiock, & Handy, 2009).

In this study, we build on the literature on urban adaptive capacity by using logistic regression to assess the importance of different indicators of adaptive capacity. We draw on the responses from 156 U.S. cities that participated in a 2011 global survey of climate adaptation planning, 60% of which have begun adaptation planning. We model the effect of 13 measures of cities' resources, local leadership, information for climate adaptation, and state policies in predicting whether or not a city has begun to engage in adaptation planning.

We find that greater commitment by local elected officials, higher municipal expenditures per capita, and perceptions that the climate is already changing are statistically significantly associated (p = .05) with cities engaging in adaptation planning. Surprisingly, state policies, income per capita, public and business awareness, and challenges obtaining staff time, funding, and scientific data are not statistically significant predictors of planning for our sample. Larger cities are more likely to engage in adaptation planning, but this finding is of borderline statistical significance and may be due to an oversampling of larger and more progressive cities in our study.

[. . .]

PROGRESS AND BARRIERS TO LOCAL GOVERNMENT ADAPTATION

Climate adaptation planning helps cities identify specific climate impacts, develop options for responding to these impacts, and mobilize the resources to implement these options. [. . .] Strategies that cities have developed include investments in ecological and engineering infrastructure, institutional reforms to existing plans, codes, insurance policies, and development approval processes, as well as programs to alter cultural and behavioral practices (Carmin et al., 2015; Ebi & Burton, 2008; Hamin & Gurran, 2009; Lemieux & Scott, 2011; Solecki, Leichenko, & O'Brien, 2011).

Adaptation planning processes require substantial technical capacity, financial resources, and political support (National Research Council, 2010). Adaptation plans task local governments with translating scientific projections of future climate conditions into tangible impacts on local operations through risk and vulnerability assessments, and selecting from potentially costly and controversial adaptation options in the face of uncertain climate impacts over long planning horizons (Berrang-Ford, Ford, & Paterson, 2011; Carmin, Dodman, & Chu, 2013; Füssel, 2007; Moser & Ekstrom, 2010; Preston, Westaway, & Yuen, 2011). Around 59% of the nearly 600 cities that are members of ICLEI— Local Governments for Sustainability in the United States have initiated explicit adaptation planning, a proportion that is likely higher than that of the country's 14,000 urban areas and clusters[1] (Aylett, 2014; Bierbaum et al., 2013; Carmin et al., 2012).

Scholars have tried to catalyze more widespread adaptation planning by identifying the conditions that prevented or enabled cities such as Keene (New Hampshire), Baltimore, Boston, and Chicago to start planning at an early stage. Qualitative research on local adaptation planning has found that the lack of policy mandates from state governments as well as the lack of resources, leadership, ability to access and communicate climate information, and supportive cultural values among local governments all constrain adaptation planning at the local level (Aylett, 2014; Carmin et al., 2012; Hamin et al., 2014; Moser & Ekstrom, 2010, 2012). However, while researchers generally agree on the importance of these broad categories of adaptive capacity, there is less agreement on specific metrics that predict cities' likelihood of actually engaging in adaptation planning (Moser, 2009, 2015). In the following review, we discuss the first four types of barriers to adaptation planning listed previously, as well as potential measures of these barriers.

RESOURCES

The lack of resources is one of the most cited barriers to adaptation (Anguelovski, Chu, & Carmin, 2014; Carmin et al., 2012; Hunt & Watkiss, 2010; Moser & Ekstrom, 2012). Studies report that smaller cities have a particularly difficult time raising the fiscal and staffing resources for adaptation planning (Hamin et al., 2014). As a result, relatively few small cities have undertaken adaptation planning without the support of regional planning agencies and foundations, such as the Kresge, Rockefeller, and Barr Foundations (Bryan, 2015; Hamin et al., 2014; Moser & Ekstrom, 2012; Shi, Chu, & Carmin, 2016). Larger cities tend to have more stable tax bases and technically trained staff, greater regulatory and political autonomy, and more access to environmental and municipal networks, such as ICLEI (International Council for Local Environmental Initiatives) and the Urban Sustainability Directors Network, that provide additional resources for adaptation planning (Homsy & Warner, 2015; Westerhoff, Keskitalo, & Juhola, 2011). Nevertheless, even large cities report challenges dedicating staff and funding, given competing priorities, particularly after the 2008 recession (Carmin et al., 2012).

[. . .] Administrative capacity for adaptation planning can also be difficult to gage. While some cities have established climate change offices and funded dedicated climate staff (Carmin et al., 2013), others have integrated climate considerations into ongoing planning processes by reallocating the time of existing staff (Halsnæs & Trærup, 2009; Klein, 2011).

LOCAL LEADERSHIP

Many studies cite the lack of leadership, especially among planning staff and local elected officials, as an important barrier to adaptation planning. Planning staff in cities that pursued adaptation early on pushed for climate impact assessments and plans even without state or federal policy mandates because they were motivated by their own beliefs, perceptions of climate impacts, or participation in global forums and networks where these ideas were gaining traction (Anguelovski & Carmin, 2011). These adaptation champions helped build local coalitions and political support for adaptation planning (Bulkeley, 2010; Lowe, Foster, & Winkelmand, 2009; Roberts, 2010). Still, many planners report difficulty in gaining support from their mayors and city councilors (Carmin et al., 2012) due to the pervasiveness of climate change denial (Germain, Ellingboe, & Kroh, 2015), the uncertainty of climate projections and impacts (Amundsen, Berglund, & Westskog, 2010; Bedsworth & Hanak, 2010; Moser, 2009), or the prioritizing of day-to-day operations (Carmin et al., 2013; Measham et al., 2011). In a vicious cycle, low political support then translates into difficulties increasing staffing capacity, allocating funding, and coordinating with other departments for adaptation planning (Aylett, 2014; Gurran, Norman, & Hamin, 2013). [. . .]

INFORMATION AND COMMUNICATION

The difficulties associated with obtaining, interpreting, and communicating data on climate change present a third set of barriers to advancing local adaptation planning (Fünfgeld, 2010; Tribbia & Moser, 2008). Even though federal and state agencies are increasingly making climate models available to local governments, cities often still need to hire technical consultants to interpret these models into specific impacts on local infrastructure and services.

Planners have found it even more challenging to build broad-based support and communicate the importance of climate adaptation to their elected officials, the public, and the business community (Brulle, Carmichael, & Jenkins, 2012; Carmin et al., 2012; Howe, Mildenberger, Marlon, & Leiserowitz, 2015; McCright & Dunlap, 2011). Although natural disasters often trigger greater public awareness and political impetus for local adaptation planning, adaptation champions often find it difficult to sustain this "window of opportunity" (Birkmann et al., 2010, p. 639). [. . .]

STATE POLICY FRAMEWORK

A final barrier is the lack of federal and state policies on urban climate adaptation, which means there is little pressure on, resources for, or guidance to local governments on adaptation planning (Amundsen et al., 2010; Measham et al., 2011). Since 2013, the Obama administration has issued several executive orders mandating federal agencies to plan for adaptation, but these new policies have yet to trickle down to the state and local levels. According to the Georgetown Climate

Center (n.d.), 14 states have developed adaptation plans and policies, and six others have issued plans for sectors such as transportation, water, and energy. With few exceptions, most of these policies do not mandate local action, but instead recommend that state and local agencies consider climate impacts in their planning processes (Cruce, 2009; Schectman & Brady, 2013) or monitor ongoing adaptation activities (Herzog, Moser, & Newkirk, 2015).

Although some early adopter cities have initiated adaptation planning without state mandates, less progressive cities are unlikely to do so absent stronger regulatory carrots and sticks (Barbour & Deakin, 2012; Bedsworth & Hanak, 2010; Betsill & Rabe, 2009). Experiences enforcing past environmental policies demonstrate that strong regulatory frameworks are critical for promoting local policy adoption, especially when local actions require difficult tradeoffs in resource allocation between development and environmental priorities (Amundsen et al., 2010; Dalton & Burby, 1994; Haughton & Counsell, 2004; Measham et al., 2011).

[. . .]

SURVEY OF ADAPTATION PLANNING PROGRESS

This study contributes to the literature on adaptive capacity by quantitatively comparing the responses of climate and sustainability staff from 156 cities to a survey on climate adaptation (Carmin et al., 2012). The survey defined adaptation as "any activity you are pursuing to address the impacts climate change could have on your community." This definition emphasizes the consideration of future climate conditions, not just present climate risks. The survey instrument[2] asked respondents 40 closed-ended questions on whether their cities had initiated adaptation planning, their strategies and motivations, and the barriers and support they faced along the way. These responses, along with supplementary census and municipal fiscal data, allow us to statistically evaluate the relative importance of different adaptive capacity measures in predicting the status of adaptation planning. We model three of the crosscutting barriers that Moser and Ekstrom (2010) identify—leadership, resources, and information and communication—as well as additional indicators for population size and the presence of state adaptation policies.[3]

The survey, of which the research reported here is a part, used ICLEI's network of 1,200 municipalities in 86 countries as a sampling frame to describe global urban adaptation trends. ICLEI members commit to addressing climate change and sustainability and are likely to include many early adopters of adaptation planning. [. . .]

Nearly 300 U.S. local governments completed at least part of the survey (a 52% national response rate). We exclude county governments and those cities that did not fully respond to the six survey questions on which we base our analyses. Those questions sought information on whether or not cities have experienced climate impacts, the status of adaptation planning in their city, the commitment of local elected officials to adaptation planning, the challenges staff face in adaptation planning, and whether or not cities have climate offices and dedicated staff. This created a sample of 156 diverse U.S. cities [. . .].

CONSTRUCTING THE MODEL

We use logistic regression to assess the relative importance of different indicators of adaptive capacity in predicting whether or not a city engages in adaptation planning. A city's planning status is based on the survey question, "Have you completed or are you working on some form of climate adaptation planning? Answer 'yes' even if you are in the earliest phases of planning or action, such as having informal discussions and meetings." We include cities in the early planning stages because getting climate adaptation onto the local agenda may already be an initial indicator of a city's adaptive capacity. We then use additional survey questions and census data to develop a list of 13 explanatory variables representing leadership, resources, information and communication, and state climate adaptation policies that may be associated with adaptation planning. [. . .]

MODELING RESULTS

Overall, 60% of cities are engaged in adaptation planning, with 24% in the early scoping stage, 27% in the planning and analysis stage, and 9% in the implementation stage. The average city in our sample has a population of 116,000, income per capita of $33,700, and municipal expenditure rate of $2,900 per capita. In the sample, 24% of cities report that their elected officials are extremely or highly committed to climate adaptation, 20% have dedicated climate staff, 78% have experienced one or more climate impacts, and 73% are located in a state with a climate adaptation policy. On average, respondents found reallocating staff time, reallocating resources, and securing funding much more challenging than obtaining scientific data, communicating with the public, and generating interest among business. [. . .]

We find that only 3 out of the 13 variables are statistically significant ($p = .05$) in predicting adaptation planning status: municipal expenditures per capita, experience of climate impacts, and commitment by local officials. The final model explains 26% of the variation in cities' adaptation planning status. These findings corroborate past research on the importance of leadership, resources, and information and communication to adaptation planning (Carmin et al., 2013; Hamin et al., 2014; Moser & Ekstrom, 2012). They also highlight the relative importance of local leadership in predicting adaptation planning, identify fiscal capacity and communication variables that are more effective in predicting adaptation planning, and suggest that state policies at this time are not associated with adaptation planning, at least for our sample.

First, the model highlights the strong predictive power of local leadership. [. . .] The importance of leadership persists even when controlling for expenditure rates and population size, indicating that strong leadership helps overcome resource constraints (Carmin et al., 2013).

The importance of leadership in predicting adaptation planning underscores the need for better measures on the conditions that promote political leadership. Past research has found that political commitment to adaptation builds on the efforts of local adaptation champions, who are often staff in planning and environment departments, to compile climate data and build interest across departments

(Bulkeley, 2010; Lowe et al., 2009; Roberts, 2010). Political and organizational cultures—such as local governments' flexibility, openness to new ideas and experimentation, and incentives for departmental staff to go beyond existing policy mandates—create the conditions for local adaptation champions and political commitment to emerge (Leck & Roberts, 2015; Moser & Ekstrom, 2012). [. . .]

Second, the model shows that municipal expenditures per capita is a more effective predictor of adaptation planning than income per capita, dedicated climate staff, and challenges securing funding for adaptation. [. . .]

As in past studies (e.g., Krause, 2010, 2012), we find that income per capita is not a statistically significant predictor of adaptation planning, likely because personal wealth does not necessarily translate into higher local government spending capacity. More surprising is the lack of significance of dedicated climate staff and challenges securing funding for adaptation. These findings may reflect the fact that many cities in our sample are in the early stages of adaptation planning, when dedicated climate staff and access to specific adaptation funds are not as critical. In these early stages, staff from many different agencies are participating in informal discussion and data gathering, thereby reducing the demand for time from any one staff member.

Third, the experience of changing climatic conditions is the only significant predictor related to obtaining information on and communicating the need for climate adaptation. The model predicts that the odds of a city planning for adaptation will triple when respondents say that their city has witnessed changes in precipitation, temperature, and coastal conditions. Better data on climate impacts, such as the economic damages of disasters or the number of federally declared disasters in a city, would help clarify the predictive power of experiences of climate change. Worryingly, this finding suggests that many cities are reactively responding to past impacts rather than proactively anticipating future change. [. . .]

Fourth, contrary to existing literature, we do not find the presence of state adaptation policies to be a significant predictor of local adaptation planning for our sample. This is not evidence that state policies are irrelevant so much as an indication that most state adaptation policies are still advisory rather than mandatory, and do not link their recommendations to new sources of funding. [. . .]

Our sample of larger and more environmentally progressive cities, however, likely understates the degree to which state policies, climate staff, and funding resources could be associated with adaptation planning in most U.S. cities.

Cities in our sample are more likely to engage in adaptation planning regardless of state policies on climate adaptation, which is not representative of environmental planning in most cities (Barbour & Deakin, 2012; Betsill & Rabe, 2009). In addition, dedicated staff and funding resources may become more important in later planning stages involving assessments, plan development, and implementation.

IMPLICATIONS FOR POLICYMAKERS AND PLANNERS

Above all, our findings point to the importance of generating political support to advance adaptation planning. The question for planners is how they can better leverage existing resources to build political leadership, short of waiting for a major climate disaster or budgetary reforms. Early adopter cities, which our sample represents, have successfully put adaptation on the local political agenda, initiated adaptation planning by tapping into foundation grants and environmental networks, and embedded climate considerations into existing planning processes, such as those for hazard mitigation and coastal zone management. Planners in other cities can learn from their experiences, draw on the data generated from earlier climate risk and vulnerability assessments, and use existing plans, policies, assessments, and models as templates.

However, catalyzing adaptation planning across U.S. cities, which tend to have fewer resources than those in our sample, will require other levels of governments to develop regulatory and fiscal mandates and incentives for climate adaptation planning. States can facilitate local adaptation planning by requiring local governments to account for climate impacts in environmental permitting requests for new developments, as done in Maine, or to account for them in local comprehensive plans, as done in Rhode Island. These policy changes can help elected officials overcome local opposition and climate denial, and empower planners to initiate adaptation planning. States can also require projects that they fund to consider climate impacts, which would facilitate the integration of adaptation objectives into local expenditure plans. These approaches build on the emerging national policies for federal facilities, investments, and planning processes.

Regional planning entities—such as councils of government, planning councils, metropolitan planning organizations, county governments, and water and conservation districts—can also help local governments overcome barriers to adaptation planning. Regional entities can foster local leadership by facilitating the exchange of information between cities, and communicating why and how some cities have translated their awareness of climate impacts into actual adaptation plans and projects. Many regional entities are already taking on these roles. [. . .]

In this study, we have demonstrated the degree to which strong political leadership, high municipal expenditures, and perceptions that the climate is already changing are associated with adaptation planning among environmentally progressive cities. As more cities begin to plan and progress along the adaptation planning process, there is an opportunity for future research to focus on the factors that help planners implement adaptation plans, and the conditions under which implementation results in actual reductions in damages from climate change. Future models of adaptation planning, drawing on representative samples of U.S. cities, can help policymakers assess and benchmark municipalities with each other and evaluate how governments at different levels can better support local adaptation planning and implementation.

ACKNOWLEDGMENTS

We dedicate this article to JoAnn Carmin (1957–2014), associate professor at MIT, who conducted the survey (supported by National Science Foundation Grant No. 0926349) used in this article. We thank Alex Aylett and three anonymous reviewers for their insightful comments.

NOTES

1. The U.S. Census defines urban areas as those with a population of 50,000 and urban clusters as those with a population between 2,500 and 50,000.
2. The full survey instrument is available online at http://dspace.mit. edu/handle/1721.1/89521
3. We do not evaluate the fourth barrier, cultural values, because the survey did not ask questions on this topic.

REFERENCES

Amundsen, H., Berglund, F., & Westskog, H. (2010). Overcoming barriers to climate change adaptation: A question of multilevel governance? *Environment and Planning C: Government and Policy, 28*(2), 276–289. doi:10.1068/c0941

Anguelovski, I., & Carmin, J. (2011). Something borrowed, everything new: Innovation and institutionalization in urban climate governance. *Current Opinion in Environmental Sustainability, 3*(3), 169–175. doi:10.1016/j.cosust.2010.12.017

Anguelovski, I., Chu, E., & Carmin, J. (2014). Variations in approaches to urban climate adaptation: Experiences and experimentation from the global South. *Global Environmental Change, 27,* 156–167. doi:10.1016/j.gloenvcha.2014.05.010

Aylett, A. (2014). *Progress and challenges in the urban governance of climate change: Results of a global survey.* Cambridge, MA: MIT Press.

Barbour, E., & Deakin, E. A. (2012). Smart growth planning for climate protection: Evaluating California's Senate Bill 375. *Journal of the American Planning Association, 78*(1), 70–86. doi:10.1080/01944363.2011.645272

Bassett, E., & Shandas, V. (2010). Innovation and climate action planning: Perspectives from municipal plans. *Journal of the American Planning Association, 76*(4), 435–450. doi:10.1080/01944363.2010.509703

Bedsworth, L. W., & Hanak, E. (2010). Adaptation to climate change: A review of challenges and tradeoffs in six areas. *Journal of the American Planning Association, 76*(4), 477–495. doi:10.1080/01944363.2010.502047

Bedsworth, L. W., & Hanak, E. (2013). Climate policy at the local level: Insights from California. *Global Environmental Change, 23*(3), 664–677. doi:10.1016/j.gloenvcha.2013.02.004

Berrang-Ford, L., Ford, J. D., & Paterson, J. (2011). Are we adapting to climate change? *Global Environmental Change, 21*(1), 25–33. doi:10.1016/j.gloenvcha.2010.09.012

Betsill, M. M., & Rabe, B. G. (2009). Climate change and multilevel governance: The evolving state and local roles. In D. A. Mazmanian & M. E. Kraft (Eds.), *Toward sustainable communities: Transition and transformations in environmental policy* (pp. 201–225). Cambridge, MA: MIT Press.

Bierbaum, R., Smith, J. B., Lee, A., Blair, M., Carter, L., Chapin, F. S., . . . Verduzco, L. (2013). A comprehensive review of climate adaptation in the United States: More than before, but less than needed. *Mitigation and Adaptation Strategies for Global Change, 18*(3), 361–406. doi:10.1007/s11027-012-9423-1

Birkmann, J., Buckle, P., Jaeger, J., Pelling, M., Setiadi, N., Garschagen, M., . . . Kropp, J. (2010). Extreme events and disasters: A window of opportunity for change? Analysis of organizational, institutional and political changes, formal and informal responses after mega-disasters. *Natural Hazards, 55*(3), 637–655. doi:10.1007/s11069-008-9319-2

Brulle, R. J., Carmichael, J., & Jenkins, J. C. (2012). Shifting public opinion on climate change: An empirical assessment of factors influencing concern over climate change in the U.S., 2002–2010. *Climatic Change, 114*(2), 169–188. doi:10.1007/s10584-012-0403-y

Bryan, T. K. (2015). Capacity for climate change planning: Assessing metropolitan responses in the United States. *Journal of Environmental Planning and Management, 59*(4), 573–586. Advance online publication. doi:10.1080/09640568.2015.1030499

Bulkeley, H. (2010). Cities and the governing of climate change. *Annual Review of Environment and Resources, 35*(1), 229–253.

Carmin, J., Dodman, D., & Chu, E. (2013). *Urban climate adaptation and leadership* (OECD Regional Development Working Papers No. 2013/26). Retrieved from http://www.oecd-ilibrary.org/urban-ruraland-regional-development/urban-climate-adaptation-andleadership_5k3ttg88w8hh-en

Carmin, J., Nadkarni, N., & Rhie, C. (2012). *Progress and challenges in urban climate adaptation planning: Results of a global survey.* Cambridge, MA: MIT Press.

Carmin, J., Tierney, K., Chu, E., Hunter, L., Roberts, J. T., & Shi, L. (2015). Adaptation to climate change. In R. E. Dunlap & R. J. Brule (Eds.), *Sociological perspectives on climate change* (pp. 164–198). Oxford, UK: Oxford University Press.

Cruce, T. L. (2009). *Adaptation planning: What U.S. states and localities are doing, 2009 update.* Arlington, VA: Pew Center on Global Climate Change.

Cutter, S. L., Solecki, W. D., Bagado, N., Carmin, J., Fragkias, M., Ruth, M., & Wilbanks, T. J. (2014). Urban systems, infrastructure, and vulnerability. In J. M. Melillo, T. Richmond, & G. W. Yohe (Eds.), *Climate change impacts in the United States: The third national climate assessment* (pp. 282–296). Washington, DC: U.S. Global Change Research Program.

Dalton, L. C., & Burby, R. J. (1994). Mandates, plans, and planners: Building local commitment to development management. *Journal of the American Planning Association, 60*(4), 444–461. doi:10.1080/01944369408975604

Ebi, K. L., & Burton, I. (2008). Identifying practical adaptation options: An approach to address climate change-related health risks. *Environmental Science and Policy, 11*(4), 359–369. doi:10.1016/j.envsci.2008.02.001

Fünfgeld, H. (2010). Institutional challenges to climate risk management in cities. *Current Opinion in Environmental Sustainability, 2*(3), 156–160. doi:10.1016/j.cosust.2010.07.001

Füssel, H.-M. (2007). Adaptation planning for climate change: Concepts, assessment approaches, and key lessons. *Sustainability Science, 2*(2), 265–275. doi:10.1007/s11625-007-0032-y

Georgetown Climate Center. (n.d.). *State and local climate adaptation plans.* Retrieved from http://www.georgetownclimate.org/adaptation/state-and-local-plans

Germain, T., Ellingboe, K., & Kroh, K. (2015, January 8). *The anti-science climate denier caucus: 114th congress edition.* Retrieved from http://thinkprogress.org/climate/2015/01/08/3608427/climate-deniercaucus-114th-congress/

Gurran, N., Norman, B., & Hamin, E. (2013). Climate change adaptation in coastal Australia: An audit of planning practice. *Ocean & Coastal Management, 86,* 100–109. doi:10.1016/j.ocecoaman.2012.10.014

Halsnæs, K., & Trærup, S. (2009). Development and climate change: A mainstreaming approach for assessing economic, social, and environmental impacts of adaptation measures. *Environmental Management, 43*(5), 765–778. doi:10.1007/s00267-009-9273-0

Hamin, E. M., & Gurran, N. (2009). Urban form and climate change: Balancing adaptation and mitigation in the U.S. and Australia. *Habitat International, 33*(3), 238–245. doi:10.1016/j.habitatint.2008.10.005

Hamin, E. M., Gurran, N., & Emlinger, A. M. (2014). Barriers to municipal climate adaptation: Examples from coastal Massachusetts' smaller cities and towns. *Journal of the American Planning Association, 80*(2), 110–122. doi:10.1080/01944363.2014.949590

Haughton, G., & Counsell, D. (2004). Regions and sustainable development: Regional planning matters. *The Geographical Journal, 170*(2), 135–145.

Herzog, M. M., Moser, S. C., & Newkirk, S. (2015). *Tracking coastal adaptation: Implementing California's innovative sea level rise planning database* (Policy Brief No. 7). Los Angeles: University of California Press.

Homsy, G. C., & Warner, M. E. (2015). Cities and sustainability polycentric action and multilevel governance. *Urban Affairs Review, 51*(1), 46–73. doi:10.1177/1078087414530545

Howe, P. D., Mildenberger, M., Marlon, J. R., & Leiserowitz, A. (2015). Geographic variation in opinions on climate change at state and local scales in the USA. *Nature Climate Change, 5*(6), 596–603. doi:10.1038/nclimate2583

Hunt, A., & Watkiss, P. (2010). Climate change impacts and adaptation in cities: A review of the literature. *Climatic Change, 104*(1), 13–49. doi:10.1007/s10584-010-9975-6

Intergovernmental Panel on Climate Change. (2014). Summary for policymakers. In C. B. Field, V. R. Barros, D. J. Dokken, K. J. Mach, M. D. Mastrandrea, . . . L. L. White (Eds.), *Climate change 2014: Impacts, adaptation, and vulnerability, Part A: Global and sectoral aspects* (pp. 1–32). Contribution of Working Group II to the Fifth Assessment Report of the Intergovernmental Panel on Climate Change. Cambridge, UK: Cambridge University Press.

Klein, R. J. T. (2011). Mainstreaming climate adaptation into development: A policy dilemma. In A. Ansohn & B. Pleskovic (Eds.), *Berlin workshop series 2010: Climate governance and development* (pp. 35–52). Washington, DC: World Bank.

Krause, R. M. (2010). Policy innovation, intergovernmental relations, and the adoption of climate protection initiatives by U.S. cities. *Journal of Urban Affairs, 33*(1), 45–60. doi:10.1111/j.1467-9906.2010.00510.x

Krause, R. M. (2012). Political decision-making and the local provision of public goods: The case of municipal climate protection in the U.S. *Urban Studies, 49*(11), 2399–2417. doi:10.1177/0042098011427183

Leck, H., & Roberts, D. (2015). What lies beneath: Understanding the invisible aspects of municipal climate change governance. *Current Opinion in Environmental Sustainability, 13*, 61–67. doi:10.1016/j.cosust.2015.02.004

Lemieux, C. J., & Scott, D. J. (2011). Changing climate, challenging choices: Identifying and evaluating climate change adaptation options for protected areas management in Ontario, Canada. *Environmental Management, 48*(4), 675–690. doi:10.1007/s00267-011-9700-x

Lowe, A., Foster, J., & Winkelmand, S. (2009). *Ask the climate question: Adapting to climate change impacts in urban regions.* Washington, DC: Center for Clean Air Policy.

Lubell, M., Feiock, R., & Handy, S. (2009). City adoption of environmentally sustainable policies in California's Central Valley. *Journal of the American Planning Association, 75*(3), 293–308. doi:10.1080/01944360902952295

McCright, A. M., & Dunlap, R. E. (2011). The politicization of climate change and polarization in the American public's views of global warming, 2001–2010. *Sociological Quarterly, 52*(2), 155–194. doi:10.1111/j.1533-8525.2011.01198.x

Measham, T. G., Preston, B. L., Smith, T. F., Brooke, C., Gorddard, R., Withycombe, G., & Morrison, C. (2011). Adapting to climate change through local municipal planning: Barriers and challenges. *Mitigation and Adaptation Strategies for Global Change, 16*(8), 889–909. doi:10.1007/s11027-011-9301-2

Moser, S. C. (2009). Governance and the art of overcoming barriers to adaptation. *Magazine of the International Human Dimensions Programme on Global Environmental Change, 2009*(3), 31–36. Retrieved from https://www.bonn-dialogues.org/file/get/7169.pdf#page=31

Moser, S. C. (2015, March 19). Why we need to do better on adaptation indicators. *SciDev. Net.* Retrieved from http://www.scidev.net/global/climate-change/opinion/better-climate-change-adaptation-indicators.html

Moser, S. C., & Ekstrom, J. A. (2010). A framework to diagnose barriers to climate change adaptation. *Proceedings of the National Academy of Sciences, 107*(51), 22026–22031. doi:10.1073/pnas.1007887107

Moser, S. C., & Ekstrom, J. A. (2012). *Identifying and overcoming barriers to climate change adaptation in San Francisco Bay: Results from case studies* (White Paper). Sacramento: California Energy Commission.

National Research Council. (2010). *Adapting to the impacts of climate change*. Washington, DC: National Academies Press.

Preston, B. L., Westaway, R. M., & Yuen, E. J. (2011). Climate adaptation planning in practice: An evaluation of adaptation plans from three developed nations. *Mitigation and Adaptation Strategies for Global Change, 16*(4), 407–438. doi:10.1007/s11027-010-9270-x

Roberts, D. (2010). Prioritizing climate change adaptation and local level resilience in Durban, South Africa. *Environment and Urbanization, 22*(2), 397–413. doi:10.1177/0956247810379948

Schectman, J., & Brady, M. (2013). *Cost-efficient climate change adaptation in the North Atlantic*. Washington, DC: NOAA Sea Grant and North Atlantic Regional Team.

Shi, L., Chu, E., & Carmin, J. (2016). The effects of city size and governance capacity on urban climate adaptation planning and implementation: Results from a global survey. In K. Seto & W. D. Solecki (Eds.), *Handbook on urbanization and global environmental change*. Philadelphia, PA: Taylor and Francis.

Solecki, W., Leichenko, R., & O'Brien, K. (2011). Climate change adaptation strategies and disaster risk reduction in cities: Connections, contentions, and synergies. *Current Opinion in Environmental Sustainability, 3*(3), 135–141. doi:10.1016/j.cosust.2011.03.001

Tribbia, J., & Moser, S. C. (2008). More than information: What coastal managers need to plan for climate change. *Environmental Science and Policy, 11*(4), 315–328. doi:10.1016/j.envsci.2008.01.003

Westerhoff, L., Keskitalo, E. C. H., & Juhola, S. (2011). Capacities across scales: Local to national adaptation policy in four European countries. *Climate Policy, 11*(4), 1071–1085. doi:10.1080/14693062.2011.579258

While, A., & Whitehead, M. (2013). Cities, urbanisation and climate change. *Urban Studies, 50*(7), 1325–1331. doi:10.1177/0042098013480963

31 Urban Wildscapes and Green Spaces in Mombasa and Their Potential Contribution to Climate Change Adaptation and Mitigation

Anna Lyth and Justus Kithiia

EDITOR'S INTRODUCTION

This article is unique in that few studies have looked at the implications of green infrastructure for climate change adaptation and mitigation in rapidly urbanizing Africa. The authors, doctoral student Justus Kithiia (Macquarie University, Australia) and Ann Lyth, a geographer from the University of Tasmania in Australia, argue that green space provides a low-cost approach to adaptation compared to the traditional "hard-infrastructure" approach. They illustrate their argument with a case study of a cement quarry rehabilitation initiated by a corporate owner that created an "urban wildscape" with wildlife habitat and much-needed parkland in densely populated Mombasa, Kenya.

The rehabilitation of this quarry was not mandated by the government, but was voluntarily initiated by the corporation. This presents a contrast to the government-initiated projects in developed countries as described in the previous chapter, but one which the authors say is more viable in less developed countries where government agencies are extremely underfunded and lack the resources to implement adaptation projects. Public-private partnerships allow local governments to take the lead in creating the green structure framework and then facilitate implementation with a range of private and or non-profit interests.

This case study also illustrates how climate change adaptation benefits can derive from projects that began with other goals, in this case, industrial land rehabilitation. The Mombasa project increased tree canopy and carbon sequestration (to offset carbon use in the nearby cement factory), while providing adaptation measures, including a cool respite for local residents escaping the tropical heat in nearby neighbourhoods and social learning from tree stewardship initiatives directed by local forestry agencies.

URBAN WILDSCAPES AND GREEN SPACES IN MOMBASA AND THEIR POTENTIAL CONTRIBUTION TO CLIMATE CHANGE ADAPTATION AND MITIGATION

INTRODUCTION

As in many parts of the world, most of the existing and proposed adaptive responses to climate change in East African cities are biased towards using "hard engineering" solutions such as building sea walls, levees and channels or relocating infrastructure to control flooding. Such hard infrastructural responses, although necessary in some cases, can present a number of challenges and costs that bring us to question both the effectiveness and efficiency of such solutions relative to the techno-institutional and financial barriers faced by low-income countries. [. . .] For low-income countries, this emphasizes the need to explore less expensive but multi-beneficial strategies. One such strategy for urban areas is the provision and protection of blocks of contiguous land and improvements in the connectivity of areas of natural resource or ecological value, with the aim of establishing a network of natural areas and working landscapes. This ecosystems approach or "soft engineering" solution can be achieved through the protection of urban wildscapes and the provision of green spaces, which are viable climate change response options and "no-regrets" measures capable of yielding multiple benefits.

Experiences from around the world tend to show that "soft engineering" solutions to climate change impacts (including the use of ecosystems-based strategies, wetlands and green spaces, green infrastructure and land use planning) are more cost effective and sustainable in the long run than hard technical solutions, and also provide a range of other benefits to society. However, it must be stated from the outset that no single solution or approach is likely to fit all future challenges posed by climate change. [. . .]

While promoting urban wildscapes, green spaces and green infrastructure for urban environmental quality and community health is not new, the application of a management approach that accounts for the full values of these urban landscapes in climate change adaptation and mitigation is less widely understood and advocated in the African region, particularly in urbanized areas, and is therefore worthy of further exploration.

The contribution of this paper is two-fold. First, it explores the potential of utilizing the moderating influence of wildscapes and green spaces to address the challenges posed by climate change in Mombasa, Kenya. Second, it presents an example of an innovative and novel approach to urban landscape rehabilitation in Mombasa and draws on lessons learnt from this example to identify the need for improved stewardship of green infrastructure resources to help urban residents in low-income countries adapt to the effects of climate change.

Mombasa is a seaport island city in Kenya, lying within a coastal strip in the hot tropical region that is influenced by the monsoon. Its rapidly increasing population is growing at a rate of 3.6 per cent per annum and now stands at close to one million (Kenya, Ministry of Planning and National Development 2002). Although the scale of climate change risk in Mombasa is yet to be established due to the lack of local analysis, it is expected that climate change will exacerbate current problems such as flooding, storm damage and seashore erosion with serious consequences for infrastructure, coastal assets and human health. [. . .]

The phrase "urban wildscapes" has been used to describe those urban spaces where natural processes (as opposed to human intervention) such as the spontaneous growth of vegetation appear to be shaping the land. According to Jorgensen (2004), urban wildscapes often emerge from the aftermath of development. In other words, it is what remains after the programmed uses have ceased. This paper extends this description to include those spaces where human agency has also contributed to the ecological revitalization of destructed urban spaces to create a new wilderness environment. [. . .]

Urban wildscapes and green spaces provide a unique opportunity to address both climate change mitigation and adaptation, in addition to maintaining, restoring and enhancing the natural environment services and offering other socioeconomic functions. They have a crucial role to play in response to the impacts of climate change whether through providing temporary holding grounds for stormwater runoff, reducing the risk or extent of flooding or improving the microclimate of an urban environment. [. . .]

To be able to provide multiple benefits, the green landscapes must be resilient enough to accommodate gradual changes associated with climate change and return towards their prior condition after disturbance, either naturally or with management assistance. [. . .] [I]nterconnected systems of green landscapes and infrastructure is broadly recognized as the optimum approach to protecting or enhancing the resilience of ecosystems and maximizing the return on investment in urban green spaces.

GREEN LANDSCAPES IN THE CONTEXT OF MOMBASA

This section outlines the necessity of buttressing the use of urban green landscapes (wildscapes and green spaces), in the context of green infrastructure, as a "no-regrets", "soft engineering" strategy for addressing the effects of climate variability and change in Mombasa. [. . .]

Mombasa occupies a low-lying, often flood-prone, coastal location and lacks adequate protection against extreme events. The city is characterized by substantial and growing social and environmental problems, including those that are associated with pressures of population growth, housing quality, air pollution and water and sanitation. Climate change is expected to exacerbate these problems, contributing to a heightened risk of flooding, coastal storm damage and seashore erosion, and vulnerability to diseases associated with climatic conditions and land uses, such as malaria and other vector-borne diseases. These will result in costs associated with the loss of infrastructure, biodiversity and natural resource assets (such as fisheries and recreational resources), as well as costs to human health. In addition, socio-economic factors such as population trends and housing conditions are also changing, altering exposure and sensitivity to flood risks as well as increasing the frequency of flood disasters. Sea level is predicted to rise by 0.1–0.9 metres by 2100, which will aggravate flooding, while it has been estimated that the overall adaptation bill will rise to 10 per cent of the Gross Domestic Product. Yet, the municipal authority has limited assets and capacity to cope with and adapt to the implications of climate change. Therefore, the challenge of urban management in the face of climate change risks points to the need for "no- regrets" and pro-poor interventions. [. . .]

The powers and duties to spearhead local environmental planning and management, and to execute local land use planning, are critical in shaping the capacity of municipal councils such as Mombasa to roll out urban green infrastructure and, by extension, use the implications of climate change risk as an opportunity to expand (and not necessarily change) their existing mandates. However, in order to use these powers effectively, any such authority requires political will and local support to be able to allocate resources.

[. . .]

Thus, if well supported, a range of different stakeholders in cities such as Mombasa can facilitate the establishment of cost-effective, citywide green infrastructure systems through urban greening. Furthermore, given the recent occurrences of flooding, wind destruction and increased average temperatures that have exposed the vulnerability of Mombasa to the impacts of climate change, the challenge facing the municipal authority is to try to establish a system of land use management for open green landscapes to help buffer floods, provide natural stormwater management and reduce energy use (through shading and/or evapotranspiration), as well as reduce costs associated with engineered systems.

FROM WILDSCAPE TO GREENSCAPE: MOMBASA'S HALLER PARK

This section describes an innovative urban landscape management activity in Mombasa that involves the transformation of a wildscape into a thriving urban wilderness. This particular example is not intended to provide proof of how the rehabilitation of the wildscape into a thriving ecosystem has helped in responding to climate change risks in Mombasa; rather, it is a demonstration of how a key stakeholder has engaged in successful urban ecosystem management that may have consequences for climate change adaptation and mitigation among other socio-ecological and economic benefits. [. . .]

History: Quarry to Park

Bamburi Cement Factory, now a subsidiary of the French multinational Lafarge Group, is located in the Kisauni area of Mombasa (Figure 31.1). Through the Lafarge Ecosystems Programme, the company has become world famous for its rehabilitation of quarry mines. The Mombasa rehabilitation programme, initially called the Bamburi Quarry Nature Park and now renamed Haller Park, was initiated in 1972. The mines formed wildscape areas which had been left when quarried materials were taken away for cement manufacture, leaving an inhospitable wasteland. Although north Mombasa benefited from the location of the cement factory (particularly through the creation of employment), the large area of bushland was converted into a wasteland that expanded every year by tens of thousands of square metres. At the time operations commenced, no environmental law required mining industries in Kenya to rehabilitate exploited land. However, the management of the cement factory believed it had a responsibility to do so long before the subject of environmental protection became a worldwide issue (Haller and Baer, 1994). [. . .] After about 25 years, the former quarry has become forested and ecologically and economically self-sustaining. [. . .]

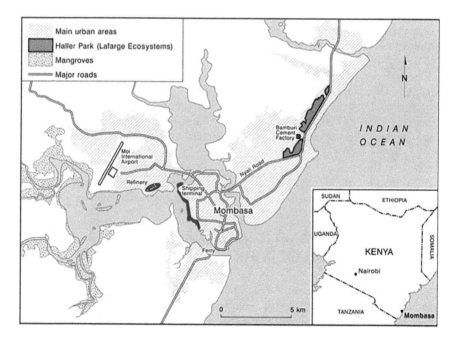

Figure 31.1 Map of Mombasa showing the location of Lafarge Ecosystems.
Source: Adapted from a map drawn by the author

Current Status

The company has 250 hectares of mined land, of which 220 hectares have been rehabilitated. Currently, Haller Park is home to 400 different varieties of indigenous trees, including bushes and herbs; also 230 species of birds, some of which have been classified by the International Conservation Union (IUCN) as endangered species; and mammals, reptiles and small cats (including giraffe, waterbuck, hippopotamus, eland, oryx, buffalo and crocodile). In addition, a large number of insects have been observed in the forest, ensuring a diversity of life, with every species making a unique contribution. The result has been the creation of a wilderness park in the city, bringing Mombasa residents into contact with nature, providing socio-psychological benefits, and promoting both educational and recreational activities. Observing the number of people visiting the park, especially at weekends and on public holidays, the eco-tourism value is also evident. According to official records, the park receives about 150,000 visitors per year (Kenya National Bureau of Statistics, 2007). The value of the park was captured by one Mombasa resident during a visit: "Since I do not enjoy going to the beach, on hot days when I'm not at work I come here to do some bushwalking. I find it cooler . . . and there is fresh air"[1] [. . .].

Haller Park is also demonstrating other social, educational and economic benefits to the wider community. For example, a Kenya Forest Service (KFS) official in Mombasa explained that his department had been organizing local user group members to visit the park for training and demonstrations on effective tree management.[2] Community groups are sub-contracted to undertake rehabilitation works, especially the replanting of trees, thus helping them to "learn by doing" [. . .].

DISCUSSING THE LAFARGE ECOSYSTEMS PROGRAMME AND RELATED ACTIVITIES IN THE CONTEXT OF CLIMATE CHANGE RISK RESPONSE AND OTHER SOCIO-ECOLOGICAL BENEFITS

The ensuing discussion revolves around four recurring themes: mitigation, adaptation, local sustainable development and socio-economic benefits. These could be viewed as signifying both the actual and the potential contribution of the Lafarge Ecosystems Programme and related activities to the city of Mombasa amidst the likely impacts of climate change.

It is clear from the history of the Lafarge Ecosystems Programme that responding to climate change was not one of the original objectives of rehabilitation 25 years ago. This is not surprising since, at the time, climate change was not a prominent issue in the development agenda generally. [. . .]

Regardless of the motivation for climate change adaptation, both purposeful and unintentional adaptation can generate short- and long-term benefits. Haller Park as a well-maintained ecosystem has the potential to create adaptation co-benefits, despite this not being the original intent. [. . . .]

The local corporation (Bamburi Cement Factory) may be unaware of its role both as a driver and responder to climate change. However, its involvement in corporate social response shows an understanding of how context shapes socio-ecological interactions within the city, hence its potential contribution to building resilience to climate change impacts. Furthermore, for a resource-poor city like Mombasa, where the state of knowledge about the most effective ways in which institutions can facilitate local climate change risk responses is sparse and where no blueprints exist for planning such responses, the municipal government cannot be expected to be the main stakeholder in spearheading climate responsive measures. The Lafarge Ecosystems Programme demonstrates an alternative role for municipal authorities; that is, one of facilitator of specific opportunities and sustainable initiatives, which initiatives may be implemented by a range of stakeholders (including local communities, private corporations or other opportunistic partnerships between different agencies). However, given the generally low priority given to climate change issues in Mombasa, coupled with ineffective urban governance in Kenya in general, it may take further incentives or other agencies to encourage the take up of such "value-adding" initiatives. This, however, does not negate the fact that the Lafarge Ecosystems Programme could serve as an indication of how climate change response actions can cascade across a landscape and be initiated by agents ranging from individuals to corporations and public bodies as well as governments.

Due to its tropical location, Mombasa can be very hot, averaging 65 per cent humidity and 32°C heat (Kenya Ministry of Planning and National Development, 2002). The fact that some people visit Haller Park on hot afternoons to experience its cool temperatures shows the potential of urban green landscapes in alleviating outdoor thermal discomfort in the urban environment. While the likely extent of changes to ambient temperature due to climate change is uncertain for East Africa, the chapter on Africa in the IPCC Fourth Assessment Report (2001) notes limited increases in temperatures in the tropics compared to other latitudes based on global warming models; similarly, the chapter alerts us to the combined impact of local land use change, land clearing and deforestation on micro-climates and thereby an increase in local temperatures in regions such as East Africa. An increase in ambient temperature due to these combined effects could potentially increase mortality among the urban poor and vulnerable populations who tend to lack the economic means and social support systems necessary to avoid the adverse health impacts associated with extreme temperatures. However, as is characteristic of most benefits of urban green landscapes, a citywide effect in reducing thermal discomfort and air pollution is only achievable in the presence of well-designed systems of green spaces and green infrastructure, and not just isolated green landscapes such as Haller Park.

To the local community, the park also provides an opportunity to be close to nature, with the associated positive impacts that this can bring in terms of mental health and the simple pleasure of experiencing trees, birds and other wildlife in an urban situation. This is apparent in the high number of people who visit the park each year. By involving the community in its activities through local partnerships, the Lafarge Ecosystems Programme adds to the broader social dimension that has the potential to facilitate adaptive ecosystem management. [. . .]

In order to enhance the value of such initiatives and provide long-lasting social, educational and adaptive benefits, it is necessary for the planning, design and management of such programmes to have an understanding of how residents interact, value and understand the environment, rather than just support planting and maintenance of vegetation. [. . .]

Although Bamburi Cement Factory, through the Lafarge Ecosystems Programme, has demonstrated the possibility of achieving well-maintained green landscapes in Mombasa, the municipal authority has yet to supply the frameworks for the provision of quality control. This could be attributed to the institutional fragmentation of the planning systems in Kenya in general, which makes it difficult to adopt local planning frameworks within which the importance of green infrastructure can be addressed. Notwithstanding the resource deficiency of the local authority, with more effective planning, existing funding and skill capacities can be better tailored towards value-adding development, promoting best practice such as green infrastructure-based projects.

CONCLUSIONS

The multi-functional nature of urban green infrastructure consisting of wildscapes and green spaces necessitates the application of management approaches that account for the full value of these urban landscapes. This is especially so in the face of predicted changes in future climate and parallel pressures of land use development and change. For low-income countries, the implications of climate change create a new urgency to seek ways of building general resilience through cost effective "no-regrets" interventions. Pursuing adaptive governance in poorly resourced urban areas requires that efforts be directed towards green infrastructure as opposed to expensive grey infrastructure development, for the simple reason that well-planned systems of green landscapes have the potential to generate net social and ecological benefits under a range of future scenarios. [. . .]

The Lafarge Ecosystems Programme and related activities show that the development of green landscapes may involve voluntary actions by various stakeholders in the city. Although the municipal authorities have the overall mandate to provide frameworks for quality control and ensure systematic planning of green landscapes, stakeholder involvement can ease the burden of implementation from the frequently cash-starved authorities. To ensure full cooperation from businesses and corporations, which are not only major responders but also drivers of climate change, their involvement should be viewed as a social *response* rather than a social *responsibility*. The synergies necessary in addressing the uncertainties surrounding climate change require that corporations, governing authorities and other players do not get stuck in the legalities of social responsibility. What is required is a framework that relies on collaborations of a diverse set of stakeholders in the city as well as approaches that embrace flexibility, learning from experience and continuous incorporation of lessons into future plans. [. . .]

The "no-regrets" interventions are not cost free and therefore expanding the green landscapes will attract both direct and indirect costs. This is especially true in Mombasa and other cities in low-income countries, where the built form does not normally allow for significant sites for the establishment of green spaces for public or ecological good. A major task for planners and decision makers will therefore be to ensure both innovation and cost effectiveness; for example, by optimizing scarce resource investments and identifying initiatives that are implementable by a range of stakeholders.

NOTES

1. Interviews were conducted by the authors in 2009.
2. Interviews were conducted by the authors in 2009.

REFERENCES

Haller, R. & Baer, S. (1994). *From Wasteland to Paradise: A Breathtaking Success Story of a Unique Ecological Experiment on the Kenya Coast.* Germany: Hans H. Koschany Publishers.

Intergovernmental Panel on Climate Change (IPCC) (2001). *Climate Change 2001: Impacts, Adaptation and Vulnerability.* Cambridge, UK: Cambridge University Press.

Jorgensen, A. (ed.) (2008). *Urban Wildscapes.* Sheffield, UK: University of Sheffield and Environmental Room Ltd.

Kenya, Ministry of Planning and National Development (2002). *Mombasa District Development Plan.* Nairobi: Government Printer.

Kenya National Bureau of Statistics (2007). *Update on Tourism Statistics.* Nairobi: Government Printer.

32 Making Climate Change Visible

A Critical Role for Landscape Professionals

Stephen R.L. Sheppard

EDITOR'S INTRODUCTION

Landscape architect Stephen Sheppard at the University of British Columbia, Canada hones in on the challenges of making climate change more visible to local residents as a catalyst for change. Sheppard argues that there is a dissonance between media coverage of climate change which focuses on major impacts (i.e. major flooding, wildfires) and climate change causes that are better displayed at the local landscape level (i.e. suburban sprawl). He argues that the local neighbourhood scale is more relevant to the public and their connection to place is a strong motivator to take planning action.

Sheppard proposes a three-prong approach for engaging the public in climate change: (1) make it local, (2) make it visual, and (3) make it connected to larger-scale issues. Creative examples of visualizing climate change locally include showing sea level rise in local shoreline landscapes, such as new infrastructure projects. Visualizing climate change builds upon a trend in landscape design to reveal ecological processes. For example, the Philadelphia rain gardens described earlier in this reader in Chapter 24.

Sheppard emphasizes the role of landscape professionals in climate change planning as having the skills for visualization, public engagement, and scenario planning (i.e. developing visually engaging designs that illustrate future alternatives). He calls for a participatory visioning process for planning and decision-making that is holistic and flexible. He talks about the idea of using 'visual learning tools' images that show climate change impacts in a scientifically accurate manner in local places. These images become the catalyst to discuss and visualize potential climate change adaptation and mitigation strategies. He also sees this role of visualization to empower local community members who are advocates for addressing climate change, as well as foster increased advocacy in the larger public. Compelling, engaging, and forward thinking, this article positions the reader for further exploration into creative climate change planning and implementation.

INTRODUCTION

Climate change is getting worse, but society is not responding accordingly (IPCC, 2014). [. . .] However, psychological research and the evidence of global politics confirm that science and science communication are not enough to stimulate behaviour change or substantive action on the climate crisis (Moser & Dilling, 2007). This essay discusses the need for experiential learning, place attachment, and social pressure at the local level, as well as enhanced planning, to help mobilize community-level awareness and action on climate change. It explores the unique potential of *local landscapes, landscape professionals, and their visual media* in helping to deliver or reinforce these as catalysts of social change, through making climate change more visible where people live.

This essay draws on concepts and examples advanced in the author's book on *Visualizing Climate Change* (Sheppard, 2012), in order to convey some of its key messages to a wider readership [. . .]

PROBLEMS AND PRINCIPLES IN ENGAGING SOCIETY ON CLIMATE CHANGE

Even in America, where climate change is still denied by some, a majority of the public has long had a concern about climate change (Leiserowitz, Maibach, & Roser-Renouf, 2009; Nordhaus & Shellenberger, 2009). Yet, despite this and the scientific consensus, society at large has been slow to act. [. . .]

The social and psychological literature on climate change suggests that we need more than information alone to bridge these perceptual gaps and reach the public. Van Der Linden (2014) argues that public campaigns need to make the climate change context explicit, and argues for integrating the knowledge/information approach with the 'affective-experiential' and 'social-normative' approaches, in order to influence behaviour.

Recommendations often invoke the following specific approaches:

- *Experiential learning* (Weber, 2006), involving personal experience with emotional meaning in order to engage people in active social environments.
- *Place attachment*, caring about your 'hood' due to individually or collectively determined meanings, related to spatial characteristics and the prominence of specific social or physical elements in the landscape (Scannell & Gifford, 2010).
- *Social or peer pressure*, motivating behaviour through comparison with others. Our neighbours can be a powerful force, encouraging uptake of climate change solutions or representing a critical barrier to behaviour change. [. . .]

- *Use of visual learning tools* to make climate change attributes more 'concrete' to people (Leiserowitz, 2007) and act as prompts for behaviours (McKenzie-Mohr & Smith, 1999). [. . .]

These findings can be distilled into three broad *principles* for engaging the public on climate change more meaningfully (Sheppard, 2012).

- *Make it local*: making climate change more salient and immediate by pulling it into a community context that people care about, using the local landscape to express climate change issues and focus action.
- *Make it visual*: harnessing the power of visual perception and imagery in making concepts and realities of climate change and carbon both clear and compelling; showing what climate change really looks like.
- *Make it connected*: looking holistically at the 'big picture' on climate change, integrating all aspects of climate change that interact with society and affected environments across scales [. . .]

THE SPECIAL ROLE OF LANDSCAPE IN ENGAGING SOCIETY ON CLIMATE CHANGE

The role and scale of landscape as a social mobilization device appears to have been largely neglected in the mainstream climate change discourse. [. . .] Yet, landscapes appear to offer the kind of integrative frame or context that Van Der Linden (2014) advocates for climate change engagement. They are by their nature local, visual, and holistic. [. . .] Through analysis of and interventions in this 'perceptible realm' (Gobster, Nassauer, Daniel, & Fry, 2007), the local and visible aspects of climate change may be highlighted to make climate change real and meaningful for people where they live, as in photographs of climate-related conditions [. . .]. A more tangible, immediate, and recurring image of climate change that is 'in your face' may help break down what Marshall (2014, p. 82) calls "the silence of climate change", whereby it remains off the table for serious ongoing discussion among affected parties (i.e. all of us).

For many in developed countries, the dominant stream of information on climate change has come from scientists and their opposition—the so-called 'two sides of the debate', but mostly filtered by the media (Boykoff, 2011). "Perhaps the most important rationale for a landscape-based perspective is to provide a third way for people to know about climate change" (Sheppard, 2012, p. 44). Local landscapes provide an alternative channel, the evidence of our own eyes, which offers a third and largely independent way to learn about climate change (i.e. first hand), in the here and now. It can triangulate the science, making it easier for communities to make sense of scientific information by contextualizing it in real places.

This essay argues that seeing evidence of climate change locally matters a lot, through reinforcing with visible evidence what people already know about climate change. In Sheppard (2012), the author describes a new Community Awareness to Action (C2A) Framework, which adds the experience of *seeing* climate change to earlier simpler models of factors contributing to action on climate change solutions [. . .]

Figure 32.1 provides a more complete and nuanced version of the simple relationships theorized in the C2A framework diagram [. . .] The current reality is that reliance on media for information about climate change, the weakness of current planning and policy mechanisms in reaching the public, and the stilted conversations about climate change in society amount to weak drivers of caring and action. Figure 32.1 represents the much stronger role that the landscape could play in enabling fuller recognition of climate change messages among citizens, bringing home the reality of climate change in a way that relates to the individual's sense of identity, security, and responsibility. This improved climate literacy may in turn result in people *caring* and *acting* more.

[. . .]

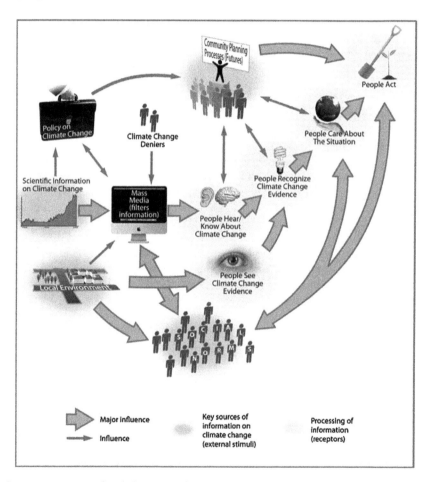

Figure 32.1 A more detailed version of the Community Awareness to Action Framework, reflecting more factors and showing potentially enhanced sources of climate change information (including strong signals from local landscapes) and their influence on peoples' responses.

Source: J. Myers. Reproduced from *Visualizing Climate Change* (Sheppard, 2012) with permission from Taylor and Francis

Most people seldom directly experience extreme events associated with climate change; these are still rare episodic events for most communities. They are, however, starting to see perceived evidence of climate change more often in the media. These periodic vicarious experiences may contribute to general awareness, but they usually do not directly affect the viewers' family and neighbourhood. Emerging evidence suggests that those who directly experience impacts such as flooding (e.g. Spence, Poortinga, Butler, & Pidgeon, 2011) express more concern over climate change, see it as less uncertain, recognize more their vulnerability to climate change impacts, and have more confidence in their agency to take action.

In community landscapes of temperate Western nations, signs of climate change may be visible but subtle, e.g. gradual changes in plant phenology, species distributions, or water levels. In order to recognize such creeping effects, observation and visual literacy must be improved. While many urban communities have relatively poor observational skills related to natural conditions and trends, some sectors of society are well placed to observe subtle signs and/or track long term trends, due to frequent or repeated activities outdoors; for example, farmers, fishermen, joggers, and dog-walkers (Sheppard, 2014). Could these be the early adopters of a new climate change lens?

There are other precedents for substantive shifts in visual literacy in response to improved knowledge and experience. There is recent quantitative evidence from California suburbs that the spread of solar roofs has accelerated in proportion to their visibility to neighbours (Bollinger & Gillingham, 2012). [. . .] It seems therefore that literacy can be built, and that the local landscape can function as a clear signal of important trends, threats, and solutions. Perhaps then the landscape can serve more systematically as a motivator for behaviour change, changing perceptual frames and social norms.

LEARNING TO RECOGNIZE CLIMATE CHANGE HOLISTICALLY IN OUR LANDSCAPES

The public is starting to connect the dots between extreme weather events and climate change, but they may not make the connection to other vital aspects of climate change, such as community vulnerability to other future threats or effective solutions. In field trips with students taking classes on climate change at the University of British Columbia, it is often difficult to find visible examples of actual impacts; it is somewhat easier to identity potential vulnerabilities, such as low spots susceptible to flooding, or hotspots without shade or cooling features, but even these require knowledge of likely threats and a certain amount of imagination.

Public recognition of carbon as a central cause and driver of climate change is also critical. Can the landscape help us build 'carbon consciousness' (Boardman & Palmer, 2003)? We know that among those who acknowledge that global warming is real, many in America do not believe it is anthropogenic (Maibach, Roser-Renouf, & Leiserowitz, 2009). Even those of us who do believe in the human causes of climate change routinely employ cognitive dissonance (Gifford, 2011) to disconnect ourselves from the many local causes of climate change that we could influence.

[. . .]

The media's selective focus on more dramatic aspects of the climate change system is problematic when they fail to direct public attention to subtle changes and practical positive local solutions. In fact, many aspects of climate change are visible in local communities, but often we just don't know where to look or how to recognize them. . . . The causes of climate change may be the most clearly visible sign of climate change in many communities, where GHG emissions are elevated by vehicle fuel use, heating and cooling of buildings, and embodied energy in infrastructure, food, and consumables. Still, these signs are usually ignored and reframed as normal and socially acceptable, while the underlying fossil fuels themselves are usually kept out of sight. Other aspects of climate change are usually much less visible or less easily recognized. Many impacts are gradual and subtle. Some mitigation measures are iconic and easily recognized (e.g. wind turbines or solar panels), but others, "ranging from backyard chicken coops and push-mowers to infill housing and district energy plants" (Sheppard, 2012, p. 239), are either still rarely or not recognized as related to climate change. In landscapes, adaptation as a concept is perhaps the least well understood and the least prominent of the four components; measures such as enlarging drainage culverts to handle more intense rainstorms go largely unrecognized.

[. . .]

In transitioning towards climate-friendly communities, how can people distinguish low-carbon from high-carbon, and vulnerable from resilient landscapes? What are the most effective ways to open people's eyes to climate change, and foster new social norms so that solutions can be scaled up?

The following sections describe some possible answers, enabled by landscape professionals. However, in addressing this challenge, we must recognize that the very aspect of local landscapes that makes them potentially powerful drivers of positive social change—place attachment, aesthetic qualities, keeping up with the Jones's—can also stymie needed change. There is the issue of resistance to new technologies such as solar panels or wind turbines that conflict with local character (Pasqualetti, Gipe, & Righter, 2002), and policy conflicts with low-carbon measures, as in prohibition of washing lines on balconies or in front gardens. We need to learn to love low-carbon resilient landscapes (Selman, 2010), and perhaps also to turn against high-carbon or vulnerable landscape features such as leaf-blowers and wind-prone exotic tree species. What we need most are low-carbon, *attractive*, resilient communities (Sheppard, Pond, & Campbell, 2008).

CRITICAL ROLES FOR LANDSCAPE PROFESSIONALS

The challenges just described call for the approaches and skills of landscape professionals. Climate scientists generally are not trained or well equipped to engage communities in climate change. They speak of science and global risks, their goal is primarily to inform. I believe that landscape professionals, on the other hand (preferably working with scientists), are better equipped to move society towards action: they intervene physically at various scales in the landscapes where people live, commute, and recreate. They work at the community or site level using local and science-based information, they engage stakeholders in planning and design processes, they talk about opportunities and design solutions which they bring to life with visual tools, and they care about aesthetics and are sensitive (usually!) to people's reactions to what things look like. They can therefore play key roles as integrators, facilitators, visualizers, visionaries, and creators, working in collaboration with other experts.

[. . .]

Such a responsible advocacy position, however, requires a solid ethical base. This essay advances five general guidelines for engaging communities on climate change using visual learning tools responsibly and effectively (described in more depth in Sheppard, 2012):

- Make climate change easily seen and understood (clarity).
- Link climate change to people, place, and context (connectivity).
- Keep the process interesting and inclusive (engagement).
- Keep the presentations honest, balanced, and verifiable (trust).
- Keep the engagement practical and cost-effective (feasibility).

Making climate change visible and meaningful under these guidelines calls for landscape techniques which range from physical design at the neighbourhood level to the use of visual learning tools in community engagement. These may address two main functions: making climate change more visible in existing landscapes, and bringing people's possible future landscapes closer to them. The author here suggests four possible pathways for implementation, addressing site design, production of compelling graphics, enhanced planning processes, and public awareness-building. The following sections describe each pathway and its purpose, briefly summarize how it works (with examples and precedents), and considers how it may be implemented effectively.

Landscape Messaging on Climate Change

What if we saw the landscape as eco-label? Landscape messaging refers to onsite "techniques for revealing the signs of a major phenomenon like carbon/climate change, by modifying the community landscape" (Sheppard, 2012, p. 285). It can be considered an extension of eco-revelatory design (Brown, Harkness, & Johnston, 1998) and landscape agency (Meyer, 2008), focusing more deliberately on informing the public through explicit displays and imaginative design to convey important and verifiable messages or learning outcomes; in this case, on climate change. This can be done through a variety of means, from explicit interpretative signage and labelling (e.g. of buildings' carbon emissions), to visible volunteer work programmes on climate change solutions, or large-scale landscape redesign of daylighted waterways to reveal changing hydrological or ecological systems (Figure 32.2).

The purpose of landscape messaging on climate change would be to increase the visibility of climate change features in local landscapes, and perhaps build broader acceptance of low-carbon resilient solutions. Various authors (e.g. Brown et al.,

Figure 32.2 Design concept for an outdoor exhibit using shoreline terraces to demonstrate sea level rise over time.
Source: Michelle Tustin

1998; Gobster, 1999; Nassauer, 1992, 1994; Sheppard, 2001, chap. 11; Thayer, 1998) have argued that the visual landscape can and should be manipulated to communicate and foster sustainability through mechanisms such as culturally recognized cues, transparency of function, and visible stewardship. Examples applied to climate change are still rare; their effectiveness has only been sporadically evaluated and established, such as Baldwin and Chandler (2010) using citizen photographs and events to build public awareness of climate change in Australia. However, interest in landscape messaging appears to be growing, with blue lines being painted on ground or bridges to mark future sea levels in several cities, or the public documentation of a block's collective daily energy usage, charted in chalk on the road surface of Tidy Street in Brighton (Sheppard, 2012), to stimulate social action.

Landscape messaging is then an opportunity not for landscape professionals alone, but also for local governments to go beyond a public art commitment to prioritize landscape messaging in infrastructure projects, in hopes of building public capacity and support for climate-friendly policy and action.

Visualization and Other Visual Learning Tools

Landscape professionals routinely use a range of graphics to represent local environments, including diagrams, infographics, maps, sections, renderings, models, and animations (Amoroso, 2015; Ervin & Hasbrouck, 2001). In particular, we use *landscape visualization* to depict actual places in 3D perspective views, often with a high degree of experiential realism (Bishop & Lange, 2005). Visualizations can be usefully applied to the climate change context by: (1) explicitly aligning the visible and the invisible (Nassauer, 2012), through augmented reality or simply combining conceptual and real-world imagery; and (2) 'time travel', showing future conditions that make long term consequences more immediate and compelling (Sheppard, 2005). The objectives here are to improve people's *understanding* of climate change by communicating complex information more clearly, "to convey what it might be like to experience climate change" (Sheppard, 2012, p. 355) in specific places, and to spark the imagination on possible solutions.

Personal experience in public engagement suggests that many people feel little connection with community planning, and most people have never seen a picture of what climate change could look like in their area. Seeing an image of their community's future can be a transformative moment for local citizens. Documented examples include Swiss ski-hill operators who experienced 'Aha!' moments when the projected effect of a dwindling snowpack on existing ski runs was visualized (Schroth, 2010); and residents of Kimberley, British Columbia who experienced emotional reactions to a virtual forest fire threatening their town, simulated in Google Earth (Schroth et al., 2011; Schroth, Pond, & Sheppard, 2015).

Because of their dramatic power, it is important that this imagery be scientifically grounded. The goal should be to achieve honest and accurate, defensible visualizations. We might call this 'permissible drama' (Sheppard, 2012): it may include dramatic content such as forest die-back or dike failures based on empirical evidence or plausible projections, [. . .]

However, the context, uncertainties, and basis of such projections should always be disclosed, and visualizations should not exaggerate the effects of climate change, distort landscape features, or selectively omit key elements. More complete guidance has been put forward in various principles and a code of ethics for landscape visualization (see for example Mulder, Sack-da-Silva, & Bruns, 2007; Sheppard & Cizek, 2009).

Without such guidelines, there is considerable risk that contested or discredited visualizations may harm the appropriate use of much-needed visual learning tools, and that useful images will be suppressed for fear of negative outcomes (such as polarizing public debates or plummeting property values for depicted coastal properties). A professionally endorsed code of ethics or standards is thus long overdue, together with supportive training programmes for practitioners.

Visioning Studies for Planning and Decision-Making

An important vehicle for making visual learning tools both accessible and defensible is to embed them within structured participatory visioning processes that explore "alternative future landscapes" (Nassauer, 2012, p. 224), explicitly incorporating climate change conditions. This amounts to better participatory planning, engaging more people, explaining local climate change issues, building community capacity, and articulating practical choices. In some jurisdictions, practitioners are increasingly conducting vulnerability studies or community energy plans, but all too often these are carried out as separate studies, losing the opportunities for synergies and efficiencies in joint adaptation and mitigation planning (Bizikova, Neale, & Burton, 2008). Communities need a simple but more holistic, flexible framework to integrate the best available knowledge into policy and decision-making, while fostering social learning with citizens and stakeholders as active participants.

Various approaches to visioning have been attempted with embedded visual media and future scenarios, such as integrated modelling and mapping of land use change with climate change in South Oxfordshire (Wood, Berry, & Lonsdale, 2006; Perez-Soba, Paterson, & Metzinger, 2015); and the City of North Vancouver's 100 Year Vision charrette (Condon, Muir-Owen, & Miller, 2009) with spatial modelling of alternative GHG emission outcomes. The New York Harbor shoreline design exhibition Rising Currents used multiple media to re-envision adaptive infrastructures for sea level rise, fostered considerable public dialogue (Bergdoll, 2011). Kwartler (2005) reports an urban visioning study with residents of Santa Fe, New Mexico, that led to a consensus on doubling densities that was otherwise unlikely to have been supported.

Some evaluation of the effectiveness of visioning has been carried out with an integrated approach termed Local Climate Change Visioning (Pond et al., 2010; Shaw et al., 2009). This process addresses elements included in the CIMA framework described earlier, through a form of participatory integrated assessment (Salter, Robinson, & Wiek, 2010) to develop future scenarios, with GIS mapping, and systematic use of 3D visualizations. Researchers at the Collaborative for Advanced Landscape Planning (CALP) worked with the coastal community of Delta facing sea level rise, and the urban fringe of Vancouver's Northshore mountains, affected by reduced snowpack and other hazards. In both communities, visioning packages with maps, diagrams, and landscape visualizations were organized around four alternative local landscape scenarios out to 2100, advised by a multi-stakeholder working group. [. . .]

This approach raised citizens' awareness of climate change, improved support for local mitigation and adaptation policies, and in some cases increased reported motivation to change behaviour (Cohen et al., 2012; Sheppard et al., 2011). In pre [and]post evaluation workshops with environmental practitioners, for example, participants' views on climate change became more urgent when serious local climate change effects were described as 'now' rather than 20 years away (Sheppard, 2012). In another planning process in Kimberley, British Columbia, residents recorded a significant increase in concern about local impacts of climate change, and improved understanding of links between climate change and land use decisions. Longitudinal studies have documented several policies and projects implemented as an outcome of Kimberley's adaptation planning process (Schroth et al., 2015). Guidance on more integrated approaches to climate change planning and communications is now emerging (e.g. Barry & Weigeldt, 2012; Pond et al., 2010). However, this needs to be accompanied by upgrading of professional skills through training and adoption of best practice procedures by local government.

Fostering Local Learning and Community Action on Climate Change

Community members who can recognize climate changes in their surroundings and champion local action should be supported and encouraged. Landscape professionals have the potential to catalyze community-led activities with support and training for residents using do-it-yourself (DIY) visual tools, community mapping, citizen science, and volunteer networks. Direct interaction with place-based communities, (i.e. local climate change tours, mapping, and labelling local climate change features, social media activities, etc.) could stimulate learning. New and visually attractive forms of online local data are becoming available for citizens' use in learning about climate change solutions such as community energy (e.g. Barron et al., 2013). Using social media, citizens can reveal, record, and share the signs of climate change and neighbourhood actions for mitigation or adaptation.

Precedents for these kinds of grass-roots activities include mapping of urban trees ('Neighbourwoods') by citizens of Sarnia, Ontario (Kenney & Puric-Mladenovic, n.d.), and the Project Neutral campaign in Toronto to encourage neighbourhoods to transition towards carbon neutrality (Project Neutral, 2014). Few of these projects have been rigorously evaluated, although relevant guidance is emerging; for example, on developing a composite foodshed map for self-sufficiency in local food (Hopkins, Thurstain-Goodwin, & Fairlie, n.d.), and on exploring sea level rise solutions with visual media (SFU, 2014).

CONCLUSIONS

Given how far we are globally and locally from meeting GHG reduction targets for avoiding catastrophic climate change, there is an urgent need to reveal the signs of climate change in local landscapes and develop strong images of attractive, low-carbon resilient futures. This essay has tried to make the case for broad, local climate change engagement and awareness-building, using the medium of landscape (and its representation in visual media) as a major stimulus. Everyday landscapes offer opportunities for experiential learning on climate change and for the leveraging of place attachment and social pressure, to help mobilize climate change literacy and action on solutions. The essay argues for the development of a new 'climate change lens' through which citizens can see and recognize climate change in their local landscapes, leading perhaps to more caring and more action. This new way of seeing needs to embrace the causes, impacts, mitigation, and adaptation of climate change as a way to make it more connected to everyday life.

If such approaches are to succeed, landscape practitioners (and their professional organizations) can and should play a critical role, expanding beyond more traditional areas of practice such as site design and construction. A range of landscape design and community engagement techniques with compelling visual learning tools will be needed, with governments mainstreaming these into enhanced planning and structured visioning processes. The potential for more work of this type in the landscape field grows every day as the climate changes and communities react. Four ways that landscape professionals can contribute to social change are recommended: design and development of landscape messaging to reveal climate change in current landscapes, production of compelling visualization of climate change in current and future landscapes, leading visioning processes that engage communities in planning for future scenarios with climate change, and helping neighbourhoods to self-educate and mobilize for local deliberation and action. There is a need for more testing of methods, guidance, and training of professionals in effective use of visualization tools and visioning processes that integrate climate science and landscape planning, and can empower communities to take action. This essay calls for a more systematic use of visual learning tools, and for ethical standards set by professional organizations to produce compelling, credible visualizations. There can hardly be a more important cause or professional opportunity than this, in taking a leadership role in making climate change (and its solutions) visible to the public.

REFERENCES

Amoroso, N. (Ed.). (2015). *Representing landscapes: Digital*. London and New York: Routledge.

Baldwin, C., & Chandler, L. (2010). At the water's edge: Community voices on climate change. *Local Environment*, 15(7), 637–649.

Barron, S., Tooke, T. R., Cote, S., Sheppard, S. R. J., Kellett, R., Zhang, K., et al. (2013). *An illustrated guide to community energy*. Vancouver, BC: Collaborative for Advanced Landscape Planning, UBC. Available at http://www.energyexplorer.ca/guide/?p=490

Barry, L., & Weigeldt, N. (2012). *Having the climate conversation: Strategies for local governments*. ICLEI – Local Governments for Sustainability (Management) Inc.

Bergdoll, B. (2011). *Rising currents: Projects for New York's Waterfront*. New York: Museum of Modern Art. Available at http://www.momastore.org/webapp/wcs/stores/servlet/ProductDisplay?langId=-1&storeId=10001&catalogId=10451&productId=187628&promoCode=8H104&categoryId=55161&parentcategoryrn=26683&cm mmc=MoMA-Other-Exhibitions-NA

Bishop, I. D., & Lange, E. (Eds.). (2005). *Visualization in landscape and environmental planning: Technology and applications*. London and New York: Taylor & Francis Group.

Bizikova, L., Neale, T., & Burton, I. (2008). *Canadian communities' guidebook for adaptation to climate change* (first ed.). Vancouver: Environment Canada and University of British Columbia.

Boardman, B., & Palmer, J. (2003). *Consumer choice and carbon consciousness for electricity*. 4CE Final Report, sponsored by the European Commission. Available at http://www.electricitylabels.com/downloads/4CE Final Report.pdf

Bollinger, B., & Gillingham, K. (2012, September). Peer effects in the diffusion of solar photovoltaic panels. *Marketing Science*, 900–912.

Boykoff, M. T. (2011). *Who speaks for the climate?* Cambridge: Cambridge University Press.

Brown, B., Harkness, T., & Johnston, D. (1998). Eco-revelatory design: Nature constructed/nature revealed. *Landscape Journal*, (Special issue), 138.

Cohen, S., Sheppard, S. R. J., Shaw, A., Flanders, D., Burch, S., Taylor, W., et al. (2012). Downscaling and visioning of mountain snow packs and other climate change implications in North Vancouver, British Columbia. *Mitigation Adaptation Strategies for Global Change*, 17(1), 25–49.

Condon, P., Muir-Owen, S., & Miller, N. (2009). *100 year sustainability vision*. Vancouver, Canada: The Design Centre for Sustainability, UBC.

Ervin, S. M., & Hasbrouck, H. H. (2001). *Landscape modelling*. New York: McGraw Hill.

Gifford, R. (2011). The dragons of inaction: Psychological barriers that limit climate change mitigation and adaptation. *American Psychologist*, 66(4), 290–302.

Gobster, P. H. (1999). An ecological aesthetic for forest landscape management. *Landscape Journal*, 18(1), 54–64.

Gobster, P. H., Nassauer, J. I., Daniel, T. C., & Fry, G. (2007). The shared landscape: What does aesthetics have to do with ecology? *Landscape Ecology*, 22, 959–972.

Hopkins, R., Thurstain-Goodwin, M., & Fairlie, S. (Undated). *Can Totnes and districtfeed itself? Exploring the practicalities of food relocalisation*. Working Paper Version 1.0. Totnes, UK: Transition Network. Available at http://transitionculture.org/wp-content/uploads/cantotnesfeeditself1.pdf

IPCC. (2014). Summary for policymakers. In C. B. Field, V. R. Barros, D. J. Dokken, K. J. Mach, M. D. Mastrandrea, T. E. Bilir, et al. (Eds.), *Climate change 2014: Impacts, adaptation, and vulnerability. Part A: Global and sectoral aspects. Contribution of Working Group II to the Fifth Assessment Report of the Intergovernmental Panel on Climate Change* (pp. 1–32). Cambridge, UK and New York, NY, USA: Cambridge University Press.

Kenney, W. A., & Puric-Mladenovic, D. (Undated). *Neighbourwoods: Community-based urban forest stewardship*. Available at http://www.forestry.utoronto.ca/neighbourwoods/web/

Kwartler, M. (2005). Visualization in support of public participation. In I. Bishop, & E. Lange (Eds.), *Visualization in landscape and environmental planning: Technology and applications*. London and New York: Taylor & Francis Group.

Leiserowitz, A. (2007). Communicating the risks of global warming: American risk perceptions, affective images, and interpretive communities. In S. Moser, & L. Dilling (Eds.), *Creating a climate for change: Communicating climate change and facilitating social change*. Cambridge, UK: Cambridge University Press.

Leiserowitz, A., Maibach, E., & Roser-Renouf, C. (2009). *Climate change in the American mind.* George Mason University, Centre for Climate Change Communication.

Maibach, E., Roser-Renouf, C., & Leiserowitz, A. (2009). *Global warming's six Americas 2009: An audience segmentation.* Available at http://www.americanprogress.org/issues/2009/05/pdf/6americas.pdf

Marshall, G. (2014). Don't even think about it: Why our brains are wired to ignore climate change. New York: Bloomsbury USA.

McKenzie-Mohr, D., & Smith, W. (1999). *Fostering sustainable behavior: An introduction to community-based social marketing.* Gabriola Island, BC, Canada: New Society Publishers.

Meyer, E. K. (2008, Spring). Sustaining beauty: The performance of appearance: A manifesto in three parts. *Journal of Landscape Architecture*, 6–23.

Moser, S., & Dilling, L. (Eds.). (2007). *Creating a climate for change: Communicating climate change and facilitating social change.* Cambridge, UK: Cambridge University Press.

Mulder, J., Sack-da-Silva, S., & Bruns, D. (2007). Understanding the role of 3D visualizations: The example of Calden Airport expansion, Kassel, Germany. In A. van den Brink, R. van Lammeren, R. van de Velde, & S. Dane (Eds.), *Manschold publication series* (Vol. 3) *Geo-visualisation for participatory spatial planning in Europe: Imagining the future.* Wageningen, NL: Wageningen Academic Publishers.

Nassauer, J. I. (1992). The appearance of ecological systems as a matter of policy. *Landscape Ecology*, 6(4), 239–250.

Nassauer, J. I. (1994). Messy ecosystems, orderly frames. *Landscape Journal*, 14, 161–171.

Nassauer, J. I. (2012). Landscape as medium and method for synthesis in urban ecological design. *Landscape and Urban Planning*, 106, 221–229.

Nordhaus, T., & Shellenberger, M. (2009). *Apocalypse fatigue: Losing the public on climate change. Environment* (Vol. 360) Yale School of Forestry and Environmental Studies. Posted 16 November 2009. Available at http://e360.yale.edu/feature/apocalypsefatiguelosingthepubliconclimatechange/2210/

Pasqualetti, M. J., Gipe, P., & Righter, R. W. (2002). *Wind power in view: Energy landscapes in a crowded world.* New York: Academic Press.

Perez-Soba, M., Paterson, J., & Metzinger, M. (2015). *Vision of future land use in Europe: Stakeholder visions for 2040 VOLANTE.* Project Report. Alterra Wageningen UR., pp. 24. ISBN 978-94-6257-406-9.

Pond, E., Schroth, O., Sheppard, S. R. J., Muir-Owen, S., Liepa, I., Campbell, C., et al. (2010). *Local climate change visioning and landscape visualizations: Guidance manual.* Version 1.0 Prepared for the BC Ministry of Community and Rural Development. Vancouver, Canada: CALP, UBC.

Project Neutral. (2014). Available at http://www.projectneutral.org/make-your-neighbourhood-carbon-neutral

Salter, J., Robinson, J., & Wiek, A. (2010). Participatory methods of integrated assessment: A review. *Wiley Interdisciplinary Reviews*, 1(5), 697–717.

Scannell, L., & Gifford, R. (2010). Defining place attachment: A tripartite organizing framework. *Journal of Environmental Psychology*, 30, 1–10. http://dx.doi.org/10.1016/j.jenvp.2009.09.006

Schroth, O. (2010). *From information to participation: Interactive landscape visualization as a tool for collaborative planning* (PhD thesis). Zurich, Switzerland: Swiss Federal Institute of Technology, ETH.

Schroth, O., Pond, E., Campbell, C., Cizek, P., Bohus, S., & Sheppard, S. R. J. (2011). Tool or toy? Virtual globes in landscape planning. *Future Internet*, 3, 204–227. Available at www.mdpi.com/journal/futureinternet

Schroth, O., Pond, E., & Sheppard, S. R. J. (2015). Evaluating presentation formats of local climate change in community planning with regard to process and outcomes. *Landscape and Urban Planning*. Special Issue on Critical Visualization. Available at http://www.sciencedirect.com/science/journal/aip/01692046

Selman, P. (2010). Learning to love the landscapes of carbon-neutrality. *Landscape Research, 35*(2), 157–171.

Shaw, A., Sheppard, S. R. J., Burch, S., Flanders, D., Wiek, A., Carmichael, J., et al. (2009). How futures matter: Synthesizing, downscaling, and visualizing climate change scenarios for participatory capacity building. *Global Environmental Change, 19*, 447–463.

Sheppard, S. R. J. (2001). Beyond visual resource management: Emerging theories of an ecological aesthetic and visible stewardship. In S. R. J. Sheppard, & H. W. Harshaw (Eds.), *IUFRO research series* (No. 6) *Forests and landscapes: Linking ecology, sustainability, and aesthetics* (pp. 149–172). Wallingford, UK: CABI Publishing.

Sheppard, S. R. J. (2005). Landscape visualization and climate change: The potential for influencing perceptions and behaviour. *Environmental Science and Policy, 8*, 637–654.

Sheppard, S. R. J. (2012). *Visualizing climate change: A guide to visual communication of climate change and developing local solutions.* Abingdon, UK: Earthscan/Routledge. Available at http://visualizingclimatechange.ca

Sheppard, S. R. J. (2014). *Dog walker blog post.* Available at http://visualizingclimatechange.ca/blog/

Sheppard, S. R. J., & Cizek, P. (2009). The ethics of Google-Earth: Crossing thresholds from spatial data to landscape visualization. *Journal of Environmental Management, 90*, 2102–2117.

Sheppard, S. R. J., Pond, E., & Campbell, C. (2008). *Low-carbon, attractive, resilient communities: New imperatives for sustainable retrofitting of existing neighbourhoods.* Paper presented at Council for European Urbanism Third International Congress, Oslo, Norway.

Sheppard, S. R. J., Shaw, A., Flanders, D., Burch, S., Wiek, A., Carmichael, J., et al. (2011). Future visioning of local climate change: A framework for community engagement and planning with scenarios and visualisation. *Futures, 43*(4), 400–412.

Simon Fraser University (SFU). (2014). *RISE: An ideas competition addressing sea level rise – 5 tools to enhance your presentation.* Vancouver, BC: SFU Public Square. October 1, 2014. http://www.sfu.ca/rise/news/blog/5-tools-enhance-presentation.html

Spence, A., Poortinga, W., Butler, C., & Pidgeon, N. F. (2011). Perceptions of climate change and willingness to save energy related to flood experience. *Nature Climate Change, 1*, 46–49.

Thayer, R. (1998). Landscape as an ecologically revealing language. *Landscape Journal*, (Special Issue on Eco-revelatory Design), 118–129.

Van Der Linden, S. (2014). Towards a new model for communicating climate change. In S. Cohen, J. Higham, P. Peeters, & S. Gössling (Eds.), *Understanding and governing sustainable tourism mobility: Psychological and behavioural approaches* (pp. 243–275). London: Routledge and Taylor and Francis Group.

Weber, E. U. (2006). Experience-based and description-based perceptions of long-term risk: Why global warming does not scare us (yet). *Climatic Change, 77*, 103–120.

Wood, P., Berry, P. M., & Lonsdale, K. (2006). *Future landscape scenarios around Little Wittenham, South Oxfordshire.* Report to the Northmoor Trust.

List of Articles

Abunnasr, Yaser & Hamin, Elisabeth M. (2012). The Green Infrastructure Transect: An Organizational Framework for Mainstreaming Adaptation Planning Policies. *Resilient Cities 2*. 205–217. doi:10.1007/978-94-007-4223-9.

Adger, W. Neil, Hughes , Terry P., Folke, Carl, Carpenter, Stephen R. & Rockström, Johan. (2005). Social-Ecological Resilience to Coastal Disasters. *Science*. 1036–1039.

Boswell, Michael R., Greve, Adrienne I. & Seale, Tammy L. (2010). An Assessment of the Link between Greenhouse Gas Emissions Inventories and Climate Action Plans. *Journal of the American Planning Association*. 76 (4). doi.org/10.1080/01944363.2010.50331.

Cutter, Susan L. & Finch, Christina (2008). Temporal and Spatial Changes in Social Vulnerability to Natural Hazards. *PNAS*. 105 (7). 2301–2306; published ahead of print February 11, 2008, doi:10.1073/pnas.0710375105.

Dodman, David. (2011). Forces Driving Urban Greenhouse Gas Emissions. *In Current Opinion in Environmental Sustainability*. 3 (3). 121–125, ISSN 1877–3435, https://doi.org/10.1016/j.cosust.2010.12.013. (www.sciencedirect.com/science/article/pii/S1877343510001521).

Elisabeth M. Hamin & Gurran, Nicole. (2009). Urban Form and Climate Change: Balancing Adaptation and Mitigation in the U.S. and Australia. *Habitat International*. 33. 238–245. doi:10.1016/j.habitatint.2008.10.005.

Frosch, Rachel Morello, Pastor, Manuel, Sadd, Jim & Shonkoff, Seth. (2009). The Climate Gap: Inequalities in How Climate Change Hurts Americans & How to Close the Gap. *PERE Publications*. May.

Gill, Susannah, Handley, J.F., Ennos, Roland & Pauleit, Stephan. (2007). Adapting Cities for Climate Change: The Role of the Green Infrastructure. *Built Environment*. 33. 115–133. doi:10.2148/benv.33.1.115. www.alexandrinepress.co.uk/built-environment.

Harlan, Sharon L. & Ruddel, Darren M. (2011). Climate Change and Health in Cities: Impacts of Heat and Air Pollution and Potential Co-Benefits from Mitigation and Adaptation. *Current Opinion in Environmental Sustainability*. 3 (3). May. 126–134. https://doi.org/10.1016/j.cosust.2011.01.001

Hoornweg, Dan, Sugar, Lorraine & Lorena Trejos Gomez, Claudia. (2011). Cities and Greenhouse Gas Emissions: Moving Forward. *Environment and Urbanization*. 23. 207–227. doi:10.1177/0956247810392270.

IPCC. (2012). Managing the Risks of Extreme Events and Disasters to Advance Climate Change Adaptation. A Special Report of Working Groups I and II of the Intergovernmental Panel on Climate Change [Field, C.B., Barros, V., Stocker, T.F., Qin, D., Dokken, D.J., Ebi, K.L., Mastrandrea, M.D., Mach, K.J., Plattner, G.-K., Allen, S.K., Tignor, M. & Midgley, P.M. (eds.)]. Cambridge University Press, Cambridge, UK, and New York, NY, USA, 582 pp.

Kirshen, Paul, Ruth, Matthias & Anderson, William. (2008). Interdependencies of Urban Climate Change Impacts and Adaptation Strategies: A Case Study of Metropolitan Boston USA. *Climatic Change*. 86. 105–122. doi:10.1007/s10584-007-9252-5.

Kithiia, Justus & Lyth, Anna. (2011). Urban Wildscapes and Green Spaces in Mombasa and Their Potential Contribution to Climate Change Adaptation and Mitigation. *Environment and Urbanization*. 23. 251–265. doi:10.1177/0956247810396054.

Kleerekoper, Laura, Esch, M.M.E. & Salcedo Rahola, Tadeo Baldiri. (2011). How to Make a City Climate-Proof, Addressing the Urban Heat Island Effect. *Resources Conservation and Recycling*. 64. doi:10.1016/j.resconrec.2011.06.004.

Kousky, Carolyn. (2014). Managing Shoreline Retreat: A US Perspective. *Climatic Change*. 124. 9–20. doi:10.1007/s10584-014-1106-3.

Lee, Sungwon & Lee, Bumsoo. (2014). The Influence of Urban form on GHG Emissions in the U.S. Household Sector. *Energy Policy*. 68. 534–549. doi:10.1016/j.enpol.2014.01.024.

Leichenko, Robin & Solecki, William. (2013). Climate Change in Suburbs: An Exploration of Key Impacts and Vulnerabilities. *Urban Climate*. 6. 82–97. doi:10.1016/j.uclim. 2013.09.001.

Lennon, Mick, Scott, Mark & O'Neill, Eoin. (2014). Urban Design and Adapting to Flood Risk: The Role of Green Infrastructure. *Journal of Urban Design*. 19. doi:10.1080/1357 4809.2014.944113?journalCode=cjud20#.VHBsqsmsnK0.

Mycoo, Michelle. (2014). Sustainable Tourism, Climate Change and Sea Level Rise Adaptation Policies in Barbados. *Natural Resources Forum*. 38. doi:10.1111/1477-8947.12033.

Norton, Briony, Coutts, Andrew, Livesley, Stephen, Harris, Richard, Hunter, Annie & Williams, Nicholas. (2015). Planning for Cooler Cities: A Framework to Prioritise Green Infrastructure to Mitigate High Temperatures in Urban Landscapes. *Landscape and Urban Planning*. 134. 127–138. doi:10.1016/j.landurbplan.2014.10.018.

Orr, David W. (2008). Optimism and Hope in a Hotter Time. *Conservation Biology: The Journal of the Society for Conservation Biology*. 21. 1392–1395. doi:10.1111/j.1523-1739. 2007.00836.x.

Pacala, S. & Socolow, R. (2004). Stabilization Wedges: Solving the Climate Problem for the Next 50 Years with Current Technologies. *Science*. 305 (5686). 968–972. www.jstor.org/stable/3837555.

Popkin, Gabriel. (2015) Breaking the Waves. *Science*. 350 (6262). 13 November. 756–759. doi:10.1126/science.350.6262.756.

Rouse, David C., AICP & Bunster-Ossa, Ignacio. 2013. Excerpted from Green Infrastructure: A Landscape Approach (PAS Report 571). Copyright January 2013 by the American Planning Association. Reprinted by Permission of APA.

Salick, J. & Ross, N. (2009). Traditional Peoples and Climate Change. *Global Environmental Change*. 19 (2). 137–139.

Sheppard, Stephen. (2015). Making Climate Change Visible: A Critical Role for Landscape Professionals. *Landscape and Urban Planning*. 142. 95–105. doi:10.1016/j.landurbplan. 2015.07.006.

Shi, Linda, Chu, Eric & Debats (now Debats Garrison), Jessica. (2015). Explaining Progress in Climate Adaptation Planning Across 156 U.S. Municipalities. *Journal of the American Planning Association*. 81. 1–12. doi:10.1080/01944363.2015.1074526.

Stone, B., Jr., Vargo, J., Liu, P., Habeeb, D., DeLucia, A., Trail, M., et al. (2014). Avoided Heat-Related Mortality through Climate Adaptation Strategies in Three US Cities. *PLoS One*. 9 (6). e100852. https://doi.org/10.1371/journal.pone.0100852.

Summary for Policymakers from Climate Change. (2014). Synthesis Report. Contribution of Working Groups I, II and III to the Fifth Assessment Report of the Intergovernmental Panel on Climate Change [Core Writing Team, Pachauri, R.K. & Meyer, L. (eds.)]. IPCC, Geneva, Switzerland.

Wilby, Robert. (2007). A Review of Climate Change Impacts on the Built Environment. *Built Environment*. 33. 31–45. doi:10.2148/benv.33.1.31. www.alexandrinepress.co.uk/built-environment.

Editor Biographies

Elisabeth M. Hamin Infield is a Professor of Regional Planning at the University of Massachusetts Amherst in the Department of Landscape Architecture and Regional Planning, where she teaches graduate and undergraduate courses on climate change adaptation and land use planning. Her current research focuses on the intersection of climate change, municipal planning, infrastructure, and regionalism. A major research effort is the SAGE (Sustainable Adaptive Gradients in the coastal Environment) Research Collaboration Network funded by the National Science Foundation, with a goal of increasing interdisciplinary communication on and the adoption of greener, resilient infrastructure (www.resilient-infrastructure. org), for which she is Principal Investigator. She was a co-Principal Investigator for an NSF-funded program to increase graduate education in off-shore wind energy (IGERT). She regularly works with communities in western Massachusetts on planning projects. Professor Hamin Infield serves on the UMass Chancellor's Sustainability Advisory Committee and was previously Department Chair for Landscape Architecture and Regional Planning (2012–2017). She is on the editorial board for the Journal of the American Planning Association. She previously taught at Iowa State University (1995–2001). She holds a Ph.D. from the Department of City and Regional Planning at the University of Pennsylvania (1997) and a Master of Management from the J.L. Kellogg Graduate School of Management at Northwestern University (1986). Between those two degrees, she worked in the private sector. Professor Hamin Infield has authored or co-authored more than 30 peer-reviewed articles and book chapters and three books including this Routledge Reader.

Yaser Abunnasr, Ph.D., M.L.A., B.Arch., Fulbright Scholar is an Associate Professor of Landscape Architecture and Planning at the American University of Beirut in the Department of Landscape Design and Ecosystem Management, Beirut, Lebanon. He teaches undergraduate design courses in landscape architecture and graduate courses in green infrastructure and urban design. Prior to his academic career, he practiced in the fields of Architecture, Landscape Architecture, and Urban Planning. He continues to consult internationally. His current research is on green infrastructure systems in the context of planning for climate change adaptation. A current multi-scalar research project is in collaboration with UC Davis on the effectiveness of vegetated green infrastructure to ameliorate urban climates in desert cities. He is also a main contributor to the SAGE Research Collaboration Network funded by the National Science Foundation, to increase interdisciplinary adoption of greener, resilient infrastructure. He is also principal investigator of a European Union-funded project on building capacities in integrated energy planning. He also partnered with the Chief Government Architect of the Netherlands to develop an open space system to increase resilience of refugee and host communities in a rural village in Lebanon. Professor Abunnasr holds a Ph.D. in Regional Planning from the Department of Landscape Architecture and Regional Planning at the University of Massachusetts Amherst (UMass, 2013), Master of Landscape Architecture from UMass (2007), and a Bachelors of Architecture from the American University of Beirut (1989). Professor Abunnasr has authored and/or co-authored several manuscripts and presented his research and lectured internationally.

Robert L. Ryan, FASLA is professor and chair of the Department of Landscape Architecture and Regional Planning, University of Massachusetts Amherst where he teaches courses on landscape planning and assessment, environment and behavior, and green infrastructure planning.

His research explores the role of place attachment as a motivation for stewardship of urban green spaces and the factors that influence public acceptance for sustainable landscapes, including green infrastructure. He is the co-author with Rachel and Stephen Kaplan of the award-winning book, *With People in Mind: Design and Management of Everyday Nature* (Island Press, 1998), as well as over 35 journal articles and book chapters in his research areas. He serves on the Editorial Board of the international journal *Landscape and Urban Planning*, and was a technical advisor to the ASLA's Sustainable Sites Initiative Human Health and Well-being Technical sub-committee. Professor Ryan holds a Ph.D. in Natural Resources (Environment and Behavior Concentration), Master in Landscape Architecture and Master of Urban Planning degrees from the University of Michigan-Ann Arbor and Bachelor of Science in Landscape Architecture from California Polytechnic State University, San Luis Obispo. In 2013, he was honored as a Fellow of the American Society of Landscape Architecture for his scholarly contributions to the profession.

Index

Note: page references in bold indicate tables and page references in italic indicate figures.

Abunnasr, Yaser 172
acclimatization 36
accommodate or retreat approach to climate change 288, 310
adaptation to climate change: balancing with mitigation to climate change and 331–338; Barbados tourism and 318; built environments and 39; climate change planning and 2; climate change risks reduced by 32–33; conflict between mitigation of climate change and 336–337; defining 10; future pathways for 31–33; green infrastructure and 185, 200–202; interdependencies within cities and 107–108; Intergovernmental Panel on Climate Change and 110; land-use conflict and 336; microclimate and 222; overview 107–110; policy goals 335–336; social vulnerability to natural hazards and 109–110; successful 261; over time **44**, 45; *see also* cities' adaptation to climate change and green infrastructure; suburban areas' adaptation to climate change and green infrastructure
adaptation over time gradient **44**, 45
Adger, W. Neil 110, 152
agricultural production concerns 214–215
agricultural soils management 60
Ahern, Jack 223
air pollution 35, 38, 100–101, 140–141, 143
air quality 38–39
albedo enhancement and materials 222, 226, 228, 230–232, 242, 251, 253, 256, 260
American Planning Association (APA) 88, 273
American Society of Landscape Architects (ASLA) 174–175
Anderson, William P. 306–307
Andrew (1992 hurricane) 151, 153
Arctic region 27, *27*, 29
Arnstein, S.R. 330
Asian tsunami (2004) 152, 154–156
Atlanta (Georgia) 222, 225, 227–228, *229*, 230–232

Atmosphere-Ocean ModelE 228
Australia: international comparison approach and 329, 333–338; koala habitat plan of management in 338; Melbourne 235, 240; Port Stephen 338; urban form in 329, 333–338

backing away from the shore strategy 292, 294–295
balancing feedback loop 180
Baldwin, C. 369
Bamburi Cement Factory 356–357, 359
Bamburi Quarry Nature Park (now Haller Park) 352, 355–357
Bamford, H. 286
Barbados tourism sector: Accra/Rockley beach redevelopment and 315–316; adaptation to climate change and 318; background information 317–318; beach nourishment and 320; capacity-building and 322–323, *323*; Coastal Zone Management Unit and 317, 320–321, 323; ecosystem-based adaptation and 320–321; future work and 324; infrastructure policies and 322; Integrated Coastal Zone Management and 319–322, *319*, *323*; methodology of study 317; overview 288–289, 315–317; physical planning policy and practice and 318, 321; planned retreat and 320; policies 315–316, 321–323, *323*; protection measures and 319–320; sustainable tourism and 318, 321–322; TCPD policy and 318, 323, *323*; water conservation and 322
basic necessities, price of 141
beach nourishment 320
behavioural exposure 238
Benedict, Mark A. 170, 175
Berlin (Germany) 268
Biddle, P.G. 201
Bilkovic, Donna 303
biodiversity 38–39, 154, 163
biofuels 145
biophysical changes 197

Biotape Area Factor 268
Bloch, Ernst 12
Bloomberg, Michael 52
Boston (Massachusetts): Build Your Way
    Out approach to climate change 288,
    306–307, 310; CLIMB project 288,
    308–314; Emerald Necklace project
    in 169; geography of 308, *309*; Green
    (accommodate or retreat) approach to
    climate change and 288, 310; metropolitan
    park system case study 169, 185, 189–190,
    191, 192–193; population in 308; Ride It
    Out approach to climate change and 288,
    306–307, 310–311, *312–313*
Boswell, Michael R. 53, 83–84
breakwaters 319, *319*
Bridges, K. 162–163
Brown, Robert 222
Brundtland Commission 85
Bryon Shire (Australia) 336–337
Budd, L. 95
Building Albedo Enhancement (BAE) 228
building form *see* urban form
buildings, more efficient 60
Build Your Way Out (BYWO) approach to
    climate change 288, 306–307, 310
built environments and climate change:
    adaptation and 39; air quality 38–39;
    biodiversity 38–39; drainage 37; flood
    risk 37, **37**; mitigation and 39; observed
    changes 35–39; overview 34–35;
    ventilation and cooling 36; water resources
    38; *see also* cities; urban form and
    greenhouse gas emissions
built-form responses to climate change 4,
    169–172, 255–256
Bunster-Ossa, Ignacio 172, 174, 184–185,
    224, 273
business-as-usual (BAU) trajectory and
    approach 18, 57–59, *57*, 227, 230,
    280, 306
buyout programs 296
Byg, A. 163

California Air Resources Board (CARB) 86
Canada: greenhouse gas emissions
    responsibility and 64–66, *65*; Project
    Neutral campaign in 371
capacity building 322–323, *323*
carbon consciousness 365–366
carbon dioxide (CO_2) 56–57; *see also*
    greenhouse gas (GHG) emissions;
    stabilization of carbon emissions
Caribbean 156–157, 316; *see also* Barbados
    tourism sector
Caribbean Planning for Adaptation to
    Climate Change (CPACC) 317
Carpenter, Stephen R. 152
Cayman Islands 156

Census Public Use Microdata Sample (PUMS)
    74, 80
Cesanek, Bill 280
challenges facing cities' mitigation of
    greenhouse gas emissions: climate change
    63; empowering change 70–71; inventory
    of greenhouse gases 70; mitigation of
    climate change 66, **67–69**; overview
    62–63; policy tools and 66, **67–69**;
    pragmatic approach to 63; responsibility
    for emissions, assigning 64–66, **64**, *65*
Chandler, L. 369
Chesapeake Bay shoreline 302
Chincoteague National Wildlife Refuge 294
Churchill, Winston 13–14
CIMA framework 370
cities: C40 members 64, **64**; climate change
    in 2, 63, 99–101; compact, building
    more 80–81; disadvantaged populations
    in, vulnerability of 108–109; expansion
    of, during last century 108; gardens in
    38; green spaces in 39; impact of climate
    change and 171; interdependencies within
    107–108; mitigation of climate change
    and 66, **67–69**; policy tools of 66, **67–70**;
    remedial action and 2; as urban heat
    islands 35–36; *see also* built environments
    and climate change; cities' adaptation to
    climate change and green infrastructure;
    health in cities; local government
    adaptation in United States; *specific name*;
    urban form and greenhouse gas emissions
cities' adaptation to climate change and green
    infrastructure: drought-resistance plantings
    and 201, 203; energy exchange model
    and 199; Greater Manchester (United
    Kingdom) case study 198–203; moisture
    deficit and 201; overview 172, 195–197;
    quantifying environmental functions and
    199, 202–203; surface runoff model and
    199–200; sustainable urban drainage and
    202; urban morphology types and 195,
    198–199
Cities for Climate Protection campaign
    (ICLEI) 85
Clean Water Act 175, 277
climate: impacts of 2–3; importance of 1;
    projected changes in 26–29; variability
    of 108–109; *see also* climate change;
    specific issue
Climate Action Plans: best-practice standards
    for 88; Boston metropolitan region case
    study and 189–190; historical perspective
    of 85–86; inventory of greenhouse gases
    and 53, 83–84, 86–88; overview 83–84;
    purpose of 85–86
climate-beneficial actions 3
climate catastrophes 1, 11; *see also*
    specific name

climate change: acceptable, threshold of 9; accommodate or retreat approach to 288; Build Your Way Out approach to 288, 306–307, 310; built-form responses to 4, 169–172, 255–256; causes of 21, *22*, *23*, *23*; challenges facing cities' mitigation of greenhouse gas emissions and 63; in cities 2, 63, 99–101; coastal areas and 285; as collective action problem 31–32; communication 343; community action on 363–364, *364*, 371; complications of 1–2; decision-making about, foundations of 31–32; density conundrum and 337–338; displacement of people and 30; dramatic, media's focus on 366; economic losses and 30; food security and 30; future 26–31; future impacts 29–31; Green (accommodate or retreat) approach to 288, 310; hard engineering solutions to 223, 269; health and 30; hope and 4, 11–14, 42; human causes of 1, 156; human rights and 139; impacts of 9, 24, *25*; indigenous peoples and 160–164; information 343; job opportunities and 141–142; in landscapes, recognizing 365–366; local learning about 371; mainstreaming 330–331; observed changes 19, *20*, 21; overview 1–5, 9–10; price of basic necessities and 141; Ride It Out approach to 288, 306–307, 310–311, *312–313*; science on 4, 11, 13, 85; soft engineering solutions and 268–270, 353; truth telling and 13–14; beyond 2100 31; urban heat island effect and 252; violent conflicts and 30–31; water scarcity and 322; worsening of 362; *see also* adaptation to climate change; built environments and climate change; engaging public in climate change; mitigation of climate change; New Jersey suburbs and climate change; social vulnerability to climate change; urban form and climate change

Climate Change Action Plan (Clinton) 85

climate change planning: adaptation and 2; education of planners and 88; greenhouse gas mitigation and 196; integrating into overall planning 3; local government in 329–330; local leadership in 330; mitigation and 2–3; variability of climate and 108–109; *see also* Climate Action Plans; local government adaptation in United States

climate experts on global warming 12–13

climate gap, defining and examples of 138

Climate Gap report (PERE): air pollution health hazards and 140–141; air pollution mitigation and 143; closing gap and 142–146; conversation gap and, closing 147; economic impacts of 146; extreme heat waves and 140; fees for investing in

hard-hit communities and 143; findings of 140–142; greenhouse gas emission mitigation and 143; health impacts of 145–146; job opportunities and 141–142; methodology of 139; new fuels and 145; overview 138–140, 147; permits and, auctioning 143; policymakers and 147; price of basic necessities and 141; regional focus and, moving beyond 144; regional versus local issues and 138, 144

Climate Protection Agreement 85

CLIMB project: hypothesis of 314; interdependencies of impacts and adaptation and 311, *312–313*; methodology of study 308, *309*, 310–311; overview 307–308; Ride It Out approach and 288, 306–307, 310–311, *312–313*; Stakeholder Advisory Group and 310; themes of 311; zones in 308, *309*

Clinton, Bill 85, 170

Coastal Barrier Resources System (CBRS) 293

coastal defenses 286, *287*; *see also specific type*

coastal hazards and resiliency: Asian tsunami (2004) and 152, 154–156; biodiversity and 154; building resilience and 158; challenges to 286, 288–289; climate change and 285; coping with hazards and 152–154, *157*; ecological memory and 154; globalization and 153; hurricanes and 156–157; mobility and 153; overview 151–152, 158; population and 292; protecting coasts and 286, *287*; rebuilding resilience and 153; reef damage and 155; responding to changes and 154–157; social memory and 154; social resiliency and 153, 155, *157*; socio-ecological resiliency and 155, *157*, 158; spatial heterogeneity and 154; *see also* sea level rise (SLR)

Coastal Zone Management Unit (CZMU) 317, 320–321, 323

cold winter extremes 28

Collaborative for Advanced Landscape Planning (CALP) 370–371

collective action problem 31–32

Colorado fires 215

combined sewer overflows (CSOs) 210, 276–278

Commonwealth Scientific and Industrial Research Organization (CSIRO) 337

communication about climate change 343

community action on climate change 371, 363–364, *364*

Community Awareness to Action (C2A) 363–364, *364*

community indicators 177–178

Compact of Mayors 10

Congressional Budget Office study (2007) 143

connectivity 275

Conservation Fund 173, 175
conservation improvements 59–60
consumption-based approach to assessing greenhouse gas emissions 96–97
conversation gap, closing 147
cooling in built environment 34–36, 202, 221–222, 228, 230–232, 235–236, 253–255
cool materials 228
coral reef damage and protection 153, 155–156, 286, 288, 317–318, 320–322, 323
Corporate Average Fuel Economy (CAFE) 85
cost efficiency gradient 44, **44**
Coutts, Andrew M. 240
Currin, Carolyn 302–303
Cutter, Susan L. 110, 129–130

Davis, J.L. 303
Den Haag (Netherlands) case study 257–258, 259, 260
density conundrum and 337–338
Design with Nature (McHarg) 170
Dickhaut, W. 268
disasters as opportunities strategy 292, 295–296
disparities in climate change impacts *see* Climate Gap report (PERE)
displacement of people 30
Dobshinsky, Andrew 280
Dodman, David 52–53, 91–92
do-it-yourself (DIY) visual tools 371
drainage, urban 37, 202
drought-resistant plantings 201, 203

Earth Summit (1992) 84–85
easements, rolling 294
Easterling, W. 314
Eckaus, R. S. 87
Eco Art 275
Ecological Art 275
ecological enhancement gradient 44, **44**
ecological memory 154
economic indicators 178
economic losses from climate change 30
ecosystem-based adaptation 320–321
ecosystem services 154, 169, 173–174, 176, 211
ecotourism concerns 215; *see also* sustainable tourism
efficiency improvements 59–60
Eisenman, T.S. 169
Ekstrom, J.A. 344
electricity, decarbonization of 60
Eliot, Charles 169
Eliot, T.S. 13
Emerald Necklace project (Boston) 169
emissions stabilization *see* stabilization of carbon emissions
energy exchange model 199
energy use and urban form 335

engaging public in climate change: carbon consciousness and 365–366; Community Awareness to Action Framework and 363–364, *364*; fostering local learning and community action 371; in future 372; guidelines for 367; landscape in 363–365; landscape messaging and 367, *368*, *369*; landscape professionals' role in 366–367, 372; make it connected principle 361, 363; make it local principle 361, 363, 371; make it visual principle 361, 363, 367, 369–370; overview 330, 361–362, 372; principles in 363; problems in 362–363; visioning studies for planning and decision-making 370–371; visualization and other visual learning tools and 369–370
environmental indicators 178
environmental performance and urban form 51
Environmental Protection Agency (EPA) 173, 175
ethanol 145
evaluation process in guide to resiliency project: collect relevant information 46–47; form evaluation team 46; move forward 48, *48*; present shared averages for each gradient 47; score project 47, *47*
evaporation: cooling and 202, 253–255; drought and 213; impervious materials and 251, 256; pervious materials and 250–251, 256–257; salinity and 19; through vegetation 173, 175, 195, 221–222, 253
evapotranspiration 230, 253
evolutionary resiliency 265, 267
Ewing, R. 334
experiential learning 362
exposure reduction gradient 43, **44**
extreme heat events (EHEs) 100, 140, 234–235
extreme weather events 24, 28, 100; *see also specific disaster*
exurban areas' adaptation to climate change and green infrastructure 214–216

Federal Emergency Management Agency (FEMA) 294
feedback loops and green infrastructure 180
fees for investing in hard-hit communities 143
Fifth Assessment Report (AR5) (IPCC): extreme weather events 24; future climate changes, risks and impacts 26–31; future pathways for adaptation, mitigation and sustainable development 31–33; observed climate changes and their causes 19–25, *20*; overview 16–18; sustainability and 31–33; United Nations Framework Convention on Climate Change and 18; Working Groups and 16–18
Finch, Christina 110, 129–130
fire concerns 215

Firehock, Karen 175
First Assessment Report (IPCC) 16
Fish, M.R. 318, 320
flexibility 280
flooding: built environments and, risk of
37, 37; causes of 264–265; literature on
264; of Missouri and Mississippi Rivers
296; mitigating 223; resiliency to 223;
risk of, calculating 265; suburban areas'
adaptation to climate change and 212; see
also stormwater management
Florida Greenways Commission 175
Florida's rental tax 295
Floyd (1999 tropical storm) 209–210
Fodrie, Joe 303
Folke, Carl 152
food security 30
forces driving urban greenhouse gas
emissions: assessment of emissions and
92–95, 93, 94, 97; consumption-based
approach and 96–97; debate about 92;
economic activities 96; frameworks for
producing accounts of contributions to
climate change and 94, 94; geography
93; overview 91–92; production-based
approach and 96; range of 95–96; spatial
organization 95–96; underlying 96–97;
see also urban form and greenhouse
gas emissions
forests and forest management 39, 60, 171,
175, 187, 189, 211–212, 214
Forman, Richart T.T. 170
Fourth Assessment Report (AR4) (IPCC) 21,
25, 112, 162
freedom of speech 14
Fricke, Rebecca 42–43
Frontiers in Ecology and the Environment
(Gittman and colleagues) 301
fuels: decarbonization of 60; economy
improvements in 59, 85, 102; new
clean 145

gardens 38; see also vegetation
Gill, Susannah E. 172
Gittman, Rachel 300–301, 303
glacial volume, shrinking 19, 21, 23, 29
global catastrophe 13
globalization 153
global mean temperature (GMT) 73
Global North countries 52
global and regional climate modeling 228
Global South countries 52
global warming 12–13, 19, 20, 21; see also
climate change
Goddard Institute for Space Studies (GISS)
228
Godron, Michel 198, 202
Goleta Beach (Santa Barbara) 294
Gómez, Claudia Lorean Trejos 62–63
Google Earth 369

Gottdiener, M. 95
Grabherr, G. 163
Granite Garden, The (Spirn) 170
gray approaches to coastal defense 286, 287,
300, 301
gray infrastructure 181, 181, 238, 278
Great Britain see United Kingdom
Greater Manchester (United Kingdom) case
study 198–203
Green (accommodate or retreat) approach to
climate change 288, 310
green approaches to coastal defense
299–304, 301
Green City, Clean Waters program
(Philadelphia) 273, 276–279
green facades 241–242
Green Factor 268–269
greenhouse gas (GHG) emissions:
anthropogenic, total 21, 22; consumption-
based approach to assessing 96–97; future
climate changes and 26; of Global North
countries 52; of Global South countries
52; as networked system 171, 187; peaks
in 9–10; per capita basis of 52, 65, 65, 70;
production-based approach to assessing
96; responsibility for, assigning 64–66,
64, 65; as spatial planning tool 170–171;
sustainable materials and 45; urban form
and 51–52; see also forces driving urban
greenhouse gas emissions; greenhouse gas
mitigation; urban form and greenhouse gas
emissions
greenhouse gas mitigation: challenges for
cities 52, 62–71; climate action plans
and 83–88; climate change planning
and 196; Climate Gap report and 143;
corporate actions and 53–54; forces
driving urban greenhouse gas emissions
and 91–97; health in cities and 101–103;
individual actions and 53–54; inventory
of greenhouse gases and 52–53; local cost
and 52; overview 51–52; stabilization of
carbon emissions 55–61; urban form and
72–81; vegetation and 45, 202
greenhouse gas reduction gradient 44, 45
green infrastructure (GI): adaptation to
climate change and 185, 200–202;
advantages of 185–186; approaches to
173; benefits of 278; concept and practice
of 2, 170; connectivity and 275; cross-
scale conception of 173; defining 174–176;
feedback loops and 180; flexibility and
280; habitability and 273, 275; historical
perspective of 169; identity and 273,
275; interconnections and 171, 180, 187;
leadership and 279; lessons learned from
279–280; leverage point and 180; literature
on 172; living shorelines 288, 299–304,
301; microclimate and 226; multi-
functionality and 171, 273–275; multiple

benefits and 280; overview 171–172; partnerships and 280; passion and 280; patience and 280; principles 273–276; principles of, primary 185; public health concerns and 178–179; research and 280; resiliency and 172, 180, 187, 273, 275; return on investment and 273, 276; role of 195–203; stock and 180; stormwater management and 267–270; subsystems of 180–181, *181*; sustainability and 170, 172, 176–178; urban heat and 230–232; vision and 279; *see also* cities' adaptation to climate change and green infrastructure; Green Infrastructure Transect; landscape approach to green infrastructure; suburban areas' adaptation to climate change and green infrastructure; urban green infrastructure (UGI)

Green Infrastructure Transect: Boston metropolitan region case study and 169, 185, 189–190, *191*, 192–193; concept of 186–187, *188*, 189; horizontal integration and 187; natural transect and 186–187; overview 172, 184–186, 193; policies appropriate for 192; urban transects and 184, 186; vertical integration and 187, 189; zones in 184–185, 187

Greenland ice sheet 23

green landscapes *see* Mombasa (Kenya) project

GreenPlan Philadelphia 273–274

green roofs 38, 242, 253

green spaces 39, 197, 200, 222; *see also* green infrastructure (GI)

Green Streets project of Red Rose Forest (United Kingdom) 203

Greenway plans 170; *see also* green infrastructure (GI)

Greenworks Philadelphia plan 224, 276–278

Greve, Adrienne I. 83–84

guide to resiliency project evaluation: adaptation over time gradient **44**, 45; cost efficiency gradient 44, **45**; ecological enhancement gradient 44, **44**; evaluation process 46–48, **47**, *48*; exposure reduction gradient 43, **44**; gradients of resiliency and 43–46, **44**; institutional capacity gradient 44, **44**; overview 42–43; participatory process gradient **44**, 46; policies and 42–43; purpose of 43; social benefits gradient **44**, 46; sustainable materials available and 45, *45*, *48*

Gulf of Mexico coast 302–303

Güneralp, B. 285

Güneralp, İ 285

Gurran, Nicole 331

habitability 273, 275

Hall, C.M. 316

Haller Park (Kenya) 352, 355–357

Hamin, Elisabeth M. 43, 172, 331

hard engineering solutions to climate change 223, 269

Harlan, Sharon L. 52–53, 98–99

Harries, T. 264

Harris, Richard J. 240

health in cities: adaptation and co-benefits 101–102; air pollution and 100–102, 140–141; climate change in cities and 99–101; extreme heat and 100, 102; greenhouse gas mitigation and 101–103; microclimate and 252; mitigation and co-benefits 101–102; overview 98–99; risk management strategies and 102–103; various risks and 101; vulnerable populations and 102

health effects modeling 228, *229*

heat exposure 237

heat-related mortalities 222, 230–231

heat waves 36, **36**, 140; *see also* extreme heat events (EHEs)

Hoornweg, Daniel 53, 62–63

hope 4, 11–14, 42

Hopkins, D. 208

Hoyer, J. 268

Hughes, Terry P. 152

human rights 139

hybrid approach to coastal defense 286, *287*

ICLEI method of inventorying greenhouse gas emissions 53, 85

identity 273, 275

impervious materials and evaporation 251, 256

implementation of ideas and vision: effective 33; experience with climate change and, first-hand 330; local climate change planning and 330; local government and 329–330, 341–342; local leadership and 330, 343; overview 4–5, 329–331; public participation and 330; themes in 329–330

indigenous peoples and climate change 160–164

information on climate change 343

infrastructure concerns 212–213, 215–216

institutional capacity gradient 44, **44**

institutional change, achieving 296–297

Integrated Coastal Zone Management (ICZM) 288, 319–322, *319*, *323*

interconnections of green infrastructure 171, 180, 187

Intergovernmental Panel on Climate Change (IPCC): adaptation and 110; assessing urban greenhouse gas emissions and 92–93, *93*; Assessment Reports of 16–18; global warming and 12; indigenous peoples and 161–162; influence of 4, 10; mitigation and 3; risk and 110; science and 4, 85; stabilization of carbon emissions and 56; terminology of 10; work of 10;

see also Fifth Assessment Report (AR5); Summary for Policymakers report (IPCC)
international comparison approach 329, 333–338
International Council for Local Environmental Initiative (ICLEI) 85, 94–95, **94**, 335–336
International Energy Agency (IEA) 63
inventory of greenhouse gases 52–53, 70, 83–84, 86–88
Ireland's flooding events 264
Irene (2011 hurricane) 299–300
Ivan (2004 hurricane) 156

job opportunities 141–142
Jorgensen, A. 354

Kato, S. 189
Katrina (2005 hurricane) 295, 300, 302
Keene (New Hampshire) adaptation planning 335–336
Kimberly (British Columbia) 371
King County (Washington) adaptation planning 336
Kirshen, Paul 288, 306–308
Kithiia, Justus 330, 352
Kleerekoper, Laura 222–223, 250
koala habitat plan of management 338
Kousky, Carolyn 286–287, 290, 293
Kwartler, M. 370
Kydland, F.E. 293
Kyoto Protocol 66, 85

LaFarge Ecosystems Programme (Kenya) 356–359, *356*
land cover modeling 227–228
landscape: climate change in, recognizing 365–366; defining 174–176; in engaging public in climate change 363–365; messaging on climate change 367, *368*, 369; recreational 192, 193n1; utilitarian 192, 193n1
landscape approach to green infrastructure: community and 177–178; concepts of 176; connectivity and 275; definitions of landscape and green infrastructure and 174–176; economy and 177; ecosystem services provided by 173–174, 176; environment and 177; flexibility and 280; habitability and 273, 275; identity and 273, 275; indicators and 178; leadership and 279; multi-functionality and 273–275; multiple benefits and 280; overview 172–174, 273–274; passion and 280; patience and 280; in Philadelphia (Pennsylvania) 273, 276–280; principles of 273–276; public health and 178–179; quantitative measurement of 178; research and 280; resiliency and 273, 275; return on investment and 273, 276; sustainability

and 176–179; systems thinking and 174, 179–182, *181*; vision and 279
landscape professionals' role in engaging public in climate change 363–365, *364*, 372
landscape visualization 369–370
land-use conflict 333, 336
land-use policies 333, 335–336
Lawrence, A. 164
Lee, Bumsoo 52–53, 72–73
Lee, Sungwon 52–53, 72–73
Leichenko, Robin M. 172, 206–207
Lennon, Mick 223, 263, 273
leverage point and green infrastructure 180
Lincoln, Abraham 13–14
Liu, Y. 285
living shoreline coastal defense 288, 299–304, *301*
Local Agenda 21 Model Communities Program (ICLEI) 85
Local Climate Change Visioning 370–371
local government adaptation in United States: barriers to local government and 341–342; communication about climate change and 343; experience of climate change and 346; implications for policymakers and planners 346–347; information about climate change and 343; local leadership and 343, 345; modeling 345–346; municipal expenditures per capita and 346; overview 340–341, 347; progress and local government and 341–342; qualitative research on 342; regional planning entities and 347; resources and, lack of 342; state policies and 343–344, 346; survey of progress and 344
local government in climate change planning 329–330, 341–342
Local Governments for Sustainability Cities for Climate Protection (CCP) campaign (ICLEI) 85
local leadership 330, 343, 345
local learning about climate change 371
London (United Kingdom), urban heat in 36
Loughnan, M. 237
Louv, Richard 179
Lynch, K. 237
Lyth, Ann 330, 352

make it connected principle 361, 363
make it local principle 361, 363, 371
make it visual principle 361, 363, 367, 369–370
Malmö (Sweden) 268
managerial realignment coastal defense 286, *287*
Marshall, G. 363
marshes, artificial 302–303; *see also* wetlands
Maryland coast 302–303
Maryland Department of Natural Resources 292

Maryland's living shoreline law 299
McClatchey, W. 162–163
McHarg, Ian 170
McInnes, J. 237
Medical Mile greenway (Little Rock, Arkansas) 179
Melbourne (Australia) 235, 240
Merseyside study (United Kingdom) 200
metropolitan statistical areas (MSAs) *see specific name*
microclimate: adaptation to climate change and 222; ecosystem services and 169; evaporation cooling and 202, 235–236; green infrastructure and 226; green spaces and 197; gray infrastructure and 238; health in cities and 252; measuring temperatures in 101; in Ondiep 260; planning 222, 224; street canyon 239–240; urban form and 221; urban wildscapes and 354
minimal coastal defenses 286, 287
Mississippi River flooding (1993) 296
Missouri River flooding (1993) 296
Mitch (1998 hurricane) 157
mitigation of climate change: balancing with adaptation to climate change and 331–338; built environments and 39; cities and 66, **67–69**; climate change planning and 2–3; climate change risks reduced by 32–33; conflict between adaptation to climate change and 336–337; defining 3, 10; delaying 31; of human causes of climate change 1; IPCC and 3; land-use conflict and 336; overview 4, 51–54; policy goals 334–335; risk and 32–33; *see also* greenhouse gas mitigation
mobility 153
moisture deficit 201
Mombasa (Kenya) project: community groups and 357; green landscapes in context of 354–355; Haller Park and 352, 355–357; LaFarge Ecosystems Programme and 356–359, *356*; overview 330, 353–354, 359–360; from wildscape to greenscape and 355–357
Mono County (California) 134
Morello-Frosch, Rachel 110, 139
Morris, Marya 178
Moser, S.C. 344
MTBE 145
multi-functionality 171, 273–275
Mycoo, Michelle 288–289, 315–316

National Combined Sewer Overflow Control Policy 277
National Flood Insurance Program (NFIP) 290, 293–294
National Household Travel Survey (2001) 74–75, 80
National Land Cover Database 227

natural disaster insurance 290
natural ecosystem protection 286, 287
natural transects 186–187
NECIA report (2007) 190
Netherlands and urban heat island effect 250, 257–259, *259*, 260
New Jersey suburbs and climate change: agricultural production and 214–215; ecotourism and 215; exurban areas and 214–216; fire concerns and 215; flooding and 212; in high-density suburbs 209–211; infrastructure and 212–213, 215–216; in low-density suburbs 214–216; in medium-density suburbs 212–214; overview 172, 206–207; public health and 210–211, 213, 215–216; public transportation and 209–210, 213; variability of impacts and vulnerabilities and 208–216, *209*; water supplies and 213; woodlands and 211
New Orleans (Louisiana) 302
New South Wales Department of Environment and Climate Change 337
New York City adaptation planning 336
New York Harbor shoreline design exhibition 370
Nicholls, R. 321
NOAA 304
no-regrets policies 3, 171, 185, 288, 353–355, 359–360
North Carolina coast 299–300, 302–303
North Dakota's population 133–134
North West Regional Assembly (NWRA) 198
Norton, Briony 222, 233
Nutter, Michael 276

Obama administration 340, 343
ocean acidification 24
Ocean Beach (San Francisco) 294
ocean salinity 19
ocean warming 19, 21, 28
Olmstead, Frederick Law 170
Ondiep (Netherlands) case study 258, *259*, 260–261
O'Neill, Eoin 263
Open Space Plan for the Commonwealth of Massachusetts 169, 185, 189–190, *191*, 192–193
open space planning 170
optimism 11–13
Orange County (California) 134
Orr, David 10–12
oyster reef protection 286, 300, *301*, 303–304

Pacala, Stephen 51, 55–56
Paris Climate Accords 2
participatory process gradient **44**, 46
passion 280
Pastor, Manuel 139
patience 280

peer pressure 362
Penning-Rowsell, E. 264
people-beneficial actions 3
per capita greenhouse gas emissions 52,
    65, *65*
permits, auctioning 143
pervious materials and evaporation 250–251,
    256–257
Phan, T. 237
Philadelphia (Pennsylvania): Green City,
    Clean Waters program in 273, 276–279;
    GreenPlan in 273–274; landscape
    approach to green infrastructure and 273,
    276–280; stormwater management in 276,
    277–278; urban heat 222, 225, 227–228,
    229, 230–232
Philadelphia Water Department (PWD)
    277–279
Phoenix (Arizona) 222, 225, 227–228, *229*,
    230–232
physical planning policy and practice
    318, 321
Pilkey, Orrin 303
Pine Knoll Shores (North Carolina)
    299–300, 302
Pitkin County (Colorado) 134
place attachment 362
Plan for the Metropolitan Park System of
    Boston 169, 185, 189–190, *191*, 192–193
planned retreat 20
Platt, R.H. 293
policies: adaptation to climate change goals
    and 335–336; Build Your Way Out 288,
    306–307, 310; Green (accommodate
    or retreat) 299–304, *301*; guide to
    resiliency project evaluation and 42–43;
    infrastructure 322; land-use 333, 335–336;
    mitigation of climate change goals and
    334–335; no-regrets 3, 171, 185, 288,
    353–355, 359–360; physical planning 318,
    321; Ride It Out 288, 306–307, 310–311,
    312–313; state 343–344, 346; TCPD
    318, 323, *323*; *see also* guide to resiliency
    project evaluation
Popkin, Gabriel 288, 299
population growth 72, 133–134
Portland (Oregon) 268
Port Stephen (Australia) 338
post-disaster planning 295–296
power plants, improving efficiency of 60
precipitation changes 28
predisaster planning 295
Prescott, E.C. 293
price of basic necessities 141
Private Greening (PRG) 228
production-based approach to assessing
    greenhouse gas emissions 96
Program for Environmental and Regional
    Equity (PERE) 139; *see also* Climate Gap
    report (PERE)

Project Neutral campaign (Toronto) 371
Public Greening (PUG) 228
public health concerns: green infrastructure
    and 178–179; landscape approach to
    green infrastructure and 178–179; in
    suburban areas' adaptation to climate
    change and green infrastructure 210–211,
    213, 215–216; urban heat and 226; urban
    heat island effect and 252; *see also* health
    in cities
public transportation concerns: suburban
    areas' adaptation to climate change and
    green infrastructure and 209–210, 213;
    urban form and greenhouse gas emissions
    72–77, 79

quarry rehabilitation (Kenya) 352, 355–357

rebuilding 295–296
recreational exercise 192, 193n1
Red Rose Forest (United Kingdom) 203
reducing or restricting new development in
    high-risk areas strategy 292–294
reef damage and protection: coral 153,
    155–156, 286, 288, 317–318, 320–322,
    323; oyster and shellfish 286, 300, *301*,
    303–304
Regional Clean Air Incentives Market
    (RECLAIM) 144
regional planning entities 347
reinforcing feedback loop 180
reliance on cars, reduced 59
relocation 295–296
Representative Concentration Pathways
    (RCPs) 18, 26–27
resiliency: defining 180; evolutionary 265,
    267; to flooding 223; gradients of 43–46,
    44; green infrastructure and 172, 180,
    187, 273; landscape approach to green
    infrastructure and 273, 275; overview 4,
    107–110; social 153; social-ecological
    157; social vulnerability to natural hazards
    and 109–110; in subsystems of green
    infrastructure 180; of vegetation 300; *see
    also* coastal hazards and resiliency; guide
    to resiliency project evaluation
resources, lack of 343
return on investment (ROI) 273, 275
Ride It Out (RIO) approach to climate
    change 288, 306–307, 310–311, *312–313*
rising sea levels *see* sea level rise (SLR)
risk: adaptation in reducing 32–33;
    Intergovernmental Panel on Climate
    Change and 110; mitigation in reducing
    32–33; overview 4, 107–110; social
    vulnerability to natural hazards and
    109–110
Road Albedo Enhancement (RAE) 228
Rodriguez, Antonio 303
rolling easements 294

Ross, Nanci 110, 160–161
Rouse, David C. 172, 174, 184–185, 224, 273
Royal Dutch Meteorological Institute (KNMI) 252
Ruddell, Darren M. 52–53, 98–99
Ruth, Matthias 306–308

Sadd, Jim 139
SAGE project 42–43
Salick, Jan 110, 160–161, 163
Sandy (2012 hurricane) 210, 212, 300, 302
Sanoff, H. 330
science on climate change 4, 11, 13, 85
Scott, Mark 223, 263
sea-ice 29
Seale, Tammy L. 83–84
sea level changes 29, 37, 37; see also sea level rise (SLR)
sea level rise (SLR): increases in 21; living shorelines coastal defense and 299–304, 301; marshes and, artificial 302–303; overview 4, 285–289, 287; problem of, constant 285; projections 291; shellfish habitat and 286, 300, 301, 303–304; over time 367, 368; small island developing states and 316; see also shoreline retreat management
Seattle (Washington) 228, 268–269
shellfish habitat as coastal defense 286, 300, 301, 303–304
Sheppard, Stephen R.J. 330, 361–362
Shi, L. 329–330
Shonkoff, Seth 139
shoreline retreat management: backing away from the shore strategy 292, 294–295; institutional change and, achieving 296–297; market and 291–292; overview 286, 288, 290–292; reducing or restricting new development in high-risk areas strategy 292–294; using disasters as opportunities strategy 292, 295–296
small island developing states (SIDS) 288–289, 316, 324; see also Barbados tourism sector
Smith, I. 208
social benefits gradient 44, 46
social-ecological resiliency 157
social indicators 178
social memory 154
social mobility 153
social model of health 178
social pressure 362
social resiliency 153, 155–156, 157
social response 359
social responsibility 359
social vulnerability to climate change: adaptation and 109–110; changes in, temporal and spatial 130–131, 135–136; characteristics associated with 129;

consistency of components studied 131; defining social vulnerability and 129; forces behind increasing 135; future, anticipating 134–136; geography and 129–130; mapping 132, 132, 133; natural hazards and 130–131; overview 129–130, 135–136; population growth and 133–134; resiliency and 109–110; risk and 109–110
Socolow, Robert 51, 55–56
soft engineering solutions to climate change 268–270, 353
Solecki, William D. 172, 206–207
South Carolina's rebuilding restrictions 296
spatial heterogeneity 154
spider diagram 48, 48
Spirn, Anne 170
stabilization of carbon emissions: action versus delay in 60–61; business-as-usual trajectory and 57–59, 57; conservation improvements and 59–60; decarbonization of electricity and fuels and 60; efficiency improvements and 59–60; goal of 55; IPCC and 56; natural sinks 60; overview 55–56, 60–61; solving carbon and climate problem and 56–57, 57; stabilization triangle and 58; wedges in 55, 58–60; see also greenhouse gas mitigation
stabilization triangle 58
Stakeholder Advisory Group (SAG) 310
state policies 343–344, 346
Stern review 162
stock and green infrastructure 180
Stone, Brian Jr. 222, 225, 250
stormwater management: adaptation and 266; challenge of 221; designing for 265–267; green infrastructure and 267–270; overview 4, 221–224, 263–265; persistence and 266; in Philadelphia (Pennsylvania) 224, 276–278; sustainable urban drainage and 38, 202; transformation and 267
Strategic Planning and Climate Change approach 337
street canyon microclimate 239–240
structural equation model (SEM) 74, 80
Subramanian, Bhaskar 300, 302
suburban areas' adaptation to climate change and green infrastructure: agricultural production and 214–215; combined sewer overflow and 210; ecotourism and 215; exurban areas and 214–216; fire concerns and 215; flooding and 212; in high-density suburbs 209–211; infrastructure and 212–213, 215–216; literature on 207; in low-density suburbs 214–216; in medium-density suburbs 212–214; overview 172, 206–208; public health and 210–211, 213, 215–216; public transportation and 209–210, 213; variability of impacts and vulnerabilities and 208–216, 209; water supplies and 213; woodlands and 211

Sugar, Lorraine 62–63
Summary for Policymakers (IPCC) report:
    adaptation to climate change and
    117–118; climate extremes and impacts
    and 116–119; context of 112, *113,
    115*, 116; disaster losses and 117, 119;
    disaster risk management and 117–118;
    exposure and 116; future climate extremes
    and 118–119; human impacts and 119;
    lessons learned from, major 111–112;
    managing changing risks of climate
    extremes and 119–121, **122–126**; metrics
    for communicating certainty of findings
    and *114*; observed changes and 116–117;
    overview 111–112; past experience
    with climate extremes and 117–118;
    sustainability and, implications for
    127–128; uncertainty and, treatment of
    114; vulnerability and 116
surface runoff model 199–200
sustainability: Fifth Assessment Report and
    31–33; green infrastructure and 170, 172,
    176–178; landscape approach to green
    infrastructure and 176–179; Summary
    for Policymakers and, implications for
    127–128; three Es of 174, 176–179;
    tourism and 288–289, 315–317; urban
    development and, understanding 79–81;
    see also Barbados tourism sector
Sustainable Communities Programme 200
sustainable materials available 45, *45*, 48
sustainable tourism 288–289, 315–317; *see
    also* Barbados tourism sector
sustainable urban drainage (SUDS) 38, 202
Sutton-Grier, Ariana E. 286, 300
Swiss Re (insurance company) 142
systems thinking 174, 179–182, *181*

Tapper, N. 237
Tel Aviv (Israel) study 253
temperatures, rising 9, 23, *23*, 27, *27, 28*,
    36, **36**, 141, 221–224; *see also* global
    warming; urban heat
Teton County (Wyoming) 134
Tibetan people and climate change 163
Tidy Street in Brighton (United Kingdom) 369
Tobey, J.P. 319
Toronto (Canada) per capita greenhouse gas
    emissions 65, *65*, 70
Toward a Sustainable America Report
    (1999) 170
traditional peoples and climate change
    160–164
transect approach to green infrastructure *see*
    Green Infrastructure Transect
transfer of climate knowledge 257
transformations 32–33, 267, 331
trees 241, 243; *see also* vegetation
truth telling 13–14
Turner, N. 164

UNECLAC 316
United Kingdom: biophysical changes in
    197; flooding events in 264; Greater
    Manchester case study in 198–203;
    Green Streets project of Red Rose Forest
    in 203; London's urban heat and 36;
    Merseyside study in 200; population in
    197; Sustainable Communities Programme
    in 200; Tidy Street in Brighton 369
United Nations 2
United Nations Framework on Climate
    Change 9, 18
United Nations Framework Convention on
    Climate Change (UNFCCC) 85, 93
United Nations World Commission on
    Environment and Development 85
United States: Army Corps of Engineers 304;
    Environmental Protection Agency in 173,
    175; Federal Emergency Management
    Agency in 294; international comparison
    approach and 329, 333–338; National
    Flood Insurance Program in 290, 293–294;
    state policies and 343–344; urban form in
    329, 332–338; *specific city or state*
urban adaptive capacity 341
urban cooling island (UCI) 222
urban development and nature 170
urban environments *see* built environments
    and climate change; cities
urban flooding *see* stormwater management
urban form: in Australia 329, 332–338;
    density and 72; energy consumption and
    74; energy use and 335; environmental
    performance and 51; greenhouse gas
    mitigation and 72–81; microclimate and
    221; in United States 329, 332–338; *see
    also* urban form and climate change; urban
    form and greenhouse gas emissions
urban form and climate change: adaptation
    goals and 335–336; conflict between
    adaptation and mitigation and 336–337;
    density conundrum and 337–338;
    international comparison of 333–338; land-
    use conflict and 333, 336; limitations to
    study 334; methodology of study 333–334;
    mitigation policy goals and 334–335;
    overview 329, 331, 332–333, 337–338
urban form and greenhouse gas emissions:
    assessment of emissions and 92–95, *93,
    94*; compact cities and, building more
    80–81; connections between, studying
    73–74; debate about 92; household carbon
    dioxide emissions in urbanized areas and
    75–76, *75, 77, 78, 79*; limitation of study
    80; methodology of study 74–75; overview
    51–52, 72–73, 79–81; population density
    and 72–73, *76, 78*; residential buildings
    carbon dioxide emissions and 79; results
    75–76, *75, 77, 78, 79*; structural equation
    model analysis and 74, 80; sustainable

urban development and, understanding 79–81; transportation concerns 72–77, 79
urban green infrastructure (UGI): cooling benefit from existing UGI and, maximising 238–239; framework for mitigating excess urban heat and 236–242, 236; gray infrastructure and, characterising 238; green facades and 241–242; green roofs and 242; hierarchy of streets for new UGI integration and, developing 239–240; new UGI based on site characteristics and cooling potential and, selecting 240–242; overview 233–235; priority neighborhoods and, identifying 236–238; trees and 241, 243; urban green open spaces and 241; urban heat mitigation and 242–244; vegetation and 238–240, 243
urban green open spaces 241; see also urban green infrastructure (UGI)
urban heat: in Atlanta, Georgia 222, 225, 227–228, 229, 230–232; behavioural exposure and 238; benefits of mitigating 231; challenge of 221; cool materials and 228; effectiveness of management strategies 230–231; global and regional climate modeling 228, 231; green infrastructure and 226, 230–232; health effects modeling 228, 229; heat exposure and 237; heat-related mortalities and 222, 230–231; land cover modeling 227–228; in London (United Kingdom) 36; overview 221–223, 225–227; in Philadelphia, Pennsylvania 222, 225, 227–228, 229, 230–232; in Phoenix, Arizona 222, 225, 227–228, 229, 230–232; public health concerns and 226; urban heat island effect and 100, 221; vulnerability to 237; see also urban heat island (UHI) effect
urban heat island (UHI) effect: built form for mitigating 255–256; causes of 251–252; climate change and 252; heat-related mortalities and 225–226; in Netherlands 250, 257–259, 259, 260; overview 250–251, 261; permeable materials for mitigating 256–257; public health concerns and 252; temperatures in cities versus rural areas and 100; transferring climate knowledge and 257; urban heat and 100, 221; vegetation for mitigating 250–251, 253–254, 256; ventilation and cooling and 36; water applications in mitigating 254–255; see also urban heat
urban morphology types 195, 198–199
urban transects 184, 186; see also Green Infrastructure Transect
urban wildscapes 354; see also Mombasa (Kenya) project
U.S. Army Corps of Engineers 304
using disasters as opportunities strategy 292, 295–296

U.S. National Climate Assessment 9
U.S. Residential Energy Consumption Survey (RECS) 74
utilitarian exercise 192, 193n1
Utrecht (Netherlands) case study 257–258, 259, 260
Uyarra, M. 317

Van Der Linden, S. 362–363
vegetation: connected corridor of 274–276; for cooling 34–35, 202, 221–222, 228, 230–232; drought-resistant 201, 203; evaporation through 173, 175, 195, 221–222, 253; evapotranspiration and 230, 253; extreme heat events and 235; greenhouse gas mitigation and 45, 202; protecting endogenous 337–338; replacement of, with impervious surfaces 234, 256, 266; resiliency of 300; small island developing states and 322; socio-economic deprivation and reduced 200; in urban green infrastructure 235, 238–240, 243; urban heat island effect mitigation and 250–251, 253–254, 256; in urban wildscapes 354; water supply for, in drought 203; see also green infrastructure (GI)
vehicle miles traveled (VMT) 74, 76, 80, 88
ventilation in built environments 34–36
violent conflicts and climate change 30–31
visioning studies 370–371
visual learning tools 363, 369–370
vulnerability to urban heat 237

Waldo Canyon fire 215
Washington, District of Columbia 228
water applications 254–255
water conservation 322
water resources 38, 322
water scarcity 322
Weather Research Forecasting (WRF) 228
Weber, B. 268
wedges in stabilization of carbon emissions 55, 58–60
wetlands 39, 45, 171, 187, 189, 209, 212, 214, 223, 292, 294, 335
White, I. 264–265
Whitford, V. 199–200
Wilby, R.L. 34
wildscapes 354; see also Mombasa (Kenya) project
Willamette River 268
Williams, K. 208
Wing, S. 87
woodlands 39, 171, 175, 187, 189, 211–212, 214
World Development Report (2009) 63
World Resources Institute (WRI) 9–10
World Wide Fund for Nature 196
Wowka, K. 286